LEADERSHIP EMERGENCE THEORY

A Self-Study Manual
For Analyzing the Development of a Christian Leader

by Dr. Bobby Clinton
Associate Professor of Leadership
School of World Mission
Fuller Theological Seminary

ISBN 0-9741818-2-X

This manual is available from:

Dr. Bobby Clinton
Barnabas Resources
2175 N. Holliston Ave
Altadena, CA
                91001

Printed by:
Printing Plus, 2326 Daniels St., Madison, WI 53718
(608) 222-7505

(This page deliberately left blank)

PREFACE--An Update

This manual represents the fourth revision of a self-study text that was originally designed for ML 530 Leadership Emergence Patterns--a course offered in the leadership concentration of the School of World Mission of Fuller Theological Seminary. The end result of the course was two-fold: 1) changed lives of students who knew God's sovereignty in a fresh way, 2) the production of leadership development studies of leader's lives. In terms of producing a life history study there were four options. The study could be a self-study done by some missionary or national leader on his/her own life. It could be a study of a biblical leader. A third option involved the study of a Christian leader from history. A final option was the study of a contemporary Christian leader.

Thirteen classes over a period of seven years have been taught. Nearly 400 students have studied leadership emergence theory. Nearly 500 leaders have been studied over this period of time. Biblical leaders studied include such characters as Joseph, Moses, Joshua, Jephthah, David, Daniel, Jeremiah, Nehemiah, Barnabas, Paul, and Peter. Many historical leaders have been studied including such giants as Hudson Taylor, Andrew Murray, A. B. Simpson, Phineas Bresee, Henrietta Mears, Mary Slessor, Maria Atkinson, and J. O. Fraser. By far the majority of case studies have been of contemporary leaders--current missionaries and national leaders from around the world. Out of this research a theory for organizing, interpreting, and perhaps even predicting a leader's development is emerging. This theoretical framework looks promising as an aid to personal growth and to the selection and development of Christian leaders.

Leadership Emergence Theory (LET), the label describing the emerging theory, traces the emergence of leaders over the span of their lives. Those traces necessitate the construction of life history cases. More than 10,000 pages of life history data was developed in constructing these life history cases. Comparative study of these many cases, led to theory as to how leaders emerge. The research framework for the comparative study utilized "Grounded Theory" techniques developed by Glaser and Strauss (1967).

What have we learned? Several important items. One, our definition of a Christian leader is becoming clearer. **A Christian leader is a person with God-given capacity and God-given responsibility who is influencing a specific group of God's people toward God's purposes.** Two, leadership emergence is a process in which God intervenes throughout a lifetime in crucial ways, to shape that leader towards His purposes for the leader. Three, when viewed from a whole life perspective, it can be seen that God's intervention or shaping is intentional. His processing is intended to develop the leader's capacity. It moves the leader to operate at realized potential in terms of giftedness--natural abilities, acquired skills and spiritual gifts. However, His shaping also allows for a given leader's response. Leadership emergence can be thwarted or enhanced due to the emerging leader's response to God's shaping. Four, we are beginning to get an overall picture of how a leader develops or fails to do so.

The overall picture of a leader's development hinges around three major variables. That is, to a large extent the development of an individual Christian leader can be explained by the use of and relationship between three important umbrella-like concepts: processing, time analysis, and patterns of response. The development moves toward goals focusing on three kinds of formation: spiritual formation, ministerial formation, and strategic formation. These three formations correspond roughly to God's activity to form leadership character, leadership skills, and a set of coherent leadership values.

In the intervening time between the production of this manual and the last (done in early 1987) I have completed a PhD on this topic which integrated my seven years of research. Major advances include: integration of the theory (4 major levels); addition of several process items; analysis of the nature of process items; extensive development of time analysis particularly in boundary analysis and use of generic time-lines; identification, clarification, and more careful description of response patterns; extensive progress in describing and/or defining measures used to evaluate a leader's development; leadership problems; ultimate contribution of a life.

This draft of the manual is more than a major revision. It benefits from the intensive effort of the PhD research. Students of the old manuals will recognize many of the process items contained herein and some of the time-line concepts. But for the most part it is a new manual. The organization of chapters, which focuses on the advances in integrating the theory, is totally new. The format too has changed. The old manuals, heavy into the concept of referential learning, were designed using information mapping techniques as integrating concepts for page formats and chapter organization. This manual uses information mapping only for the crucial definition sections of the theory and for feedback pages. A lessening of information mapping means a corresponding increase in use of narrative. You will see this especially in the introduction to the definition sections, commentaries on definitions, and chapter summary sections. This increase of narrative enhances the facility of initial learning. The end result means that this latest manual appears more like standard texts that are familiar to students. Hopefully, this increase in initial learning isn't at the expense of referential learning--a strength of the old information mapped manuals. Referential learning techniques, in addition to information mapping of important definitions, are bolstered by the use of cue headings and marginal labels in the narrative portions and by the design of the extensive index.

Structure of the Manual

The manual is organized into three parts.

Part I introduces Leadership Emergence Theory and provides the overall framework for understanding the extended treatment of concepts which follow.

Part II describes the three major variables of the theory. It has three sections--one for each variable. Section A of Part II treats the processing variable. Chapters 3, 4, 5, 6, 7, and 8 describe the fundamentals of the processing variable. These chapters define the many process items that are helpful in describing God's intervention in a leader's life. Section B of Part II discusses the time variable. Chapter 9 introduces the time concepts. Chapter 10 details the two most useful generic time-lines. Section C of Part II describes the response patterns. Chapter 11 overviews the the notion of response pattern and keys the important patterns discovered to date to the ministry time-line. It then lists the detailed definitions/descriptions of the patterns.

Part III is integrative in nature. It discusses the overall effect of processing and development in terms of three goals: leadership character which is the goal of spiritual formation, leadership skills which is the goal of ministerial formation, and ministry philosophy (the integrated set of leadership values) which is the goal of strategic formation. Chapter 12 describes processing and the three formations--spiritual formation, ministerial formation, and strategic formation (the shaping that results in an articulated ministry philosophy). The concept of development of ministry philosophy is still very much in infancy but its outlines are becoming bolder as we continue research on it.

Seven measures are introduced in Chapter 13. Finally, some suggestions are given concerning the ultimate goals of a lifetime of leadership. Taken together, Chapters 12 and 13 gives first steps toward evaluating and measuring an individual leader's development.

Theme of the Manual

The theme of this manual is fairly clear. The emergence of a leader is a life-time process in which God both sovereignly and providentially is active in the spiritual formation, ministerial formation and strategic formation of a leader. All of life is used by God to develop the capacity of a leader to influence. Internal processes (individual psychological shaping) and external processes (social, cultural and contextual shaping) are combined with divine processes (divine shaping) in the activities and events of life to develop the capacity and responsibility a leader has to influence specific groups of God's people toward God's purposes for the leader and groups being influenced. Leadership Emergence Theory provides a discovery and evaluative

framework for a leader to use to evaluate all of these shaping
processes in his/her life and the lives of others.   Let me state
it more concisely.

The evaluation of development of a given individual leader,

- can be explained to a large degree by the use of and
  relationship between three sets of variables--processing,
  time, and response--which give the backdrop for
  understanding spiritual formation, ministerial
  formation, and strategic formation,
- can be evaluated over time by use of seven measures which
  indicate progress in response patterns or other like
  development: major lessons, development tasks, giftedness,
  sphere of influence, influence means, pattern assessment,
  and convergence factors,
- can be extremely insightful for a mid-career leader who
  uses it for self-analysis, since it provides coherence to
  past processing, and gives indications of future
  direction, and instills confidence in God's
  overall control of the whole process.

Twofold Purpose of the Manual

My purpose in providing this detailed treatment of
Leadership Emergence Theory is purely applicational in nature. I
want mid-career leaders, both men and women, to understand what
God has done in shaping them in the past and to confidently
expect God to continue that shaping in the future. I want them
to believe that God will make them quality leaders whom He will
use to accomplish His purposes. I further want these quality
leaders to use leadership emergence theory concepts to help
select and develop the future leaders who are emerging all around
us. If we, first of all **become** the leaders God wants us to be,
and then secondly reach out to **mentor** the more effective
development of younger leaders we will decrease the leadership
gap and do our part in hastening the coming of the Kingdom.

Bobby Clinton
Summer 1989

CHAPTER 1. A LETTER TO RANDY

The Leadership Mandate

"Remember your former leaders who spoke God's message to you.
Think back on how they lived and died, and imitate their faith.
Jesus Christ is the same yesterday, today, and forever."
                    Hebrews 13:7,8 Good News Bible

A Letter To Randy

Clara communicated clearly. Here was Clara's request

Dear Dr. Clinton,
    I'm sending you an invitation to Randy's
birthday party because of all the men besides his
father, you have had a great impact in my husband's
life.
    I don't really expect the honor of your presence
physically, but would like to ask you a favor.
    We will be having a time of verbal blessing and
prayer given to Randy. If you could prepare something
in writing, I could have it read to him during his
party. I know it would be significant to him.
    I also would like to thank you for the life and
encouragement you have given Randy throughout your
encounters with him. As a wife, I am thankful to see
godly, wise men be spokesmen, on behalf of the Lord,
to my husband. You helped remove that "edge" that has
been leaving Randy almost hopeless and feeling
purposeless.
    I am grateful to my Jesus for sending you in our
path.
    With lots of respect and gratefulness to you,

        Clara

P.S.
Send what you write, if you can, to this address. It
is my business address and I generally get the mail.
Thanks!
P.P.S.
I have been reading your book and am really enjoying
it. I feel stretched, enlightened and more at ease.

Randy had been in the very first leadership emergence
patterns class in 1982 when he was 25 years old. Now he had been
through some tough sledding in his entrance into ministry as a
leader. I had contact with Randy off and on over the ensuing
seven years. In fact, just about six weeks before her letter I
had spent two hours with Randy in my office. I had listened to
him describe his first seven years in ministry and the ups and
downs he had seen. I had given some of my insights on that.
Then I had counseled him about finishing his Master's program and

designed for him two independent studies he could do to round out
his program.

     Randy was in midst of struggles concerning his leadership.
For the immediate past he had been involved in a church planting
situation--always a difficult entry situation. He needed
assurance from someone older--someone who had passed this way
before. He needed someone who could help him see what was going
on--in short, perspective from a mentor. Ministry entry requires
a discerning perseverance. The discerning of God's special
shaping of the leader is critical during this time. Lack of
discernment at this early stage of ministry development
frequently leads to leadership drop out described by the label,
the abbreviated entry pattern.[1] Mentors are needed to offset this
early drop-out.

     Clara was right. They lived in Phoenix and I in Altadena.
It wasn't feasible for me to make the trip in person. So I chose
the following substitute--a personal letter (Clinton 1989). It is
rather a lengthy letter but I think well worth a careful reading.
For it illustrates several important concepts from **leadership
emergence theory (LET)**. Please note that the original letter
didn't have these academic footnotes. I include them to
foreshadow some of the concepts that you will be seeing in the
manual and to point out that the letter is indeed the fruit of a
serious application of the leadership mandate.

                                             11 May 1989
     Dear Randy,

          Oh, to be 32 again. Age is a matter of
     perspective you know. From where I stand, 32 seems so
     young and fresh with vibrancy and the prospect of
     accomplishing so much for God. You have just begun to
     learn about life and leadership. And if the Lord
     should allow you there will be a long time of
     effective ministry ahead.

          You have begun well. But remember the chess
     analogy. You must have a good opening game, a good
     middle game, and a good end game to come out on top.
     So now, you must continue well.

          Over the past six to eight years you have gone
     through the early part of your Growth Ministry Phase.[2]
     During that phase of life much is learned negatively.
     Roles, relationships, giftedness are often discovered

---

[1]Studies have shown that a large number of pre-service graduates
of seminaries drop out of ministry in the first three to five
years. I discuss this later in Chapter 9. See also Harbaugh
et al, **Beyond the Boundary--Meeting the Challenge of the First
Years of Ministry**, New York: Alban Institute.
[2]He was in the provisional sub-phase of his Growth Ministry

via negative processing--what not to do, what you
ought to do but can't yet. Early indications of the
giftedness set[3] began to emerge. That is normal and
right. So cheer up and remember that God has a
lifetime of processing in mind for you. You must
continue well.

In wishing you a happy birthday and God's best I
wouldn't be me if I didn't also give some exhortation.
So I want to pass on to you six major leadership
lessons[4] that have been emerging in my classes. Keep
them in mind as you celebrate this 32 birthday and
begin to think ahead to what God is going to lead you
into. Age 32 is a good time to take stock and make
some future resolutions by God's grace. So I have a
few questions to ask that perhaps may challenge you as
you think of continuing well.

1. **EFFECTIVE LEADERS MAINTAIN A LEARNING POSTURE
   THROUGHOUT LIFE.**

How are you doing on this one? Informal
training--personal growth projects, personal research
projects, reading, informal apprenticeships; non-
formal training--workshops, seminars, conferences;
formal--continuing education thoughts, bringing
closure on your previous program.[5]

Phase. I will discuss the generic Ministry Time-Line briefly in
Chapter 2 and in-depth in Chapter 9.
[3]Giftedness set is a term describing the stewardship potential
in a leader's life. It refers to the set of three elements
that are symptomatic of a leader's capacity to influence:
natural abilities, acquired skills and spiritual gifts.
[4]Not all of these six major lessons necessarily appear in any
one historic leader. They have been synthesized over many
lives. Nor is there yet hard evidence that they are causal to
the effectiveness in leadership though I believe there is a
strong connection.
[5]Three modes of learning are indicated here. Informal describes
the deliberate use of daily activities and self-initiated
growth projects as training means. Non-formal refers to
organized yet non-programmatic learning which is experiential
in focus and usually delivered via conferences, seminars,
workshops or local church institutes. Formal refers to
programmatic institutionalized training. Historical leaders
were strong in utilizing informal training. The other two modes
were not that available. Today, in the light of the continuing
education movement necessitated by the rapid pace of social
change, all three modes are available. Learning must be a
continuing process in the complex world of today. Leaders must
know how to learn and must continue to learn as the dynamics of
ministry change to meet the changing needs of society. Randy
needed to bring closure to a formal program.

2. **EFFECTIVE LEADERS VALUE SPIRITUAL AUTHORITY AS A PRIMARY POWER BASE.**

If it is true that your natural abilities (organizational bent) and acquired skills along that line are focal[6] in your giftedness set, then this will be a crucial principle for you. One of the major problems of people who work in an organizational context with management skills is their lack of spiritual authority[7] (and consequently their reliance on positional authority). You must cultivate your spirituality--for it is spirituality from which spiritual authority flows.

3. **EFFECTIVE LEADERS RECOGNIZE LEADERSHIP SELECTION AND DEVELOPMENT AS A PRIORITY FUNCTION.**

Think back on your recent experience. Have you been developing people?[8] Are you alert to the potential leaders God is bringing around You? You should help people move further along in their development patterns. The basic principle underlying II Cor 1:3,4, applies: **You are being taught by God in situations in order to share with others answers that ring with spiritual authority.** God has met you. You should be able to help others see God meet them. This leadership lesson especially applies to your giftedness set. Remember that like-attracts-like so that people will be drawn to you who reflect some similarity to your gifting. Watch for them. Help them along. Whatever God has taught you is worth passing on to others in such a way as to move them along in their own development.

---

[6]The focal element of a giftedness set refers to the dominant motivational capacity of a leadership. In this case I am suggesting that Randy's natural ability to organize is central to his life. When Randy took the leadership emergence patterns course in 1982 he studied the life of Samuel Mills (Maranville 1982), an early historical leader whose focal element was the natural ability to organize and motivate people toward mission causes. If I am right about Randy, this fact of who he studied illustrates the concept of "the like-attracts-like" giftedness pattern discussed in Chapters 10 and 11.

[7]Power bases, the leader's perceived source of capacity to influence, are discussed in Chapter 15. Spiritual authority is one power base. It flows from perceived spirituality. Positional authority flows from an office held by the leader.

[8]Charles Simeon (McDonald 1985, Cook 1987) demonstrates this attitude superbly and certainly stands as one who should be imitated in the truest sense of the leadership mandate. See also the following remarks on ministry philosophy and Charles Simeon.

4. EFFECTIVE LEADERS WHO ARE PRODUCTIVE OVER A LIFETIME HAVE A DYNAMIC MINISTRY PHILOSOPHY.

Three basal factors (the scriptures, giftedness, situation) define the dynamic quality of a ministry philosophy.[9] You will find that as you experience life you will see things in the Scriptures that you had not previously seen which will affect your ministry philosophy. Your discovery of your giftedness set will also affect your ministry philosophy. Some of your giftedness set is just now becoming clear to you. You minister out of being--who you are. Giftedness is part of that. Your philosophy will be deeply affected by your giftedness. And since giftedness is not revealed all at once, your ministry philosophy can be expected to change as discovery prompts it. A third factor affecting your ministry philosophy involves the "situation" in which you are ministering. No two situations are the same. Your Baptist situation was not like your Phoenix situation. Followers are different. Demands on leadership are different. These demands and situational differences will force you to alter your ministry philosophy. **Focus** in ministry philosophy usually begins to emerge in mid to late thirties. **Articulation** begins to emerge in mid forties to mid fifties. How are you doing on your personal ministry philosophy? You should be seeing hints of focus now. If you want to study someone who had focus in ministry read Charles Simeon's life.

5. EFFECTIVE LEADERS EVINCE A GROWING AWARENESS OF THEIR SENSE OF DESTINY.

You are not in this endeavor of leadership alone. Remember God has touched your life several times in destiny experiences to assure you that He is going to

---

[9]My thinking in part is based on D. Allen's special research project on ministry philosophy which was an in-depth case study of Charles Simeon (Allen 1988). From it and from comparisons with other historical case studies I have tentatively identified the following theoretical relation. The three basal factors (scriptures, giftedness, situation) will result in a Ministry philosophy which is dynamic. That ministry philosophy can in turn be traced to the interplay of three ministry philosophy variables: **blend** (an integration of past and present leadership values--both of these the result of processing), **focus** (destiny convergence, giftedness) and **articulation** (the movement from implicit to explicit organization of leadership values into a strategy for ministry which has the ministry philosophy focus as its driving force). See Chapter 12 where I discuss this in detail.

use you.[10] Never take these experiences lightly.
They are the divine road signs along the journey which
affirm, begin to clarify the route, and open up final
accomplishments at the destination. Sometimes I find
it helpful to stop and go back over my list of destiny
experiences and praise God and deliberately remember
them before God. How are you doing on your awareness
of destiny items?

6. EFFECTIVE LEADERS INCREASINGLY PERCEIVE THEIR MINISTRY IN TERMS OF A LIFETIME PERSPECTIVE.

We are back to where we started. Look at what
has happened to you in terms of your whole life-time
and God's intentions in developing you. Remember that
most of your Growth Ministry Phase has more to do with
developing you than accomplishing great ministry
accomplishments. So rejoice in all that God has
taught you in these past six to eight years. And look
forward to the coming years with a view toward seeing
God bring focus to your life.

Happy Birthday. Oh, to be 32 again.

Sincerely,

Bobby Clinton

The letter to Randy illustrates, in a small way, one of the
five results that come when one applies the leadership mandate,
Hebrews 13:7,8, seriously.

Five Results of Applying the Leadership Mandate

I like to interpret the command in the leadership mandate
this way. "Think back on how respected Christian leaders lived
and died and learn vicariously for your own lives." That is,
lessons can be experienced "second hand" and learned much more
rapidly than otherwise might be the case if they were to be
learned via direct experience only. I think that is the intent
of the mandate.

What happens if leaders do seriously apply this command? Of
course it depends on the leaders themselves. My experience with

---

[10]Destiny Processing is discussed in Chapter 4. In essence, it
is that touch of the Divine onto a life which gives ultimate
purpose to a life beyond the finite.

about 400 leaders who have seriously done this shows that five
things happen to them. They,

1. experientially learn the providence of God.
2. sense a continuity of God's working in their past.
3. go away from the study with a high degree of
   anticipation that God is going to use them in the future.
4. learn vicariously through the experiences of those they
   study.
5. began to perceive others in terms of the concepts learned
   from leadership emergence theory and thus become more
   deliberate in their use of these ideas in training of
   others.

The letter to Randy illustrates, at least in a token way, the
fifth item.

We apply the leadership mandate in two major ways. One, we
actually study leader's lives and learn lessons. Two, we learn
how to study leader's lives. The methodology for studying
leader's lives is leadership emergence theory. We then apply
this theory to the study of our own lives. Results 1 through 3
above are realized from the self-study of one's own life. Result
4 happens as lives of others--Biblical or historical or
contemporary leaders, are examined. Result 5 happens
spontaneously as a natural outflow of the paradigm shift[11]
experienced in learning the theory.

Result 1, the providence of God, becomes real for leaders
when they analyze their own past using the concepts of leadership
emergence theory. The perspectives help them see "old familiar
things" with new eyes. They personally perceive the providential
working of God in many incidents of their past. Their renewed
reflection of past incidents with these new perspectives often
results in "fresh learning" or "closure" which was not there
previously. In short, they now see more clearly what God
intended to teach them through those experiences.

Result 2, sensing a continuity of God's working, leads in
turn to result 3. After the first step of sensing God's hand in
many of the past incidents, a logical next step and one that many
take is to begin to see a continuity between God's providential
working in these incidents. Patterns begin to emerge. There is
a sense of an overall intent in the many incidents. There is a
growing sense of destiny--an affirmation of God's working in
their lives. Looking back and sensing the continual working of
God up to the present naturally leads to result 3, anticipating

---

[11]A paradigm shift is a radical change in one's mental
perspectives such that new things can be seen even from previous
experiences. This is discussed further in Chapter 6 in the
processing section dealing with God's means of expanding a
leader.

God's hand in their lives in the future.

Result 3, anticipating God's use of them in the future, is probably the most worthwhile serendipity of the whole experience. The joy, in seeing God's past working and identifying some patterns leading toward convergence, gives rise to a firm anticipation that God is indeed going to use them greatly in the future. This anticipation becomes even stronger for some and becomes a sense of destiny. I have seen numerous missionaries coming to the School of World Mission in a burned out condition or in the midst of uncertain boundary processing or in crises in their lives. Many are ready to turn in their missionary badges and try some other vocation. And I have seen God turn them around and give a renewed sense of His presence and a Holy Motivation to accomplish something for the expansion of the Kingdom.

But it isn't just ability to perceive things through leadership emergence theory concepts that is helpful. God actually changes values through the principles seen in the lives of those studied. Many learn for their own lives the lessons that Daniel and Joseph learned about integrity and sense of destiny and the sovereignty of God. Lessons of spiritual authority flow out of Watchman Nee's life. Those who study his life find that they desire spiritual authority to be their dominant power base. They are challenged by the word items in Nee's life. Those who study J. O. Fraser get a heavy dose of the power of imitation modelling. They get a fresh appreciation for the foundational place of power released in ministry through prayer. From Barnabas many catch the mentoring spirit. And many more will benefit from the future mentoring that will result. Those who study Titus see the value of ministry task as an informal training model that can be used to spot emerging leaders. It is amazing how many principles studied about someone of another culture have a cross-cultural application. Vicarious learning, the fourth result of seriously applying the leadership mandate, allows one to gain experience through another's life, often speeding up the process of personal development.[12]

Once you understand leadership emergence theory concepts it will be almost impossible for you ever again to look at leaders and emerging leaders in the same way as you did previously. You can't help using these concepts to help you evaluate where they are and what God is doing and where they might be going next. And you can suggest lessons that God is intending with the items

---

[12]The Response Premise is an articulation of this fact and is one of the powerful motivating factors for studying this manual. This premise is a theoretical formulation worded as follows. THE TIME OF DEVELOPMENT OF A LEADER DEPENDS UPON RESPONSE TO PROCESSING. RAPID RECOGNITION AND POSITIVE RESPONSE TO GOD'S PROCESSING SPEEDS UP DEVELOPMENT. SLOWER RECOGNITION OR NEGATIVE RESPONSE DELAYS DEVELOPMENT.

they are experiencing. In short, you will be able to more
effectively mentor leaders and emerging leaders with whom you
come in contact.

     This manual will help you obey the leadership mandate. By
learning its concepts and applying them you will experientially
learn how to assess good leadership and to see how it emerges.
You will learn how God intervenes in a leader's life to shape a
good leader. You will find that you can readily apply these
concepts to your life. In fact, I really want you to do that.
It is with this intent that I leave you with the following
challenges.

     My studies of many leaders have led me to some convictions.
I'll voice them in the form of four challenges.

The Four Challenges

     I'll first word the challenges. Then I'll explain each.

CHALLENGE 1. **WHEN CHRIST CALLS LEADERS TO CHRISTIAN MINISTRY HE
INTENDS TO DEVELOP THEM TO THEIR FULL POTENTIAL.
EACH OF US IN LEADERSHIP IS RESPONSIBLE TO CONTINUE
DEVELOPING IN ACCORDANCE WITH GOD'S PROCESSING ALL
OUR LIVES.**

CHALLENGE 2. **A MAJOR FUNCTION OF ALL LEADERSHIP IS THAT OF
SELECTION OF RISING LEADERSHIP. LEADERS MUST
CONTINUALLY BE AWARE OF GOD'S PROCESSING OF YOUNGER
LEADERS AND WORK WITH THAT PROCESSING.**

CHALLENGE 3. **LEADERS MUST DEVELOP A MINISTRY PHILOSOPHY WHICH
SIMULTANEOUSLY HONORS BIBLICAL LEADERSHIP VALUES,
EMBRACES THE CHALLENGES OF THE TIMES IN WHICH THEY
LIVE, AND FITS THEIR UNIQUE GIFTEDNESS AND PERSONAL
DEVELOPMENT IF THEY EXPECT TO BE PRODUCTIVE OVER A
WHOLE LIFETIME.**

CHALLENGE 4. **MINISTRY ESSENTIALLY FLOWS OUT OF BEINGNESS. YOU
MUST CONTINUALLY ASSESS YOUR SPIRITUALITY AND
MAINTAIN IT IF YOU ARE TO GIVE SPIRITUAL LEADERSHIP
IN THE KINGDOM.**

Challenge 1: Personal Leadership Development

     Leadership emergence theory is based on the assumption that
God is in the business of raising up leaders and intervening in
their lives to develop them for carrying out His purposes. Jesus
still calls people to follow him and influence many others. My
studies of those whom God has used in the scriptures as leaders
to accomplish his purposes led me to my working definition of a
leader.

definition   A leader, as defined from a study of Biblical
                    leadership, and for whom we are interested in
                    tracing leadership emergence is a person,

——————→   1) with God-given capacity AND

——————→   2) with God-given responsibility,

                    WHO IS INFLUENCING

                    3) specific groups of God's people

                    4) toward God's purposes for the group.

It is the first and second concepts that I am highlighting in
challenge 1.

      The "God-given capacity" denotes giftedness. I use
giftedness to mean natural abilities, acquired skills and
spiritual gifts. This giftedness is inherent in the leader. The
God-given responsibility includes not only a burden for the work
that God calls one to but also a sense of accountability before
God for that work. My studies in New Testament philosophical
leadership models,[13] particularly the stewardship model have
reinforced my conviction about challenge 1. Passages such as
those focusing on stewardship of spiritual gifts (Romans 12 and
Ephesians 4) and those emphasizing stewardship in general, like
the stewardship parables (particularly Luke 19, The Pounds, and
Matthew 25, The Talents) have led me to the conclusion that
leaders have capacities which must be developed and used.

      So then, let me repeat the challenge.

**CHALLENGE 1. WHEN CHRIST CALLS LEADERS TO CHRISTIAN MINISTRY
                HE INTENDS TO DEVELOP THEM TO THEIR FULL
                POTENTIAL. EACH OF US IN LEADERSHIP IS
                RESPONSIBLE TO CONTINUE DEVELOPING IN
                ACCORDANCE WITH GOD'S PROCESSING ALL OUR LIVES.**

      I believe the perspectives in leadership emergence theory
can help you personally as a leader to perceive where you are in
your own development, to more clearly evaluate it, and to sense
God's hand in it. This in turn will make you operate in tandem

———————————————

[13]At this point I have theorized four such models: The Servant
Leadership Model, The Stewardship Model, the Harvest Model, the
Shepherd Model. Two of these, Servant and Stewardship, are
value driven models. That is, they deal with fundamental
"oughts" of leadership which apply to all Christian leaders.
Two, Shepherd and Harvest, are gift driven. That is, the
Shepherd and Harvest Models, while having some items applying to
all Christian leaders, apply more forcefully to certain leaders
who have gifts which correlate with the ultimate functions of
these models.

with God's developmental purposes for you. Priority wise I
believe this is the most important challenge. Unless we as
leaders are experiencing God's ongoing development personally we
will not be able to help others develop their leadership
capacity. So I would exhort you, "How are you doing in your
development as a leader?" And I would challenge you, be all you
are meant to be as God's leader.

Challenge 2. Developing Other Leaders

I am firmly convinced that a major function of all
leadership is the selection of rising leadership. Now I should
explain what I mean by selection. I don't mean picking some
young people to send off to Bible College or seminary. I mean
observing who God is selecting and processing and finding ways to
enhance their development. Awareness of processing concepts can
mean that you can much more efficiently advise and mentor
emerging leaders. You can point them to informal and non-formal
training which you know can move them along in several of the
developmental patterns. In each of our ministries God is
developing leaders and followers. As leaders we must work with
God to see leadership needs continually being met by emerging
leaders. So read it again and let it be embedded deeply.

**CHALLENGE 2. A MAJOR FUNCTION OF ALL LEADERSHIP IS THAT OF
          SELECTION OF RISING LEADERSHIP. LEADERS MUST
          CONTINUALLY BE AWARE OF GOD'S PROCESSING OF
          YOUNGER LEADERS AND WORK WITH THAT PROCESSING.**

Challenge 3. Develop an Explicit Ministry Philosophy

Discernment[14] is crucial to effective leadership. Leaders
must be able to see God's working in events and people and
situations around them. They must recognize God's processing in
their own lives. A discerning leader will identify a ministry
philosophy. A discerning leader is a leader with a solid
ministry philosophy. The ministry philosophy pattern is
essential for effective leadership that will carry through to the
end.

_____

[14]During ministry processing four repetitive functions occur:
entry, training, relational, discernment. These functions are
discussed further in Chapter 9 which deals with the time
variable. Discernment is that trait in a leader which allows
the leader to understand what is happening and what has
happened. It is at the heart of developing a ministry
philosophy.

It is my opinion that Ministry Philosophies will be as diverse as there are leaders. We can not carbon copy some successful leader's philosophy and simply put it in to our situation. The ministry philosophy of a given leader must arise out of that person's actual leadership development. For it must fit the lessons learned by that leader, that is, it must grow out of the unique processing that God has for that leader. It must fit that leader's giftedness development pattern. And it must fit the situation to which God places that leader. And it will harmonize with the destiny processing of that leader.

There are of course some base values in the scriptures concerning leadership ethics, leadership styles, ends and means, and the basic overarching attitude of servant leadership which apply to all leaders. And we can, of course, profit greatly from studying the ministry philosophies of leaders whom God has greatly used. However, the vast majority of values learned will be unique to a leader because of the unique situation. That is, the situation will force a closer scrutiny of the scriptures for truth that fits that situation.

A ministry philosophy does not have to be explicitly stated in logical propositional statements, though that is very helpful. But it has to be there and has to give that overarching integration of a leader's ministry. I am highlighting concepts 3 and 4 of my leader definition when I work on challenge 3. Read again the definition and look closely at those last two concepts.

definition   A leader, as defined from a study of Biblical leadership, and for whom we are interested in tracing leadership emergence is a person,

1) with God-given capacity AND

2) with God-given responsibility,

WHO IS INFLUENCING

------->   3) specific groups of God's people

------->   4) toward God's purposes for the group.

The central ethic of leadership is INFLUENCING GOD'S PEOPLE TOWARD GOD'S PURPOSES. This will not be maintained over over an entire life-time without an adequate ministry philosophy. Let me repeat challenge 3 for emphasis.

CHALLENGE 3. LEADERS MUST DEVELOP A MINISTRY PHILOSOPHY WHICH SIMULTANEOUSLY HONORS BIBLICAL LEADERSHIP VALUES, EMBRACES THE CHALLENGES OF THE TIMES IN WHICH THEY LIVE, AND FITS THEIR UNIQUE GIFTEDNESS AND PERSONAL DEVELOPMENT IF THEY EXPECT TO BE PRODUCTIVE OVER A WHOLE LIFETIME.

How are you doing on your ministry philosophy? Or to say it
another way, How is God doing in developing the discernment
function in you as a leader?

Challenge 4. Maintain Your Spirituality

Plateaued leadership and leadership which is set aside
(disciplined by God) usually can be traced back to problems in
spirituality. While there are of course some leaders who fail
in leadership due to lack of ministry skills it is probably
more true that the majority of failures in leadership come due
to failure in the area of spirituality. Every leader should
have an explicit theology of spiritually which guides him/her
as development proceeds along the three major goals of
spiritual formation, ministerial formation, and strategic
formation. As Willard (1988:26) has so aptly pointed out,
your thoughtless and heretofore unorganized theology of
spirituality guides your life with just as much force as a
thoughtful and informed one. Kingdom leadership demands
spiritual leadership. An informed theology of spirituality is
vital to this kind of leadership. Your application of
leadership emergence theory to your own life should result in
a much clearer understanding of your personal view of
spirituality. Think again on the challenge to assess and
maintain your spirituality.

CHALLENGE 4. MINISTRY ESSENTIALLY FLOWS OUT OF BEINGNESS. YOU
          MUST CONTINUALLY ASSESS YOUR SPIRITUALITY AND
          MAINTAIN IT IF YOU ARE TO GIVE SPIRITUAL LEADERSHIP
          IN THE KINGDOM.

Well I've finished voicing my convictions in challenge
format.

I hope you'll take up the gauntlet.

Closing--Returning To The Leadership Mandate

When I began my own pilgrimage into the study of leader's
lives I was personally challenged by the leadership mandate.
Read it again.

Remember your former leaders, who spoke God's message
to you. Think back on how they lived and died, and
imitate their faith. Jesus Christ is the same
yesterday, today, and forever. Hebrews 13:7,8

When I read those verses, two questions came to mind. The
first question is how do I "think back on how they lived and
died?" The second is how do I "imitate their faith?"

Over the last seven years at the School of World Mission I have been privileged to start answering those two questions. The answer to those questions has resulted in leadership emergence theory and this manual.

The reason I think it is important to answer those questions for myself and others is that Jesus Christ is the same yesterday, today, and forever. It is no accident that those very words follow the admonition to "think back" and "imitate." The same lessons that He taught in the past, apply to me today. The same Jesus Christ who enabled those leaders to live lives of faith will enable me to live a life of faith today. He is both the source and the reason for our study of leadership.

Leadership evolves and emerges over a lifetime. In fact, leadership is a lifetime of God's lessons.

I trust that you, too, will accept the challenge of Hebrews 13:7,8 and that you will be much better equipped to do it than I was when I started. That is the intent of this manual.

DISCUSSION

1. How is a learning posture indicated in your culture? To what extent is learning posture determined by literacy? Can one maintain a learning posture and be illiterate?

2. Suggest some leaders you have known or seen in the past who evince spiritual authority? On what is their spiritual authority based?

3. Suggest some leaders you have known or seen in the past who have excelled in leadership selection and development. What traits or giftedness were evident in their lives and ministry?

4. Give illustrations or examples, if you can, of both the positive and negative side of the RESPONSE PREMISE (see footnote 12). What Biblical evidence is there of this notion?

5. Consider the five results normally experienced by those who study leadership emergence theory. Which of these do you think will be most important for you personally?

6. Consider the four challenges which close out this chapter. Which of these is most likely to motivate you to study leadership emergence theory? With which of these are you least familiar?

FOR FURTHER STUDY

1. Major Lesson 1 [LEARNING POSTURE]. See **Leadership Training Models**, 1983 by J. Robert Clinton; Malcolm Knowles, **The Modern Practice of Adult Education**, 1980.

2. Major Lesson 2 [SPIRITUAL AUTHORITY]. See Watchman Nee's **Spiritual Authority**. See also J. Robert Clinton's unpublished PhD Tutorial, "Leadership Development Theory--Influence Concepts." On file In Leadership Department.

3. Major Lesson 3 [LEADERSHIP SELECTION]. See life of Charles Simeon. See J. Robert Clinton's, **Barnabas--Encouraging Exhorter, A Study In Mentoring.**

4. Major Lesson 4 [MINISTRY PHILOSOPHY]. See Chapter 8, Integrating the Lessons of Life: Toward a Ministry Philosophy, in **The Making of a Leader**, by J. Robert Clinton.

5. Major Lesson 5 [SENSE OF DESTINY]. See Bertelsen's "When God Gives a Sense of Destiny," unpublished research paper, School of World Mission, Fuller Theological Seminary. On file In Leadership Department.

6. Major Lesson 6 [LIFETIME PERSPECTIVE]. See Clinton's **The Making of a Leader** as well as this entire manual. See also Clinton's PhD dissertation, **Leadership Development Theory: Comparative Studies Among High Level Christian Leaders.**

(This page deliberately left blank)

CHAPTER 2. FOUNDATIONAL CONCEPTS

Introduction

Chapter 2 gives an overview of leadership emergence theory, places it in the context of overall leadership research, and introduces some fundamental leadership definitions which are foundational to leadership emergence theory. References to these foundational definitions and concepts behind them will frequently be made throughout this book.

Overview of Leadership Emergence Theory

Leadership emergence theory traces the expansion of leadership capacity in a Christian leader over a life-time. It assumes that throughout a lifetime a leader continues to learn about leadership. In particular, that the lifetime of learning involves the intervention of God. Christian leaders perceive that God superintends their development. Sometimes the intervention manifests itself more directly (sovereignly) through critical spiritual incidents which most leaders remember well. At other times the interventions are less direct (providential) and are seen primarily through retrospective reflection. The development involves internal psychological shaping, external sociological shaping, and internal/external divine shaping.

The theory evolved from a comparative study of numerous Christian leader's analysis of their own lives, analysis of historic Christian characters, and studies of Biblical leaders. Technically the theory is called a grounded substantive theory subsumed under the general category of middle-range theories. That is, the theory flows directly from reflective inductive thinking generated from a comparative study of data. Theoretical sampling of data is controlled by the emerging theory which dictates the categories and properties that need further data. This study has been limited to a specific focus--evangelical Christian leaders with a missiological bent. Further, the type of leaders studied primarily fall into those who are influencing Christianity on a regional or national basis. In contrast, a formal theory would apply to development of any leaders, anywhere, regardless of their orientation to Christianity or level of leadership.

Description

Figure 2-1 gives an integrative bird's eye view of leadership emergence theory. Leadership emergence theory, (LET), can be explained for the most part, in the life of a given leader by the use of three important variables.[1] While not intending

---

[1] Variables is used here more in the linguistic sense of "slots" (with fillers) or in the sense of "parameter,"--a set of

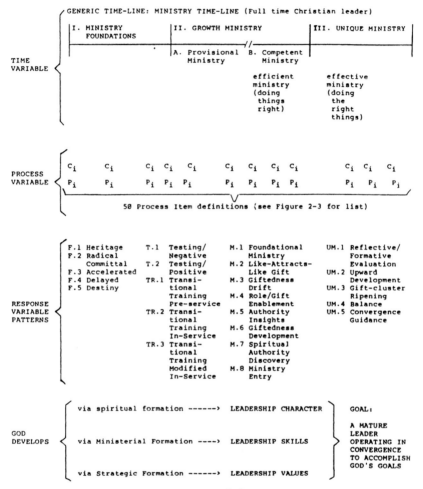

FIGURE 2-1
INTEGRATION CHART--AN OVERVIEW OF
LEADERSHIP EMERGENCE THEORY

properties whose values determine the characteristics or
behavior of a system--than in the strict mathematical sense of a
variable. These three variables, processing, time, and response
are generic umbrella-like labels which subsume sets of entities
under them. These sets of entities taken collectively give
labels and concepts for describing and explaining how a leader
develops.

mathematical precision, the symbolic notation, given below, is helpful in succinctly stating the major relational idea of leadership emergence theory.

$$L = f(p,t,r)$$

where L means "development of a given leader," f means a "function of," or "can be explained by," p means "processing," t means "time," r means "response patterns of a leader."

Processing is the core variable around which the theory integrates. That is, critical spiritual incidents in the lives of leaders are sprinkled densely throughout their lives. These incidents are often turning points in terms of leadership insights. These incidents are perceived by the leaders as God's work of **developing them for leadership.** This is called **processing.** The actual incidents can be identified, labeled and defined. The categorical term for defining these incidents is, process items.

The umbrella category under which all other items of the theory is subsumed involves the concept of developing. A leader is developed by God over a lifetime in order to expand leadership capacities to fulfill God's purposes for that leader. Developing is in turn broken up into three major areas: spiritual formation ministerial formation and strategic formation. These major areas of development occur simultaneously throughout a lifetime. Though all are present throughout development over a lifetime the focus may change during various time periods in the life.

Each individual leader can analyze his/her life in terms of time periods. Comparative analysis of the resulting unique time-lines has resulted in two overall major time groupings, (i.e., referred to as generic time-lines). The first time-line, called the generalized time-line focuses on individual personal development. The second, the ministry time-line, focuses on the leader's development in regards to ministry. Figure 2-2 gives these two generic time-lines. Notice that the integration diagram of Figure 2-1 used the ministry time-line. The ministry time-line deals with full time Christian workers, the focus of this manual.[2]

Unique time-lines (a time-line of a specific person) can be profitably compared to these two generic time-lines. Patterns of development have been generalized for the various time periods. Dominant process items have been identified for the various time periods, as well.

---

[2] The other generic time-line, the Generalized time-line, is the focus of **The Making of a Leader** (Clinton 1988). That book seeks to apply leadership emergence theory to lay as well as full time Christian leaders.

THE MINISTRY TIME-LINE

```
| I. MINISTRY    | II. GROWTH MINISTRY               | III. UNIQUE         |
|    FOUNDATIONS |                                   |    MINISTRY         |
| ---------------| ------//------------------------- |-------------------- |
|                | A. Provisional  B. Competent      |                     |
```

THE GENERALIZED TIME-LINE

```
PHASE I.      PHASE II.    PHASE III.   PHASE IV.  PHASE V.      PHASE VI.
Sovereign     Inner-Life   Ministry     Life       Convergence   Afterglow
Foundations   Growth       Maturing     Maturing
|-----------|-----------|------------|----------|----------|---------|
```

FIGURE 2-2
TWO GENERIC TIME-LINES

Studies of **response** patterns (see Figure 2-1: symbols F.1, F.2, F.3, F.4, F.5, T.1, T.2, TR.1, TR.2, TR.3, M.1, M.2, M.3, M.4, M.5, M.6, M.7, M.8, UM.1, UM.2, UM.3, UM.4, UM.5) point out stages of development and explanations as to why and when these patterns have exceptions. Pinpointing a leader's location along a pattern is one kind of development measure. Movement along patterns can be sped up or retarded. Retarded development along a pattern usually indicates a problem. Problems (not shown on the chart of Figure 2-1) have also been identified, labeled, and defined.

The process item is the core variable, the major concept around which the whole theory can be discussed and integrated. A leader is perceived to be developed via numerous process items. Process items occur throughout all time periods and form the basis for determining relationships which integrate the theory. Relationships between these process items and development are identified and labeled under patterns, principles, problems or clusters of these elements.   It is the description of these process items, patterns, problems, and principles related to time periods and measures of expansion which integrate the theory. Figure 2-3 lists the fifty process items identified to date. These will be discussed in depth in Chapters 4-8.

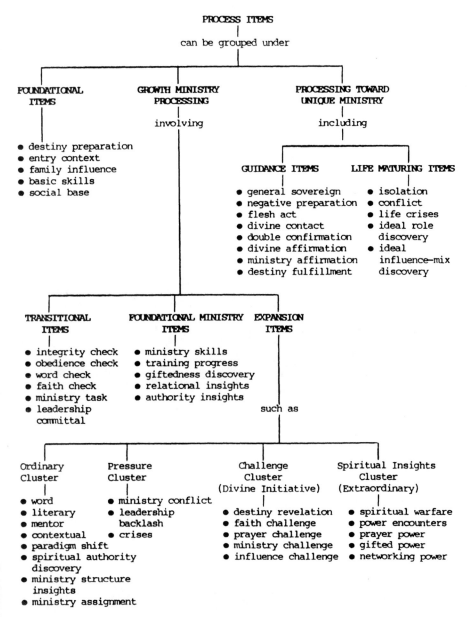

PROCESS ITEMS

can be grouped under

FOUNDATIONAL ITEMS

- destiny preparation
- entry context
- family influence
- basic skills
- social base

GROWTH MINISTRY PROCESSING

involving

PROCESSING TOWARD UNIQUE MINISTRY

including

GUIDANCE ITEMS

- general sovereign
- negative preparation
- flesh act
- divine contact
- double confirmation
- divine affirmation
- ministry affirmation
- destiny fulfillment

LIFE MATURING ITEMS

- isolation
- conflict
- life crises
- ideal role discovery
- ideal influence-mix discovery

TRANSITIONAL ITEMS

- integrity check
- obedience check
- word check
- faith check
- ministry task
- leadership committal

FOUNDATIONAL MINISTRY ITEMS

- ministry skills
- training progress
- giftedness discovery
- relational insights
- authority insights

EXPANSION ITEMS

such as

Ordinary Cluster

- word
- literary
- mentor
- contextual
- paradigm shift
- spiritual authority discovery
- ministry structure insights
- ministry assignment

Pressure Cluster

- ministry conflict
- leadership backlash
- crises

Challenge Cluster (Divine Initiative)

- destiny revelation
- faith challenge
- prayer challenge
- ministry challenge
- influence challenge

Spiritual Insights Cluster (Extraordinary)

- spiritual warfare
- power encounters
- prayer power
- gifted power
- networking power

FIGURE 2-3
CATEGORIZED LIST OF PROCESS ITEMS

So then, in summary, moving from lower categories to higher categories the theory builds as follows. Process items, daily observable critical spiritual incidents, develop a leader and give insights which expand leadership capacity. Time analysis of the leader's life then breaks the life up into developmental phases. Various process items dominate developmental phases. Some process items are multi-phased and occur throughout all time periods. Patterns relating to various process items can be identified. These patterns also relate across time periods and in terms of expansion measurements. The process items, patterns, principles, and problems associated with them all contribute to development of the leader. Development at the highest level is related to three basic kinds: spiritual formation which deals with internal character formation, ministerial formation which deals with capacities to relate to groups and lead them, and strategic formation which deals with the underlying ministry philosophy derived from leadership values taught in processing.

How Leadership Emergence Theory Fits

Leadership emergence theory is part of the broader study of leadership in general. A tracing of the research paradigms (Clinton 1985) relating to the study of leadership in general identified five major paradigmatic eras: Great Man Era 1848-1903, Trait Era 1903-1948, Ohio State Behavioral Era 1948-1967, Contingency Era 1967-1985, Complexity Era 1985--present. Each of these eras focused on a specific aspect of leadership theory. A simplified synthesis of the theoretical notions underlying each of the major eras resulted in the balanced framework for studying leadership as given in Figure 2-4. This diagram is expanded later in this chapter.

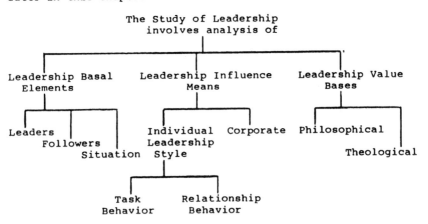

FIGURE 2-4
A BALANCE FRAMEWORK FOR ANALYZING LEADERSHIP

Leadership emergence theory focuses primarily on the major
component of the leadership basal elements and studies how one
becomes a leader. Analysis of processing will touch every aspect
of the framework. Spiritual formation deals dominantly with the
basal elements. Ministerial formation will focus primary on
influence means. Strategic formation will focus on the value
bases for leadership.

Foundational definitions relating to the above leadership
framework in general, and to leadership emergence theory in
particular, follow in an information mapped form. This is a
format which unpacks information into blocks of integrated focus
with labels which allow for easy referential use. Read as little
or as much of a given map as is necessary to learn the major
concept (map label) being detailed. Usually a single page is
dedicated to one definition--occasionally two pages--to make up
the map. Following each map is a feedback section forcing a
learning response. At the conclusion of a map and its feedback
there is sometimes a commentary suggesting implications,
importance, related reflections and further study.

The order of the maps is suggestive. **LEADERSHIP ACTS** (p.
34) are the lowest component of demonstrated leadership.
Potential leaders are identified in the context of leadership
acts. Those who persist in leadership acts are **LEADERS** (p. 36).
The study of leaders and what they do results in the
identification of what the essentials of **LEADERSHIP** (p. 40) are.
LEADERSHIP FUNCTIONS (p. 42) spell out the three major areas of
Christian leadership activities and give some specifics. Which
of these specifics or the extent that they are done depends on
which of the **5 TYPES OF LEADER** (p. 46) a person is. The
LEADERSHIP FRAMEWORK (p. 54) gives three important categories
used to analyze any type of leader. The third category deals
with value bases of a leader, the "Why" of leadership. The **4
BIBLICAL LEADERSHIP MODELS** (p. 56), give a beginning framework
for the "why" of Christian leadership. Both the **STEWARDSHIP** (p.
57) and **SERVANT LEADER** (p. 60) models pose broad theological
values that apply generally to all leaders. The **SHEPHERD** (p. 63)
and **HARVEST** (p. 66) models apply less broadly to some and most
specifically to others depending on giftedness. **LEADERSHIP
EMERGENCE** (p. 69) is the application of the leadership mandate
(Hebrews 13:7,8) to the tracing of the development of a given
Christian leader. A **LEADERSHIP EMERGENCE STUDY** (p. 70) provides
an organized framework for tracing that development. Three types
of formation, **SPIRITUAL FORMATION** (p. 72), **MINISTERIAL FORMATION**
(p. 73), and **STRATEGIC FORMATION** (p. 74) point out the
fundamental areas that God develops in expanding a Christian
leader to accomplish His ultimate purposes.

LEADERSHIP ACT   synonym: group influence

introduction   A leadership act occurs when a given person
                influences a group, in terms of behavioral acts or
                perception, so that the group acts or thinks
                differently as a group than before the instance of
                influence. Such an act can be evaluated in terms
                of the three major leadership categories: 1)
                leadership basal elements, 2) leadership influence
                means and 3) leadership value bases. It should be
                noted that any given act of leadership may have
                several persons of the group involved in bringing
                about the influence. While the process may be
                complex and difficult to assess, nevertheless,
                leadership can be seen to happen and be composed
                essentially of influencer, group, influence means,
                and resulting change of direction by the group.

definition   A leadership act is the specific instance at a
                given point in time of the leadership influence
                process between a given influencer (person said to
                be influencing) and follower(s) (person or persons
                being influenced) in which the followers are
                influenced toward some goal.

example   Barnabas, Acts 9:26-30

example   Barnabas, Acts 11:22-24

example   Barnabas, Acts 11:25-26

example   Agabus, Acts 11:27-28

example   leaders, whole church: Acts 11:29-30

example   Paul, Barnabas, apostles and elders in Jerusalem,
                Peter, James: Acts 15:1-21

comment   One can differentiate between a momentary instance
                of leadership which I call a leadership act, as
                defined above, and leadership as an ongoing process
                which I call leadership. The momentary leadership
                act recognizes the reciprocal nature of leadership
                (that is, the impact of gifts that all have) for
                any group in a given situation. The repeated
                persistence of leadership acts by a given person
                indicates the permanence of a leader in a group
                context and specifies leadership.

comment   A major difference in one who influences
                momentarily in a group and one who persistently
                influences over time is the emergence of vision and
                sense of responsibility for seeing that vision
                fulfilled.

FEEDBACK EXERCISES ON LEADERSHIP ACT

1. Examine the leadership act given in Acts 9:26-30.   Identify
the four major parts of the leadership act.

    a. leader--

    b. followers--

    c. influence means-

    d. the influence goal (resulting change)--

2. For the leadership act in Acts 9:26-30, was the leader
successful in this leadership act? If not, why not? If so, why
do you think the leader was successful?

3. Describe a recent leadership act you have observed in
connection with some ministry you are involved in. Describe,

    a. leader--

    b. followers--

    c. influence means--

    d. results--

ANSWERS----------

    1. **a.** leader--Barnabas **b.** followers--apostles in
Jerusalem, unnamed but most likely including Peter, James, John
et al. **c.** influence means--persuasion backed by credibility.
d. the goal was to have Saul recognized as a legitimate Christian
and to have him accepted by the apostles.
    2. In my opinion, yes. Verse 28 describing Saul's staying in
Jerusalem and his ministry there indicates that Barnabas was
successful.
    3. Your choice. In doing this exercise you will probably
note that leadership acts in life are generally much more complex
than the biblical example given above (that one was probably
complex but we only have a selected summary of it). For one
thing, there is usually multiple influence going on in the group.
That is, it may not be easy to identify only one leader. For
another thing influence goals are not always straightforward or
understood by leaders and followers. Sometimes there are
differing groups of followers within the same leadership act.

LEADER

introduction   One who persists in leadership acts is a leader.
                Such an influencer is said to demonstrate
                leadership. From a study of many leaders in both
                the Old and New Testaments the following
                perspectives are offered as a synthesis of a
                biblical leader.

definition   A leader, as defined from a study of Biblical
                leadership, and for whom we are interested in
                tracing leadership development is a person,
                    1) with God-given capacity AND
                    2) with God-given responsibility
                WHO IS INFLUENCING
                    3) a specific group of God's people
                    4) toward God's purposes for the group.

Biblical   Joseph, Moses, Joshua, Jephthah, Samuel, David,
examples   Daniel, Paul, Peter, Barnabas, Timothy, Titus

historical   William Carey, J. Hudson Taylor, J. O. Fraser,
examples   Cameron Townsend, Charles Simeon, Henrietta Mears,
                Phineas Bresee, Simon Kimbangi, Livingston Sohn,
                John Sung, Samuel Mills

central   The central ethic of Biblical leadership is,
ethic   INFLUENCING TOWARD GOD'S PURPOSES. That is, the
                prime function of leadership is the influencing of
                groups so as to accomplish God's purposes involving
                the group. This requires vision. This external
                direction is what distinguishes a Christian leader
                from a secular leader.

comment   The "God-given capacity" denotes giftedness
capacity   (whether an actual spiritual gift or natural talent
                or acquired skill). The capacity of a leader is
                part of the influence means component of the
                leadership framework. It also connotes leadership
                character, as well as the concept of the potential
                that is yet to be developed.

comment   The "God-given responsibility" denotes two major
responsi-   ideas concerning a sense of accountability with
bility   God for leadership. 1) There is a downward sense of
                responsibility (a burden from God) to influence
                others for God.   2) There is an upward sense of
                responsibility (to God) for the people being
                influenced.

comment   Leadership is concerned with the persistent
specific   influence of a leader upon specific groups. It is
groups   this group (the followers) for which the leader will
                be responsible and will discern God's purposes.

FEEDBACK ON LEADER

1. Give Biblical evidence for each of the four significant points in the definition of leader.

2. Choose any of the leaders mentioned in the examples (or any other one that you want to use) and illustrate how each of the significant points in the leadership definition is fulfilled.

3. Explain how you personally interpret the concept of "God-given capacity" to influence?

ANSWERS----------

1. I'll just touch on some answers. There is much more in the Bible. You probably have other answers than those I've hastily jotted down. Concept 1: see Ephesians 4:7-11, and passages on spiritual gifts of ruling, administration, apostleship, and pastoring. Concept 2: see Acts 20:28, Hebrews 13:17. Concept 3: see Acts 20:28, I Peter 5:2. Concept 4: see Acts 20:17-38. The whole passage is Paul's example of this very concept; his letters to churches illustrate this.

2. A study of Samuel Mills' leadership development (Maranville 1982) reveals that he was gifted to foster mission organizations. He had an amazing ability to organize and administer and to motivate others to take over the organizations. His influence was greatly felt in the early years of mission activity in the United States in the early 1800s. He demonstrated traits usually identified with the spiritual gifts of apostleship and administration. A study of Mills' whole life-time seems to indicate that God gave him a national responsibility to motivate North American Christians toward involvement in missions. The groups of people for whom he was responsible (indirectly) were those people already involved in churches but not in missions--which was the majority of christians in North America. In terms of God's purposes, time and time again Mills saw the need for an organization or a movement which would recruit and activate God's people into missions' involvement. He was able to sense God's timing in events and happenings and develop plans and organizations based on what he saw.

3. I interpret the phrase "God-given capacity to influence" to mean that the person is born with natural abilities for leadership as well as potential to acquire skills that will enable influence. A leader has also been imparted spiritual gifts which are important for influencing. I consider spiritual leadership gifts (that is, those gifts which allow for influence) to include what I call the word gifts. Primary word gifts include teaching, prophecy, exhortation, Secondary word gifts include: apostleship, evangelism and pastoring (and ruling). Tertiary word gifts include word of wisdom and word of knowledge and faith.

COMMENTARY ON LEADER

position
or
influence

Frequently missionaries and nationals and particularly women coming to the School of World Mission identify a leader as a person having a formal position of leadership. Notice that the focus of this definition is not on status or position but on functionality. That is, a leader is one who influences others. It is true that there are leaders who are influencing people toward God's purposes who may not have formal positions. It is also true that there are people holding formal positions who are not really functioning as leaders. One can exercise leadership even in situations where structures prohibit them from having formal positions.

women
in
leadership

Frequently, women students do not think of themselves as leaders. This can occur primarily for two reasons. One, some Christian leaders have convictions against women in leadership and teach against it. Some women who have sat under this kind of teaching find it difficult to freely see themselves as leaders. Two, many women come from male dominated cultures in which formal leadership structures are open only to males. Four basic positions on women in leadership include: can operate freely, cannot operate at all, can operate but under a male authority covering, can operate only with women. My own conviction allows for women who are gifted and developed by God for leadership to lead; the same for men. My definition of a leader can apply broadly to those who hold my conviction or not--since it is an influence based definition, not a formal/ positional one. Sometimes women who study leadership emergence theory go through a paradigm shift[3] in which they move from viewing themselves as not being leaders to being leaders. The real problem, once one admits that God has gifted one to lead, is how to exercise that leadership in terms of the cultural structures and roles available.

ordination
and
leadership

My own convictions have led me to believe that ordination is not required in order to exercise leadership. It may be important for civil or government recognition or other purposes. Ordination requirements vary greatly from group to

---

[3]A paradigm shift is a radical change in one's mental perspectives. In this case, the women students perceive that their past experience has indeed been filled with repetitive incidents of influence even if they have not held formal positions. An analysis of their giftedness confirms that they are gifted for leadership. Chapter 5 discusses the notion of a paradigm shift as an expansion process used by God.

COMMENTARY ON LEADER continued

group and are largely traditionally based. See
Warkenton (1982) on this. What this often means is
that women are excluded from ordination due to male
biased tradition. I advise sometimes for
ordination, or sometimes against it, depending on the
situation of a given leader. Regardless of gender,
ordination usually encourages the problem of
dichotomy between clergy and laity and thus
discourages lay leadership.

elements
of
emergence

Though potential leaders are born, effective
leaders are made as a result of, 1) opportunity,
2) training and 3) experience. These three components
do not automatically guarantee that one will rise
to become a great leader. But without them it is
not likely that one will realize maximum potential.

essential
difference
of
leaders and
followers

Both leaders and followers actually influence in
church and para-church situations. When Christians
use their gifts with others, these impact so as
to influence. In small groups, the sharing of both
leaders and followers will influence. There is a
mutuality of leadership in group situations.
Sometimes followers spontaneously exert influence
that is significant to a group. Le Peau (1983)
stresses that anyone can lead. He describes paths
along which anyone can develop as a leader. My
understanding of leaders and leadership disagrees
somewhat with his approach. I do allow for anyone
to lead (that is, exert influence) in the sense of
a leadership act. But I want to strongly point out
that this is different from on-going leadership.
When I think of a leader as defined herein I am
thinking of permanency, a continuing on-going
influence that can build toward accomplishment of
vision (a la Ephesians 4:7ff, Christ's gifts to the
church for leadership). I am talking about people
who have a sense, inherent or instilled, of
responsibility to carry out some aspect of God's
work and to give an account to God for others.
This sense of vertical accountability
differentiates "casual leadership" from permanent
on-going leadership. Those who do not have this
sense of accountability are basically followers.

calling
and
leadership

Leaders need a strong sense of destiny. A call is
one manifestation of that but not the only one.
Even without a supernatural call the stewardship
model can provide a pseudo-call to those who see
the implications of the model. The model, itself,
is enough to give one a sense of destiny toward
leadership. If God has given capacity then
inherent in it is the destiny to use it.

LEADERSHIP

introduction   Leadership is essentially the ongoing persistence
of leadership acts by one person. One who
consistently exerts influence over a group is said
to manifest leadership. Leadership is then seen to
be an ongoing process involving several complex
items. This definition flows from a research
project in which I studied the development of
leadership theory from 1841 till 1986.

definition   Leadership is a dynamic process over an extended
period of time in various situations in which a
leader utilizing leadership resources, and by
specific leadership behaviors, influences
followers, toward accomplishment of aims mutually
beneficial for leaders and followers.

example   Barnabas' leadership: Acts 4:32-36; 9:26-30; 11:22-
24; 11:25-26; 15:1-21. Here Barnabas is seen to
exercise influence in various situations over a
long period of time. He used various resource
means to accomplish this influence.

example   Paul's leadership (a few leadership acts cited):
Acts 11:25,26; 13:9-12; 13:13-43; 13:44-48; 14:21-
23; 20:17-38.

comment   The major items in the leadership process include:
1. It is a dynamic process over an extended
period of time.
2. It is exercised in various situations.
3. It is identified with a leader, one who
persists in exercising influence.
4. It involves the use of leadership resources
which include various power bases for
influencing.
5. It is seen overtly in leadership behaviors
which contribute to the influence process.
6. Its nature is seen as motivating followers
so that the group responds differently than
would be the case without the influence.
7. It is seen as purposeful (directive). That
is, influence which moves followers, toward
accomplishment of aims which may originate
with the leader, the followers, or some
combination of both.
8. Ideally, it results in mutual benefit for
the leader, the followers, and the
situation of which they are a part.

comment   Point eight is an ideal not always seen in secular
leadership.

see also   **LEADERSHIP FUNCTIONS** page 42

FEEDBACK ON LEADERSHIP

1. I have stated in the examples that Barnabas exercised
leadership. I pointed out several leadership acts: Acts 4:32-36,
9:26-30, 11:22-24, 11:25-26, 15:1-21. Do you agree? Quickly
scan the biblical passages giving these leadership acts. How many
of the major items of the leadership process are seen in these
leadership acts examined as a whole? Check the leadership
elements which you feel can be seen in these acts.
___ a. It is a dynamic process over an extended period of time.
___ b. It is exercised in various situations.
___ c. It is identified with a leader, one who persists in
        exercising influence.
___ d. It involves the use of leadership resources which include
        various power bases for influencing.
___ e. It is seen overtly in leadership behaviors which
        contribute to the influence process.
___ f. Its nature is seen as changing the followers thoughts
        and/or behavior so that the groups respond differently
        than would be the case without the influence.
___ g. It is seen as purposeful (directive). That is, influence
        which affects the thoughts and activity of followers,
        toward accomplishment of aims which may originate with the
        leader, the followers, or some combination of both.
___ h. It results in mutual benefit for the leader, the
        followers, and the macro context of which they are a part.

2. Take any two of the leadership elements you checked above and
explain them. That is, show what you saw in scripture that
prompted you to select the leadership element as being present.

3. If you were to examine an autocratic leader, Hitler, in terms
of his leadership acts which of the following leadership elements
most likely would not be demonstrated.
___ a. His leadership was demonstrated in various situations.
___ b. He used various power bases for influencing.
___ c. One of the overt behaviors which was tremendously
        effective was his public oratory.
___ d. His leadership was purposeful (directive). Influence which
        affected the thoughts and activity of followers, toward
        accomplishment of aims which were primarily his own.
___ e. It resulted in mutual benefit for the leader, the
        followers, and the macro context.

ANSWERS----------
    1. I checked all of them. "g" is least easiest to demonstrate.
    2. I'll explain what I saw concerning (e) and (h).
Barnabas used persuasive oratory to convince apostles to accept
Saul in Acts 9:26-30. He used modelling as well as oratory to
influence behavior in Acts 11:22-24. Barnabas' influence
resulted in Paul being accepted as a Christian leader which
significantly altered the course of history. His ministry at
Antioch provided the base for cross-cultural missionary effort
which began the worldwide expansion of the Gospel.
    3. e. My opinion of course.

LEADERSHIP FUNCTIONS

introduction   High level Christian leaders perform many
                leadership functions. In addition to direct
                ministry functions based on giftedness there are
                those additional functions that are the
                responsibility of leaders simply because they are
                people of responsibility for others. The
                inspirational functions are part of this added
                responsibility of Christian leaders. The Ohio
                State model showed that most leadership functions
                can be grouped under two major functions, those
                dealing with consideration functions and those
                dealing with initiation of structure. In addition
                to these there are the inspirational functions
                which flow from word gifted leadership. Note that
                the giftedness of the leader, that is, the direct
                ministry functions can occur in any of the three
                major categories.

description   Leadership functions describe general activities
                that leaders must do and/or be responsible for in
                their influence responsibilities with followers.

comment   The Ohio State Leadership Research paradigm (1948–
Ohio State   1967) reduced the many observed functions of
analysis   secular leadership by factor analysis to two major
                generic categories: consideration and initiation of
                structure.

comment   Consideration is the Ohio State term which groups
consideration   all of those activities which a leader does to
                affirm followers, to provide an atmosphere
                congenial to accomplishing work, to give emotional
                and spiritual support for followers so that they
                can mature, in short, to act relationally with
                followers in order to enable them to develop and be
                effective in their contribution to the
                organization.

comment   Initiation of structure is the Ohio State term
initiation   which groups all of those activities which a leader
of   does to accomplish the task or vision for which the
structure   group exists. Task behaviors involve clarifying
                goals, setting up structures to help reach them,
                holding people accountable, disciplining where
                necessary and in short, to act responsibly to
                accomplish goals.

comment   Christian leadership is externally directed. That
inspirational   is, goals result from vision from God. That
                kind of leadership must move followers toward
                recognition of and acceptance of and participation
                in bringing about that God-given vision or those
                goals.

LEADERSHIP FUNCTIONS continued

Consideration Functions (relationship behaviors)

Christian leaders,

1. must continually be involved in the selection and development and release of emerging leaders.
2. are continually called upon to solve crises which involve relationships between people.
3. will be called upon for decision making focusing on people.
4. must do routine people related problem solving.
5. will coordinate with subordinates, peers, and superiors.
6. must facilitate leadership transition; their own and others.
7. must do direct ministry relating to people (extent depends on giftedness).

Initiation of Structure Functions (task behaviors)

Christian leaders,

1. must provide structures which facilitate accomplishment of vision.
2. will be involved in crisis resolution which is brought about due to structural issues.
3. must make decisions involving structures.
4. will do routine problem solving concerning structural issues.
5. will adjust structures where necessary to facilitate leadership transitions.
6. must do direct ministry relating maintaining and changing structures (extent depends on giftedness).

Inspirational Functions (motivating toward vision)

Christian leaders,

1. must motivate followers toward vision.
2. must encourage perseverance and faith of followers.
3. are responsible for the corporate integrity of the structures and organizations of which they are a part.
4. are responsible for developing and maintaining the welfare of the corporate culture of the organization.
5. (especially higher level) are responsible for promoting the public image of the organization.
6. (especially higher level) are responsible for the financial welfare of the organization.
7. are responsible for direct ministry along lines of giftedness which relate to inspirational functions.
8. must model (knowing, being, and doing) so as to inspire followers toward the reality of God's intervention in lives.
9. have corporate accountability to God for the organizations or structures in which they operate.

FEEDBACK ON LEADERSHIP FUNCTIONS

1. The two Ohio State behavioral functions of consideration and initiation of structure are commonly referred to in the leadership concentration as relational behavior and task behavior, terms more directly appropriate to Hersey and Blanchard's (1982) leadership theory. The Ohio State findings indicated that the two were independent of each other. That is, a given leader could operate freely in both functional areas. Fiedler (1967) and others generally disagreed and posited that leaders usually are "bent" toward one or the other as dominant in their leadership. What has been your experience? Are leaders in your culture generally task oriented or relationally oriented or some combination? Explain.

2. Give here the name of a leader that you have known who is highly task oriented. Give also an example of a task which has driven this leader.
      a. leader--   b. cultural origin--
      c. culture ministering in--
      d. illustration of task--

3. Give here the name of a leader that you have known who is relationally oriented. Give an example of relational behavior from that leader's ministry.
      a. leader--   b. cultural origin--
      c. culture ministering in--
      d. illustration of relational behavior--

4. Give here the name of a leader that you have known who operates well in the inspirational functions. Identify a specific inspirational function and illustrate it.
      a. leader--   b. cultural origin--
      c. culture ministering in--
      d. illustration of inspirational function--

5. Do this exercise after you have studied the 5 Types of Leaders. Consider the total list of functions under the three categories. Beside each function place each type of leader (A,B,C,D,E) if you think that type of leader is heavily responsible for that leadership function.

ANSWERS----------
    1. In my culture I have experienced a mix of both although task behavior seems to be more valued and espoused by leadership in general. In the West Indies I found the reverse was more generally true. In either case leaders were not usually both task and relational--one usually dominated to the detriment of the other.
    2. your choice. 3. your choice. 4. your choice.
    5. The point of this exercise is to see that Types A and B are dominantly involved in direct ministry functions. Type C is usually involved in both depending on the size of organization involved in. Type D and Type E will be concerned more with indirect functions.

COMMENTARY ON LEADERSHIP FUNCTIONS

essentials
of
leadership
activities

There are common activities and unique activities
for the three categories of leadership functions.
Listing them in a single list helps identify the
essential activities of Christian leaders.

1. Utilize their giftedness for direct ministry for
   all those within their sphere of influence.
2. Solve crises.
3. Make decisions.
4. Do routine problem solving.
5. Coordinate people, goals, and structures.
6. Select and develop leaders.
7. Facilitate leadership transition (adjustments
   with people and structures) at all levels.
8. Facilitate structures to accomplish vision.
9. Motivate followers toward vision. This usually
   involves changing what is, and providing/
   promoting a sense of progress.
10. Must encourage perseverance and faith of
    followers. This usually involves maintaining
    what is and creating a sense of stability. This
    is usually in dynamic tension with activity 9.
11. Accept responsibility for corporate functions of
    integrity, culture, finances, and accountability.
12. Must model so as to inspire followers toward the
    reality of God's intervention in lives and
    history.

direct
versus
indirect

Direct ministry involves ministry which produces
growth such as evangelism (quantitative growth) or
teaching (qualitative growth). Usually the word
gifts (apostleship, prophesy, evangelism,
pastoring, teaching, exhortation) are thought of as
involving primarily direct ministry. Indirect
ministry involves activities which enable direct
ministry to happen. While it is true that most of
the activities on the condensed list above involve
both direct and indirect ministry it is also true
that the larger majority are dominantly indirect.
As leaders move along the Typology continuum they
will increasingly be involved in more indirect
ministry and will embrace it as primary because of
their understanding of capacity entrusted them.
The enablement of others to do direct ministry is
the thrust of indirect ministry. This means
creating and keeping healthy organizations and
structures through which it can happen. On the
typology continuum the move from Type B to C
involves a shift toward indirect ministry. The
shift from C to D is a major shift toward indirect
ministry. Processing which develops a leader for
these shifts focuses on the first two elements of
the leader definition--capacity and
responsibility.

5 TYPES OF LEADERS

introduction   It is sometimes helpful to recognize differences in
                 influence capacities in Christian leadership. This
                 is so since sub-categories under the three basic
                 leadership categories--leadership basal elements,
                 leadership influence means, and leadership value
                 bases--frequently vary depending on the sphere of
                 influence of the leader, the financial base for the
                 leader, and the ministry thrust of the leader. This
                 classification follows along earlier lines by
                 McGavran and McKinney.

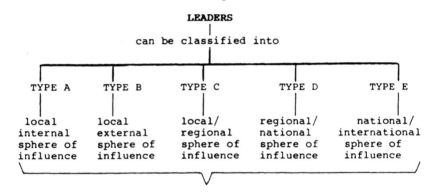

LEADERS

can be classified into

TYPE A	TYPE B	TYPE C	TYPE D	TYPE E
local internal sphere of influence	local external sphere of influence	local/ regional sphere of influence	regional/ national sphere of influence	national/ international sphere of influence

which can be further delimited by
the para-professional/professional continuum

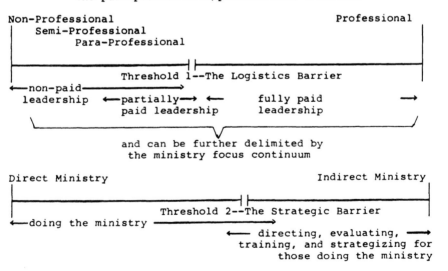

Non-Professional   Professional
    Semi-Professional
        Para-Professional

Threshold 1--The Logistics Barrier

←—non-paid————————→
   leadership   ←—partially—→ ←—   fully paid   —→
                 paid leadership   leadership

and can be further delimited by
the ministry focus continuum

Direct Ministry   Indirect Ministry

Threshold 2--The Strategic Barrier

←—doing the ministry ————————→

                    ←— directing, evaluating, —→
                    training, and strategizing for
                    those doing the ministry

EXAMPLES OF 5 TYPES OF LEADERS

introduction   Below are given a list of general examples of the
                five types of leaders.

examples   Sunday School workers in local church, home group
Type A   leaders, youth workers.

comment   Type A leaders primarily work with small groups
Type A   within a local church. Their basic ministry thrust
                is edification and service within the local body.
                They are para-professional Christians in that they
                see their main contribution in life as ministry to
                the church. Their vocation supports this purpose.

examples   visitation workers, bi-vocational pastor, part-time
Type B   evangelist, part-time pastor, pastor shared between
                two small congregations, evangelist/church planting
                paid worker

comment   Type B leaders can work both within the local
Type B   church and beyond it. Their basic ministry thrust
                goes beyond edification to evangelism and other
                outreach ministries beyond the confines of the
                local church. The sphere of influence is beyond
                small groups but usually limited to small churches.
                They are para-professional Christian workers in
                that they see their main contribution in life as
                ministry to the church. Their vocation supports
                this purpose.

example   full-time paid pastor, youth worker, evangelist,
Type C   other staff workers in a larger local church.

comment   Type C leaders usually are senior pastors of large
Type C   churches or those on staff who have large spheres
                of influence. Usually Type C leaders will have
                external influence upon other churches or pastors
                of churches. These are professional Christian
                workers who are paid to do Christian ministry.
                Usually these workers will meet ordination
                requirements and will be recognized by the
                government as ministers with legal status as such.

examples   heads of small mission organizations working in a
Type D   region or country, denominational workers with
                regional or national influence, national
                evangelists, teachers in seminaries or other
                training institutes training full-time christian
                workers, national strategists, authors of training
                materials and books which are used nationally
                across denominations and in seminaries and
                institutes, theologians of national influence

EXAMPLES OF 5 TYPES OF LEADERS continued

comment
Type D

Type D leaders primarily give direction to Type A, B, and C leadership in a region or a country. They are people who influence Christianity throughout a region or nation. They set trends in terms of evangelistic strategies, training strategies, methodology, evaluation, organizational cooperation, contextualization of theology, and the founding of new organizations. They are usually people who are known widely by Type C leaders.

examples
Type E

heads of international organizations, Christian statesmen who travel internationally and influence several nations, prominent theologians, trainers who are training Type D leadership (multi-country), prominent authors of Christian materials which set trends or support wide-spread movements, charismatic leaders who begin movements and organizations which expand worldwide or at least across many nations

comment
Type E

Often Type E leaders will control large resources of people, finances, and facilities. They will have very broad personal networks with other international leaders and national leaders. They will often be on boards of very influential organizations.

comment

It should be explicitly stated here that there is no inherent value attached to any of the types. That is, a Type E leader is not better than a Type A leader. All of the various types are needed in the church. More types A and B are needed than say Type E. The type of leader we become depends on capacity that God has given and God's development of us toward roles which use that capacity. To be gifted for Type B leadership and to aspire for Type D is a mismanagement of stewardship. So too, to be gifted for Type E and yet remain at Type C. None of the types are better than any other. All are needed. We need to operate along the continuum so as to responsibly exercise stewardship of our giftedness and God's development of our leadership.

FEEDBACK ON TYPES OF LEADERS

1. The essential difference between a Type A leader and a Type C
leader are (check the one correct answer):
____ a. a Type A leader is a full time Christian worker while a
      Type C worker is usually a bi-vocational worker.
____ b. a Type A worker is usually not paid and works with groups
      primarily within the local church while a Type C worker is
      paid and works with people both in and out of the church.
____ c. neither (a) nor (b)
____ d. both (a) and (b)

2. The essential difference between Types A, B, C and Types D,E
is (choose any answers which are correct):

____ a. Types D,E have a different ministry focus; indirect as
      opposed to direct.
____ b. Types D,E are fully supported while Types A, B, C are not.
____ c. Types D,E usually have formal training to do indirect
      ministry functions while Types A, B, C usually have non-
      formal and in-formal training to do direct ministry.

3. Give here an example of each of the Types of leaders and a
qualifying phrase showing their ministry focus to show that you
understand the basic types.

Type	Name	Descriptive Phrase
A		
B		
C		
D		
E		

ANSWERS----------

See next page.

FEEDBACK ON TYPES OF LEADERS continued

ANSWERS----------

    1. b.
    2. a.
    3.

Type	Name	Descriptive Phrase
A	Althea Penner	Participates in and leads worship for "Cornerstone," an adult Sunday School class. has exhortive gift; occupation is nursing.
B	Mike Plessett	Leadership responsibilities in "Cornerstone." Involved in social and evangelistic ministries outside the church as well. His vocation is a financial investor.
C	Richard Clinton	Pastor in Anaheim Vineyard Church, a full time Christian worker supported by the church; formal training acquired Fuller Theological Seminary.
D	John Tanner	Denominational executive with the Queensland Baptist (Australia); also heads a mission organization for church planting and is on several other mission boards
E	C. Peter Wagner	Professor of Church Growth at Fuller Theological Seminary; trains type D leaders; has written many books used as texts all around the world; has international ministry in conferences, seminars, and workshops; has influence with several internationally influential organizations

COMMENTARY ON TYPES OF LEADERS

application   Below is given a specific example of the typology
of   continuum as perceived by Queensland Baptist
continuum   Pastors. During a week long seminar in Brisbane
                   they applied the standard typology continuum to
                   their situation with the following result.

Example: Australian Baptists (Queensland)

<--doing the ministry ---------->
                         <------ directing, evaluating,   --->
                         training and strategizing for
                         those doing the ministry

```
|              Threshold 1    Threshold 2                            |
|--------------||-------------||----------------------------------|
|A             B             C                    D               E |
```

small   small to   large church   state/   Inter-
local   middle   with senior pastor national   National
church   size local   and pastoral staff denomi-   statesmen
               church   national
                                                leaders

(0-50)   (50-150)   (150+)   groups of
people   people   people   churches

<--non-paid-->
  leadership   <--partially/full-->   <-- full paid   -->
                          paid leadership   leadership

McGavran's   Various profiles of the continuum can be described.
ideal   McGavran's (1981) original use of the continuum
profile   was for showing profiles which represented growing
                   church denominations and and plateaued church
                   denominations. He showed that for churches that
                   were growing quantitatively the following profile
                   was needed. The profile is not exact but relative.

```
            ^      |              x
            |      |              x
        number    |              x
          of      |      x       x
        leaders   |      x       x       x
                  |      x       x       x       x
                  |      x       x       x       x       x
                  |_____
                      Type A   Type B  Type C  Type D  Type E
```

COMMENTARY ON TYPES OF LEADERS continued

further
use of
continuum

Plots of current leadership in a denomination or country along the continuum will be helpful in analysis of the health or sickness of a church. If such a plot is correlated with age of leaders it can prove helpful in anticipating future needs for selection and development of leaders. Elliston (1989:190) has suggested an ideal profile based on numbers of churches and size of churches.

problem

One problem which the continuum helps visualize is often associated with the pre-service transitional training pattern, TR.1 (see Chapter 11). Leaders often skip Type A and Type B leadership and are trained formally to enter at the level of Type C. Normally, healthy development for a leader involves experiencing each of the previous types before moving to a new type. Skipping any type makes one vulnerable in overseeing leaders of that type. This same kind of problem exists for those who are trained formally at Type C and enter at Type D (say in a Bible College or seminary which is training Type C or B people). Without experiencing Type C functions it is difficult for one to adequately train others for it.

projection
tendency

There is a tendency to seek to pressure good Type A and B leaders to "go full time." The idea being that full time Christian leaders are more dedicated to God than lay leaders. Agnes Sanford (1983: 71,72, 146,147) points out the fallacy of this in two excellent examples describing lay people, their giftedness and their accomplishment for God.

problems
crossing
the
thresholds

The two thresholds present problems that leaders should be aware of. Crossing the logistics barrier, threshold 1, involves a major status change for leaders. Laity perceive full time Christian workers differently than lay leaders. Movement across the threshold means that people will view them differently (perhaps have higher expectations of them) even though their roles may not change. And there is the basic problem of how to finance full time Christian work. Type C leaders are usually unprepared to cross threshold 2, the strategic barrier, for two reasons. Responsibilities that Type D and E leaders perform dominantly require indirect ministry functions, something most Type C leaders were not trained for. So problem 1 in crossing threshold 2 means that most leaders are not prepared to handle the ministry activities of that level and will grope for a period of time as these activities

COMMENTARY ON TYPES OF LEADERS

crossing
the
thresholds
continued

are learned experientially (mainly via negative
processing). A second problem of crossing the
strategic barrier is that most leaders think
tactically and not strategically. That is, they
have been rewarded psychologically (affirmation,
feeling of competency) for doing direct ministry
which involves their gifts. Now they must do
indirect ministry (problem solving, crises
resolution, structural planning, strategizing,
etc.) which does not reward one in the same way as
direct ministry. Two things can help overcome the
psychological loss perceived by leaders crossing
the strategic barrier. One, they can from time to
time do forays back into direct ministry which
bring satisfaction that was experienced previously.
Two, they can learn to see that what is being
accomplished has broader potential and more far
reaching results than their former direct ministry
which had to be sacrificed in accepting Type D
ministry. This is strategic thinking and an
application of the servant leadership model at a
higher capacity level.

why
distinguish
types

Types of leaders are distinguished not to imply
that bigger is better but to indicate that sub-
category items under the basic three leadership
categories (leadership basal elements, leadership
influence means, and leadership value bases) will
vary noticeably with the different types of
leaders. For example, Types D and E will be much
more concerned with the leadership means/resource
items of organizational structure, culture,
dynamics, and power. They will usually be leaders
available to utilize many leadership styles. They
are people who will be much more concerned with
leadership value bases and will have heavy
accountability to God in these areas. They will be
concerned with macro-contextual factors.
Leadership functions, too, will vary greatly along
the continuum. This means that different training
is needed for the roles implied by each type.
Informal and non-formal training which focuses on
skills for direct ministry is needed for Type A and
B and should usually be in-service. All three
modes (informal, non-formal, and formal) are
needed to provide skills and perspectives for
Types C, D, and E. In-service and interrupted
in-service should dominate for Types C, D, and
E.

I CATEGORIES OF LEADERSHIP ANALYSIS--THE LEADERSHIP FRAMEWORK

;ynonym: A Balanced Framework for Analyzing Leadership

.ntroduction   Leadership anywhere in the world is concerned with
               some basic common issues. These can be grouped and
               organized under three major categories. The first
               category concerns the basal elements of leadership
               which occur wherever leadership exists: the leader,
               the followers, and the situational context
               affecting both leader and followers. The second
               category involves the ways and means whereby a
               leader actually influences the followers. This
               second category includes the leader behavior and
               means/resources. The third category, leadership
               value bases, is often implicit and not expressed
               openly. It refers to the underlying purpose,
               motivation, ethics and philosophy governing the
               leadership basal elements and the leadership
               influence means. These 3 major categories are
               relatively generic and can be used as a framework
               for leadership analysis in various cultures. Sub-
               categories under these major categories are less
               cross-culturally valid directly but most likely
               have dynamic equivalent forms/functions in various
               cultures. This is a first-draft attempt at
               organizing a leadership framework for analysis.

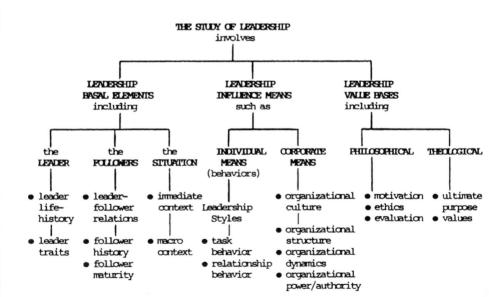

THE STUDY OF LEADERSHIP
involves

LEADERSHIP BASAL ELEMENTS including			LEADERSHIP INFLUENCE MEANS such as		LEADERSHIP VALUE BASES including	
the LEADER	the FOLLOWERS	the SITUATION	INDIVIDUAL MEANS (behaviors)	CORPORATE MEANS	PHILOSOPHICAL	THEOLOGICAL
• leader life-history	• leader-follower relations	• immediate context	Leadership Styles	• organizational culture	• motivation • ethics • evaluation	• ultimate purpose • values
• leader traits	• follower history • follower maturity	• macro context	• task behavior • relationship behavior	• organizational structure • organizational dynamics • organizational power/authority		

FEEDBACK ON 3 CATEGORIES OF LEADERSHIP ANALYSIS

1. If the leadership basal elements answers the "what" of
leadership, that is,

   What are the essential elements of leadership?

and leadership influence means answers the "how" of
leadership, that is,

   How do leaders accomplish leadership?

what question(s) does leadership value bases answer?

2. The balanced analytical framework can be used to analyze any
specific leadership act (or a series of them). Each of the major
items or sub-categories can be used as a screen through which to
view the leadership act. Suggested exercises include analysis of
the last public act of Samuel's leadership and/or the Jerusalem
counsel deliberations of Acts 15 from the standpoint of Barnabas'
leadership.

ANSWERS----------

   1. The "leadership value bases" answers the "why" of
leadership. Why does leadership exist? And what are the
standards by which leadership is judged?
   2. I'll leave this exercise to you. But if you have access
to the Fuller School of World Mission campus then these two acts
and many others have been evaluated using this framework and are
worth one's reading in order to see these concepts fleshed out in
terms of specific situations.

4 BIBLICAL LEADERSHIP MODELS

introduction   More New Testament philosophical models may exist,
                      but the following four models are the most
                      important ones noted in Christian literature.
                      These models are not exhaustively treated in one
                      unified source in the New Testament. Much of the
                      descriptive analysis comes as much from
                      observations of practice of New Testament leaders
                      as from explanatory passages. The framework below
                      is built on a premise that foundational models have
                      more widespread application, while superstructural
                      models apply less widely. The foundational models
                      apply to all leaders. The superstructural models
                      apply somewhat to all leaders but more specifically
                      to certain gifted leaders.

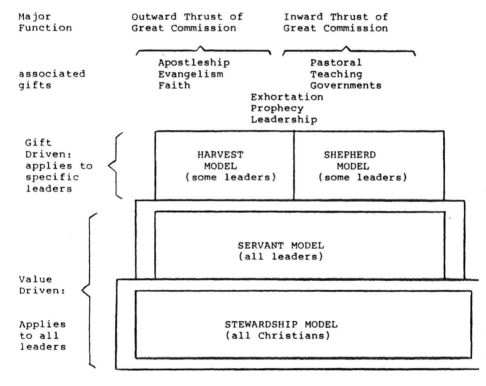

Major   Outward Thrust of   Inward Thrust of
Function   Great Commission   Great Commission

                      Apostleship   Pastoral
associated   Evangelism   Teaching
gifts   Faith   Governments
                                    Exhortation
                                    Prophecy
                                    Leadership

Gift
Driven: HARVEST   SHEPHERD
applies to   MODEL   MODEL
specific   (some leaders)   (some leaders)
leaders

                              SERVANT MODEL
                              (all leaders)

Value
Driven:

Applies   STEWARDSHIP MODEL
to all   (all Christians)
leaders

comment   Value driven means the essence of the model is
                      found in the values it promotes. It applies to all
                      to whom the values are appropriate. Gift driven
                      means that leaders with certain gifts will be drawn
                      to the values of the models.

MINISTRY PHILOSOPHY MODEL--THE STEWARDSHIP MODEL
synonym: Accountability Model

introduction   Ministry philosophy refers to a related set of
values that underlies a leader's perception and
behavior in his/her ministry. The values may be
ideas, principles, guidelines or the like which are
implicit (not actually recognized but part of
perceptive set of the leader) or explicit
(recognized, identified, articulated). For any
given leader a ministry philosophy is unique. It is
dynamic and related to three major elements:
Biblical dynamics, giftedness, and situation.
Though a ministry philosophy is dynamic there are
core issues which are stable and apply to all
leaders. The stewardship model is one such set of
stable Biblical values.

definition   Ministry philosophy refers to ideas, values, and
principles whether implicit or explicit which a
leader uses as guidelines for decision making, for
exercising influence, and for evaluating his/her
ministry.

definition   The stewardship model is a philosophical model
which is founded on the central thrust of several
accountability passages, that is, that a leader
must give account of his/her ministry to God.

passages   Accountability parables: Matthew 20 Laborers in the
Vineyard, Matthew 24 The Waiting Servants, Matthew
25 The Ten Virgins, Matthew 25 The Ten Talents,
Luke 16 The Worldly Wise Steward, Luke 19 The
Pounds.

General Judgment Passages: Romans 14:11,12,
I Corinthians 3:5-9, 12-15, II Corinthians 5:10,
Philippians 2:10,11, Hebrews 9:27.

Special Leadership Responsibility: James 3:1,
Daniel 12:1-3, Hebrews 13:17.

Other Passages Indicating Accountability/ Rewards:
I Corinthians 4:1-5, II Corinthians 4:1-6, Acts
20:17-38, I Peter 5:1-4.

Cases: See Moses especially for severity of
judgment due to leadership position and influence.

MINISTRY PHILOSOPHY MODEL--THE STEWARDSHIP MODEL continued

basic values
1. Ministry challenges, tasks, and assignments ultimately come from God.
2. God holds a leader accountable for leadership influence and for growth and conduct of followers.
3. There will be an ultimate accounting of a leader to God in eternity for one's performance in leadership.
4. Leaders will receive rewards for faithfulness to their ministry in terms of abilities, skills, gifts and opportunities.
5. Leaders are expected to build upon abilities, skills, and gifts so as to maximize potential and use them for God.
6. Leaders will be uniquely gifted both as to gifts and the degree to which the gift can be used effectively.
7. Leaders will receive rewards for their productivity in terms of zealously using abilities, skills, gifts, and opportunities for God.
8. Leaders frequently must hold to higher standards than followers due to "the above reproach" and "modeling impact" they must have on followers.

implications
1. Leaders must be persons who maintain a learning posture all of their lives--growing, expanding, developing.
2. Leaders must make certain of ministry tasks, challenges, and assignments in terms of God's guidance (calling) for them.
3. Leaders must perform in ministry as unto the Lord in all aspects of ministry.

comment
The Stewardship Model is the most general of the New Testament Philosophical models in that it applies to followers as well as leaders. Servant leadership applies only to leaders as does the Shepherd and Harvest Models.

FEEDBACK ON STEWARDSHIP MODEL

1. Scan the list of values for the Stewardship Model. Assess your own personal preference for these values by placing an "x" in the appropriate column for each value. (MP = my personal ministry philosophy)

values	Column 1 Does not affect MP	Column 2 Loosely Held in MP	Column 3 Definitely affects MP	Column 4 Deliberately used and vital to MP
1.				
2.				
3.				
4.				
5.				
6.				
7.				
8.				

2. What other values has God taught you that are not listed but somewhat compatible with the central thrust of this philosophical model?

3. For any one of the values in exercise 1 for which you checked the right most column (deliberately used and vital to my personal ministry philosophy) suggest implications of this value for your ministry.

Value Number   Implication for Me:

4. Which of the values or implications of this model do you think God is impressing upon you, especially at this time in your life, to learn more about or apply more definitely in your life?

ANSWERS----------

    1. all of mine are column 4.
    2. your choice.
    3. Value 8. Implication: Particularly in disputed practices I must sometimes forego a Christian liberty for the benefit of others. That is, I must adhere to a more strict standard than I think is Biblical. This is necessary because my actions as a leader are constantly under scrutiny by followers and may be harmful to a "weaker brother."
    4. Values 1 and 7.

MINISTRY PHILOSOPHY MODEL--THE SERVANT LEADER

introduction Ministry philosophy refers to a related set of values that underlies a leader's perception and behavior in his/her ministry. The values may be ideas, principles, guidelines or the like. Each Christian leader will have a unique ministry philosophy that generally differs from others due to values God has taught experientially. But there will be some items in common with other leaders. The Servant Leader Model provides a set of values that should be common to the ministry philosophy of each Christian leader. Its central thrust says in essence that a leader's main focus is to use leadership to serve followers. A leader is great whose leadership capacities are used in service vertically to God and horizontally to followers.

definition The servant leader model is a philosophical model which is founded on the central thrust of Jesus' teaching on the major quality of great Kingdom leaders. That is, a leader uses leadership to serve followers. This is demonstrated in Jesus' own ministry.

primary Matthew 20:20-28, Mark 10:35-45.
passages

secondary Parable of the Waiting Servant--Matthew 24:42-51,
passages   Luke 12:35-40, 41-48.
   Parable of the Unprofitable Servant--Luke 17:7-10.
   Isaiah's suffering Servant--Isaiah 52:13-53:12.

basic values 1. Leadership is exercised primarily as service first of all to God and secondarily as service to God's people.
2. Service will require sacrifice on the leader's part.
3. Servant leadership is dominated by an imitation modelling leadership style. That is, the dominant form of influence is modelling for the followers and setting expectancies for them to do the same.
4. Abuse of authority, "Lording it" over followers in order to demonstrate one's importance, is incompatible with servant leadership.
5. A major motivational issue for leadership is anticipation of the Lord's return.
6. One ministers as a duty expected because of giftedness. Hence, there is no expectancy or demand or coercion for remuneration--no demanding one's due.

MINISTRY PHILOSOPHY MODEL--THE SERVANT LEADER

implications   1. A servant leader does not demand rights or expect
                   others to see him/her as one with special
                   privileges and status.
                2. A servant leader can expect God to give ministry
                   affirmation and does not demand it from
                   followers.
                3. A servant leader expects to sacrifice. Personal
                   desires, personal time, and personal financial
                   security will frequently be overridden by needs
                   of service in ministry.
                4. The dominant leadership style to be cultivated is
                   imitation modelling. While there is a place for
                   other more authoritarian styles this style will
                   dominate.
                5. Spiritual authority, with its earned credibility,
                   will be the dominant element of one's power-mix.
                6. Leadership functions are performed always with a
                   watchful spirit anticipating the Lord's return.
                7. Finances will not dominate decision making with
                   regard to acceptance of ministry.

comment   "Servanthood is an attitude and a set of values, not
                a specific job description, or form of organization,
                or leadership style." (Bennett 1988:7)

comment   Balance is important, for the servant leader must
                lead and must serve. The servant leader must
                maintain a dynamic tension by recognizing Butt's
                (1975) assertion that a leader leads by serving and
                serves by leading.

comment   The servanthood Model is a general leadership model
                which applies to all leaders.

comment   Kirkpatrick (1988) identified eight common
                characteristics of Biblical leaders in the Old and
                New Testaments whom he considered servant leaders.
                While these commonalities do not give values that
                define what servant leadership is, they do identify
                broad areas of processing that can be expected and
                some character traits that will surface in servant
                leaders. These nine commonalities include: called
                by God, cleansed by God, commissioned by God,
                preserved by God, empowered by God, guided by God,
                humble in service, rejected by the world, triumphant
                in mission. The leaders he studied included:
                Isaiah, Jeremiah, Daniel, Ezekiel, Peter, John,
                Paul, Jesus.

FEEDBACK ON MINISTRY PHILOSOPHY MODEL—THE SERVANT LEADER

1. Scan the list of values for the Servant Leader Model. Assess your own personal preference for these values by placing an "x" in the appropriate column for each value. (MP = my personal ministry philosophy)

values	Column 1 Does not affect MP	Column 2 Loosely Held in MP	Column 3 Definitely affects MP	Column 4 Deliberately used and vital to MP
1.				
2.				
3.				
4.				
5.				
6.				

2. What other values has God taught you that are not listed but somewhat compatible with the central thrust of this philosophical model?

3. For any one of the values in exercise 1 for which you checked the right most column (deliberately used and vital to my personal ministry philosophy) suggest implications of this value for your ministry.

Value   Implication for Me:

4. Which of the values or implications of this model do you think God is impressing upon you especially at this time to learn more about or apply more definitely in your life?

ANSWERS----------

     1. Column 1 = value 5. Column 2 = values 2, 6.
        Column 3 = value 1. Column 4 = values 3, 4.
     2. Your choice.
     3. Value 3--I must deliberately use what happens
in my life (positive and negative lessons) as a means towards influencing my students.
     4. In reviewing the values and implications for this model I have been impressed by how little the Servant Model has affected my leadership. There is much improvement for me in making the values and implications of this model real for me.

MINISTRY PHILOSOPHY MODEL--THE SHEPHERD LEADER

introduction   Each Christian leader will have a unique ministry
                philosophy that generally differs from others due
                to values God has taught experientially. Leaders
                whose giftedness and calling line up with the
                central function of the Shepherd Leader Model will
                find that its values are enmeshed in their own
                unique ministry philosophy. Leaders not so gifted
                may or may not have experienced processing leading
                to these particular ministry philosophy values. In
                any case the values are worth evaluation. Shepherd
                leaders tend to have a leadership style bent which
                is fundamentally relational in nature.

definition   The shepherd leader model is a philosophical model
                which is founded on the central thrust of Jesus' own
                teaching and modelling concerning the
                responsibilities of leadership in caring for
                followers as seen in the various Shepherd/ Sheep
                metaphors in scripture.

central   Its central thrust is concern and care for the
thrust   welfare of followers--that is, growth and
                development of the members in the Kingdom so that
                they know God's rule in their lives and can in turn
                productively impact on God's righteousness in
                society. This model is concerned primarily with the
                inward aspects of the Great Commission--teach them
                to obey all that I have commanded.

primary   Matthew 28:19,20, Great Commission, Inward Aspect.
passages   Matthew 9:36,37 Shepherd Aspect of the Analogy.
                Matthew 18:12 Parable of Lost Sheep.
                Luke 15:1-7 Parable of Lost Sheep.
                John 10:1-18 The Good Shepherd.
                John 21:15-17 Feed My Sheep.
                I Peter 5:1-4 Peter's View, Shepherd Leadership.
                Acts 20:17-38 Paul's View, Watching for the Flock.

archetypes   Peter and Barnabas are significant examples of
                the shepherd leaders in the New Testament.

values   1. Shepherd leaders value personal kingdom growth
                   in each follower. That is, they have a strong
                   desire to see realization of kingdom truth in
                   followers that is, they have a drive to see
                   followers increasingly experiencing the rule of
                   God in their lives. (Matthew 28:20, John 21,
                   Acts 20)

MINISTRY PHILOSOPHY MODEL--THE SHEPHERD LEADER continued

values
continued

2. Shepherd leaders have a strong empathy with followers which seeks to assess where they are and to help meet their needs in order to develop them toward their potential for the kingdom. (Matthew 9:36,37)

3. Shepherd leaders value each follower as important to the whole body and want to keep them incorporated in the body. (Acts 20:28 Luke 15:1-7, Matthew 18:12,13)

4. Shepherd leaders value a personal relationship with followers. (John 10:3, 4, 14)

5. Shepherd leaders give personal guidance to followers by setting examples--particularly in the area of kingdom values. They value the importance of imitation modelling as an influence means with followers. (John 10:4)

6. Shepherd leaders protect followers from deviant teaching by giving positive truth that will aid them in assessing counterfeit teaching. (John 10:5, 10, 12 Acts 20:28)

7. Shepherd leaders want followers to experience abundant life in Christ. (John 10:10)

8. Shepherd leaders are willing to sacrifice and know that personal desires, personal time, and personal financial security will frequently be overridden by needs of service in ministry. (John 10:11)

9. Shepherd leaders are willing to persevere through persecution or hard times in order to better the condition of followers. (John 10:11)

10. Shepherd leaders are open with followers exposing weaknesses and strengths and their heart with followers. (John 10:14)

11. Shepherd leaders value unity in body and wider body. (John 10:16)

12. Shepherd leaders willingly take responsibility for followers. (I Peter 5:2)

13. Financial gain is secondary to performing ministry in the values of a Shepherd leader. I Peter 5:2)

implications   see feedback exercise

comment   Gift-mixes of leaders which correlate strongly with the Shepherd Leader model include the various combinations of: the word gifts of pastor and teaching; the love gifts of mercy and helps and governments; the power gifts of healing and word of wisdom.

comment   The word gifts of prophecy and exhortation and leadership can operate with both Shepherd and Harvest leader models.

FEEDBACK ON SHEPHERD MODEL

1. Scan the list of values for the Shepherd Model. Assess your
own personal preference for these values by placing an "x" in the
appropriate column for each value. (MP = my personal ministry
philosophy)

values	Column 1 Does not affect MP	Column 2 Loosely Held in MP	Column 3 Definitely affects MP	Column 4 Deliberately used and vital to MP
1.				
2.				
3.				
4.				
5.				
6.				
7.				
8.				
9.				
10.				
11.				
12.				
13.				

2. Suggest one or two implications that in your opinion are
necessitated if one is to hold these values with a high preference.

3. Is God impressing a need for you to learn more about or apply
more definitely in your life one or more of the values or
implications of this model?   If so which?

ANSWERS----------
        1. No Column 1 entries. Column 2 = values 3, 6, 9, 13.
        Column 3 = values 8, 11.
        Column 4 = values 1, 2, 4, 5, 7, 10, 12.
        2. Implication of value 10: Leaders must share openly of
God's processing in their lives. Implication of Value 4 (in my
culture): Leaders must be on a first name basis with as many
followers as practical.
        3. Value 7 has been reaffirmed for me. Just this summer God
gave a special word to me on this.

MINISTRY PHILOSOPHY MODEL--HARVEST

introduction   Ministry philosophy refers to a related set of
                  values that underlies a leader's perception and
                  behavior in his/her ministry. The values may be
                  ideas, principles, guidelines or the like. Each
                  Christian leader will have a unique ministry
                  philosophy that generally differs from others due
                  to values God has taught experientially. Leaders
                  whose giftedness and calling line up with the
                  central function of the Harvest Leader Model will
                  find that its values are enmeshed in their own
                  unique ministry philosophy. Leaders not so gifted
                  may or may not have experienced processing leading
                  to these particular ministry philosophy values. In
                  any case the values are worth evaluation. Harvest
                  leaders tend to have a leadership style bent which
                  is fundamentally task oriented in nature.

definition   The harvest leader model is a philosophical model
                  which is founded on the central thrust of Jesus'
                  teaching which seeks to expand the Kingdom by
                  winning new members into it as is demonstrated in
                  the agricultural metaphors of growth in scripture.

central   Its central concern is with expansion of the
thrust   Kingdom so as to bring new members into the Kingdom
                  as forcefully commanded in the outward aspect of
                  the Great Commission--Go ye into all the world and
                  make disciples of all people groups.

primary   Matthew 28:19,20: Great Commission--Outward Aspect.
passages   (See also Mark 16:15, Luke 24:46,47, John 20:21,
                  Acts 1:8).
                  Kingdom Growth Parables:
                  Matthew 13:24-30 Tares.
                  Matthew 13:31,32 Mustard Seed.
                  Mark 4:30-32 Mustard Seed.
                  Matthew 13:33-35 Leaven.
                  Luke 13:33-35 Leaven.
                  Mark 4:26-29 Mysterious Growth of Seed.

                  Sending Passage:
                  Luke 10:1-12 Sending of 70.

archetype   Paul is the archetype of a harvest leader
                  in the New Testament.

values   1. Harvest leaders have a strong concern for those
                     outside the kingdom and want to give them a
                     choice to hear and enter the kingdom. (Great
                     Commission Passages)

MINISTRY PHILOSOPHY MODEL--HARVEST continued

2. Harvest leaders have a strong desire to motivate
   followers to take the kingdom message to others.
   (Luke 10:1-12)
3. Harvest leaders have a strong concern for power
   in ministry--they know the value of power to
   gain a hearing for the gospel of the kingdom.
   (Matthew 28:20, Mark 16:16,17, Luke 24:49,
   Acts 1:8)
4. Harvest leaders are more concerned with the
   ultimate destiny of those outside the kingdom
   than the present state of those in the kingdom.
   (Matthew 28:19 emphasis on outward not inward)
5. Harvest leaders recognize that Kingdom expansion
   means will not always sift out the real from the
   unreal but know that ultimately there will be
   resolution. (Matthew 13:24-30)
6. Harvest leaders by and large exercise faith.
   They believe God will accomplish His expansion
   work and hence are not afraid of small
   beginnings. (Matthew 13:31,32, Mark
   4:30-32)
7. Harvest leaders recognize the evangelistic
   mandate as taking priority over the cultural
   mandate since the cultural mandate will require
   large numbers before impact on a non-kingdom
   society can be made. (Matthew 13:33-35,
   Luke 13:20-21)
8. Harvest leaders value receptivity testing in
   order to discover movements of God. (Mark 4:26-
   29)

implications   see feedback exercise

comment   Gift-mixes of leaders which correlate strongly with
                the Harvest Leader model include the various
                combinations of: the word gifts of apostle,
                faith, evangelist; the love gifts of mercy;
                the power gifts of healing, miracles, word
                of knowledge.

comment   The word gifts of prophecy and exhortation and
                leadership can operate with both Harvest and
                Shepherd leader models.

comment   See Wagner's **Leading Your Church To Growth** and
                Church Growth and The Whole Gospel which espouse
                Harvest leader values. See also Tippett's **Verdict
                Theology in Missionary Thought.**

FEEDBACK ON HARVEST MODEL

1. Scan the list of values for the Harvest Model. Assess
your own personal preference for these values by placing an "x"
in the appropriate column for each value. (MP = my personal
ministry philosophy)

values	Column 1 Does not affect MP	Column 2 Loosely Held in MP	Column 3 Definitely affects MP	Column 4 Deliberately used and vital to MP
1.				
2.				
3.				
4.				
5.				
6.				
7.				
8.				

2. What other values has God taught you that are not listed but
somewhat compatible with the central thrust of this philosophical
model?

3. Suggest one or two implications that in your opinion are
necessitated if one is to hold these values with a high preference.

4. Is God impressing a need for you to learn more about or apply
more definitely in your life one or more of the values or
implications of this model? If so which?

ANSWERS----------

        1. Column 1 = value 4.   Column 2 = values 1, 2, 3, 6.
        Column 3 = value 7, 8. Column 4 = value 5 (Used in a
negative way. I am vitally concerned with the sifting process.
My strong bias to the Shepherd Leader Model makes me want to
assess genuineness of those professing to be in the kingdom.)
        2. Your choice.
        3. If one held value 8 on receptivity high then that person
would by necessity do studies in futurology--future trends, since
receptivity is often correlated with various trends.
        4. No, I don't think so.

LEADERSHIP EMERGENCE

introduction   Leadership selection is a major function of all
Biblical leadership. Leadership selection refers
to the human side of recognizing potential for
leadership. That is, leaders are constantly to be
looking for potential leaders who are emerging.
Leadership emergence also deals with selection. It
encompasses leadership selection, the human side of
recognizing potential for leadership, but it does
more. It looks at the total selection process
which includes God's part in development.
Leadership emergence refers to the overall process
in which God is at work in selecting that leader.
It is the broad life-time process in which a
potential leader expands capacity for influencing
to become the leader God wants him/her to be.

definition   <u>Leadership</u> <u>emergence</u> refers to a leader's changing
capacity to influence and is measured or evaluated
in a longitudinal study over time in terms of
various factors.

comment   Three important generic factors include internal
psychological processes and external
sociological/contextual processes and divine
processes. The total effect of the forces bring
development in terms of capacity to influence.
Various process items are defined which relate to
these three generic factors. Some process items
have been grouped longitudinally. Other patterns
indicate process items which occur over shorter
spans of times.

comment   Longitudinal study indicates a tracking over time
of the changing capacity to influence.

comment   Longitudinal studies usually view emergence in
terms of development phases. These development
phases usually follow cycles of boundary turmoil,
decision formulation, consolidation or outworking
of decisions followed by a new boundary turmoil and
the cycle repeats. The boundary turmoil usually
involves backward reflection, evaluation, and
forward looking formulation which affects new
decision making.

comment   Measurement of capacity to influence involves
evaluating growth both in spiritual formation and
ministerial formation and strategic formation.

comment   Immediate lessons, development tasks, giftedness,
sphere of influence, influence means, assessment
along patterns and convergence factors are measures
used to indicate development.

LEADERSHIP EMERGENCE STUDY   abbreviation: LES

introduction   Hebrews 13:7,8 admonishes us to study Christian
               leaders and learn from their lives. It further
               encourages us to trust the ever constant source of
               leadership, Jesus Christ, to enable us to also
               imitate those admirable qualities and
               characteristics which made their lives count for
               God. A leadership emergence study is a systematic
               approach for carrying out the implications of that
               admonition. Using a time-line format, it integrates
               findings in terms of leadership emergence patterns,
               identifiable processes, and constant leadership
               principles. These findings are displayed
               systematically for both initial study and
               referential study. One can learn greatly from
               studying the life of a leader used by God. A
               leadership development study serves to facilitate
               that learning.

definition   A leadership emergence study is the end product
               of a research approach which assesses emergence of
               leadership potential, that is, leadership
               development, by utilizing a life-history analysis
               of a leader which integrates internal influences
               (personal/psychological), external influences
               (social/contextual), and divine influence (God's
               providential working) upon the leader's influence
               capacity.

contents   A leadership emergence study normally includes:
full
range   ● a Summary Sheet
               ● Expectations/Motivations for the study
               ● a Running Capsule of the Life
               ● an Overview Chart Listing Process Incidents
               ● an Overview Chart Listing Development Measures
               ● detailed phase charts showing process items
               ● explanation of major process items for each
                 detailed phase chart
               ● principles derived in each phase
               ● summary of development measures for each phase
               ● conclusions

comment   The heart of the study is the Overview Charts.
               These charts contain a time-line along the
               horizontal axis, which is broken up into
               development phases. Each development phase follows
               a basic overall development pattern of boundary
               turmoil, decision formulation, consolidation or
               outworking of decisions and further boundary
               turmoil. The vertical axis is divided into
               categories which allow for display of issues
               relating to processing or development.

COMMENTARY ON LEADERSHIP EMERGENCE STUDY

examples

Approximately 500 or more leadership development studies have been produced at the School of World Mission. Some historical leaders that have been studied include: Phineas Bresee, A.B. Simpson, Maria Atkinson, Jim Elliot, Samuel Mills, etc. Biblical characters include: Joseph, Daniel, David, Peter, Jephthah, Barnabas. The vast majority of studies are of contemporary leaders. These are self-studies and have proved of tremendous benefit not only to those who did them but to those who have followed after them.

vicarious
learning

The power of the leadership mandate focuses on learning vicariously from previous leaders. The analysis of past leadership emergence studies meets the leadership mandate at its power focus. Careful study of God's processing and lessons seen in other leader's lives will result in the living Christ intervening to put those same lessons in your own life. Many studies are available on file for those who want to profit from direct application of the leadership mandate. For those not having access to these studies I suggest doing your own analysis using Christian biographies or autobiographies of leaders.

range
of
studies

Various kinds of leadership emergence studies are available on file. In-depth studies (Gripentrog 1987, Hawthorne 1989) include the full range of contents listed. Full studies (McConnell 1985, Newton 1983) include much of the contents listed (missing overview chart of development measures and analysis of development measures). Lesser studies (Chao 1982, Clinton 1984, Myers 1989, Strong 1989, Stalnaker 1989) involve various parts of the contents. Minimum studies (Hollis 1985) include a time-line with some back up information. The range of studies evolved over the seven years of research. Each of these kinds of studies (in-depth, full, lesser, minimum) can be profitable.

suggestion

For those studying this manual and having access to Fuller Theological Seminary I recommend that you scan the bibliography list of available leadership emergence studies. They are grouped in terms of historical, Biblical, contemporary men, contemporary and historical women. Then I suggest that you select five or so and study through them with a propensity for vicarious learning.

SPIRITUAL FORMATION

introduction   A leadership emergence study seeks to assess the
                 emergence of leadership potential. It utilizes a
                 life-history analysis of a leader which integrates
                 internal, external, and divine influences upon the
                 development of a leader. Spiritual formation
                 refers to the inner development of character of a
                 leader. Internal, external, and divine influences
                 all affect that inner development.

definition   Spiritual formation refers to development of the
                 inner-life of a person of God so that,

                 ● the person experiences more of the life of
                   Christ,
                 ● reflects more Christ-like characteristics in
                   personality and in everyday relationships, and
                 ● increasingly knows the power and presence of
                   Christ in ministry.

comment   Spiritual formation is one of four major components
                 in Holland's Two-Track analogy (Clinton 1985:41),
                 a model for evaluating balance in training. There
                 is input, experience, dynamic reflection, and
                 spiritual formation. Holland stresses that
                 spiritual formation is the end result of training
                 and therefore must be designed into training
                 programs and accounted for explicitly not
                 implicitly. These same four components can be
                 applied to life activities as well as formal and
                 non-formal training.

comment   Spiritual formation is the application of the
                 process of Romans 8:28,29 to a leader's life. It
                 recognizes that God utilizes life processes to
                 "conform a leader to the image of Christ." That
                 conformation process is spiritual formation.

comment   Spiritual formation relates directly to a leader's
                 power base for influencing. Power base refers to
                 the source of credibility which enables a leader to
                 have authority to influence followers. Spiritual
                 authority is that source of credibility perceived
                 as from God which permits leaders to influence
                 followers. Spiritual authority characteristics
                 presuppose spiritual formation. While there are
                 other power bases which are legitimate for a
                 Christian leader, spiritual authority is
                 foundational and should be the central means of
                 power for influencing followers.

MINISTERIAL FORMATION

introduction   Spiritual formation is concerned with "being."
Ministry formation is concerned with "doing." It
focuses on the leader's ability to function as a
leader. It seeks to identify and measure the
skills and abilities and knowledge needed to
operate as a leader in ministry. These skills have
to do with "innate" skills as well as "acquired
skills." They have to do with spiritual gifts.
They have to do with sensitivity to God's purposes
in a leadership situation. They have to do with
the use of influence means in order to motivate
followers toward ministry goals.

definition   Ministerial formation refers to development of
ministry skills and knowledge, which are reflected
by a leader's

- growth in experiential understanding of
  leadership concepts,
- growing sensitivity to God's purposes in terms of
  the leadership basal elements (leader, follower,
  and situation),
- identification and development of gifts and
  skills and their use with increasing
  effectiveness with followers,
- ability to motivate followers toward beneficial
  changes which will harmonize with God's purposes.

comment   Experiential understanding of leadership concepts
means the ability to dynamically reflect on and use
concepts dealing with leadership basal elements,
leadership influence means, and leadership
philosophy to local situations. This may be a
studied thing or it may be intuitive.

comment   At every level of influence a leader must be able
to sense the important elements of the leadership
triangle--leader, follower, and situation. Crucial
leadership decisions should reflect an awareness of
important patterns of interplay between these
elements.

comment   Deliberate development of natural abilities and
acquisition of skills not only indicates maturity
in ministerial formation but also a responsible
attitude toward capacities God has given the
leader.

comment   By definition, the central ethic of a leader is the
motivation of followers toward God's purposes. An
increased ability to do this indicates development
in ministerial formation.

STRATEGIC FORMATION

introduction   Development of leadership involves three primary
                formational thrusts. The third, strategic formation
                refers to an overall ministry perspective.

definition   Strategic Formation refers to an overall ministry
                perspective, a ministry philosophy, which emerges
                from a lifetime of formational thrusts and
                interweaves lessons learned into an increasingly
                clear ministry framework that gives direction and
                focus and ultimate purpose to a leader's life.

comment   The heart, or idealized goal, of strategic
                formation is its end result--a well articulated
                lived-out ministry philosophy which usually
                develops in three stages.

Stage	General Description	Some Functions
1. Osmosis	Leader learns implicit philosophy experientially.	1. Operate with implicit philosophy of sponsoring group.
2. Baby Steps	Leader discovers explicit philosophy through experience and philosophy.	2. Personal lessons in ministry. 3. Questioning/ evaluation of implicit philosophy of ministry. 4. Evolving of a modified philosophy; some implicit some explicit.
3. Maturity	Leader formulates, uses and articulates his/her ministry philosophy. He/she passes on to others the key ideas and retrospective reflection of what ministry is about.	5. Develops a growing sense of uniqueness and ultimate accountability. 6. Sees need for evaluation of ministry. 7. Recognition of need for focus and unique ministry. 8. Formulation of focused ministry philosophy. 9. Internalization of the philosophy. 10. Articulation of the ministry philosophy which has been worked out in practice.

comment   The set of factors contributing to strategic
                formation includes lessons learned from all process
                incidents but especially those from the discernment
                cluster of process items, guidance cluster of
                process items and destiny cluster process items.

FEEDBACK ON THREE FORMATIONS

1. The root concept underlying all of the three formations is spirituality. Most leaders do not have an adequate understanding of their own view of spirituality. Nevertheless they are controlled by their uninformed implicit view of spirituality. Spiritual formation deals primarily with the vertical aspect of spirituality, as it applies to character. Ministerial formation deals with the horizontal aspect of spirituality as it applies to performance in ministry and relationship to others. Strategic formation deals with spirituality and ultimate contribution. A step forward for any leader is to identify an explicit "informed" theology of spirituality.

a. define spirituality:

b. How does spirituality relate to the Kingdom?

2. It is not unusual for a leader to be developed further in one formation than another. Comparatively evaluate your general overall development in terms of the three formations.
    a. Further along in development of:
    b. Next further along in development of:
    c. Least further along in development of:
    d. Other:

3. If failure in leadership can be attributed to lack of development in one of the formations more than the others, which one would you suggest it to be?

ANSWERS----------

    1. a. In my opinion spirituality is a measure of control by the spirit of my holistic being and is a state of relationship with God in which God is manifested through me, a total being, to accomplish His purposes in me and to others so that Kingdom values are proliferated. **b.** The Kingdom is the realm of God's rule. Spirituality is a measure of that rule in an individual.
    2. In my opinion, comparatively, my development would rank the three formations in this order: spiritual formation, ministerial formation, and strategic formation. It is not unusual for strategic formation to lag behind. Most leaders when they first start out are ahead in spiritual formation. But in their growth ministry--provisional and competent ministry sub-phases ministry formation usually moves ahead (doing takes precedence over being). Strategic formation lags well behind. Toward the end of the competent sub-phase spiritual formation again usually overtakes ministerial formation with significant development having taken place in strategic formation. In the unique ministry phase the three usually come into balance.
    3. Spiritual formation is usually considered to be more foundational although all are necessary. People can have power in ministry and maintain an apparently outward success and yet fail fundamentally in character development. Sooner or later it will catch up.

SUMMARY OF FOUNDATIONAL LEADERSHIP CONCEPTS

This self-study text approaches leadership through the study of individual leaders. It is essentially the outworking of the command given in Hebrews 13:7,8. From a comparative study of many individual leaders various common patterns, processes and principles can be suggested which can be of use in formulating leadership theory which is applicable to ministry situations.

A given leader is one who persists in leadership over time and with various followers in various situations. The development of that leader, both in maturity of character and maturity of influence ability and maturity of understanding how ministry should be carried out can be traced via the use of a leadership emergence study. A leadership emergence study is a systematic approach to measuring and evaluating the development of a leader to influence followers over his/her lifetime. Leaders usually pass through various stages of ministry including those described by the typology of leaders, Types A,B,C,D,E.

General leadership theory is concerned with leadership basal elements (leader, followers, situations), leadership influence means (both individual and corporate means of influence), and leadership value bases (the moral aspects of leadership). A leadership emergence study touches on every area of leadership categories but focuses on the basal elements and individual influence means.

Of particular importance to Christian leadership is that which can be learned about spiritual formation (the development of the inner person toward spiritual maturity), ministerial formation (the development of the person in terms of doing ministry) and strategic formation (development of an underlying philosophy of ministry). A ministry philosophy will be unique to a person. But an informed ministry philosophy will be aware of New Testament philosophical models and incorporate appropriate values from them. Patterns, processes, and principles concerning these three areas of development can be useful both in the on-going development of leaders and the selection of potential leaders. These findings can affect training designs.

CHAPTER 3. INTRODUCTION TO PROCESSING

OVERVIEW

Section A of the manual, Chapters 3-8, describes the processing variable. The grouping of the process items in Section A are categorized within basic time periods identified as pre-ministry, early and middle ministry, and latter ministry. Later in Section B, when we talk about the time variable we shall identify these same three time periods as ministry foundations, growth ministry, and unique ministry.

Chapter 3 introduces the basic notion of processing. Chapter 4 discusses some foundational process items, those which occur in the early childhood and adolescence, and some transitional items, those which are preliminary or concurrent with movement into ministry. Chapters 5,6, and 7 identify process items that occur during the growth ministry time period. Chapter 8 points out processing items which may occur throughout ministry but which point to a latter and more effective ministry.

The Major Processing Concepts

Five concepts which are foundational to the nature of processing are given in this chapter. **Critical incidents** and **process incidents** are described and differentiated. Also, the **process item,** a concept distinct from the process incident, is defined. It is a perspective for viewing and analyzing and evaluating a process incident. A series of typical process incidents are compared to define a given process item--the integrity check. The process item, thus defined, is used to illustrate **process item properties.** Finally, the **process awareness continuum** is introduced. All of these concepts are simply constructs, that is, perspectives, defined to help us perceive the reality of God's sovereign shaping in our lives.

Review of Three Variables

Let's place the notion of processing, the thrust of this chapter, in the context of the three variables which were briefly discussed in chapter 2. You will remember that leadership emergence can be explained in the life of a given leader by the use of three important variables: processing, time, and leader response. While not intending mathematical precision, the symbolic notation, given below, is helpful in succinctly stating the major relational idea of leadership emergence theory.

$$L = f(p,t,r)$$

where L means "the development of any given leader," f

means "a function of," or "can be explained by," p denotes the "processing variable," t stands for the "time variable," and r symbolizes the "leader's response as seen in various patterns."

Another way of stating the symbolic notation of the formula in words is as follows.

The unique development of a given leader can be expressed in terms of various significant processes experienced and responded to over his/her lifetime.

Research done on the most recently written contemporary case studies revealed that, on the average, 34 important process items were identified and explained in a typical study. Three time phases, with varying number of sub-phases, and hence varying numbers of boundaries, are usually described. The writers also analyze eight response patterns in explaining their own unique development. Summaries of the three variables, on five typical contemporary cases, are shown in Table 3-1.

TABLE 3-1
THREE VARIABLES--FIVE TYPICAL CASES

	Case Length in pages	Process Items	Time-Line Phases	Response Patterns
Gripentrog	92	60	3	15
Finzel	72	56	4	13
Waldner	51	30	3	11
Baumgartner	67	27	3	12
Belesky	52	35	2	8

The above cases are all contemporary studies. They are current leaders now in process and in various stages of their development.

On the average, whole life cases derived from biographical or autobiographical sources will have from 30-75 process items, 4-5 five time-line phases, and 10-20 response patterns. Some examples of these studies include: A. B. Simpson (Chuang 1982; Pease 1983; Takatori and Kropp 1983), J. H. Taylor (Lee-Lim 1982), R. C. McQuilkin (Clinton 1984b), A. W. Tozer (Clinton 1984a), A. Carmichael (Reid and Van Dalen 1985), F. Asbury (Callendar 1983), du Plessis (Turkot 1987), P. Bresee (Tink 1982).

The development of a leader is complex. Not all can be explained by this generalized statement. But much of what characterizes a given leader can be explained in terms of the timing of significant processing and the leader's response to it. This chapter intends to define the foundational concepts underlying the process variable and its significance.

The Processing Variable

Christian leaders, in looking back over their lives, perceive that God has worked to develop and bring about their leadership. Incidents stand out in which they sense the involvement of God either directly or indirectly. The cumulative effect of these incidents over a lifetime indicates the integrative working of God to shape the leader for His purposes. Comparative study of many lives makes even more evident this involvement by God. It is a long-term process. Each of the incidents, big or small, fits as part of the process of this lifetime of shaping. The set of concepts categorizing and describing this "processing" by God make up the processing variable. The basal concepts include critical incidents, process incidents and process items. Secondary concepts include process item properties and the process awareness continuum.

I can best introduce the notion of processing by giving some highlights from the early history of my leadership research.

The Emergence of the Process Incident

All biographic data centers around the selection of important incidents. In the earliest cases whether historical, Biblical, or contemporary, it was clear from the start that certain incidents were formative.[1] Historical writers select certain issues to highlight in biographies. Biblical writers also intentionally selected. I found this to be true also when I interviewed Peter Kuzmic. He intuitively selected formative items, at least from his own viewpoint, which had shaped his leadership. The basis for his selection of incidents was not clear. The earliest analysis among this research simply involved collection of these important incidents. (Later however, these incidents were analyzed in such a way as to categorize their occurrence, explain their importance and/or to evaluate the selection criteria used.) These incidents, however selected, were found to be important enough to be remembered and somehow had significantly been used in shaping the leader. These significant incidents came to be called, **critical incidents.**

Many of these critical incidents could be correlated to leadership development. Earliest comparisons of these incidents pointed out that important people, events, circumstances,

----

[1]Earliest Biblical studies involved Nehemiah and Daniel. The earliest contemporary study was of Peter Kuzmic, a Christian leader from Yugoslavia. Earliest historical studies included Charles Wesley, a leader in the formation of a movement which later became a denomination, Samuel Mills, who was instrumental in founding several mission sodalities, Alexander Mack, a denominational leader and Watchman Nee, a Chinese church and para-church leader. All of these studies listed incidents, roles, etc. which somehow significantly shaped the leaders.

educational experiences (formal and informal), and perceived
interventions by God, were all important categories. Table 3-2
shows some of the earlier incidents listed from each of the three
kinds of cases, historical, Biblical, or contemporary.

TABLE 3-2
LISTS OF PROCESS INCIDENTS FROM EARLY CASES

+Mother strong in
  child training
+Lord's prayer learned
  as soon as could
  speak
+Taught piety,
  methodical routine
+Experienced Melancholy
  on shipboard trip
+Evangelical conversion
  "new song in my mouth"
+Struggle to know God
  and be pure within
+Matched every crisis
  with a song which
  reflected mood and
  learning
+People Influences—
  John Wesley, George
  Whitefield
+Traveled widely

From (King 1982) on
Charles Wesley

+Taken captive
+Selected for
  special training
+First religious
  integrity stand
  (wine issue)
+Giftedness noted
+Appointment as member
  of king's court
+Giant statue incident
  (self-initiative)
+Crisis—reliance upon
  prayer band
+Exercises God-given
  interpretation gift
+Appointed head of
  Babylonia province
+Reveals meaning
  of tree dream
+Studies Jeremiah—
  bases for vision

From (Clinton 1982a)
on Daniel

+Father's radical
  conversion at 35
  (alcoholic)
+Father—lay pastor
+Home birth—Prophetic
  utterance
+6 years old; Police
  search home, dad
  hides Bible
+Avid reader
+Natural leader
+Stole egg money
+Aunt's compromise
+Dad's fervent prayers
+Radical conversion
+Assigned 5 minute talk
+Reads Scripture
  through and through
+Scholarship checks
+Military experience—
  isolation

From (Clinton 1982b)
on Peter Kuzmic

   Notice these incidents occurred throughout a life time.
They were seen as processes in the shaping of a life over an
entire lifetime. Terms like leadership selection processes,
process incidents, and process items which, arose in early
attempts to analyze these incidents, signaled this on-going idea
and were forerunners of the notion of processing. Even in earlier
cases it was evident that a leader was shaped (that is,
developed) over time by many events.

   Particularly in the Biblical cases, it was frequently very
evident that these emerging leaders (and the Biblical authors)
perceived that God was doing the processing. The Daniel study
(Clinton 1982a) and Joseph studies (Harris 1982, Clinton 1985b)
particularly support this perspective of God intervening in the
lives of leaders to direct them toward His purposes.

   The first attempt to define or categorize these incidents
broadly defined them in terms of four categorical bases according
to their importance for leadership development. The primary
criteria was how they functioned.

Leadership selection processes refers to anything in
the life-history of a person which God uses, to
indicate leadership potential, to train a person for
leadership, to confirm his or her appointment to a
role/task/given responsibility, and to bring the
leader along into God's continued appointed ministry
for him or her. (Clinton 1982a:11).

As more attention was placed on what these processes were, as
well as what they did, the definition was refined. Those
critical incidents which could be correlated to leadership
shaping were called process incidents. Further refining included
distinguishing between the occurrence of an actual incident and
generalizations which could more generically describe certain
kinds of incidents and their properties. This was the first level
of abstraction concerning processing which entailed identifying
critical incidents which could be labeled **process incidents**. The
second level, the inductive generalization of process incidents,
became known as **process items**. Table 3-3 highlights the
distinction between process incidents and process items.

TABLE 3-3
COMPARISON--PROCESS INCIDENTS AND PROCESS ITEMS

definition	examples	difference
Process incidents are the actual occurrences from a given life of those providential events, people, circumstances, special divine interventions, inner-life lessons, and/or other like items which God uses to develop that person by shaping leadership character, leadership skills, and leadership values so as to 1) indicate leadership capacity (such as inner integrity, influence potential), 2) expand potential, 3) confirm appointment to roles or responsibilities using that leadership capacity, and 4) direct that leader along to God's appointed ministry level for realized potential.	Peter Kuzmic steals from Mom's egg money; conviction requires confession Daniel takes a stand on wine issue in court; later chosen for special study Joseph chooses not to sin with Potiphar's wife	actual real life things
A process item is a label inductively drawn from a comparative analysis of process incidents which categorizes incidents into groups with like properties and functions.	Integrity Check (the three process incidents above are grouped under this item.)	construct under which several incidents can be grouped

The distinction is not always seen in the early case studies. Researchers overlap the notions frequently.

Emergence of A Typical Process Item--the Integrity Check

As indicated previously a process item emerges from the comparative analysis of numerous process incidents. Table 3-3 listed three incidents, one from a contemporary case on Kuzmic (Clinton 1982b) and two from Biblical cases on Daniel (Clinton 1982a) and Joseph (Clinton 1985b). The following series of process incidents is given for the use of illustrating how the concept of a process item emerges from comparative analysis. The incidents are taken from Biblical, historical, and contemporary cases.

A process item is a label inductively drawn from a comparative analysis of process incidents which categorizes those incidents into groups having similar properties and functions. It is a construct under which several incidents can be grouped and properties identified. This example will focus on the integrity check process item. The integrity check is informative both for its illustration of the comparative procedure in action and for its conceptual value. It is one of the major process items used to form character early in a leader's emergence process.

Process Incident Examples

The first two incidents come from Biblical cases. These are typical Biblical incidents as have been identified in the case studies. The first shows a positive response to the character testing while the second illustrates a negative response.

Example 1: Biblical Case Study--Daniel

In Daniel 1:8-21, there is a process incident concerning the Biblical character, Daniel.

> Daniel made up his mind not to let himself become ritually unclean by eating the food and drinking the wine of the royal court, so he asked Ashpenaz to help him, and God made Ashpenaz sympathetic to Daniel. Ashpenaz, however, was afraid of the king, so he said to Daniel, "The king has decided what you are to eat and drink, and if you don't look as fit as the other young men he may kill me."
> So Daniel went to the guard whom Ashpenaz had placed in charge of him and his three friends. "Test us for ten days," he said. "Give us vegetables to eat and water to drink. Then compare us with the young

men who are eating the food of the royal court, and
base your decision on how we look."
      He agreed to let them try it for ten days. When
the time was up, they looked healthier and stronger
than all those who had been eating the royal food. So
from then on the guard let them continue to eat
vegetables instead of what the king provided.
      God gave the four young men knowledge and skill
in literature and philosophy. In addition, he gave
Daniel skill in interpreting visions and dreams.
      At the end of the three years set by the king,
Ashpenaz took all the young men to Nebuchadnezzar.
The king talked with them all, and Daniel, Hannaniah,
Mishael, and Azariah impressed him more than any of
the others. So they became members of the king's
court. No matter what question the king asked or
what problem he raised, these four knew ten times
more than any fortune teller or magician in his whole
kingdom. Daniel remained at the royal court until
King Cyrus of Persia conquered Babylonia (Daniel 1:8-
21 TEV).

In this incident, Daniel, a teenager away from home and
parental influence, must decide if the convictions he grew up
with were his own. In this case the inner conviction was a
religious one involving food. Daniel was under pressure to
violate this conviction, but he stuck to his conviction. God gave
him relationships that allowed him to work out a plan which did
not compromise his convictions. Following the check on his
character Daniel was moved along toward a role which suited God's
purposes for him. God honored Daniel's firmness of character.
Daniel and his friends were respected for their knowledge and
skills and were given top level government jobs.

Example 2: Biblical Case Study--Saul

      In I Samuel 15 an incident is recorded concerning Saul, the
first king of Israel. I Samuel 15 tells the sad story. In
essence, the story is this. God, through the prophet Samuel, told
Saul to utterly destroy the Amalekites and all their possessions.
Saul defeated them but he didn't utterly destroy them or their
possessions as he was commanded to do.

      Samuel said to Saul, "I am the one whom the Lord sent
      to anoint you king of his people Israel. Now listen
      to what the Lord Almighty says. He is going to punish
      the people of Amalek because their ancestors opposed
      the Israelites when they were coming from Egypt. Go
      and attack the Amalekites and completely destroy
      everything they have. Don't leave a thing; kill all
      the men, women, children, and babies; the cattle,
      sheep, camels, and donkeys" (I Samuel 15:1-3 TEV).

The chapter goes on to describe what Saul actually did.

> Saul defeated the Amalekites, fighting all the way
> from Havilah to Shur, east of Egypt; he captured King
> Agag of Amalek alive and killed all the people. But
> Saul and his men spared Agag's life and did not kill
> the best sheep and cattle, the best calves and lambs,
> or anything else that was good; they destroyed only
> what was useless or worthless (I Samuel 15:7-9 TEV).

Samuel is sent to reprove Saul for this incomplete obedience
and Saul's first comments indicate that he has rationalized his
compromising actions.

Saul's first words upon seeing Samuel are, "The Lord bless
you Samuel! I have obeyed the Lord's command." Samuel then
replies, "Why, then, do I hear cattle mooing and sheep bleating?"
Samuel then went on to confront Saul and told him that God had
rejected his leadership. Verses 10-13 of the same chapter give
God's assessment of the action. Two phrases sum it up, "turned
away from me" and "disobeyed my commands." Again the incident is
dealing with inner convictions of a leader. In this case the
leader's character was found lacking and he was removed (though
the actual removal took place over a number of years).

The next two incidents are drawn from historical cases.

Example 3: Historical Case Study--Carmichael

Patricia Reid and Norma Van Dalen describe an incident that
occurred in early in the life of Amy Carmichael. She later became
the founder of the Dohnavur Fellowship, that famous mission
organization which worked with temple children in India.

> The lessons Amy had learned concerning life values and
> priorities were challenged often during these years of
> preparation. On one particular occasion while
> shopping for new clothes with her mother, Amy was
> especially tested regarding these convictions. When
> the dressmaker brought out his finest and gayest
> materials, Amy sensed the Holy Spirit's convictions
> about such an "extravagant and unpractical" dress.
> Surprising her mother and the dressmaker, Amy obeyed
> the still small voice and resisted the temptation to
> enjoy a beautiful dress she didn't really need. This
> lesson became the foundation of Amy Carmichael's
> simplistic lifestyle with regard to her personal needs
> (Reid and Van Dalen 1985:24,25).

A life-time conviction concerning an inner value of a
simplistic lifestyle was established in an instant of time. Reid
and Van Dalen point out that God knew Amy would need this value
in her 55 years on the mission field in India.

Example 4: Historical Case Study--Booth

In his autobiography, Carlton Booth relates an incident that occurred just after his conversion.

> I had been converted to Christ shortly before going to work for Sears; but up on that second floor, all alone, I found myself subjected to strong temptation. Some of the orders that came down to me from floors above included unwrapped boxes of chocolates, and I convinced myself that one chocolate lifted from the second layer of a box now and then would never be missed. Candy was a rare treat which we could not afford in those days, and this made the temptation so irresistible that I yielded to it several times (Booth 1984:32).

Booth's conscience began to bother him. The Lord convicted him of the need to tell his supervisor about what he had done. He saved up a dollar to cover the cost of the items he had taken. He then confronted his supervisor. The rest of the account follows,

> He neither chided nor congratulated me when I said my conscience had been troubling me. Those gimlet eyes looked straight through me and he said, "Well, son, what shall I do with this money?"
> I told him I didn't care what he did with it, all I wanted was to have relief from this thing that had been troubling me for many days. So he took the money and said quite calmly, and I think a bit sympathetically, "I shall turn this into the office marked 'conscience money'" (Booth 1984:33)!

Booth learned something in this incident concerning the inner value of restitution. It established another inner value, honesty. Booth was later used by God in an evangelistic music ministry and in a training ministry. He looked back to this incident as one of real significance to his progress as a Christian (and I would add Christian leader). The early occurrence of such an incident (labeled honesty check) to a relatively new Christian is seen repeatedly in other lives.

The next several incidents come from contemporary case studies. I have chosen to include the following examples so that most of the categories and properties which will later be listed in reference to the integrity check will be represented through an illustration.

Example 5: Contemporary Case Study--Student 1

Throughout these early teenage years there was a deep earnestness about the things of God. I attended the school Christian fellowship. My intense dislike

of that meeting was not the tedium with which it was
conducted, nor was it the fact that I was the only boy
attending. It was because it further separated me
from my class mates. Yet, such was my earnestness,
that I was not willing to compromise in what I
regarded as a matter of Christian witness for the sake
of acceptance (Student 1 1982:19).

Here the emerging leader sticks by a conviction, demonstrating
ultimate allegiance (loyalty to things of God), even though it
brought negative consequences. Compromise with what the leader
believed to be God's desires could not be condoned. This basic
test of conviction was on-going, occurring many times over a
period of time.

Example 6: Contemporary Case Study--Student 2

One summer day, about four or five of us decided
to bike the five miles into our little town to just
see what was happening. Once in the grocery store,
someone came up with the idea of trying to steal some
candy without getting caught. It would have been easy
since there were enough of us to keep the clerk busy.
I did not participate in this game and left the store
with an empty feeling inside.
I was thankful to be brought up with the teaching
that stealing was wrong, and that I was able to pass
this test. It was very difficult because my friends
were present, however they did not put any pressure on
me (Student 2 1987:19).

Pressures concerning conviction are frequently most sorely tested
by peer pressure. This was a surprise test; there was not time
to prepare for it.

Example 7: Contemporary Case Study--Student 3

Also during this time, in one of my schools I had
befriended an unpopular girl--rather she befriended
me. At one point I was made to choose between this
girl's friendship and the friendship of the 'in'
group. I chose the 'in' group. Being sensitive, I
felt miserable. I realized the value of loyalty, and
it kindled in me the desire to reach out to those in
need. From this experience and my own along these
lines, God began developing in me a heart of
compassion (Student 3 1983:6).

Here retrospective reflection points out learning from
failure and the establishment of an inner value which determined
future actions and which set a direction for ministry. This

incident took place in a relatively short time.

Example 8: Contemporary Case Study--Student 4

     This process incident is important for several reasons.
One, it shows that processing can be extended over time to
include several incidents. Two, it tests or checks several
character traits. Three, it reflects more than just one process
item.

     My fourth year at Bible School became one of major
     crisis and change. The "problems" began when I was
     asked to sign the school's confession of faith as a
     requirement for graduation. During the first three
     years I had been questioning some of my dispensational
     background, so I felt I could not honestly sign the
     confession of faith. After a great deal of inner
     turmoil I decided to sign the confession, but soon
     afterwards had to go to the dean of students to tell
     him that my signature was not valid.
          I was accused of being a spiritual rebel because
     I would not submit to the teaching leadership over me.
     I was publicly accused of this before the student body
     and was asked to publicly confess my rebellious
     spirit. (I did speak before the student body, but
     only stated my willingness not to share my beliefs
     with any of the students as I had been instructed to
     by the dean as a requirement to be allowed to finish
     the last semester.) One of the professors accused me
     of pride during an "inquisition" by twisting what I
     said in confidence to him. I was not allowed to
     graduate and because I was blacklisted in the world I
     had grown up in I was very unsure as to where all
     this would end.
          I was able to survive this experience due to the
     support of several key people. One of my professors,
     B. H., had an open door policy for me during all this
     time. He was a shoulder to cry on, but also he
     challenged me to look beyond Bible School. He
     encouraged me to read widely and to look into the
     possibility of attending seminary.
          H.M. was a handyman on campus who helped me work
     through my questions related to dispensationalism. He
     helped me realize there were other points of view
     (something one does not learn in a small town
     dispensational church) and encouraged me to read other
     views. A missionary (B.C.) who was studying Spanish
     at the school, allowed me to struggle with the issue
     with him, even though he did not agree with me.
     Without the support of these three and others I
     probably would not have survived the experience
     intact.
          God would later use this experience to guide me

into the future He had for me. I would not be where I
am today if I had not "passed" the test (Student 4
1987:4,5,19).

The immediate results of this incident were negative for the
student. But the incident taught many lessons (concerning
mentoring, perspectives, etc.), gave direction for the future,
and was significant in establishing a tolerant viewpoint toward
those differing in various Christian convictions--a necessary
trait in one who would work at higher levels and direct various
minority leaders in Christian work. This incident was spread
over time.

Example 9: Contemporary Case Study--Student 5

...One evening coming home late off work, I turned to
the London evening newspaper to discover an ad for
airline stewards, with B.O.A.C. That was for me!
Young man, see the world. I didn't have the
qualifications, but I committed it to the Lord, and
applied. I was accepted. And there followed four
years of the most useful and maturing experience I had
ever had. The experience took me around the world,
and I loved it. It taught me something of working
with a team. It taught me a lot about how to get
along with and handle people. It also brought me to a
new stage of commitment to the Lord. Drinking was
part of the life-style, and it was easier to go along
with the crowd. But my testimony at home among the
church young people brought home to me the importance
of setting a right example. This led me to give up
drinking, and immediately opened the door of
opportunity to witness among the air-crews (Student 5
1983:22).

This incident points out testing of conviction in which
inconsistency was faced and eliminated.

Example 10: Contemporary Case Study--Student 6

At the time I was being visited by J.K., an
evangelist from Africa (who later became Bishop of
N.). As Captain L, J.K, and myself were praying I
heard a voice speak to me and say, "Go to Africa!" I
said, "I will." This command was repeated twice more
and twice more I responded, "I will." This
overpowering experience was to be with me as I
encountered obstacle after obstacle with the faith
that God would enable me to do what He commanded.
    Five days later in the mail I received a request
from the Bishop of N. for me to come and work there.
There was no money to bring me over or to pay me, but
help was needed.

>   The first obstacle was securing a visa.
> Religious workers are prohibited immigrants in South
> Africa; residence permits are difficult to obtain.
> Meanwhile how was I to live? I asked the Bishop of V.
> if there was a place I could be of service to him in
> his diocese. He sent me to preach at a college parish
> across the river from Dartmouth. They were looking
> for a new rector and asked me to accept the call.
> This was a great temptation. I declined, and the
> Bishop was kind enough to send me to another place as
> locum tenans until my visa came (Student 6 1986:28).

After several other trials and obstacles this missionary did
indeed make it to Africa. Once a direction was set conviction
was tested concerning it.

Example 11: Contemporary Case Study--Student 7

>   Another test presented itself one year after our
> marriage. I had been working in retail during our
> Bible school days. Upon completion of this training,
> I did not know what was to lay ahead in terms of
> ministry opportunity. I began to pursue a career
> toward becoming a buyer. The door opened and I was to
> sign a contract with F. and N. in High Women's'
> Fashions. King's Temple was coming to a decision on
> whether or not to hire me on the staff. This was all
> happening on the same day. I felt up for grabs by the
> highest bidder.   The church called me at work with
> an affirmative decision an hour before I was to sign
> the contract downtown (Student 7 1986:7).

In addition to working in retail this student had been working
part time in the church. The past direction had been toward full
time ministry. The choice was between that direction (which was
tested at the last minute) and an attractive financial future.

Example 12: Contemporary Case Study--Student 8

>   I was hired by the elementary school that I had
> just completed to do janitorial work for two hours
> every day after the remedial reading and math student
> had left. This work was done when the entire school
> was empty except for a secretary or two in a distant
> part of the building. I felt proud to have such a job
> as a young boy. One day as I swept the teacher's
> lounge (I was allowed in there!) I noticed that
> someone had left an old cigarette lighter on a coffee
> table. It had only a little lighter fluid left in it
> and was all scratched up. I thought it would be nice
> to have one--not to smoke or to start fires, but "just

to have one." After all, I was old enough not to do
lots of things that I was too young for before, like
having a job. So went my logic. But I was troubled
by my conscience which warned of stealing. So I left
it.
     The next day, however, the lighter was there
again in the same position. My desires said that it
was obviously abandoned and forgotten--no one would
miss it. So I took it home and put it in my drawer.
I finally had a lighter. But the joy I expected to
have was not there. My conscience bothered me
continually. So the following day, I took it back.
When I had it in my pocket, on the way to the
teachers' lounge, the principal met me in the hall and
thanked me for doing such a good job. I was sure she
could see the bulge in my pocket from the lighter and
could hear my heart's pounding. I managed to grunt a
nondescript thank you and hurried on, later returning
the contraband with a sigh of relief.
     In the Lutheran liturgy for baptism, there is
mention of the empty promises of the devil--promises
of joy and fulfillment only to deliver shame and fear.
The integrity of an obedience, Spirit-directed life is
not only a solid foundation for the building of future
Christian leadership but it also brings the true joy
and peace in the present.
     I learned through this experience that stealing
(and all sin) does not deliver the promised joy. I
learned that the principles of honesty and
faithfulness to the Word of God as taught in my family
and church were true. One might wonder if I did not
fully pass the integrity check since I did not admit
my guilt to the principal, only secretly returning the
stolen lighter. I believe that at that point in my
life, simply returning the item, having had a "close
call," was sufficient to achieve God's purposes. At a
later stage of maturity, perhaps more public
repentance would be necessary to achieve the same
results in the inner life (Student 9 1987:22,23).

This incident occurred in the foundational phase of this emerging
leader and shows the value of early character formation. It set
a value which lasted on into leadership. The heart of this test
was that in essence it was between the emerging leader and God
alone. No one else knew about it or may ever have known about
it. Such is the ultimate issue with all of these incidents--the
issue of conscience before God.

Integrity Check Defined

     An integrity check refers to a special kind of process
test which God uses to evaluate heart-intent. God uses such tests
as foundations from which to expand the leader's capacity to

influence and/or to expand one's actual sphere of influence.
There are three parts to an integrity check: the challenge to
consistency with inner convictions, the response to the
challenge, and, if passed successfully, the resulting expansion.
Sometimes evidence of the resulting expansion may be delayed or
take place over a period of time, but it can definitely be seen
to stem from the integrity check.

Common to all of the previous incidents is the essential
idea of inner convictions being tested. But there were also
subtle differences which help an analyst delineate incidents into
different kinds of integrity testing. Table 3-4 lists the kinds
of integrity checks which have been identified.

TABLE 3-4
NINE KINDS OF INTEGRITY CHECKS

1. temptation (conviction test--Example 1)
2. restitution (honesty testing--Example 4)
3. value check (ultimate value clarification testing)
4. loyalty (allegiance testing--Examples 2,5)
5. guidance (alternative better offer after Holy Spirit led
   commitment to some course of action--Example 10, 11)
6. conflict against ministry vision (guidance/faith testing--
   See Jeremiah's ministry which was generally never
   confirmed by followers he was to influence)
7. word conflict or obedience conflict (complexity testing
   usually in guidance--See Clinton 1982a, Nee example of
   guidance to do ministry which was in conflict with obedience
   to parents who opposed it)
8. leadership backlash (perseverance/faith/guidance testing--See
   Moses in Exodus 5:20ff)
9. persecution (a steadfastness check; may come through
   prophecy or contextual situation--See Paul in Acts 20:22,23)

While all integrity checks have the same common idea of testing
inner conviction there are a number of purposes for which the
integrity check seems to be used.

TABLE 3-5
SEVEN USES OF INTEGRITY CHECKS

Integrity Checks are used:

1. to see follow-through on a promise or vow
2. to insure burden for a ministry or vision
3. to allow confirmation of inner-character strength
4. to build faith
5. to establish inner values very important to later
   leadership which will follow
6. to teach submission
7. to warn others of the seriousness of obeying God

General Nature of Properties of Process Items

These last two tables illustrate the notion of properties of a process item. Comparative analysis of similar incidents representing a given process item results in a list of properties associated with it, such as were described for the integrity check process item. Generalizations concerning **properties of process items** were derived from a comparative analysis of all process items.

Table 3-6 lists the range of properties identified thus far in the study of process items. A name or label, a brief description, and a process item[2] which typically exemplifies each specific property is included. It has been seen that having a knowledge of properties, when a leader is going through processing, amplifies the leader's sensitivity to God in it.

At this point in your study you may not understand the implications of all these properties. It is included here as part of the initial learning because it is integral to these processing concepts. Its most valuable use is for referential learning. As you are introduced to each of the process items in the following chapters, refer back to this table and these properties will become clearer. So keep this table in mind and return to it as you study each of the process item definition.

---

[2]The process items listed on Table 3-6, (obedience checks, mentoring, influence challenge, integrity check, double confirmation, divine contact, divine affirmation, networking power, relational insights, life crises, leadership backlash, ministry task, giftedness discovery, spiritual authority discovery) are all defined and carefully described in later chapters. Their insertion here is simply to illustrate the notion of process items exemplifying given properties. You are not expected to know them at this point in your study.

TABLE 3-6
RANGE OF PROPERTIES SEEN IN PROCESS ITEMS

Property Label	Basic Description	Example--Process Item
kinds	differentiates types of same process items	7 kinds of Obedience Checks
specific uses	differentiates actual contextual applications	Mentoring, 8 Ways Mentors Aid Proteges
timing	general placement along generic time-line: specific phase, or other time indicator	Influence Challenge: late; Integrity Check: early; Double Confirmation: anytime
causal source	identifiable catalytic prod of the processing: person, divine intervention, event, thing, providential circumstances	Divine Contact: a person; Divine Affirmation: vision (divine intervention); Networking Power: leadership conference
developmental focus	effects of processing; specific area developed character, skills, values lessons, principles	Relational Insights: develops the ministry relational function
patterns affected	identification of response variable patterns affected	Life Crises: UM.1 Reflective/ Formative Evaluation Pattern; Isolation: UM.2 Upward Development Pattern
order	stages, steps, cycles, continuum analysis or other sequential analysis of incidents	Leadership Backlash: 8 stages in the the cycle; Ministry Task: task continuum
trigger incidents	a key specific incident stimulates awareness of process item; usually in cumulative process items with several incidents	Giftedness Discovery: some specific incident affirming fruitful use of a gift
build-up incidents	supportive incidents in cumulative process item over time	Spiritual Authority Discovery: series of clashes with a leader abusing authority

Awareness of Processing

The final processing concept to be discussed is that of awareness of processing. Emerging leaders usually sense some process items more readily than others. The **Process Awareness Continuum** shown in Figure 3-1 helps give further perspective on the sensitivity of leaders to processing. Ontologically, processing is going on whether or not a leader is aware of it fully. The continuum suggests that awareness of processing varies with kinds of process items.

Christian leaders are generally much more aware of incidents which they attribute to sovereign intervention as being significant to their development than they do to incidents which are more providential (God's circumstantial arrangement of factors).[3] The continuum simply recognizes that certain incidents toward the left are more easily attributable to God's intervention than those to the right. Recognition that incidents all along the continuum can indicate God's involvement is a step forward to further development. A heightened awareness of processing and various kinds of process items allows the leader to more effectively work with that processing towards its goal for his/her life. That is, knowledge of process items with their properties (kinds, uses, steps, etc.) allows the leader to shift those process items more to the left on the continuum in terms of

```
| HIGH                            HIGH                          |
| <--SOVEREIGN INTERVENTION    PROVIDENTIAL INTERVENTION -->    |
| ----------------------------------------------------------- |
| <--HIGHER AWARENESS                     LOWER AWARENESS -->  |

  • sensed divine intervention    • providential circumstances
  • sensed immediately            • sensed upon retrospective
  • relatively short time           reflection
  • few incidents                 • often over extended time
                                  • often combination of
                                    incidents
```

FIGURE 3-1
PROCESS AWARENESS CONTINUUM

---

[3] I am using these two notions, sovereign intervention and providential intervention, in a special technical sense in leadership development theory to indicate the extremes of sovereign action described in the Bible. Two Biblical examples of these extremes of processing are Moses' encounter at the burning bush (sovereign intervention) and God's saving of the Jews through Esther's leadership committal decision (providential intervention). Many of the incidents seen in Joseph's life when analyzed in retrospect were incidents of providential intervention.

sensing God in them. The numerous classes that have studied
leadership development theory have confirmed this. This is one
indication of the importance of leadership development theory.
Understanding of God's processes helps bring more effective
processing toward leadership development issues.

A growing sensitivity to God's direct or indirect
intervention in life incidents is indicative of development.
Once there has been a significant incident with positive results,
then later incidents are easier to recognize and hence more rapid
learning occurs.

All processing, as perceived by Christian leaders, falls
under the general theological notion of the sovereignty of God.
Some of it is more easily identifiable with sovereign acts and
direct intervention, while other parts seem more providential--
God is at work behind the scenes in less direct circumstantial
ways.

Figure 3-2 lists fifty process items on the awareness
continuum. Again, as in the case with process item properties,
this table will be an important referential tool. Your response
to this table now should be to recognize that items to the right
should be studied very carefully in order to heighten your
sensitivity to them (in effect to move them to the left on the
continuum in your particular case).

As the discernment development task (part of ministerial
formation and strategic formation) is increasingly accomplished a
leader shifts those process items such as spiritual authority
discovery, structure insights, influence challenge, training
progress, ministry skills, and flesh act toward the left. That
is, the leader is more likely to see God's intent in these
"otherwise circumstantial" items and development is increased.

```
  HIGH                               HIGH
|<--SOVEREIGN INTERVENTION          PROVIDENTIAL INTERVENTION -->|
|------------------------------------------------------------------|
|  <--HIGHER AWARENESS                          LOWER AWARENESS -->|
```

- double confirmation   • social base
- divine contact   • flesh act
  • obedience check   • influence challenge
  • faith check
  • prayer power   • ideal role discovery
  • power encounter   • ideal influence-mix
   • leadership   discovery
   committal   • ministry
   • general sovereign   structure insights
   guidance   • training progress
   • destiny revelation
   • destiny fulfillment   • ministry skills
    • word check   • entry context
    • int grity   • basic skills
    check   • contextual
    • word item
    • divine affirmation

      • spiritual warfare
        • ministry affirmation
        • destiny preparation
          • gifted power

          • crisis
          • life crisis
          • isolation
          • ministry challenge
            • giftedness discovery
            • paradigm shift
           • faith challenge

              • prayer challenge
             • ministry conflict
             • mentoring
             • spiritual authority
             discovery
             • family influence
              • negative preparation
                • networking power
               • conflict
                 • relational insights
                   • leadership backlash
                   • literary items
                    • authority insights
                   • ministry task
                   • ministry assignment
```

**FIGURE 3-2**
**PROCESS AWARENESS CONTINUUM—ALL PROCESS ITEMS DESCRIBED**
```

Summary of Processing

Life is made up of numerous incidents. Some are seemingly more important in terms of development of character, values and skills than others although all are important. A critical spiritual incident is a significant event or process involving events in a life in which a person senses divine intervention of some kind either as the event or events are unfolding or in retrospective analysis.

Process incidents are the actual occurrences from a given life of those critical spiritual incidents which can be traced to leadership development. The development may be in the nature of shaping leadership character, leadership skills, or leadership values. This shaping will have long term leadership effects such as:

1. indicating leadership capacity (such as inner integrity, influence potential),
2. expanding potential capacity,
3. confirming appointment to a role/responsibility which uses leadership capacity, and
4. directing the leader along to God's appointed ministry level for the potential.

In short, it will contribute to development of any of the five aspects of the definition of leader introduced earlier.

A **leader**, in the biblical context, is a person
1. with God-given capacity and
2. with God-given responsibility
3. who is influencing
4. a specific group of God's people
5. toward God's purposes for the group.

Critical incidents and process incidents are the lowest level of abstraction concerning the processing variable. These incidents, from a given life, form the direct data that is analyzed for development insights.

The second level of abstraction involves grouping similar kinds of incidents and studying those similar incidents for common and differing features. The term, process item, describes this grouping. Or to state it definitively, a **process item** is a label inductively drawn from a comparative analysis of process incidents which categorizes those incidents into groups having similar properties and functions. It is a construct under which several incidents can be grouped.

The process item name should be both analytic and sensitizing. Analytic refers to a slightly higher level of abstraction than the incidents being described while still explicitly relating to them. Sensitizing refers to the ability to capture something of the key notions of the item with a label that intuitively speaks to a practitioner.

The process item is the central concept of the processing variable. It occurs throughout the theory and relates either directly or indirectly to every other development theory concept.

Comparison of process incidents for the same process item results in the identification of categories of concepts for that process item. Comparisons of all of these categories for all process items leads to identification of general **properties of process items.**

One value found in these properties is their great explanatory power. Properties like, "specific uses" (e.g. two purposes of ministry affirmation, four uses of double confirmation, seven uses of integrity checks, eight ways mentors help, etc.), or "patterns affected" (positive testing or negative testing, etc.), or "developmental focus" (knowing that the processing is building toward a particular formation), or "order" (e.g. three elements of a faith challenge, six steps in a classic power encounter, eight stages in a leadership backlash cycle, etc.), help a leader to identify his/her own situation with more precision and understanding. These kind of **process** item **properties** are very useful in counseling with leaders. Insights from God's past activity with former leaders is readily transferred by the hearer to his/her present situation. Suggesting how a particular incident has been used by God in the past in the processing of leaders carries special authority with leaders who are analyzing their own situation. Pointing out a pattern or a particular leadership strength that God develops through a given kind of processing is more than suggestive. If a person can identify a time frame for what is happening it allows anticipation and mental preparation for on-going processing.

The goal of leadership development is the production of a leader who is mature in leadership character, leadership skills, and leadership values and who accomplishes the purposes of God. This chapter has suggested that the processing variable is core to that development. A typical example of one process item, the integrity check, was shown. Its extrapolation from process incidents and identification of properties served to illustrate how this theoretical process works for all of the process items identified to date.

CHAPTER 4. FOUNDATIONAL PROCESSING

Overview

Chapter 3 introduced us to the major concepts of processing. Critical incidents which correlated with leadership development were classified as process incidents. Comparative study of like process incidents resulted in the identification of process items--the label used to group like categories of process incidents. This chapter defines specific process items-- particularly those identified within two early periods--1. childhood and adolescence (sometimes including early years in the twenties) and 2. a transitional time from these foundations into leadership. Unit 1 of this chapter covers the first period. Unit 2 of this chapter covers the second period.

Unit 1. Early Foundational Processing

God providentially works through family, contextual background, and historical events including the timing of the birth of each leader. Personality characteristics are formed. These later will be reflected in the leadership style of the leader. Early skills are learned. Early lessons of life are learned. Values are inculcated. All of these will affect later leadership. God is sovereignly working in this period of time. The potential leader has relatively little say so in the majority of the foundations seen in this phase.

This period of life, early childhood and adolescence has been studied in-depth by the school of psychology known as depth psychology. It is beyond the scope of this work to analyze a leader's life using those techniques. Instead leadership development theory reviews this period in the emerging leader's life to identify in retrospect findings that will suggest God's providential working as it may affect later leadership patterns.

A major developmental task during this early period is the laying of foundations in the life that relate to leadership capacity. Leadership potential, or the capacity to influence (which includes character development that can affect this), is examined in this chapter in terms of five major process items. These five major process items have repeatedly been found significant in past leadership studies and are hence highlighted in this chapter. Additional process items may be found significant for any particular individual study. But these five are foundational and should be included in any leadership emergence study along with any other unique process items that apply to a given leader.

Process items can be broadly or narrowly defined. That is, a process item is said to be broad if it is an umbrella-like label which allows for a broad range of kinds of process incidents. A process item is said to be narrow if it includes only very specific kinds of process incidents grouped under it.

The five identified items of the early foundational period are all broad process items: destiny preparation, entry context, family influence, basic skills, and social base. When studied in retrospect (after leadership qualities have emerged) often correlation can be seen between leadership styles, leadership traits, leadership vision, and these foundational process items.

A leader should recognize his/her unique foundations, see the strengths in them, and respond to those findings. Leadership limitations strongly influenced by these foundations should also be recognized for what they are. Where there is flexibility and change is feasible, the leader should open his/her life to God's efforts concerning growth. Otherwise, the leader should learn to operate within these limitations.

God desires that a person profit from their unique foundations and set life-long habits which promote acceptance of self, particularly in regards to leadership strengths resulting from those foundations. An analysis of this early foundational phase using leadership emergence theory is often a good step toward that acceptance. Frequently, students using leadership emergence theory go through a painful but profitable time in reviewing this early foundational time. To see the providential working of God through it (especially if it was a very negative time) can bring a much needed cathartic closure which will allow a fresh new approach to the future.

In order to understand the first of the general category process items of this phase, called destiny preparation, several preliminary definitions will be given. These include SENSE OF DESTINY (p. 101) THE DESTINY CONTINUUM (p. 101), and BERTELSEN'S 3 CATEGORIES OF DESTINY EXPERIENCES (p. 102) These preliminary concepts prepare the ground for the understanding of the DESTINY PREPARATION PROCESS ITEM (p. 103). The ENTRY CONTEXT PROCESS ITEM (p. 108) follows next. These two are given first since they frequently refer to and occur before or near birth. The remaining items are given in the natural order in which they are most likely experienced: FAMILY INFLUENCE PROCESS ITEM (p. 112), BASIC SKILLS PROCESS ITEM (p. 115), and SOCIAL BASE PROCESS ITEM, (p. 118).

SENSE OF DESTINY
THE DESTINY CONTINUUM

introduction   Destiny experiences refer to those experiences
                 which lead a person to sense and believe that God
                 has intervened in a personal and special way
                 particularly in regards to encouraging the
                 emergence of leadership toward some purpose of God
                 during that leader's lifetime. Destiny experiences
                 include preparation experiences, revelation
                 experiences, and fulfillment experiences.

definition   Sense of destiny is an inner conviction arising
                 from an experience or a series of experiences (in
                 which there is a growing sense of awareness in
                 retrospective analysis of those experiences) that
                 God has His hand on a leader in a special way for
                 special purposes.

comment   Sometimes the experience is awe inspiring and there
                 is no doubt that God is in it and that the leader
                 or emerging leader is going to be used by God. Such
                 are the destiny revelation experiences of Moses in
                 Exodus 3 and Paul in Acts 9. But at other times it
                 is not so clear to the individual. Over a period of
                 time various experiences come to take on new light
                 and an awareness of that sense of destiny dawns.
                 For example, Moses' birth and deliverance into
                 Pharaoh's palace was an indicator of God's hand on
                 his life and in retrospect can be seen that way.
                 Bertelsen's study of sense of destiny in the
                 scriptures pointed out that sense of destiny may be
                 a process as much as a unique awe inspiring
                 experience. The idea of the destiny continuum
                 comes out of Bertelsen's thinking.

                      The Destiny Continuum

Destiny To Be Fulfilled   Destiny Fulfilled

time ─────────────►
emergence of leader unfolding ─────────────────►
preparation ─────► destiny revelation   destiny Realization───►
                   and confirmation ─────►

comment   This continuum describes a spiritual leadership
                 pattern in which there is a growing awareness of a
                 sense of destiny, progress seen in that destiny,
                 and finally, culmination as the destiny is
                 fulfilled. (See the F.5 Destiny Pattern in Chapter
                 11.)

BERTELSEN'S 3 CATEGORIES OF DESTINY EXPERIENCES

introduction   Walt Bertelsen (1985), in an in-depth study on the
                sense of destiny concept in the scriptures,
                identified three categories of destiny experiences
                which are outlined in the tree diagram below. He
                categorized and labeled a number of new process
                incidents as well as showed how some of the more
                familiar process items relate to the sense of
                destiny continuum. Notice that all three of these
                destiny items are broad items. That is, many kinds
                of different experiences and process items already
                previously defined could fit under the umbrella
                categories.

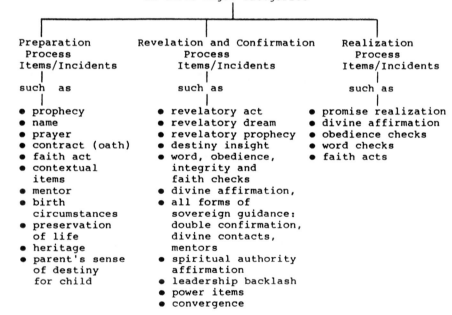

DESTINY EXPERIENCES

can be categorized in terms of the continuum
in three major categories

Preparation Process Items/Incidents	Revelation and Confirmation Process Items/Incidents	Realization Process Items/Incidents
such as	such as	such as
• prophecy • name • prayer • contract (oath) • faith act • contextual items • mentor • birth circumstances • preservation of life • heritage • parent's sense of destiny for child	• revelatory act • revelatory dream • revelatory prophecy • destiny insight • word, obedience, integrity and faith checks • divine affirmation, • all forms of sovereign guidance: double confirmation, divine contacts, mentors • spiritual authority affirmation • leadership backlash • power items • convergence	• promise realization • divine affirmation • obedience checks • word checks • faith acts

comment   A number of these process items will be defined
                later in this manual. The process incidents are
                descriptive enough for the reader to catch the
                basic idea of the term. See Bertelsen's paper
                (1985) for detailed explanations.

DESTINY PREPARATION PROCESS ITEM   Symbol: P(DP)

introduction   The Destiny Pattern is a pattern with three
               aspects. One, God's preparatory work brings a
               growing awareness of a sense of destiny. Two, the
               awareness moves to conviction as God gives
               revelation and confirmation of it. Three, there is
               movement in accomplishment of that destiny which
               often culminates in destiny fulfilled. Destiny
               preparation describes the category of process items
               which are operative in aspect 1 of the destiny
               pattern. That is, God's preparatory work in
               instilling a growing awareness that a leader is
               going to be used in a special way to accomplish
               special purposes for God.

definition   The destiny preparation process item describes a
               grouping of process items concerning significant
               acts, people, providential circumstances, or
               timing, which hint at some future or special
               significance to a life and, when studied in
               retrospect, add firmness to a growing awareness of
               sense of destiny in a leader's life.

examples   Bertelsen (1985) lists the following specific kinds
               of destiny preparation process items:

               ● prophecy   ● faith act
               ● name   ● contextual items
               ● prayer   ● mentor
               ● contract (oath)   ● birth circumstances
               ● parent's sense of   ● preservation of life
                 destiny for child   ● heritage

example   A prophecy destiny preparation process item is
prophecy   seen in Luke's account of the pre-birth prophecies
               about John the Baptist and Jesus. A contemporary
               example is the prophetic words spoken at Peter
               Kuzmic's birth by a visiting evangelist, "This
               boy will be a great preacher of the Gospel
               someday."

example   Joseph's name signifies answer to prayer by God on
name,   Rachel's behalf. The timing of his birth was seen
birth   to be controlled by God and involved as part of his
circum-   processing of Rachel as well as God's plans to
stances   later deliver Jacob's family.

example   Hannah made a contract with God. She wanted a son.
contract   God wanted a transition leader.

example   Moses parents by faith (Hebrews 11:23) saved his
faith   life in the small ark which was providentially
               discovered by Pharaoh's daughter.

FEEDBACK ON DESTINY PREPARATION PROCESS ITEM

1. One danger of exposing a concept like sense of destiny or the destiny pattern is that these concepts might tend to make people overly ambitious. One of my students once said after class that he didn't believe in such a thing as a sense of destiny because it tends to puff up the ego of Christian workers. How would you handle such a criticism? What dangers do you see in introducing such concepts as sense of destiny and the concept of the destiny process item?

2. Sometimes it is not clear that a destiny preparation process item has happened until some time in the future and one does some retrospective thinking. After some time the happening can be more clearly seen as part of a destiny pattern. Has this happened to you? If so, describe these destiny preparation experiences?

3. Can you think of incidents from the Bible which illustrate destiny preparation process items for any of the specific items for which I didn't give examples? They are listed here:

____ a. contextual items
____ b. mentor
____ c. birth circumstances
____ d. parents (sense of destiny for child)
____ e. preservation of life.

Do any you can and give Bible references.

ANSWERS----------
See next page.

FEEDBACK ON DESTINY PREPARATION PROCESS ITEM continued

ANSWERS----------

1. I'll leave the meat of this answer for discussion. But I will say that if someone feels this way about such concepts I would advise them not to use the concept at all since they would be violating their conscience, which is sin. But I think it would be tragic to miss the added confirmation of God's working in a life which can come through retrospective reflection on preparation items. I would advise also that one should not neglect a truth simply because it is abused by some.

2. I have identified 4 such experiences. I'll relate one.

When	Means	Experience	Intent/Impact
1966	home bible study with a couple	young Christian, not a charismatic, made a prophetic statement about me which I didn't recognize or understand	• to give me guidance later when I would need it. • to encourage me that God was going to use me in a much wider sphere

When this preparation process item occurred I did not know of the concept of a "word of prophecy." As I walked out of a home Bible study, after teaching for about an hour, a young man said to me, "When you get your Doctorate we'll say we knew you when you were just a Bible teacher." At the time, I was an electrical engineer, Type B leader, with local church sphere of influence. The remark seemed out of context and strange. Yet it stuck with me and I would often think about it. There came a time during conflict processing when the remark came back to my mind with force and served as confirmation in the next step of guidance.

3. a. Paul's birth and early life in Tarsus--the third
      University city of its time. Roman citizenship.
   b. Gamaliel as a mentor for Paul.

All these in retrospect fall into a pattern of a Jewish leader being prepared to bridge into the Gentile world.

COMMENTARY ON DESTINY PROCESSING

Bertelsen

Bertelsen (1985), in conjunction with a special research project, did a comparative study of destiny process incidents in the lives of ten Biblical characters. These characters included Abraham, Joseph, Moses, David, Jeremiah, Daniel, Peter, Paul, Isaac and Jacob. All the Characters were not studied with equal thoroughness, though all were done well. This study was definitive in terms of the concept, sense of destiny, the formulation of the destiny pattern, and identification of various process items that were observed to fit the destiny cluster. From this study the basic destiny pattern was derived. The various Biblical characters give ample evidence and illustrations of the pattern.

major
example--
Paul

Paul's life history follows this pattern. There was the destiny revelation experience on the road to Damascus. The three testimonies about this in Acts 9, 22, and 26 give expanded detail on it (see particularly Acts 26:19). The Galatians 1:15,16 shows retrospective reflection concerning destiny preparation. His closing words in II Timothy 4:6-8 show culmination of his destiny.

retro-
spective
discovery

Often during aspect 2 of the destiny pattern, it is in retrospect, that a leader sees earlier process items with a sense of destiny focus. The growing conviction of a sense of destiny is significantly re-enforced, which is the major development task of aspect 2 of the pattern.

importance

No leader of any significance, that has been studied and for which there is ample data, has failed to have one or more important destiny experiences. It is the accumulation of destiny experiences that frequently give one the vision that becomes the ultimate contribution for a life.

Joseph
sensitizing
factors
to
destiny

See Clinton, (1985). Joseph's life shows the importance of being sensitized to sense of destiny. The account of Joseph's life in the Bible records only two sense of destiny experiences yet it is clear that he was a person of destiny. Analysis of his life revealed eight factors that contributed to his growing awareness of a sense of destiny. The following are taken from that booklet (1985:38,39).

1) He sensed he was part of a Godly heritage (following the God of Abraham, Isaac, and Jacob and not the gods of Laban, for example).
2) He was familiar with sense of destiny occurrences in the lives of Abraham, Isaac, and

COMMENTARY ON DESTINY PROCESSING   continued

Jacob. He would have heard the stories about Abraham's call, Isaac's birth and near sacrifice, Jacob's ladder, as well as other accounts. He was conditioned by a Godly heritage. Knowing how God had intervened with his great-grandfather, grandfather, and father, he was sensitive to such a destiny for his own life. (But why were his brothers not just as sensitive?)

3) He was present when his father had major sense of destiny experiences (Peniel and Bethel).
4) He saw evidence of sovereign protection of his family. (Laban crisis).
5) He knew he, himself, was an answer to prayer. (Genesis 30:24)
6) He had personal experience with God (prophetic word given in dreams).
7) He knew his own life had been preserved (the slavery crisis).
8) His daily life, working at whatever tasks he was given, reflected the presence and blessing of God so as to be recognized by others. (Genesis 39:2,3; 21-23)

transfer-
able

Some of these kinds of factors will reappear in other leadership emergence studies. We should at least be aware of a variety of ways in which God intervenes in the destiny of a leader. They might well apply in our own lives. They may give us insights as we help develop other leaders.

mentor
and
sense of
destiny

Later when the mentoring process item is discussed I will suggest that one thing a mentor can do to help a young emerging leader is to sensitize that leader to sense of destiny experiences. A growing sense of destiny is one of the major lessons seen in effective leader's lives.

major
lesson

EFFECTIVE LEADERS EVINCE A GROWING AWARENESS OF THEIR SENSE OF DESTINY.

explanation
sequencing

In this unit I have introduced the concept of sense of destiny and the first process item label, destiny preparation. I have not given the second two labels, the destiny revelation process item and the destiny fulfillment process item. Topically speaking they should be introduced here but logically speaking they should be introduced where they occur time-wise. That is what I chose to do.

ENTRY CONTEXT PROCESS ITEM   Symbol: P(EC)

introduction   Entry contextual items, those items relating to the
                  situation or time in history into which a leader is
                  born and which will offer constraints and expansive
                  opportunities for the exercise of leadership, may
                  be unusually important to a leader--particularly
                  one with a strong destiny pattern. The entry
                  contextual items include but are not limited to:
                  cultural and linguistic factors, location,
                  regional, national and international trends, and
                  movements, etc. It is important to recognize the
                  divine determination of and placement in such
                  situations and to be "people who know the times."
                  (I Chronicles 12:32) Such a perspective allows one
                  to correlate process items with divine purpose for
                  a leader.

definition   <u>Entry</u> <u>contextual</u> <u>process</u> <u>items</u> refer to those items
                  related to the setting, both culturally and
                  historically, of the local, regional, national, and
                  international situation into which a leader is born
                  and will minister in and which will be used by God
                  to process a leader in terms of strategic guidance,
                  long term convergence, and sense of destiny.

example   Peter Kuzmic was born just after World War II, to
                  rural peasant parents in Yugoslavia, very near the
                  borders of three countries. At this time in
                  history, Tito resisted Russian influence and sent
                  Yugoslavia on its autonomous socialist path
                  giving it more freedom than other Eastern bloc
                  countries. Peter's father was converted in his
                  middle thirties out of alcoholism. He became a lay
                  preacher, founding a church in his barn. He also
                  led many of his relatives to Christ. In his
                  elementary school studies, Peter was forced to
                  learn a second language. Later this experience was
                  repeated in almost every schooling situation. Tito
                  formed the non-aligned nations association. This
                  allowed travel for Yugoslavians and communication
                  with the outside world. Later Tito opened the
                  borders so that migrant laborers could go into
                  other countries. Open borders later allowed Peter
                  to go abroad for studies. He also planted churches
                  among these ethnic groups in several locations in
                  Europe. His rural peasant background, along with
                  his brilliant educational career, put him in a
                  position to understand the anti-educational bent of
                  the peasant Christians in Eastern bloc countries.
                  He experienced, and hence understood, the dangers
                  of a communist educational system. Such
                  experiences as these prepared him to be a man
                  uniquely qualified to set up a training program in
                  Yugoslavia.

FEEDBACK ON ENTRY CONTEXT PROCESS ITEM

1. Glance again through the descriptive example on Peter Kuzmic.
Show that you understand the basic concepts of context by listing
from the description at least one factor which applies under each
of the following categories along with an implication you see the
factor has:

	Factor identified	Implications of Factor
local level		
regional level		
national level		
international level		

ANSWERS----------

1. Here are my answers. There are so many contextual facts
which have long-term leadership implications that I wouldn't be
surprised at all if you had none that I listed.

	Factor identified	Implications of Factor
local level	rural peasant by birth; borders of three countries.	could later influence peasants even though educated; grew up multi-lingual and muliti-cultural.
regional level	Communistic educational system	gave contacts in various parts of country; had to learn new languages.
national level	Tito's opposes Russian control	most free socialistic country
international level	non-aligned nations pact	gave freedom to travel, study and minister in Europe

COMMENTARY ON ENTRY CONTEXT

entry
context
part of
broader
contextual
item

The entry context process item is a specific category contained under a more general process item, called the contextual process item. (This item is defined later as one of the ordinary expansion items.) Entry contextual items have been found to be significant enough to warrant discussing separately in this section. The entry context process item is distinct from the contextual process item in that it limits itself to those factors into which a leader is born or which occur early in life. The more general context process item deals with factors that appear anytime during the on-going development of a life and which sovereignly will be used to shape the destiny of the life.

release
to
destiny

A recognition of the divine intent in general background process items such as entry context items, items can bring great release and movement later in the destiny pattern. (The family infuence process item is another example.)

Barnabas
example

Analysis of Barnabas' (Clinton and Raab 1985) life points out the importance of the entry context process item to major decision making. Barnabas grew up as a Jew in a Hellenistic island context on Cyprus. It was most logical that he bridge Jewish Christianity to Gentiles in Antioch among whom were Cyprus Christians.

entry
context
processing
significant
factor in
major
decision

Christian leaders appointed Barnabas to investigate the Antioch manifestation of Christianity. It seems clear that God was working behind the scene to insure that Barnabas was chosen for this task. God used entry context processing (island worldview, familiarity with Greeks, Cyprus connections), Barnabas's positive growth in ministry, and spiritual authority, and experiential understanding of Christianity (Cornelius's revelation) to prepare Barnabas for this apostolic ministry task.

pivotal
decisions

Some decisions in life are pivotal and swing us onward toward fulfillment of our sense of destiny. Such a momentous decision in Barnabas' life is covered over by the simple words of Acts 11:22. Note in the scriptural account the context and the simple statement of fact dealing with a key decision that will eventually lead on to God's expansion of Christianity among the Gentiles.

COMMENTARY ON ENTRY CONTEXT continued

Barnabas--
scripture
pivot

> 19 Now they which were scattered abroad upon the persecution that arose about Stephen travelled as far as Phenice, and Cyprus, and Antioch, preaching the word to none but unto the Jews only. 20 And some of them were men of Cyprus and Cyrene, which, when they were come to Antioch, spake unto the Grecians, preaching the Lord Jesus. 21 And the hand of the Lord was with them: and a great number believed, and turned unto the Lord. 22 Then tidings of these things came unto the ears of the church which was in Jerusalem: and **they sent forth Barnabas, that he should go as far as Antioch.**
>
> Acts 11:19-22

link
major
decision
to
early
processing

In doing leadership emergence studies it frequently occurs that one in maturity ministry or convergence can correlate foundational factors (like entry context process items or family influence process items) after the fact. It is more rare to see how these factors can be significant before the fact. One of the reasons for noting and defining the process items under foundational factors (destiny preparation, entry context, family influence, basic skills and social base) is to stimulate thinking when boundary decisions are to be made toward correlation with foundational factors. The entry context, family influence, and social base process items are very general yet they may contain within them seeds for later important decisions. Careful analysis of these items for correlation to anticipated ministry may be pivotal in moving one toward fulfillment of a sense of destiny. It was so with Barnabas in the decision to go to Antioch. My point here is that leaders in boundary conditions facing important ministry decisions leading into the next sub-phase or phase should search back into their foundational factors as well as forward toward anticipated challenges. I believe some major decisions can be made with destiny assurance when such correlation is seen.

FAMILY INFLUENCE PROCESS ITEM Symbol: P(FI)

introduction   Family process items relate particularly to the
                  family into which the leader was born and the
                  providential nature of this situation in terms of
                  what God intended for the leader. It is frequently
                  observed that the particular family into which a
                  leader was born significantly influenced the leader
                  in ways which proved valuable throughout the
                  leader's ministry experience.

definition   Family influence process items refer to significant
                  situations, events, and personalities that occurred
                  in the early family life of a leader which helped
                  mold character, perspectives, abilities, etc. of
                  the person and which play a significant part in
                  God's later leadership intentions.

negative   Jephthah's half-brothers ousted him from the family
example   in order to preserve their own inheritance. This
                  forced Jephthah into isolation which eventually led
                  to many crisis process items and the development of
                  a crisis leader.

positive   Hannah's dedication of Samuel to the Lord was a
example   destiny preparation process item which set the
                  pattern for Samuel's entire life. He was set aside
                  by God (double confirmation) for leadership in a
                  leadership transition time.

negative   One example from a contemporary study describes how
example   a family experience of rejection impacted one
                  person's later ministry. " This (early rejection)
                  led me in a deeper way to understand God's love and
                  acceptance of me; I can show empathy and
                  communicate God's love like few can."

sub-   Since the family influence process item is so
categories   general it is usually followed by a qualifier which
                  sub-categorizes the specific focus of the
                  processing via family influence. Examples include:

                  family influence/dominant mother;
                  family influence/heritage--godly grandfather;
                  family influence/protestant work ethic;
                  family influence/foundational moral values;
                  family influence/godly praying mother;
                  family influence/heritage, sense of destiny;
                  family influence/mentoring of older brother.

FEEDBACK ON FAMILY INFLUENCE PROCESS ITEM

1. What foundational family process items do you see indicated in
Acts 16:1,2; II Timothy 1:5 and II Timothy 3:14,15? How would
you describe them? How would you correlate them to Timothy's
later leadership development?

2. What can you imply in the way of a significant family process
item from Colossians 4:10? How would you describe it? How would
you correlate it to Mark's leadership development? (See also
Acts 15:37 and II Timothy 4:11)

3. Indicate a significant family process item in your own
background which you feel God has used or will use in your
leadership development. Give your qualifier name to the process
item and then explain its relationship to your leadership.

ANSWERS----------
   1. **Family: heritage/expectation.** Timothy came from a line of
spiritual females who had exercised faith in God. Mothers have a
significant influence on the early world view of a child.
Heritage of that nature can apply powerful pressure through the
leadership expectation principle. **Family: word grounding.** A
second family process item concerned family devotions or whatever
was the term for sharing of the word in the family during those
days. Timothy had a base of knowledge from childhood which could
be applied to his later apostolic ministry of working with
leaders. The apostolic gift requires power in the word and a
prerequisite to power in the word is knowledge of the word. A
third family process item I see is **Family: bi-cultural birth
heritage.** Timothy was born of a Jewish mother and Greek father.
This meant he most likely was bi-cultural and bilingual. He was
a "natural bridge" between Jewish and Greek worlds. And that was
a role he was to play all his life.
   2. **Family: divine contact/mentor.** Barnabas was a patient
mentor for John Mark. His constant use of the gift of
exhortation with Mark led to the development of Mark. A New
Testament book and a good ministry were the result of this
contact with Barnabas. The kinship relationship was a natural
bridge to link Mark and Barnabas, the kind patient sort of mentor
that Mark would need to bring him through the crisis event and
later on to ministry potential.
   3. **Family: qualitative effort value.** In my own life I was
taught from the time I was a small boy to do whatever I did to
the best of my ability. An oft quoted phrase was, "Whatsoever
thy hand findeth to do, do it with all thy might!" And this was
modeled for me both by my mom and dad. This persistence of
effort has permeated my use of my "exhortation gift" and has made
me an "application to life" type of teacher.

COMMENTARY ON FAMILY INFLUENCES

family
influence
processing
two foci

Psychological studies in our century have concentrated deeply on the fact that early family life is crucial in building into and influencing a person's personality, ethics, world view values, and other formative aspects. The effects of the early family experience will be reflected throughout one's life. Analysis of the family process item should focus on two developmental thrusts: 1) how they are used to form or establish character, influence skills, and values which will be important in regards to the leader's influence array; and 2) how or why these unique foundations are important (or valuable) to God particularly in regards to His intentions for the leader's life. Both negative and positive experiences are often used by God to build into a life needed perspectives that later are found useful in leadership situations. The key in this process item is seeing the correlation between family influences and the exercise of leadership later in a leader's life. Perceiving God's purposes in those early years--whether negative or positive experiences-- can bring great release to a leader.

specific
focus

Much sub-categorization needs to be done to identify and correlate these specific items with leadership traits or qualities. A particular format when describing family influence process items should first give the generic category, family, then follow by a succinct phrase describing the unique processing involved. Finally, one should in the explanation of detail, relate the process item with its value in terms of later leadership.

cumulative
or
point
processes

Frequently, family influence will contain both point and cumulative processing. Point process items, like the integrity check incident that student 2 saw in the candy store when faced by peer pressure to steal (see page 86), occur on-the-spot. Cumulative process items refers to a series of issues over a period of time which build to a trigger incident or other means to bring awareness of the processing. Early character shaping usually involves both cumulative buildup of many incidents to produce a noticeable effect as well as memorable point incidents

BASIC SKILLS PROCESS ITEM Symbol: P(BS)

introduction   During the foundational phase the potential leader
                will participate in various life experiences
                through which he/she will learn skills and values
                which will inevitably affect later leadership
                influence capacities. Examples of such experiences
                include educational programs, various kinds of
                social activities including athletics, and kinds of
                activities for earning money.

definition   The basic skills process item refers to actual
                skills acquired and/or values learned in picking up
                those skills, during the foundational phase, which
                will later affect leadership skills, leadership
                attitudes, and leadership styles.

example   Doug McConnell's leadership development study
                (1984) is filled with entrepreneural-like instances
                of developing businesses which financed his way
                through school. Creativity, management of
                financial affairs, supervisory skills, and self-
                reliance were skills learned by McConnell through
                these foundations.

example   Michael Senyimba's leadership development study
                (1986) reveals that from an early age he was forced
                to fend for himself. He learned perseverance,
                ingenuity, the value of hard work, the value of
                money, self-reliance, and the value of an
                education.

example   Richard Loving (1986) grew up on a farm. He was
                given responsibility for basic tasks. In these he
                learned self-reliance, management of money, skills
                in repairing various equipment and a bent towards
                working with and repairing equipment.

example   Robert Edwards (1986) was highly involved with
                athletics during his time in high school and
                college. Many valuable lessons concerning
                discipline, fairness, perseverance, teamwork, and
                the desire to do one's best came out of this focus
                on athletics.

other   Other skills associated with music, the educational
examples   process, and other social activities could be
                named. Any skills or attitudes associated with
                skill acquisition which later will have a bearing
                on the exercise of leadership should be analyzed in
                conjunction with this process item.

FEEDBACK EXERCISE ON BASIC SKILLS PROCESS ITEM

1. From your general knowledge of the Apostle Paul's life what early skills or attitudes associated with those skills can you see that were gained during his foundational period? How did these relate to his later exercise of leadership?

2. From your general knowledge of King David in the Old Testament, what early skills or attitudes associated with skills can you see that were gained during his foundational period? How did these relate to his later exercise of leadership?

3. In examining basic skills processing from your own foundational phase identify any attitudes associated with skills that you learned which you feel have been foundational to your present leadership or future leadership.
____ a. teamwork
____ b. perseverance
____ c. desire to do the best
____ d. innovativeness
____ e. self-reliance
____ f. discipline
____ g. creativity
____ h. dependability
____ i. ingenuity
____ j. value of hard physical work
____ k. the value of sacrifice in developing skills
____ l. value of money
____ m. value of an education
____ n. other values--name them.

4. Check any of the following skills you gained through basic skills processing during the foundational phase.
____ a. critical/analytical thinking
____ b. management of finances
____ c. entrepreneural-like thinking
____ d. supervisory skills
____ e. relational skills
____ f. repair skills
____ g. a trade
____ h. music skills--identify specifically:
____ i. other: name them:

5. Give a major skills process item from your foundational phase. Then list skills and skill attitudes learned through it.

ANSWERS----------

    1. The vocational skills associated with the tentmaking trade. This was greatly used by Paul especially when doing apostolic church planting. This allowed him to teach on giving with great power. Paul also learned analytical skills from Gamaliel which included the skill attitude of broad mindedness which Gamaliel showed toward all kinds of learning. These skills stood Paul in great stead as he began to formulate his theology.
    2. David's shepherd experiences prepared him in many ways. Courage, the ability to believe in himself, and the ability to meditate came out of skills learned as a shepherd.
    3. a., b., c., d. These were mostly learned through sports.
    4. a., b., e. Learned through paper route, athletics, and military training.
    5. Major skills process item: Sports. Skills learned through sports: How to win. How to lose. Skill attitudes learned through sports: Perseverance, relationship skills.

COMMENTARY ON BASIC SKILLS

process
awareness
basic
skills

Reference to the process awareness continuum on page 96 shows that the basic skills item is one that is more difficult to sense as a God-given process item. Foundational processes can be correlated to later leadership functions in light of acknowledging the sovereignty of God. Correlating leadership functions with foundational processes brings a greater assurance of God's involvement in the leader's life. This has a bearing on present functions, whose seeds can be traced back to basic skills.

skills/
skill
attitudes
learned
early

Teamwork, perseverance, and the desire to do the best one can, are often skill/skill attitudes learned in athletics. Innovativeness, self-reliance, and management of finances are often learned in the foundational phase by potential leaders who hold down part-time jobs or who begin their own businesses. Early music ability may lead to discipline, the value of sacrifice in developing skills, and an ability to worship creatively.

focus

The basic skills process item seeks to correlate skills and attitudes learned via those skills with later leadership roles or leadership style or leadership character.

non-formal
informal
modes

The basic skills process item does not pertain only to formal skills learned in education, but also to skills learned non-formally or informally. The ability to orate, to relate to people, to sense people's feelings, and to sense consensus are excellent basic skills that are often taught informally in the socialization processes of some cultures. Various cultures will impart through the socialization process, crucial skills that will be basic to a leader's supposed "natural abilities" in leadership.

SOCIAL BASE PROCESS ITEM   Symbol: P(SB)

introduction   Levinson (**Seasons of A Man's Life**) uses the concept
               of the social or family factor as one form of
               measurement during the stabilization period of a
               development phase. Every person has some kind of
               social unit which they work out of. This unit
               functions as an emotional support and gives
               guidance concerning development. This is true of
               the Christian worker, especially for the missionary
               worker, who must have some sort of stable social
               base from which to draw support and minister.

definition   The social base process item refers to those
               incidents in which God gives guidance concerning
               one's social base, teaches lessons concerning the
               priority or importance of the social base to
               ministry, or teaches lessons concerning any of the
               three formations (spiritual, ministerial, or
               strategic) from the members of the social base.
               This process item may occur throughout any
               development phase.

example   See Tink (1982a), Gripentrog (1987), Waldner (1987),
               Finzel (1987), Zabriskie (1986)

kinds   In western cultures the social base revolves around
               singleness and its support elements, the nuclear
               family, and various other family patterns that are
               emerging in modern society. In non-western society
               the social base may be an extended family or other
               kinship network.

causal   In western missions, spouses are often very
source,   influential in the development of the partner.
spouse   Many relational lessons and other important
               insights crucial to development of the leader come
               via the causal source of a spouse or other
               important member of the social base.

causal   The issue of singleness can become a causal source
source,   for many important process incidents in a
singleness   missionary's life.

combinations   Frequently this process item may be combined with
               other ones such as an obedience check, word check,
               guidance processing, or structural insights.

FEEDBACK ON SOCIAL BASE PROCESS ITEM

1. Describe briefly the Social Base you experienced during your foundational years. This refers to the family situation you were raised in as a child.

2. Check any social base category for which you have experienced any process incident that may have affected your leadership.
___a. special guidance.
___b. lessons concerning relationship between ministry and social base.
___c. relationship insights from the social base that have affected leadership.
___d. issue of singleness before God.
___e. important lessons taught via spouse.
___f. in marriage--priority of ministry concerning spouse or self.
___g. combination of social base processing with other processing: specify which if you know.
___h. Other: you describe--

3. Check your present social base
___a. reluctantly single, unclear support unit
___b. single by choice, operating independently
___c. single, operating in a team environment
___d. single, backed by some friendship/support unit
___e. married--nuclear family, dominantly in social support role
___f. married--nuclear family, share social support and ministry role
___g. married--nuclear family, dominantly in ministry role
___h. married--other family, specify support/ministry profile:

4. What is the most important lesson you have learned concerning social base processing?

ANSWERS----------
    1. Nuclear family, neither parents dominantly in ministry. Mother was dominantly in social support role. Father was in vocational role. Later both were in vocational with mother still providing main social support for family.
    2. b., c., e., g.
    3. f.
    4. One, a leader must have an adequate social base to operate from--emotional and social support is necessary to effective ministry. Two, a person aspiring to ministry but having a spouse against it, will not function adequately in ministry. Three, in special cases a leader may have to sacrifice an adequate social base in order to concentrate on a highly demanding ministry situation. Four, some organizations recognize the importance of the social base for singles as well as marrieds. Five, functionally equivalent social bases must be deliberately sought and developed by singles on the mission field. Six, the social base you experienced in the foundational years will almost deterministically affect the social base you develop in adult years.

COMMENTARY ON SOCIAL BASE PROCESS ITEM

social
base
processing
an on-going
item

One of the major issues a missionary must deal with (whether single or married) is the personal social base unit that supports the mission effort. It is a special kind of on-going relationship insights process item. There is first of all the relationship with God concerning the issue of single or married. Secondly, if married there is the interplay between the worker, spouse and family throughout ministry. Or if single, there is the functional substitute for spouse and family, and relationship of the single worker to that substitute. Frequently, from time to time there will be a critical incident related to this social base which significantly affects the leadership of the worker. It may well relate to any of the formations--spiritual, ministerial or strategic.

combination
items

A social base process item will often be in combination with other process items. Conflict and crisis in a marriage is a combination involving social base processing. A decision to remain single to devote oneself exclusively to some ministry if done in response to a word or obedience item would be another example of combination of processing. One of the characteristics of process items given later is the overlap characteristic. Process incidents do not necessarily map one to one with process items. That is, a given process incident may include several process items occurring concurrently. Of these, one or more may be in focus and may be found dominate when a person analyzes the situation. This will often be the case with social base processing. See Tink (1982).

functional
equivalents

Single workers will need to find a functional equivalent for a family social base if they are to minister without facing the prospect of heavy isolation processing. For an example of a single worker who ministered for years without a good functional social base unit and experienced heavy isolation processing, see Carlson (1985).

profiles

Married workers operate in various combinations of ministry focus. Typical profiles include: spouse 1: heavy direct ministry, spouse 2: support role (or vice versea); spouse 1 and spouse 2: heavy direct ministry, share support functions; Trade off situation: spouse 1 minister for a period of time, spouse 2 heavy support; roles may switch after time. Frequently, the various profiles hinge on care of children. Ideal profiles based on giftedness are often not practical due to contextual and cultural pressures.

SUMMARY ON FOUNDATIONAL ITEMS--Unit 1

General

Leadership emergence theory analyzes the foundational phase of a leader's life in order to identify data that will shed light on the leadership functions of the person later in life. Such data may indicate limitations on leadership due to personality traits, contextual items, or cultural items that were formative during this period of time. It may indicate latent potential that needs to be exploited. It most likely will uncover divine foreshadowing in terms of destiny preparation items not seen before. Such items can only foster stronger leadership.

Two results of examining this period of time should include an acceptance of oneself as uniquely fitted for leadership in line with God's purposes for that uniqueness and a deeper appreciation for the hand of God in the early formative portion of life. That is, God was superintending during that time, as pleasant or unpleasant as it was, with a view towards a lifetime of development and service. The pieces do have meaning. We need the sovereign perspective to believe this. And remember the data is not all in. At the end of our lifetime of service we will fill in the pieces and see the whole puzzle complete. It begins to make sense as we accept this foundational time as God's time for uniquely laying foundations.

Developmental Tasks

The major developmental task of the early foundational phase is the laying of foundations that relate to leadership capacity in the life of a person. A leader's capacity to influence comes partially from character, partially from skills and abilities, and partially from values concerning leadership. Many foundations will be laid during this phase concerning character, skills and abilities, and values. Later phases will focus on the spiritual side of leadership capacity.

The laying of foundations that relate to leadership capacity will vary uniquely from individual to individual in terms of many complex factors not the least of which is the long term leadership purposes that God has for the individual. Later developmental tasks for other phases will have much more in common for all leaders than does this general task of the foundational phase. Here the laying of foundations, what they are and how it is done, varies greatly with each individual.

Present Response of Leader To This Phase

What is to be the response of a leader who is viewing this in retrospect? It is too late to change the incidents, but not too late to learn from the process items. What then can be done? One, honestly recognize this foundational time for what it was. Two, notice the destiny preparation items which now may be more evident than at the time they occurred. Reflecting on them and sensing the freshness of taking a new look at what occurred should strengthen your sense of destiny and its fulfillment in your life. Three, where there are restrictions to your leadership which are to be traced back to this phase, acknowledge them and make decisions in light of them if they are still binding and can't be changed. Four, consider your findings from this phase when making major decisions affecting further development and movement toward convergence. Five, acknowledge any potential areas of expansion that are hinted at in this phase and take steps to develop them and use them in future ministry. An in-depth study of entry context processing may help you see some of the unique aspects that are built into your leadership potential and clarify some ultimate purposes. Most of all accept what God has allowed or controlled in this phase as part of His long term formation for you.

We can not go back and change the incidents that we experienced in this foundational processing. But we can change how we interpret it. Our understanding of it in light of God's developmental purposes for us can cause us to change radically concerning this early processing.

Unit 2. Transitional Processing

Thus far we have been considering the foundational processes that can significantly affect later leadership such as destiny preparation, entry context, family influence, basic skills and social base. These foundational processes are followed by the transition to adulthood and leadership. The leader will have experienced a social base in growing up and will have to transition to a social base in the move to adulthood. God's call on the life and early character testing will form the backdrop for transition into leadership. These topics develop the theme of this unit, transitional processing into leadership.

In this unit we describe the processing which occurs as the emerging leader breaks forth into early adulthood. For some, this time of transition into leadership will last into the mid-thirties or even later. The early part of the transition concerns several development tasks which dominantly "look back." These include: 1) the "release task", breaking free from family structures which have controlled most of the previous phase, 2) the "first steps task", which involves decisions about role/structures for the coming phase, and 3) the "internalizing task", movement toward personalizing of one's previous stand for Christ. The process items during this time focus mainly on the formation of character during the stabilizing process of the "first steps task" and the "internalizing task."

As progress is made on the "looking back tasks" the "transition tasks" dealing with leadership emergence begin to occur. They include: 1) the formation of basal leadership character through testing, and 2) the continued identification of leadership potential. The leader's response is to react positively to the testing and be prepared for the expansion after the testing.

The major leadership development pattern of this transition is a testing-expansion cycle which is used to develop character. Successful response to the testing on the part of the leader results in inner growth and expansion of ministry. The testing-expansion pattern involves three aspects: the test, the response to the test, the outworking of the test. For a positive response the outworking usually involves expansion though its effects may be delayed. For a negative response there is usually remedial action involving repeated effort or correction or disciplinary action though again it may be delayed.[1]

God frequently uses three important process items to test an emerging leader's heart intent--the core of ministry character. These three are INTEGRITY CHECKS (p. 125), OBEDIENCE CHECKS (p. 129), and WORD CHECKS (p. 133). Notice these process items are

----

[1]These testing patterns, T.1 and T.2, are described more fully in chapter 11 but are mentioned here in connection with these basic process items used to launch potential leaders into leadership.

called checks. Check is used in the sense of "check and balance."
This reminds us of the testing nature of these process items.
These tests move toward achievement of the transitional
developmental task, the formation of basal leadership character
through testing.

A fourth item, the MINISTRY TASK PROCESS ITEM (p. 136),
focuses on both developmental tasks: character formation and
identification of leadership potential. It tests character in
the nature of doing some specific ministry assignment. This item
tests for and develops the qualities of availability,
faithfulness and dependability. It also points out leadership
potential. This ministry task process item not only occurs in
this transitional period but also throughout the early portion of
full time ministry.

A fifth item, less frequent, but particularly important in
developing ce tain kinds of leaders is the FAITH CHECK (p. 143).
All leaders need to trust God in leadership. Faith checks are
those initial baby steps in which a young emerging leader is
learning to do that. Some leaders, those who will go on to
apostolic leadership will find that faith checks will be
foundational to their ministry.

Finally, a sixth item, the LEADERSHIP COMMITTAL PROCESS ITEM
(p. 146) provides the solid basis for a life of leadership to
follow. Leadership committal processing is usually foundational
to destiny processing.

INTEGRITY CHECK PROCESS ITEM   Symbol: P(IC)

introduction   At the heart of any assessment of biblical
                qualifications for leadership lies the concept of
                integrity--that uncompromising adherence to a code
                of moral, artistic or other values which reveals
                itself in utter sincerity, honesty, and candor and
                avoids deception or artificiality (adapted from
                Webster).

definition   An <u>integrity</u> <u>check</u> refers to the special kind of
                process test which God uses to evaluate heart-
                intent, consistency between inner convictions and
                outward actions, and which God uses as a foundation
                from which to expand the leader's capacity to
                influence.

example   Daniel (Daniel 1,5); Shadrach, Meshach, and
O.T.   Abednego (Daniel 3); Joseph (Genesis 39), Abraham
                (Genesis 24), Jephthah (Judges 11).

N.T.   Paul (Acts 20:22,23)

kinds   ● temptation (conviction test)
                ● restitution (honesty testing)
                ● value check (ultimate value clarification)
                ● loyalty (allegiance testing)
                ● guidance (alternative testing--better offer after
                  Holy Spirit led commitment to some course of
                  action)
                ● conflict against ministry vision (guidance/faith
                  testing)
                ● word conflict or obedience conflict (complexity
                  testing usually in guidance)
                ● leadership backlash (perseverance/faith/guidance
                  testing)
                ● persecution (a steadfastness check; may come
                  through prophecy or contextual situation)

uses   ● to see follow-through on a promise or vow
                ● to insure burden for a ministry or vision
                ● to allow confirmation of inner-character strength
                ● to build faith
                ● to establish inner values very important to later
                  leadership which will follow
                ● to teach submission
                ● to warn others of the seriousness of obeying God

timing   Integrity checks usually occur early in the
                transition into leadership. Occasionally, later,
                there will be integrity checks at critical
                junctures of transition from one given ministry
                focus to another.

FEEDBACK ON INTEGRITY CHECK PROCESS ITEM

1. Read again the 4 facets of the definition of a biblical
leader.

A <u>leader</u>, in the Biblical context for which we are interested in
studying leadership development is a person
    1. with God-given capacity AND
    2. with a God-given responsibility
    WHO IS INFLUENCING
    3. a specific group of God's people
    4. toward God's purposes for the group.

As God develops a leader toward these four functions, which of
them is most likely to have integrity check process items as part
of the means for development?

2. Give here a Biblical example of an integrity check other than
those already mentioned.

Who: Where found in Scripture:

Brief description of incident:

Challenge:

Response:

Result:

3. Which of the kinds of integrity checks have you personally
experienced in your own leadership development? (Check any that
apply.)
    ___ a. temptation (conviction test)   ___ g. word conflict or
    ___ b. restitution (honesty testing)   obedience conflict
    ___ c. value check (ultimate value   (complexity testing
        clarification)   usually in guidance)
    ___ d. loyalty (allegiance testing)   ___ h. leadership backlash
    ___ e. guidance (alternative better   (faith/ perseverance/
        offer)   guidance testing)
    ___ f. conflict against ministry   ___ i. persecution (stead-
        vision (faith testing)   fastness check)

4. Which of the uses of integrity checks have you seen in your
own life? Check any which apply.
    ___ a. to see follow-through   ___ d. to build faith
        on a promise or vow   ___ e. to establish values impor-
    ___ b. to insure burden for   tant to later leadership
        ministry or vision   ___ f. to teach submission
    ___ c. to allow confirmation   ___ g. to warn others of
        of inner strength   seriousness of obeying God

FEEDBACK ON INTEGRITY CHECK PROCESS ITEM continued

5. For any one item you marked in question 3 jot down the essentials of that check and be prepared to share it with a small group or some other interested person.

The kind:

The background:

The challenge:

My response:

The result:

Effect on later leadership:

ANSWERS----------
   1. I think the integrity check process items are most likely given in conjunction with 2 and 4.
   2.
Who: Ananias and Sapphira (indirectly whole Jerusalem church)
Where found in Scripture: Acts 5:1-11.
Brief description of incident: Ananias and Sapphira sold a piece of property and then claimed to give all of the amount to the church. In actuality, they lied; they gave only a part of it. Peter confronted them.
Challenge: Ananias and Sapphira were both individually tested as to integrity when Peter confronted them.
Response: They could have recognized that they were wrong, confessed it, and repented. They did not.
Result: There were two. 1) Peter announced God's judgment. God gave ultimate discipline by taking their lives. 2) The church saw this and were made aware of God's power and of the ministry of the Holy Spirit (particularly in regards to holiness) in a new way.
   3. Here are the ones for me: a., b., e.
   4. Here are the ones for me: a., c., d.
   5. Here is one I personally experienced:
The kind: restitution
The background: when I left the military I took some items of equipment (used) which were really not mine though they were assigned to me for my use.
The challenge: God challenged me on honesty.
My response: I did not know how to return the equipment. It was used material and would be thrown away. So I talked it over with a mentor with whom I was doing a personal bible study. I had assessed the value of it. He suggested I send the money to a servicemen's center in Texas who were ministering to those in the armed forces. I would at least be returning some value back to the military.
The result: I did so. God blessed my efforts in my discipling ministry and continued to expand my sphere of influence.
Effect on later leadership: I saw first hand the value of restitution.

COMMENTARY ON INTEGRITY CHECK PROCESS ITEM

importance   As has been mentioned previously, failure in
                  ministry dominantly is rooted in spiritual
                  formation issues (spirituality) rather than
                  ministerial formation and strategic formation
                  issues. Most of these failures can ultimately be
                  traced to basic failures of integrity checks early
                  on in this transitional time.

order   There are three parts to an integrity check: the
property   challenge to consistency with inner convictions,
three   the response to the challenge, and the resulting
parts   expansion. Sometimes the expansion may be delayed
                  or take place over a period of time but it can
                  definitely be seen to stem from the integrity
                  check. Delayed expansion is seen in Joseph's
                  classic test with Potiphar's wife. Immediate
                  expansion is seen in Daniel's wine test.

preparation   Integrity is the heart of character as can be seen
for wider   by in depth analysis of the biblical leadership
sphere of   trait lists in Timothy and Titus. God often
ministry   prepares a leader for a wider sphere of influence
                  by testing the leader's integrity. Intent of the
                  heart and follow through on intent are checked in
                  an integrity check. Usually a successful passing
                  of an integrity check results in a stronger leader
                  able to serve God in a wider sphere of influence.

ongoing   Integrity checks occur as tests of entrance into
integrity   leadership or entrance into particularly demanding
                  ministries later in life. Normally, processing
                  concerning integrity during ministry is usually not
                  in the form of testing for leadership but in the
                  form of continued molding of leadership character
                  and occur in combination with processing concerning
                  guidance and word or literary or other ordinary
                  expansion items.

causal   Often the integrity check happens completely
source   unknown to people around the emerging leader. That
property   is because of its inward nature. The secondary
                  causes may be events, people, etc. They may not
                  even know that they are sources. The primary
                  causal source is inward via the conscience. The
                  Holy Spirit shapes the conscience.

OBEDIENCE CHECK PROCESS ITEM   Symbol: P(OC)

introduction   A leader must influence others toward obedience. A necessary first step is that the leader personally learns obedience. A leader must learn to recognize God's voice, and understand what God is saying, and obey when obedience is called for. Usually the obedience process item is learned rather early in the development of the leader and then repeated throughout life. Often the first lessons come as checks, that is, the leader is tested as to obedience. A proper recognition and response leads to growth and further revelation.

definition   Obedience checks refer to that special category of process items in which God tests personal response to revealed truth in the life of a person.

examples   Ananias in Acts 9, Peter in Acts 10, Barnabas in Acts 4, Philip in Acts 8

kinds   Some frequently seen obedience checks concern:

- learning about possessions/giving,
- learning about choice of mate and putting God first,
- willingness to be used by God in ministry
- willingness to trust a truth God has shown,
- willingness to forgive,
- willingness to confess something,
- willingness to right a continuing wrong,

order property   Again the pattern is threefold. There is the demand for obedience by God in terms of an issue, there is the response by the leader, and there are the results. The demand for obedience may be in terms of the written Word or as the result of some spoken Word or in terms of application of what is already known. The response can be positive or negative. A positive response may be immediate obedience, or a desire to obey but with the need for further clarification. A negative response is a refusal to obey. The results for those who respond positively is usually enlightenment with more truth; negative responses most often result in some remedial action.

importance-- use property   Leaders are those whom God is going to entrust with truth and guidance for others. Leaders will expect to be obeyed. A leader must first of all be an obedient follower of the Lord before expecting others to follow. Leaders must continually model obedience if they expect others to recognize their spiritual authority.

FEEDBACK ON OBEDIENCE CHECK PROCESS ITEM

1. Examine the obedience check which God used with Peter in reference to Cornelius. (See Acts 10)

    a. Describe the stages of the process in your own words.

    b. In what way was this process item used by God in Peter's leadership development?

    c. Why was this process item so significant from God's viewpoint? (What do you think were the wider purposes intended by God? Consider Acts 15.)

2. Think carefully on the obedience check implied in Acts 4:32-37. Suggest how this process item affected Barnabas' leadership development. (You may want to think about Acts 11:27-30, Romans 15:25-29 and 2 Corinthians 8,9).

3. Can you identify an obedience check in your own experience? Check which category it fits in and then give a short explanation of how you see this obedience check being used to develop you as a leader.
____ a. learning about possessions and giving,
____ b. learning about choice of mate and putting God first,
____ c. willingness to be used by God in ministry,
____ d. willingness to trust a truth God has shown,
____ e. willingness to forgive,
____ f. willingness to confess something,
____ g. willingness to right a wrong,
____ h. some other kind, you name it:

How has this obedience check process item affected your leadership development?

ANSWERS---------- see next page

FEEDBACK ON OBEDIENCE CHECK PROCESS ITEM continued

ANSWERS---------- continued

    1. a. Stage 1. God reveals truth to Cornelius in a vision.
Stage 2. God gives Cornelius an obedience check. Send to Joppa
for Peter. Stage 3. God used Peter's regular prayer time to
reveal truth. Stage 4. God used a natural physical craving to
get Peter's attention concerning a new truth He wanted to give.
Stage 5. God used the vision of the sheet and unclean animals to
experientially teach Peter a truth. He does not yet understand
it in the broader sense. But he is thinking about it and now
open to learn about it cognitively. Stage 6. Peter gets an
obedience check from the Holy Spirit--go with these men for I
have sent them. Stage 7. Peter obeys and sees God's wider
revelation of the vision. A gentile is not unclean. He saw this
when the Holy Spirit said "Do not hesitate to go with them for I
have sent them." His remarks to Cornelius in 10:27-29 show he
had grasped that much of the truth. Stage 8. God further
confirms the truth by using the outward sign of the Holy Spirit
as in Acts 2. Stage 9. The Gentiles are baptized as followers of
Jesus.
    Notice that this vignette also illustrates the Double
Confirmation Guidance processing. God reveals truth to Cornelius
and to Peter and then brings them together so as to have them
validate each others' revelation. The guidance needs to be sure
since this episode is a major hinge in God's purposes to reach
the world. Note also that two obedience checks were given--one
to Cornelius and one to Peter.
    b. Peter was broadened to understand that Jesus would reach
Gentiles as well as Jews with salvation. Later he would
courageously voice this conviction in the Jerusalem Council in
Acts 15 which would validate Paul's contextualization of the
Gospel to the Gentiles.
    c. God's wider purposes involve the vision and call to Paul
to reach the Gentiles. God will use this episode with Peter to
back up Paul's claim of ministry to the Gentiles.
    2. Barnabas responded to an evident obedience check
concerning possessions and giving and the essential meaning of
sharing the Christian life. His obedience shows that he had
learned to recognize the Holy Spirit's promptings. (This positive
example is especially significant in light of the negative
example which immediately follows.) That this experiential
lesson deeply impacted Barnabas' mind-set can be seen in the fact
that Barnabas influenced others to give. He did this for the
church in Antioch. It was an evident process item for Paul.
Barnabas' influence on Paul was multiplied greatly, for wherever
Paul went, the crucial truth concerning possessions and giving
and sharing with other Christians was emphasized.
    3. a. God tested me twice within my first week of Bible
College concerning my sharing of finances with other students.
God for the next three years met our financial needs. This
perspective on God's ownership of all of "our things" and sharing
and giving has influenced all of my ministry and those I have
influenced.

COMMENTARY ON OBEDIENCE CHECK PROCESS ITEM

developmental focus property-- conative goal	A leader must learn obedience in order to influence others in obedience. A will conditioned to obey God is a primary tool for all leaders. With it they have a fundamental basis for developing spiritual authority--experiencing the living God in their lives.
Abraham's classic obedience check-- character- istics	God's request for Abraham to sacrifice Isaac in Genesis 22 illustrates several important characteristics of an obedience check.

1. Obedience checks may appear to contradict some earlier leading. This obedience check was especially difficult because of a series of destiny experiences and promises concerning Isaac. Abraham knew his future line depended on Isaac, but he was still <u>willing</u> (conative function) to obey God.
2. Obedience checks are not always logical. It is one thing to obey when it seems logical and necessary, but it is quite another when obedience calls for something that doesn't make sense. Obedience doesn't always hinge on understanding. Sometimes it is true we know in order to do but it is also sometimes true that we do in order to know.
3. God requires unconditional obedience. Obedience checks often test surrender of the will.
4. God is responsible for the results. They may or may not be anything we would expect from the obedience.
5. Larger purposes may be involved than is immediately seen in the outward act. Hebrews 11:17-19 shows that faith in the living God as the source of life, was being strengthened through this obedience check.

causal source property	An obedience check tests obedience to God. The ultimate cause must be traced to the Lord no matter what the intermediate means. A leader must learn to know that it is the Lord's voice he/she is obeying.
John 7:17	The Lord's statement in this passage is often tested in an obedience check. "If any man will do his will, he shall know of the doctrine, whether it be of God, or whether I speak of myself."
major lesson	Leaders will be responsible for influencing specific groups of people to obey God. They will not achieve this unless they themselves know how to obey the thrust of this early major lesson: **OBEDIENCE IS FIRST LEARNED, THEN TAUGHT.**

WORD CHECK PROCESS ITEM Symbol: P(WC)

introduction	An essential characteristic of leadership is the ability to receive truth from God. This is a springboard to authoritative use of the word in ministry. It is also an integral part of a leader's methodology for getting guidance for the ministry. The process item used to describe this development is called the word process item. A special kind of word process item is a word check which launches a leader into other kinds of word processing.
definition	A word check is a process item which tests a leader's ability to understand or receive a word from God personally and to see it worked out in life with a view toward enhancing the authority of God's truth and a desire to know it.
example	Barnabas was sent to Antioch (Acts 11) to ascertain genuineness of the experience there. He had just been exposed to truth concerning God's acceptance of Cornelius. The test--Can he use this truth in a life situation?
example	Peter was told by the Holy Spirit (Acts 10) to go with the three gentiles to Cornelius' home. This happened concurrently with the thrice repeated vision concerning clean and unclean. He immediately perceived new truth. The Gentiles were not unclean. He was then ready for God's expansion of that truth in Cornelius' home. Peter was tested on two truths (Gentiles are clean and Jesus will baptize in the Holy Spirit).
development focus property	A successful pass of a word check results in an increased ability to discern God's voice of truth, to clarify truth, and to apply it to life's situation. This will lead to more truth and authoritative use of truth.
other word processes	The word check process item represents only one kind of word processing item. Over a lifetime a leader will see other kinds such as use of the word for guidance, for ministry, for formation of character and as a framework for interpreting life in line with the purposes of God. But the word check is that category of word item which God uses, usually in the early formative stages of an emerging leader, to test the leader's ability to understand the word, to use the word in one's own life and to transfer truth from it to life situations. In addition, it is used by God to cement in the young leader's life the authority of the Word and thus form life habits which will insure continued growth in acquiring truth.

FEEDBACK ON WORD CHECK PROCESS ITEM

1. Which of the following passages contains a Word Check Process
Item?
___ a. Acts 11:27-30   ___ c. neither of the above
___ b. Acts 23:11 and 27:13ff   ___ d. both of the above

2. Read again the 4 facets of our leadership definition.

A <u>leader</u>, in the Biblical context for which we are interested in
studying leadership development, is a person
    1. with God-given capacity AND
    2. with a God-given responsibility
    WHO IS INFLUENCING
    3. a specific group of God's people
    4. toward God's purposes for the group.

As God develops a leader toward these 4 functions, which of them
is most likely to have word check process items as part of the
processing?

3. Identify a word check process item from your own experience.
Describe it and show how it has been used to help develop you as
a leader.

4. Interview a Christian leader concerning the word process item
in general and word checks in particular. See if you can elicit
a good example of a word check process item. Describe your
findings.

5. We have been studying inner-life growth process items. We
have listed three common ones frequently seen in the early
development phases of a potential leader. These three are
obedience checks, word checks, and integrity checks. Compare and
contrast these three inner-life factors. How are they the same
and how are they different? How will they most likely be used by
God over the life-time development process?

FEEDBACK ON WORD CHECK PROCESS ITEM continued

ANSWERS----------

1. d. both of the above
2. The question called for your opinion. Here's mine: all of them.
3. In my early days of being discipled I was reading 5 Psalms and 1 chapter in Proverbs each day. I did this for about a year. God repeatedly brought attention to truth concerning my use of words. I have memorized many of the verses. God changed my use of my tongue through those many truths. I would find that it was often the case that I would be introduced to a truth in my quiet time and would be immediately confronted with its application at my job at Bell Telephone Labs. Usually the process would be: truth given, a failure at work involving that truth, recognition that God was testing, reaffirmation and progressive use of the truth. A leader must be careful concerning what he/she says. Because they influence others so much words take on added import. It is particularly true of one with an exhortation gift. I am continuing to learn to use words that not only encourage (an exhortive gift thrust) but also edify (a teaching gift thrust).
4. I interviewed Peter Kuzmic, a limited level 5 leader from Yugoslavia concerning the word process item. At one point in his life in which he was isolated from all other christians in an isolated military post where the word of God was not permitted he memorized the Gospel of John. He had a small copy of the Gospel in his billfold. Other word process items were shared with me, enough to know that Peter is a man of the Word.
5. The three have this in common, they are all **inner-life** factors. Hence, usually they are **only known to the person and God alone.** Others may never find out about them. Particularly this is true of the integrity check process item. The word check and obedience check items will frequently be shared, but usually after the fact and as part of a ministry thrust which uses imitation modelling. The word check is foundational since it deals with an authoritative base for making judgments. The integrity check is foundational since a leader is one who must elicit trust. This can not be done when a leader is inconsistent with his/her own inner-life convictions. The obedience check is foundational to followership. A leader can not expect obedience from those being influenced unless the leader is one who first models obedience.

COMMENTARY ON WORD CHECK

word checks as bridge to word gifts	Leaders usually have one or more word gifts (apostleship, evangelism, prophecy, teaching, pastoring, exhortation, faith, word of knowledge, word of wisdom) as part of their gift-mix (the set of primary spiritual gifts). The word check processing is usually a springboard leading to perception of one of these gifts and its use. Word checks usually lead to public sharing of a testimony concerning the check, a first step in experiencing use of a word gift.
timing property	Word checks usually occur early in a leader's life in order to initiate habits of intake and appreciation for the written word.
love of word	Leaders greatly used of God have evidenced a love for truth. They study the written word to feed their own souls as well as to help those to whom they minister. They are quick to discern God's truth in everyday life. They learn to hear the voice of God through the ministry of other people. So then, one would expect God to develop a leader in his/her ability to appreciate truth, and to cultivate habits of intake.
trigger property	Usually early word checks have a strong trigger incident which involves the written Word. Some verse, phrase or sentence seems to come alive and rivets one's attention until there is a recognition that it is the Lord speaking personally.
spiritual authority	Usually one aspect of perceived spiritual authority by followers is their respect for a leader's understanding and use of the word. When the word has made a powerful impact on a leader's life its spill over or by-product is spiritual authority.
balanced learning via testing items	Holland (1978) points out that balanced learning involves three goals: being, knowing, doing. The three process items, integrity check, word check, and obedience check, respectively, focus on these three learning goals for a young leader.
overlap: integrity, obedience, and word checks	I have described three major kinds of tests: integrity checks, obedience checks, and word checks. Sometimes it is not so easy to differentiate them. Life is complex and a given piece of reality does not always fit into neat analytical categories. Often a test involves a combination of one or more of these three process items. Although it is good to identify a given process item it is much more important to see the testing's significance.

MINISTRY TASK PROCESS ITEM   Symbol: P(MT)

introduction   Emerging leaders early on in their informal
               training are often given small tasks by mentors,
               masters, supervisors, pastors or other leaders
               who are associated with them. The tasks can be
               small and informal or formal. These tasks are
               often indicators of loyalty, submission, use of
               gifts, initiative, and further usefulness. God
               honors the principle of Luke 16:10, "He that is
               faithful in that which is least is faithful also in
               much; and he that is unjust in little is unjust in
               much." An important thing to keep in mind about
               ministry tasks is that the ultimate assignment is
               from God whether or not the ministry task is self-
               initiated or assigned by another. Ultimate
               accountability is to God. One of the signs of
               maturity in an emerging leader is the recognition
               of this fact and the desire to please the Lord in a
               ministry task.

definition   A ministry task is an assignment from God which
               primarily tests a person's faithfulness and
               obedience but often also allows use of ministry
               gifts in the context of a task which has closure,
               accountability, and evaluation.

example   Barnabas' trip to Antioch in Acts 11 was an
               apostolic ministry task which was definable and had
               closure, as well as accountability, and evaluation.

example   Paul's year or so at Antioch with Barnabas as
               mentor was a ministry task which was a springboard
               to the missionary task of Acts 13 with Barnabas.

example   Titus had five ministry tasks including three with
               the Corinthian church, one in Crete and one in
               Dalmatia. The ministry tasks at Corinth were
               primarily confrontational ministry tasks. In all
               of them he was essentially testing Paul's spiritual
               authority. His major task, at least from the
               standpoint of information available, was a broad
               comprehensive apostolic task at Crete. Nothing is
               known about the final ministry task at Dalmatia,
               though some have speculated that it was an
               evangelistic task.

examples   Numerous ministry tasks have been identified and
               evaluated in contemporary studies. See Baumgartner
               (1987:35), Gripentrog (1987:70).

EXAMPLE OF MINISTRY TASKS--TITUS

introduction   Titus was apparently given several ministry tasks.
We can identify five in the scriptures and draw
lessons from three of them.   The tasks are listed
below.   Dr. Edmond Hiebert (1954:146,147)
identifies the first three.   I assume his time
analysis of Titus' ministry with Paul.

TASK	WHERE	MAIN INTENT	COMMENTS
1	Corinth	Initiate giving for Jerusalem Project.	Titus completed this task. The Corinthian Church was initially enthused about giving. Titus was evidently a person of tact and persuasive ability.
2	Corinth	Ascertain accountability; take disciplinary measures.	Titus completed this task with heartfelt involvement. Discipline was applied. Apparently the problem of divisions was solved, somewhat. Paul does not deal with any of those major problems in II Corinthians where the issue is spiritual authority.
3	Corinth	1. Complete Jerusalem project. 2. Test loyalty to Pauline authority. 3. Follow-up on discipline.	Results here are unknown.
4	Crete	Apostolic 1. Appoint leaders 2. Ground in teaching/ lifestyle 3. Establish mission giving.	Here the thrust is on appointing leadership which will model a Christian lifestyle in the Cretian context.
5	Dalmatia	Evangelistic	Unknown.

MINISTRY TASK CONTINUUM

introduction   Small ministry tasks can be early indicators of
                  leadership potential. In earlier development
                  phases the thrust of these small ministry tasks is
                  INNER-LIFE GROWTH FACTORS. When ministry tasks are
                  given in later development phases they will usually
                  be under MINISTRY FACTORS. The primary thrust of
                  the ministry task when given in earlier development
                  phases will be toward the development of the person
                  given the task. Those given in later development
                  phases will have a thrust toward accomplishment of
                  the task. The continuum given below indicates
                  these thrusts. Ministry tasks are transition
                  items. They test (like integrity, obedience, and
                  word checks) and hence belong in the Inner-Life
                  Growth Phase. They also give ministry experience
                  and develop ministry skills (like many of the other
                  ministry process items) which puts them also in the
                  early part of growth ministry processing.

THE MINISTRY TASK CONTINUUM--Luke 16:10 in Action

```
LITTLE                                                          MUCH
|                                                                 |
| <------------------------------------------------------------> |
|                                                                 |
| PRIMARILY FOR                              PRIMARILY FOR        |
| PERSON DOING TASK                          DOING TASK           |
```

EXAMPLE USING TITUS' MINISTRY TASKS

```
LITTLE                                                          MUCH
|                                                                 |
| <---------------------------X----------X-----------X--------X-->|
|                             MINISTRY  MINISTRY  MINISTRY MINISTRY|
|                             TASK 1    TASK 2    TASK 3   TASK 4 |
|                             CORINTH   CORINTH   CORINTH  CRETE  |
|                                                                 |
| PRIMARILY FOR                              PRIMARILY FOR        |
| PERSON DOING TASK                          DOING TASK           |
```

ultimate   A final note of importance concerns recognition of
acount-   the ultimate source of the assignment of ministry
ability   tasks. On the human side the task may appear
                  routine, natural, or not very significant. But
                  ultimate accountability for the task is to God
                  through human authority. To be able to sense that
                  a given task is really an assignment from God can
                  bring great fervor regarding accomplishing the task
                  and a sense of contributing towards God's purposes.

FEEDBACK ON MINISTRY TASK PROCESS ITEM

1. Place the following ministry tasks on the continuum at the approximate place you feel they fit by placing the letter on the continuum line.

A. Philippians 2:25   C. Philippians 2:19   E. Luke 9:1-6
B. Luke 10:1-12   D. Acts 13:1-3   F. Acts 11:22

```
<──────────────────────────────────────────────────────────>
  PRIMARILY FOR                          PRIMARILY FOR
  PERSON DOING TASK                      DOING TASK
```

2. For the tasks given in exercise 1 above, categorize the ministry tasks by filling in the table below. I have filled in E. Luke 9:1-6 as an example.

MINISTRY TASK	WHO ASSIGNED	BASIC FUNCTION(S)
A. Philippians 2:25		
B. Luke 10:1-12		
C. Philippians 2:19		
D. Acts 13:1-3		
E. Luke 9:1-6	12 disciples	1. demonstrate kingdom: healing, exorcism. 2. Test of faith. Test of obedience. 3. Experience spiritual authority.
F. Acts 11:22		

3. Suggest here any other biblical examples of ministry tasks that you are aware of.

4. Give an example, if you can, of a ministry task you have experienced which:
    a. someone else gave.

    who   what function   results

    b. was self-initiated; describe.

    c. put your example from exercise a. on the ministry task continuum.

```
<──────────────────────────────────────────────────────────>
  PRIMARILY FOR                          PRIMARILY FOR
  PERSON DOING TASK                      DOING TASK
```

ANSWERS FOR FEEDBACK ON MINISTRY TASK PROCESS ITEM continued

ANSWERS----------
    1. Your answer is as good as mine. Here's mine.

```
<----------E--B----------------F------------D------------AC-->
```

PRIMARILY FOR	PRIMARILY FOR
PERSON DOING TASK	DOING TASK

2.

	Ministry Task:	Who Assigned:	Basic Function(s):
A.	Philippians 2:25	Epaphroditus	encouragement, unify, affirm, mission giving.
B.	Luke 10:1-12	the 72	soil testing, test faith, demonstrate the kingdom, experience spiritual warfare and spiritual authority.
C.	Philippians 2:19	Timothy	pastoral, unify, messenger.
D.	Acts 13:1-3	Barnabas, Paul	experience contextualization in evangelism and ecclesiology and Gentile Christian life-style, evangelize Gentiles, plant church groups,
E.	Luke 9:1-6	12 disciples	1. demonstrate kingdom: healing, exorcism. 2. Test of faith. Test of obedience. 3. Experience spiritual authority.
F.	Acts 11:22	Barnabas	word test, Apostolic ministry task, judge Gentile forms of Christianity, experience and develop spiritual authority, model Christian life-style and teaching

    3. I'll leave this one for you.
    4. a. who=Pastor Thompson
          what function=teach home Bible study
          one result=developed gift of teaching
       b. was self-initiated; describe. Paul Shattuck, an Air
Force enlisted man, and I, an electrical engineer, held an
evangelistic rally for youth in a small rural town in northern
Ohio.
       c. put your example from exercise a. on the ministry task
continuum.

```
<------X------------------------------------------------->
```

PRIMARILY FOR	PRIMARILY FOR
PERSON DOING TASK	DOING TASK

COMMENTARY ON MINISTRY TASKS

ministry task	A ministry task should be differentiated from ministry experience in general. A ministry task is specifically a test. Perceived as a special assignment from God, a ministry task usually pertains to a specified ministry experience that can be completed and evaluated for the purpose of testing the leader's availability, faithfulness and skills.
ministry task pattern	God's pattern seems to be to assign small ministry tasks. Usually the first ones are self-initiated in response to integrity, word, or obedience checks. Other tasks follow upon right responses until tasks of great responsibility can be given to the leader with confidence. Titus exemplifies this pattern.
kinds property	Ministry tasks are as varied as they can be. No categorization other than where they fit on the continuum has been developed.
uses property .	Ministry tasks are used in at least the five following ways: 1. Assess an emerging leader's faithfulness. 2. Assess an emerging leader's readiness to obey. 3. Facilitate emergence of gifts. 4. Actual accomplishment of task. 5. Allows closure with regard to developmental issues.
order property	The steps involved in a ministry task include: 1. recognition of the task, 2. obedient response, 3. accomplishment of task, 4. Closure assessment, 5. Expansion.
causal property	The immediate cause for a ministry task can be self or another person. Where self-initiated the prompting is usually in response to sensitivity to the Holy Spirit. The ultimate cause is God who is superintending the development process.
patterns property	The M.1 Foundational Ministry Pattern is usually first encountered via ministry task processing. See chapter 11 on response patterns.
importance	The ministry task is a valuable tool for more experienced leaders in assessing potential leaders. This processing should be deliberately used and closure assessment given as a means for leadership selection. One should guard against the assigning of ministry tasks for selfish reasons. Its primary focus should be for development of the potential leader.

FAITH CHECK PROCESS ITEM   Symbol: P(FCHK)

introduction   Leaders are people with vision from God. A response
                of faith is one that accepts and sees that vision
                worked out. The faith check is an early test in
                which God brings an emerging leader to take baby
                steps of faith so as to see them fulfilled. These
                experiences build confidence so as to encourage
                much larger steps of faith. Potential leaders need
                to learn early the truth of Hebrews 11:6, "But
                without faith it is impossible to please God, for he
                that cometh to God must believe that He is and that
                He is a rewarder of them that diligently seek Him."

definition   A faith check is an early challenge by God given to
                a potential leader concerning some issue in which
                God's reality and faithfulness can be tested and
                seen to be true and which forms a confidence
                builder for later trusting God with bigger issues.

example   David's test with the lion when he was a shepherd
                boy was a faith check which prepared him for a
                later faith check, the confrontation with Goliath.
                Both of these were faith checks which established
                David's confidence in God. David would receive
                much greater challenges as King. These were
                stepping stones to greater faith.

example   Peter's impetuous request for the Lord to bid him
                to also walk on the water was a stimulus coming
                from an underlying desire to trust Jesus and
                resulted in a faith check partially passed.

example   The Angel of the Lord's visitation to Gideon in
                Judges 6:11-32 records a faith check process item.
                God carefully built up Gideon step-by-step from the
                initial revelation all the way to the destruction
                of the Midianites. The first faith check involved
                believing that God was revealing Himself to Gideon.
                The intermediate checks involved the fleece
                praying. The final check involved selecting the
                small army. God would be the source of victory.

timing   Faith checks are part of a more inclusive process
property   item, the faith challenge. Faith checks occur in
                transition into ministry and early ministry. Faith
                challenges occur in middle and latter ministry and
                are part of the expansion cluster of items.

order   Faith checks occur in five steps: 1. a stimulus to
                faith, 2. recognition that having faith in God is
                the issue 3. insight as to what God wants to do or
                can do in the situation, 4. response which believes
                God will intervene, 5. the results through which
                faith in God is vindicated.

FEEDBACK ON FAITH CHECK PROCESS ITEM

1. If an integrity check deals with "being" goals and a word check deals with "knowing goals" and an obedience check deals with "doing" goals what kind of goals do you think are being dealt with by a faith checks?

2. Give an illustration from your own life of a faith check. Did your faith check have all the steps listed in the order property section? Check the ones you experienced and describe the process incident for your faith check.

____ a. Step 1. the stimulus to faith,
____ b. Step 2. the recognition that faith in God is the issue
____ c. Step 3. the insight on what God wants or can do,
____ d. Step 4. the response which believes God will,
____ e. Step 5. the results in which faith in God is vindicated.

3. Give any other Biblical illustrations of faith checks that you are aware of.

4. Notice that no commentary is given on the Faith Check Process item. Write a paragraph or two that from your experience you feel would be appropriate for a commentary sheet.

ANSWERS----------

see next page.

FEEDBACK ON FAITH CHECK PROCESS ITEM continued

1. Faith checks deal with a combination of knowing and doing goals. A faith check involves discerning that the issue at hand is a faith check, and that God is able and willing to intervene. Both of these are knowing goals. It also requires doing--a stepping out, a deliberate act of the will--as an outward manifestation that indicates one truly believes that God will act.

2. All of the steps occurred in my first faith check. In the early summer of 1967 we had resigned from Bell Labs in Columbus, Ohio (official termination date in September) and were planning on going to Columbia Bible College in South Carolina. We had put our house up for sale and begin to get rid of our furniture that we wouldn't be taking. About mid-summer the Lord challenged me concerning our future housing in Columbia. The issue was that of presumptious faith, that I was assuming that He would work yet I was not taking an active step of faith to believe Him for that housing. The conviction was strong and I repented of this presumption. At that time we had a young Bible College student, Jeff Imbach, staying with us for the summer. I explained to Jeff and Marilyn, my wife, what I was feeling. I think it was Jeff who suggested we should pray on-the-spot about it. We went to our living room and the three of us knelt down to pray. But before we could pray it occurred to us we didn't know what we should ask. We then got back up, got a piece of paper and wrote down what we should trust God for. The list essentially had three items: 1. size of the house, three bedrooms (we had two boys and two girls), 2. cost, $75 per month (we had only $110 per month of known income after we left the Labs), and 3. distance from school, less than three miles (we couldn't afford much in terms of gasoline). Having written these three specifics down we agreed that these were reasonable and we should take these as from God--His challenge to us to trust Him. We did, got down on our knees and prayed specifically. While we were on our knees the telephone rang--a long distance phone call from Columbia, S.C. A lady, Mrs. Westervelt, was on the phone who said we did not know her but that Dean Braswell, dean of students, had informed her that we were coming to school that fall and she happened to have a house coming available in a month. Were we interested? She then went on to say that it had three bedrooms, was 2.5 miles from the school and was renting for $75 per month. Were we interested or would we like to see it first? We took it. And we knew we could trust our God.

3. The sending of the 70 involved a combination of ministry task and faith check--they must obey and believe that God would provide.

LEADERSHIP COMMITTAL PROCESS ITEM   Symbol: P(LCOM)

introduction   The heart of the leadership committal process item
                 is an inward private agreement (though there may
                 be some public stimulus to this) between the
                 potential leader and God. The agreement pledges
                 willingness by the potential leader to be used by
                 God in service for Him as the major priority of
                 life. In essence, it is a Lordship decision with
                 regard to service for Christ. This does not
                 necessarily mean a full-time Christian vocation
                 though that is often the case. It does mean
                 that all vocational efforts will be subservient to
                 whatever service roles God gives.

definition   The <u>leadership</u> <u>committal</u> <u>process</u> <u>item</u> is a destiny
                 process item, either an event or process which
                 culminates in an acknowledgment from a potential
                 leader to God of willingness to be used in ministry
                 in whatever way God indicates.

example   Paul's crisis experience in conversion was linked
                 to a sense of destiny call which forever changed
                 his life work. The radical nature of his conversion
                 experience led him to have confidence in the Gospel
                 and its power to save. He believed it would work
                 for all kinds of people (see his descriptions in I
                 Corinthians 6:9). And he lived that conviction.

example   Kuzmic's conversion as an early teen-ager from
                 scientific-atheism through a miraculous power
                 experience was coterminous with committal to
                 ministry and can be correlated to his evangelistic
                 ministry and his training ministry.

timing   The committal process item can occur coincidentally
property   with conversion or as a second committal after
                 conversion. The committal act may occur long
                 before the actual leadership potential emerges or
                 it may initiate the process immediately.

major use   A leadership committal act often serves as a
                 benchmark upon which all future leadership
                 assessment can look back to. When the going gets
                 rough there is always that assurance that God
                 called and He knew in His call even the things
                 happening now. He will sustain.

causal   The committal may occur as result of a special
property   challenge, as a result of a special revelatory
                 act, or in terms of a growing awareness which
                 culminates in decisions reflecting steps toward
                 leadership.

FEEDBACK EXERCISE ON LEADERSHIP COMMITTAL PROCESS ITEM

1. Conversion and leadership committal may be coincidental.
Below are listed the general goals of processing. Read them and
then reflect on Paul's radical Damascus experience (Acts 9) to
note which of the items were in focus in his leadership committal
process item.

Process Incidents are the actual occurrences from a given life of
those providential events, people, circumstances, special divine
interventions, inner-life lessons, and/or other like things
which God uses to shape leadership character, leadership skills,
and leadership values so as to

    a. indicate leadership capacity (such as inner integrity,
       and influence potential),
    b. expand that potential capacity,
    c. confirm appointment to a role or responsibilities which
       use that leadership capacity,
    d. direct that leader along to God's appointed ministry level
       for the realized potential.

Which of the four do you think was in focus in Paul's radical
conversion experience? ___ a. ___ b. ___ c. ___ d.
Explain.

2. Give a Biblical example of a leadership committal process
item.

3. Give an example from your own experience in terms of the
leadership committal process item. Be prepared to discuss this
in a small group. My leadership committal processing was (choose
any which fit you):

___a. coincidental with conversion
___b. a second committal after conversion
___c. a result of a special challenge
___d. a result of a special revelatory act
___e. a growing awareness which culminated in decisions
      reflecting steps toward leadership.
___f. clear as to implications for future leadership
___g. not clear to implications for future leadership but can be
      seen in retrospect.
___h. other--explain:

4. Look again at the description of goals for process incidents
given in exercise 1 above and with your own own leadership
committal experience in view. Which of the four do you think was
in focus in your leadership committal processing? Explain.
___ a. ___ b. ___ c. ___ d.

FEEDBACK EXERCISE ON LEADERSHIP COMMITTAL PROCESS ITEM continued

ANSWERS----------

 1. I believe <u>x</u> d. It took that radical experience to alter Paul's life-ministry. Leadership potential was already seen.
 2. Moses' experience at the burning bush.
 3. b., c., e., g. In my experience, there was growing awareness which culminated in a special challenge to me in my quiet time regarding missionary service which did result in decisions reflecting steps toward leadership. There was also a latter "clarification committal" as a result of a missionary woman, Ruth Nephew, who challenged me toward the mission field. At the time it was not clear as to the implications for future leadership but it was seen more clearly in retrospect.
 4. d. I think the heart of the definition of leadership committal tends toward this last function of processing in that the committal usually breaks loose a potential leader from other focuses. When it takes place in processing over time then functions a., b., and c. may be in focus.

COMMENTARY ON LEADERSHIP COMMITTAL PROCESS ITEM

further explanation of timing property	For some who experience radical conversions like the Apostle Paul the leadership committal may be coincidental with conversion. For others who were born into a Christian heritage the agreement may not be related to the salvation experience but to some other kind of Lordship challenge. The committal may be in response to a perceived call from God to the mission field or pastorate or Christian organization. It may not be a specific call but rather a willingness to be used with a gradual clarification over time as to how. The committal may also come after some ministry has been experienced. Then suddenly there is an inner satisfaction and an inner knowledge that you want to be and will be used by God in ministry. The desire to be deeply used is a first step toward leadership emergence.
implications not clear	The implications for future leadership may not be in focus in the committal but can be seen in retrospect.
trigger and build-up incidents	Frequently a trigger incident will culminate a leadership call. Sometimes these are given in public (challenges in meetings); sometimes in private. Usually there is a series of build-up incidents taking place over an extended time which lead to the trigger.
repeated committals	Sometimes the leadership committal has an "initial challenge" (dealing with submission and surrender) which demands a response and then further along there will be a "clarification committal" in which the submission issue is reaffirmed in light of the more specific direction. There may be a great deal of time between these incidents.

SUMMARY ON UNIT 2—TRANSITIONAL PROCESSING

General

A potential leader is transitioned toward leadership via several process items which focus on basic character and desire for leadership. The foundations are laid for leadership character via **integrity checks, obedience checks, word checks** and **ministry tasks**. The turning point for entrance into ministry comes via the leadership committal process item.

Development Tasks

In general any Christian, leader or not, will be responding to some development tasks that naturally signal the boundary phase from the foundational phase into adult life.

An emerging Christian must

1. transition from the past (looking back tasks)
2. transition into his/her own social unit (the release task),
3. find beginning roles for existing in society (first steps task),
4. personalize convictions about Christianity (internalizing task).

These tasks may coincide with the transitional tasks leading to full-time Christian leadership (testing via integrity check, obedience check, word check and ministry task). Or they may occur before the transition into Christian leadership happens. If so, there will probably be a vocational switch as the leader moves from that initial vocation (those beginning roles in society) into full-time Christian leadership.

The major development task of transitional processing is to develop a positive response pattern to testing situations. When this is achieved a leader will habitually respond in positive ways to God's voice in integrity, word, obedience and ministry task issues.

FOUNDATIONAL PROCESSING--FINAL COMMENTS

Some Findings--Early Processing and Major Lessons

Five of the seven major leadership lessons have been cultivated during the foundational processing.

Touched on	Major Leadership Lesson
X	1. EFFECTIVE LEADERS MAINTAIN A LEARNING POSTURE THROUGHOUT LIFE.
X	2. EFFECTIVE LEADERS VALUE SPIRITUAL AUTHORITY AS A PRIMARY POWER BASE.
X	3. EFFECTIVE LEADERS RECOGNIZE LEADERSHIP SELECTION AND DEVELOPMENT AS A PRIORITY FUNCTION.
	4. EFFECTIVE LEADERS WHO ARE PRODUCTIVE OVER A LIFETIME HAVE A DYNAMIC MINISTRY PHILOSOPHY.
X	5. EFFECTIVE LEADERS EVINCE A GROWING AWARENESS OF THEIR SENSE OF DESTINY.
	6. EFFECTIVE LEADERS INCREASINGLY PERCEIVE THEIR MINISTRY IN TERMS OF A LIFETIME PERSPECTIVE.
X	7. EFFECTIVE LEADERS ARE PACE SETTERS.

Learning Posture Lesson

The testing items--integrity checks, obedience checks, and word checks--which operate in terms of life incidents have begun to lay seeds for a life-long learning posture.

Spiritual Authority Lesson

Direct first-hand experiences with God in these same three testing process items begin to lay a credibility base from which spiritual authority will develop. One major source of spiritual authority is direct experience with God.

Leadership Selection Lesson

Experiencing first hand the selection process of movement toward leadership is the first step in understanding and recognizing selection processes in others.

Sense of Destiny Lesson

Having experienced destiny preparation process items is the first step toward recognizing destiny processing as a major factor in one's ministry. At this point the emerging leader will usually not be aware of this. But it is ontologically true and will be used later to build upon this major leadership lesson on destiny.

Pace Setting Lesson

Leaders must be and do that which they expect of others. The testing items all teach this pace setting principle from the ground floor up.

Early Processing Other Findings

Three leadership principles and two patterns have been consistently identified over many studies from this developmental phase. These give valuable insights about leadership selection. One of the major functions of all leadership is that of recognizing and developing future leadership. Leadership selection is crucial to ongoing leadership. These principles and patterns help one discern what God is doing to select leaders and thus to move in harmony with His selection processes.

The first principle is derived from repeated observations of God's use of the integrity check process item.

PRINCIPLE 1. INTEGRITY IS FOUNDATIONAL FOR LEADERSHIP; IT MUST BE INSTILLED EARLY IN A LEADER'S CHARACTER.

Trust flows from integrity. Leaders with integrity will be trusted and their authority will be primarily that of spiritual authority because of this aura of integrity.

The second principle is derived from repeated observations of God's use of the obedience check process item. Leaders will be responsible for influencing specific groups to obey God. They will never do so unless they first know the challenge of hearing God tell them to obey, accept that challenge by responding to it, and experience God's touch upon that response. This dynamic is captured in principle 2.

PRINCIPLE 2. OBEDIENCE IS FIRST LEARNED PERSONALLY BY A LEADER THEN TAUGHT TO OTHERS BY THAT LEADER.

Leaders are pace setters. They are what they demand of others. They do or are willing to do what they require of others. The authority needed by forceful leadership has its foundation in personal experience with God. The obedience check is the springboard from personal obedience to corporate obedience.

The third principle particularly applies to leadership selection. It flows from an analysis of the word check process item in many leadership development studies and correlation of that with findings from growth ministry processing. Briefly let me give some background for the principle.

Leadership is tied strongly to giftedness. Giftedness, particularly the giftedness pattern[2] (discovery of gift ---> increased use of that gift ---> becoming effective in it ---> discovering gift-mix ---> discovering gift-cluster ---> convergence), is more properly a subject of growth ministry processing or expansion processing (given later on in this manual), but its seeds lie in this transitional processing. It is the first part of that pattern, discovery of gift, which has its seeds in word checks and ministry tasks.

A major finding of leadership emergence theory is that all leaders have at least one word gift in their gift-mix. Analysis of spiritual gifts in terms of leadership development reveals three clusters of gifts: word gifts, love gifts, and power gifts. Much more detail will be given about these later, but for now let me say that word gifts is the term describing the cluster of gifts which are specifically used by God to reveal and clarify truth about God and His purposes and which will edify the believers and instill hope in them concerning God's present and future activity. These functions, revealing and clarifying truth, edifying believers, instilling hope, guidance toward future are major leadership functions.

The primary word gifts are exhortation, prophecy, and teaching. The secondary word gifts are apostleship, evangelism, and pastoring. The tertiary word gifts are word of wisdom, word of knowledge and faith.

Let me repeat all that I have been saying in a nutshell. Leadership gifts flow from the cluster of word gifts. It is the correlation between these word gifts and the word check process item that leads to the principle:

PRINCIPLE 3. LEADERSHIP GIFTS PRIMARILY INVOLVE WORD GIFTS WHICH INITIALLY EMERGE THROUGH WORD CHECKS.

Word checks are the bridge to use of the word in ministry. Personal lessons via word processing, particularly the word check, are almost always stepping stones to group lessons. The basic pattern is: personal response to truth, leads to further truth, and to the use of that truth with others. Use of truth with others is the very heart of all word gifts.

---

[2]The M.6 Giftedness Development Pattern is discussed in much more detail in chapter 11. It is introduced here simply because transitional processing often helps stimulate movement in stage 1 of the pattern.

Two further findings from this phase are worthy of note. Both are patterns that will be discussed more fully in chapter 11 on response patterns. They are helpful in leadership selection because they represent something being learned experientially by the emerging leader during transitional processing.

    PATTERN 1.   **THE POSITIVE TESTING/EXPANSION CYCLE VIA INTEGRITY CHECKS, WORD CHECKS, AND OBEDIENCE CHECKS IS A MAJOR SELECTION PROCESS USED BY GOD TO IDENTIFY EMERGING LEADERS.**

Pattern 2^3 flows from observations on ministry task process items which are a bridge process item between the Inner-Life Growth Phase and Ministry Maturity Phase. It too is very helpful in leadership selection.

    PATTERN 2.   **SUCCESSFUL SELF-INITIATED MINISTRY TASKS ARE OFTEN IMPORTANT PREDICTORS OF EMERGING LEADERSHIP.**

Leaders are people who exercise responsibility. In early stages this is often seen as people who can see that things need to be done and find ways to attempt to do them without others having to order them to do so. The self-initiated ministry task is a good indicator of a responsible person.

Boundary Ending the Phase

All boundary times involve reflecting back and reflecting forward, followed by movement toward decisions that will be worked out in the next phase. Reflection back on the major development tasks of foundational processing reveals that God has personally interacted with a potential leader to lay character foundations for future leadership. He has also indicated possible future ministry through word checks or ministry tasks. These personal lessons will usually culminate in the emerging leader's desire to give out some of that which is being learned. The "receiving to giving" pattern is the major boundary impetus. It will lead to various ministry options which will be clarified and expanded in growth ministry processing the subject of the next chapter.

So then, the boundary involves transition toward responsible ministry. It may culminate in going to school for further training, direct involvement in ministry while maintaining a separate vocation for support, or direct involvement in some apprenticeship ministry training which leads to full-time Christian service. It is this reaching out for increased responsibility in ministry which dominates the early portion of the next phase dealing with growth ministry processing.

----

[3]Actually what is described as Pattern 2 is part of a larger pattern, M.1 Foundational Ministry Pattern, discussed in chapter 11.

CHAPTER 5. GROWTH MINISTRY PROCESSING--PART I

Overview

Chapter 4 discussed foundational processing which led up to transition into full time Christian leadership. Chapter 5 picks up at that point and discusses early ministry processing. Foundational ministry items are identified. **Growth ministry** is the term used to embrace the development of the leader who is starting to minister. **Ministry** indicates that the leader is indeed in full time Christian work. **Growth** indicates that most of what is happening is intended to shape the leader more than the followers. There will probably be some successful ministry but that is less in focus than the shaping of the leader. Ministry is the context in which it happens and indeed may be the only context in which it could happen.

Many leaders transition slowly into leadership which necessitates an extended period of bi-vocational work (a vocation that provides financial support while enabling one to carry out part time leadership activities). Many of the process items discussed in Unit 1 of this chapter, along with other testing items, will have occurred within this transition period.

Overview of Foundational Ministry Items

Two clusters of process items are important in the early shaping of a leader in ministry. While it is true that an individual process item contributes to the shaping of a leader and can be analyzed in regards to its particular impact, it is also true that several items often are shaping toward some common goal, and thus can be grouped together. Such a grouping is called a **cluster.**

The **Personal Development Cluster** combines three items which concentrate on early ministerial formation: **ministry skills, training progress,** and **giftedness discovery.** This cluster helps a leader begin to sense God-given capacity and the potential for development.

The **People Insights Cluster** points out the importance of understanding and using insights concerning relationships with people. Leadership is dominantly influencing people. Relationships are key to effective influence. The **authority insights process item** concentrates on hierarchical relationship lessons, such as how to submit to the authority of other leaders and how to use authority with followers. The **relational insights** deals with peer relationships and other people-to-people concerns. How does the leader relate to followers, and other leaders, as a person?

Both of these clusters concentrate on developing the personhood of the leader so that influence potential is recognized and efforts toward development begun.

PERSONAL DEVELOPMENT CLUSTER

introduction   Early ministry efforts force an emerging leader to
                 learn skills and obtain training which will impact
                 initial influence efforts. Three process items
                 describe these early efforts of a leader to cope
                 with basic ministry demands. The young leader will
                 not usually sense the sovereign intervention of the
                 Lord in two of them--**Ministry Skills** and **Training
                 Progress..** The third, the **Giftedness Discovery**
                 process item will usually evoke a sense of God's
                 intervention. Awareness of this cluster and its
                 threefold focus--to instill confidence, to impart
                 basic direct influence skills, and to create a
                 sense of God-given capacity yet to be developed--
                 pave the way for expansion processing which will
                 allow for stabilization of ministry entry.

definition   The <u>personal</u> <u>development</u> <u>cluster</u> refers to the
                 three process items--**ministry skills, training
                 progress,** and **giftedness discovery**--which are used
                 to move an emerging leader to a new point of
                 stabilization, at a level significantly beyond
                 entry level leadership skills.

Venn Diagram
of Cluster   PERSONAL DEVELOPMENT CLUSTER

description   The **ministry skills process item** is the focal item
                 of the cluster. Doing is emphasized at this stage
                 of development. **Training progress** and **giftedness
                 discovery** both move toward realization of influence
                 skills.

common focus   Working together, the cluster develops the emerging
                 leader to a capable level of ministry, well above
                 entry level influence skills.

threefold   The cluster purposes to,
purpose   1. instill confidence,
                 2. impart basic direct influence skills, and
                 3. to create a sense of God-given capacity yet to
                    be developed

preliminary   Two definitions must be introduced in order to lay
definitions   foundations for understanding training. See
                 3 TRAINING MODES, INFORMAL TRAINING MODELS (pages
                 160,161).

MINISTRY SKILLS PROCESS ITEM   Symbol: P(MS)

introduction   A major thrust of development during the growth
                ministry phase is the acquisition of skills which
                aid a leader in accomplishing ministry. Most
                skills are acquired in the early and middle
                portions of this phase. Important skills usually
                gained include disciplinary, relational, group,
                organizational, word, persuasive and prayer skills.
                These skills may be knowledge focused (gaining
                perspectives on leadership) or influence focused
                (learning how to exercise leadership). These skills
                may or may not be directly supportive of spiritual
                gifts the leader has already been using.

definition   <u>Ministry skills</u> refers to a definite acquisition of
                one or more identifiable skills which aids one in a
                ministry assignment.

example   how to lead various kinds of small groups: prayer
                groups, kinship groups, bible study groups,
                committees.

example   how to prepare bible study materials for small
                groups

example   how to organize committees, write proposals,
                persuade people of the importance of new ideas

example   how to persuade people so as to implement change

example   how to relate to various people in organizational
                structures including superiors, co-equals, and
                subordinates

example   conflict management

example   Bible study methods, Bible communication skills

plateau   A commonly observed pattern is the **plateau pattern.**
pattern   Often, initially a person will learn new skills
                until he/she can operate with a reasonable amount
                of comfort. After this point, if a person does not
                deliberately and habitually seek new skills but
                rather chooses to coast on prior experience and a
                minimum skills level, their development will
                plateau, levelling off.

value of   Careful analysis of one's ministry history should
dynamic   seek to identify skills learned in various
reflection   assignments. Analysis of skills learned will
                include motivation for doing so, methods for doing
                so, results of the skills, implications for future
                learning of skills.

FEEDBACK ON MINISTRY SKILLS

1. Check any of the following disciplinary skills that you acquired early in your growth ministry:
___a. self-discipline (control of tongue, other personal habits)
___b. time management
___c. personal goal setting
___d. management of personal finances
___e. ability to perceive, receive, and obey orders from those in authority (in a submissive spirit, even if in disagreement)
___f. ability to persevere through on an assignment
___g. devotional habit
___h. Other--

2. Check any of the following relational skills that you learned early in your growth ministry:
___a. how to or not to relate to superiors in your organization
___b. how to or not to relate to peers in your organization
___c. how to or not to relate to subordinates
___d. beginning strategy for how to or how not to handle conflict
___e. Other--

3. Check any of the following group skills that you learned early in your growth ministry:
___a. how to lead prayer groups
___b. how to lead growth groups
___c. how to lead evangelistic groups
___d. how to lead Bible study groups
___e. how to lead committees
___f. how to start any of the above groups/ specify which ones:
___g. Other--

4. Check any of the following organizational skills that you acquired early in your growth ministry:
___a. how to organize committees
___b. how to write proposals
___c. how to design brochures and other publicity materials
___d. how to organize a church bulletin
___e. how to assess jobs which need to be done
___f. how to assign people to jobs in order to accomplish a task
___g. how to recognize structure in an organization
___h. how to prioritize
___i. how to set goals for a group
___j. Other--

5. Check any of the following word skills that you learned early in your growth ministry:
___a. how to study the scriptures
___b. how to prepare oral presentations from the word
___c. how to use the Bible devotionally to feed one's soul
___d. how to use Bible study aids like concordances and original language tools
___e. how to prepare Bible study materials for small groups
___f. how to study the Bible topically for theological findings
___g. Other--

FEEDBACK ON MINISTRY SKILLS continued

6. Check any of the following prayer skills that you acquired early in your growth ministry:

___a. prayer discipline
___b. learning to hear God give initiative on what to pray for
___c. intercessory aids (how to use a prayer notebook, how to journal in praying, etc.)
___d. how to fast (different kinds of fasts: isolation, working, group fasting, etc.)
___e. how to use the Bible in praying
___f. how to have a day of prayer
___g. conversational praying
___h. laying hands on a person for special release of power (physical healing, inner healing, commissioning, empowerment, gifting, etc.)
___i. Other--

7. Check any of the following persuasion skills that you learned early in your growth ministry:

___a. how to convince individuals and motivate them without overriding their own desires
___b. how to be flexible while verbally interacting with followers and peers in regards to decision-making issues,
___c. how to communicate a new idea so as to excite followers
___d. motivation techniques (use of scriptural case studies, review of God's past working, demonstration of power, use of gifting)
___e. how to gain consensus in a group
___f. Other--

8. What was the most important practical ministry skill you acquired in your early growth ministry?

9. Give an example of an important practical ministry skill you have learned recently? What was the processing that God used to bring about your acquisition of that skill?

ANSWERS----------
    1. a., b., c., g.
    2. how not to's in all categories--vicariously some; some via negative processing in my own life.
    3. a., b., d., e., f.   4. d.   5. a., b., c., d., e., f.
6. a., c., e., f., g.   7. c.   8. How to hold the attention of a small group Bible study for up to two hours.   9. Writing skills--programmed instruction and information mapping. The challenge came initially through a ministry assignment to create a theological education by extension program in Jamaica. This necessitated preparation of materials forcing me to pick up programmed instruction writing skills. Information mapping followed as an attempt to improve on programmed instruction. Both of these forced me to learn more about the nature of the teaching/learning dyad. They led to pursuit of communication skills as well. All along the way there was the divine touch in getting information, books, workshops, and financing.

THREE TRAINING MODES

introduction   Training models can be classified under three major
                 modes: formal, non-formal and informal. Basically,
                 the **formal** mode refers to organized institutional
                 education recognized by the society. **Informal**
                 refers to training which takes place in the context
                 of normal life activities. **Non-formal** training
                 refers to semi-organized training which usually
                 takes place outside the jurisdiction of formal
                 training. The following categories are helpful in
                 describing the training progress item.

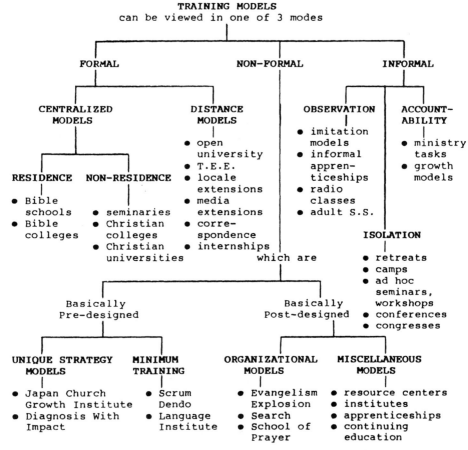

TRAINING MODELS
can be viewed in one of 3 modes

FORMAL   NON-FORMAL   INFORMAL

CENTRALIZED MODELS   **DISTANCE MODELS**   **OBSERVATION**   **ACCOUNT-ABILITY**

DISTANCE MODELS
● open university
● T.E.E.
● locale extensions
● media extensions
● correspondence
● internships

OBSERVATION
● imitation models
● informal apprenticeships
● radio classes
● adult S.S.

ACCOUNT-ABILITY
● ministry tasks
● growth models

RESIDENCE   **NON-RESIDENCE**
● Bible schools
● Bible colleges

● seminaries
● Christian colleges
● Christian universities

ISOLATION
● retreats
● camps
● ad hoc seminars, workshops
● conferences
● congresses

which are

Basically Pre-designed   Basically Post-designed

UNIQUE STRATEGY MODELS   **MINIMUM TRAINING**   **ORGANIZATIONAL MODELS**   **MISCELLANEOUS MODELS**

UNIQUE STRATEGY MODELS
● Japan Church Growth Institute
● Diagnosis With Impact

MINIMUM TRAINING
● Scrum Dendo
● Language Institute

ORGANIZATIONAL MODELS
● Evangelism Explosion
● Search
● School of Prayer

MISCELLANEOUS MODELS
● resource centers
● institutes
● apprenticeships
● continuing education

comment   Used by permission from (Clinton 1983b). Explanation
                 of models given there.

TWO CATEGORIES OF INFORMAL TRAINING MODELS

introduction   Informal training can be seen as a number of
                      training models grouped according to the time span
                      in which they occur.

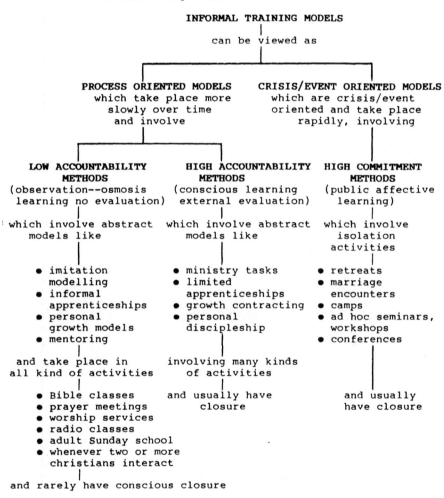

INFORMAL TRAINING MODELS

can be viewed as

PROCESS ORIENTED MODELS
which take place more
slowly over time
and involve

CRISIS/EVENT ORIENTED MODELS
which are crisis/event
oriented and take place
rapidly, involving

**LOW ACCOUNTABILITY
METHODS**
(observation--osmosis
learning no evaluation)

which involve abstract
models like

- imitation
  modelling
- informal
  apprenticeships
- personal
  growth models
- mentoring

and take place in
all kind of activities

- Bible classes
- prayer meetings
- worship services
- radio classes
- adult Sunday school
- whenever two or more
  christians interact

and rarely have conscious closure

**HIGH ACCOUNTABILITY
METHODS**
(conscious learning
external evaluation)

which involve abstract
models like

- ministry tasks
- limited
  apprenticeships
- growth contracting
- personal
  discipleship

involving many kinds
of activities

and usually have
closure

**HIGH COMMITMENT
METHODS**
(public affective
learning)

which involve
isolation
activities

- retreats
- marriage
  encounters
- camps
- ad hoc seminars,
  workshops
- conferences

and usually
have closure

comment   Used by permission from (Clinton 1983b), where
                      further explanation of models is given. The
                      training progress process item will usually involve
                      several of these informal models. In fact, many
                      more informal training models will be involved in
                      leadership emergence than will formal models.

FEEDBACK ON PRELIMINARY TRAINING DEFINITIONS

1. Most leaders have been helped by non-formal organizational training models such as Evangelism Explosion, Search Inc., School of Prayer or other similar models. List any such non-formal training model that was significant in your ministry development. Give the name of the model, when you were exposed to it, and what leadership development you can identify as a result of it.

2. Imitation modelling is defined as a training model in which the learner subconsciously or by choice observes someone further along in ministry development and seeks to reproduce in his/her own life what is observed. This can mean imitation of skills, methods of ministry, and philosophy. Frequently, the "like attracts like giftedness pattern" is observed. That is, a potential leader is drawn to a leader who demonstrates spiritual gifts like his/her own (even though the similar gift may not yet be recognized or developed). Imitation modelling along with mentoring are probably the two most prevalent low accountability informal training models. See if you can identify any leadership development through imitation modelling as to:

   a. Skills:

   b. Ministry Philosophy:

   c. Ministry Structures:

ANSWERS----------
   1. I was significantly helped by a secular non-formal training model presenting a writing technique called Information Mapping. This was a week long workshop in New York City in 1975. My teaching gift was significantly aided by the concepts given in this workshop. My <u>Spiritual Gifts</u> book was written as a project of this workshop. The workshop helped me understand how people learn cognitive information.
   2. a. how to teach home Bible studies, how to mentor through home Bible studies, how to do one-on-one Bible studies. I specifically learned the importance of visual aids in teaching Bible classes. I began to make my first Bible charts as a result of observing Pastor Thompson, my mentor in my early ministry development in the local church. b. From Pastor Thompson I learned of the vital place of the local church in God's worldwide redemption. I learned how important it was to develop people in ministry. I learned to get people to experience ministry as early as possible. I learned of the importance of sharing a pulpit and allowing young preacher boys to get public ministry experience. I saw the importance of knowing the word and its relationship to spiritual authority. I began my life-long habit of continually studying the Bible because of Pastor Thompson's modelling.
   c. I learned of the importance of the cell structure both for discipleship and for evangelism. I also learned about church government structures--advisory boards, committees. I also learned of the Bible Conference structure for teaching the Bible.

TRAINING PROGRESS PROCESS ITEM Symbol: P(TP)

introduction   In the early part of the ministry phase most skills
                are picked up through experience, observation, and
                self-study. This aspect of informal training can
                be greatly accelerated if the potential leader has
                access to leaders who are conscious of informal
                training models and use them deliberately to
                develop potential leaders. Often during the early
                or middle portion of this phase a leader will opt
                for intensive rapid acquisition of knowledge and
                skills. This training will usually be formal in
                nature and will thus require extraction from the
                normal ministry situation in which development was
                taking place. Formal training usually involves
                relocation to a centralized training institute.
                The training progress process item calls attention
                to reflection and analysis at specific periods of
                time in which formal, non-formal, and informal
                training has taken place. The thrust of the item
                is on how training has brought definite development
                in spiritual and ministerial formation, not simply
                on the completion of a program.

definition   The training progress process item refers to a
                closure experience which seeks to note identifiable
                progress in terms of influence capacity, leader
                responsibility, or self-confidence, and which
                occurs during or following a period of time in
                which there is some form of definite training
                whether formal, non-formal, or informal. Often
                divine affirmation or expectation concerning future
                leadership is revealed at this time.

example   Mark Williams, a Conservative Baptist Pastor, did
                an informal apprenticeship with Josh McDowell which
                lasted about a year. This apprenticeship developed
                skills in evangelistic methods and communication of
                faith.   In addition, it gave Mark an added
                confidence in approaching ministry problems. This
                was a major turning point in terms of training
                progress since skills and attitudes were learned
                that will last a lifetime.

example   Bob Newton, Missouri Synod missionary in the
                Philippines, studied in the leadership
                concentration at the School of World Mission. At
                the end of his study Bob had made such progress in
                training model theory that he could operate as a
                consultant in analysis and design of training
                programs. Bob has made significant use of this
                training and repercussions throughout his remaining
                ministry are likely.

FEEDBACK ON TRAINING ITEMS

1. Consider any training progress item you have had which has been significant in terms of the spiritual formation, ministerial formation, or strategic formation aspects of your development. Identify it in terms of the model categories suggested (See pages 160-161). Describe any ministerial formation or spiritual formation development which has continued to impact your ministry.

2. As you look forward to future ministry what further training do you see necessary? Can you suggest some training modes, either formal, non-formal, or informal, which you feel you will need in order to enhance your next ministry assignment?

ANSWERS----------

1. One major training progress item for me occurred through was an informal model within a formal training situation at the Columbia Graduate School, Columbia, S.C.   The particular development regarded my spiritual formation and was taught via imitation modelling.   I learned the importance of trusting God for ministry concerns.   This was learned primarily by observing the lives of many of the teachers.   I also learned a prayer skill--that of spending a whole day of prayer alone with God for spiritual refreshment and for guidance.   Through this training, the confidence that God could be trusted in regards to my future ministry was established.   I also knew that I could count upon such meetings with God to refresh me and give me guidance for my ministry.

2. I am in the midst of an on-going influence-mix challenge process item.   This challenge is forcing me to broaden my ministry to others (both in non-formal and formal models) as well as communicate my ideas popularly. Therefore, as I look forward to future ministry I see the need to develop skills in designing and conducting workshops and seminars. I need also to develop popular writing skills so that I can communicate some of my ideas to a much broader constituency.   I am presently using imitation modelling and an informal apprenticeship to help me in approaching the seminar and workshop development I need.   I am being mentored in developing popular writing skills by my daughter, Cathryn Hoellwarth, who has tremendous writing skills and a teaching gift to go along with them.

GIFTEDNESS DISCOVERY PROCESS ITEM Symbol: P(GD)

introduction   Apart from acquisition of general leadership
                  skills, the most important development during the
                  growth ministry phase involves giftedness,
                  especially in regards to discovery of spiritual
                  gifts and confident use of them. The focus of this
                  process item is the discovery of giftedness and how
                  development occurs.

definition   The giftedness set refers to the set of giftedness
                  elements: natural abilities, acquired skills, and
                  spiritual gifts.

definition   The giftedness discovery process item refers to any
                  significant advancement along the giftedness
                  development pattern and the event, person or
                  reflection process that was instrumental in
                  bringing about the discovery.

Barnabas   Barnabas discovered his exhortation gift early in
spiritual   his ministry. A destiny experience affirmed this
gift   discovery and set life-discovery time expectations
discovery   for using it. (See Acts 4:32-37.) There were
                  later significant discoveries in Acts 9 and Acts 11
                  which brought out manifestations of his apostleship
                  gift. The Galatians 2:6-10 affirmation was another
                  step forward in giftedness discovery.

general   Giftedness development, the discovery process of
time-line   identifying, adding to, and building upon one's
                  natural abilities, acquired skills, and spiritual
                  gifts, usually occurs somewhat in order of a
                  generic giftedness time-line. Some stages may
                  overlap; some may be skipped. But the general
                  tendency flows from an emphasis on natural
                  abilities to acquired skills to spiritual gifts to
                  supplemental skills.

order   1. Natural Abilities
property   2. Basic Acquired Skills
                   3. Early Spiritual Gift Indications
                   4. Further Acquired Skills
                   5. Early Identification of Spiritual Gift(s)
                   6. Late Discovery of Latent Natural Ability
                      (occasionally occurs)
                   7. Identification of Other Spiritual Gifts
                   8. Identification of Gift-Mix
                   9. Further Acquired Skills
                  10. Formation of Gift-Cluster
                  11. Discovery of Focal Element of Giftedness Set
                  12. Convergence of Giftedness

see also   Five patterns specifically focused on spiritual
                  gifts are given later in chapter 11.

GIFTEDNESS TIME-LINE EXAMPLE

introduction   "Post" discovery of giftedness development is
                stimulated by using a giftedness time-line. Below,
                a "generic time-line," followed by several examples
                of specific giftedness time-lines, is given.

General Giftedness Time-Line

```
| I. Foundational | Transi-   | II. Growth      | III Convergence   |
|    Processing   | tion      |    Processing   |    in Giftedness  |
|-----------------|-----------|-----------------|-------------------|
```
1. Natural Abilities
   2. Basic Skills   3. Early Spiritual Gift Indicators
                         4. Acquired Skills
                            5. Spiritual Gifts
                               6. Late Natural Abilities
                                  7. More Spiritual Gifts
                                     8. Gift-Mix
                                        9. Further Acquired Skills
                                           10. Gift-Cluster
                                              11. Focal Element
                                                 12. Convergence

Example: Mo Whitworth (1989a)

| 1959 1964 - 1977 | 1977-1981 | 1982 | 1983 | 1984 | 1985 | 1987-1989 |
[K-12 grade]	college	work				grad. ed.
1)optimism	2)analyt-	2)resource	2)prayer	5)teach-	5)giving	7)discern-
1)perseverance	ical	linking	5)faith	ing/	5)word of	ings of
1)high commitment	thinking	3)govern-	5)proph-	exhort-	knowl-	spirits
1)compassionate	2)writing	ments	ecy	ation	ledge	8)gift-mix
1)diversity of	2)self-	3)faith		5)pastor	3)miracles	identi-
interests	disci-			ing	9)small	fied
2)organizational	pline			5)ruling	business	
skills	1)see				skills	
2)group dynamics	overall				9)event	
skills	picture				coordi-	
3)prophetic					nation	
impressions						

Example: Kwang-Fo Teng (1989b)

| 1955 | 1970 | 1977 | 1979 | 1981 | 1983 | 1985 | 1987 | 1989 |
birth	15	22	24	26	28	30	32	34
```

1)natural        2)small            3)evangelism                     5)teaching
  leader           group             4)ruling                        5)exhortation
1)making         2)plan-                          4)Biblical         3)prophecy
  friends          ning           4)group          Theology         5)mercy
                 3)folk            Bible study   4)preaching
                   dance          4)personal
     1)speaking                    evangelism          4)youth ministry
     2)Chinese   6)analytical                          4)cross-cultural aspects
       culture     thinking                            4)leadership concepts
                                                       4)prayer/devotion
```

FEEDBACK ON GIFTEDNESS DISCOVERY PROCESS ITEM

1. It may prove helpful for you to indicate for which of the
stages you have process incidents to show development.
___(1) Natural Abilities
___(2) Basic Acquired skills
___(3) Early Spiritual Gift indications
___(4) Further Acquired skills
___(5) Early Identification of Spiritual Gift
___(6) Occasionally late discovery of latent natural ability
___(7) Identification of Other Spiritual Gifts
___(8) Identification of Gift-Mix
___(9) Further Acquired Skills
___(10) Formation of Gift-Cluster
___(11) Discovery of Focal Element of Giftedness Set
___(12) Convergence of Giftedness

2. List your dominant natural abilities.

3. List the dominant acquired skills you are presently aware of.

4. List the spiritual gifts that you are presently repeatedly
demonstrating in ministry. Identify the dominant one.

5. For any one stage you checked in exercise 1 above give the
details of an incident(s) or analysis indicating giftedness
discovery.

6. Which of the four New Testament philosophical models is most
fundamental to the concept of the giftedness discovery process
item? (See pages 53-57 for review of the models.)
___a. Stewardship ___b. Servant ___c. Shepherd ___d. Harvest

ANSWERS----------
    1. I have incidents for the first 11.
    2. Leadership and analytical sensitivity.
    3. Ability to conceptualize through models.
    4. <u>exhortation</u>, teaching, word of wisdom, leadership

    5. I'll discuss stages 3, 5, 7, and 8 and 10. My first gift
discovered was teaching in 1965. It came about through ministry
tasks relating to home Bible classes as assigned by Pastor
Thompson. I increasingly accepted openings to teach. I have
taught children classes, teen-age boy's classes, teen-age girl's
classes, collegiate classes, couple's classes, single's classes,
and old people's classes.

FEEDBACK ON GIFTEDNESS DISCOVERY PROCESS ITEM continued

I saw my effectiveness in teaching improve as I continued to have numerous opportunities to teach, as I gained a better understanding in regards to teaching methods, as I made efforts to develop my own teaching gift and as I experienced personal growth and maturity in my Christian development.

In 1968 I did a spiritual gifts paper for Dr. J. R. McQuilkin entitled, "My Spiritual Gift and How I Intend to Develop It." This outlined steps for development of my teaching gift which I have followed and added to. Books on practical communication as well as hermeneutics and writing skills have immensely aided me in improving effectiveness of the teaching gift.

In 1973,74 in conjunction with my study into spiritual gifts I recognized that I had the gift of exhortation (primarily admonition thrust). As I continued to utilize my teaching gift I began to se. that my exhortation gift dominated all that I did in teaching. [found that I had already made significant efforts towards developing my exhortation gift since I had been so diligent in applying truth to my own life. I also recognized that the basic pattern which occurs with the exhortation gift was already happening within my ministry. I was increasingly shifting the admonition thrust to the encouraging thrust so that my exercise of that gift was more balanced. Today I have seen that God has also further balanced my exhortation gift into a comfort thrust.

In 1975,76 I began to increasingly notice, especially in small group settings, that I often would speak a word of wisdom for situations. I first noticed this gift in another member of the executive team of which I was a part. I then saw that the same occurrence was happening with me. My continued study of gifts identified this as the word of wisdom gift. In the past I have been very careful about this gift and would seek outside confirmation. Increasingly in recent times I have been more free to use it and even try to put myself in situations where I can, by faith, expect to use that gift. Since 1979 I have recognized a gift-mix of exhortation, teaching, and word of wisdom with exhortation being dominant.

The cluster has begun to take shape. The teaching gift provides the base from which exhortation takes off. Ideas arising in teaching stir people and open them for change. Exhortation strongly moves people toward use of ideas. Follow-up counseling after application leads to opportunity for word of wisdom.

A most recent discovery, due to my continued study of the Stewardship Model and its implications for my life, has been my realization of my leadership ability as a natural ability. This ability supplements and fits well with my spiritual gift-mix. Thus I am sensing a responsibility to use it.

6. a. The Stewardship Model is most fundamentally related to the giftedness discovery process item. Its strong central thrust on accountability is at the heart of discovering who we are and what we have been given by God to use for Him. Shepherd and Harvest models are very related in an applicational manner.

COMMENTARY ON PERSONAL DEVELOPMENT CLUSTER

general note specifics of cluster	The ministry skills process item creates a sense of confidence by giving the leader tools that bring some success in ministry. All leaders need some positive reinforcement as they "do" ministry. Adequate skills give one a positive attitude toward ministry which in turn brings success and further positive reinforcement.
focus P(TP)	The training progress item gives a sense of closure and an expectation toward using what has been learned.
focus P(GD)	The giftedness discovery brings the divine into the picture and is a step forward in learning to use spiritual authority.
ministry skills-- informal mode	A recurring training model through which skills are often learned is the informal apprenticeship model. Personal growth models, deliberate use of limited apprenticeships, and mentoring are further informal training models that should be more systematically used to gain ministry skills.
ministry skills-- non-formal mode	Non-formal models including workshops, seminars, and conferences via organizational models should also be part of one's planning for deliberate acquisition of skills.
personal example P(MS)	In the mid-seventies I attended a week-long workshop in New York city with Bob Horne to develop information mapping writing skills. At the end of that week I began a project which eventually became my spiritual gifts book. This short non-formal organizational model of training has significantly affected my teaching ministry.
essence P(TP)	The essence of the training progress process item is found not in the completion of training, but rather in significantly altering one's understanding or learning so that all ministry hereafter is affected.
discovery stimulus P(GD)	Ministry achievement or other special ministry affirmation is frequently associated with the discovery of progress or advancement in giftedness.
forced discovery	A ministry situation may demand gifts that the leader has not previously recognized. God will reveal in that leader the needed gift in response to a step of faith. The gift might have been there in embryonic form or might be entirely new.

COMMENTARY ON PERSONAL DEVELOPMENT CLUSTER continued

early discovery stimuli P(GD)	Three patterns (described more fully in chapter 11) help one recognize early discovery of elements of the giftedness set. They are listed here in order to point out "discovery" stimuli for the giftedness discovery process item.

Pattern	Explanation
Like-Attracts-Like	Potential leaders are intuitively attracted to leaders who have like spiritual gifts.
Giftedness Drift	Potential leaders respond intuitively to ministry challenges and assignments that fit their spiritual gift even if not explicitly known.
Role/Gift Enablement	A role assigned to a person can be the stimulus for discovery of a latent gift or acquisition of new gift needed to function in the role.

further explanation on terms P(GD)	For further information on spiritual gifts, especially definitions and development suggestions, see Clinton (1985a). A **spiritual gift** is a God-given capacity to a leader for use in ministry. Leaders usually demonstrate several spiritual gifts over a life time. Some are more permanent and repeatedly used. Some occur for periods of time. Some only spontaneously appear. Those gifts which repeatedly appear make up the set of gifts called the **gift-mix**. The **gift-cluster** is a mature gift-mix in which a dominant gift is effectively supported by each other gift in the mix. The **focal element** of the giftedness set refers to the element--natural abilities, acquired skills, or spiritual gifts-- which dominates the ministry behavior of a leader.
discovery spiritual gifts, P(GD)	Usually Type A and B leaders will discover spiritual gifts experientially by using them without knowing names for them, or even that they are spiritual gifts. They will eventually use effectively at least one gift. The gift may not be identified explicitly in terms of cognitive terms but usually implicitly in terms of intuitive drift toward ministry using the gift. Type C leaders will at least implicitly identify more than one gift and use at least one effectively. Type D and E leaders will explicitly identify at least gift-mix. Often they will identify a gift-cluster and will rearrange roles and priorities in terms of this gift-mix or gift-cluster, which is a major step toward convergence.

PEOPLE INSIGHTS CLUSTER

introduction   Leaders influence people. Working with people is
                    at the heart of all leadership functions. Two
                    major problems all emerging leaders face have to do
                    with relationships with people. Leaders must learn
                    about authority in order to use it. They must
                    learn how to recognize it and submit to it if they
                    in turn are to use it properly. They influence
                    people. People are important to all leadership.
                    Leaders must learn how to relate to people and
                    learn that the end results of leadership are to
                    serve and help people. Lack of response to these
                    fundamental lessons on servant values and authority
                    will plague a leader all his/her life. The People
                    Insights Cluster occurs very frequently throughout
                    the early stages of growth ministry, and fairly
                    often thereafter. As a leader matures, the thrust
                    of the cluster becomes more subtle, moving the
                    leader toward use of spiritual authority and toward
                    effective motivation of people.

definition   The people insights cluster refers to two process
                    items--authority insights and relationship
                    insights--which are used to impress upon a leader
                    lessons concerning effective working with people, a
                    fundamental aspect of leadership.

Venn Diagram
of Cluster

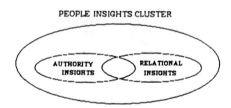

PEOPLE INSIGHTS CLUSTER

AUTHORITY INSIGHTS   RELATIONAL INSIGHTS

twofold   The people insights cluster teaches fundamental
purpose   lessons in two areas: 1. how to relate to people as
                    a servant leader (always balancing concerns for
                    serving people with the responsibility of leading
                    them toward God's purposes); 2. how to recognize,
                    submit to, and use authority as a servant leader
                    for the accomplishment of God's purposes.

most common   A survey of leadership problems among emerging
problems   leaders shows that problems concerning authority
                    and relationships with followers rank among the
                    most frequently occurring ones.

AUTHORITY INSIGHTS PROCESS ITEM Symbol: P(AI)

introduction	Authority refers to the right to exercise leadership influence. As with the centurion who recognized Jesus' authority, leaders themselves must have experienced what it means to be under authority in order to exercise it effectively. Lessons concerning submission to authority and the proper exercise of authority are preludes to efficient leadership and development in spiritual authority.
definition	The authority insights process item refers to those instances in ministry in which a leader learns important lessons, via positive or negative experiences, with regards to: 1) submission to authority, 2) authority structures, 3) authenticity of power bases underlying authority, 4) authority conflict 5) how to exercise authority.
order property	The pattern usually involves some or all of the following stages: 1. negative lessons of authority, 2. search for legitimate authority, 3. desire to model legitimate authority, 4. insights about spiritual authority, and 5. increasing use of spiritual authority as a foundational power base.
Gospel examples	● The Centurion in Luke 7:1-10. ● Request for James and John in Matthew 20:20-28. ● The disciples in Luke 8:22-25 when Jesus calms the sea. ● Pharisees, lawyers, disciples in Luke 5:17-26 at the healing of the paralyzed man.
O.T. example	Miriam and Aaron in the incident involving jealousy over Moses' authority in Numbers 12:1-16.
problem in Gospels	The issue of Jesus' authority runs throughout the Gospels and is a major source of contention with the Jews. He demonstrated authority in numerous ways: his teaching ministry, healing ministry, spiritual warfare, various miracles concerning physical creation, knowledge, prophecy, etc. He claimed that his authority came from God.
ultimate goal	The ultimate goal of authority processing is to bring a leader into an understanding of and use of spiritual authority as the primary power base. This is not to negate other kinds of authority as legitimate but to put them in proper perspective. Spiritual authority should be the dominant influence means of a servant leader.

FEEDBACK ON AUTHORITY INSIGHTS PROCESS ITEM

1. Scan again the five primary areas of insights: 1) submission
to authority, 2) authority structures, 3) authenticity of power
bases underlying authority, 4) authority conflict or the like,
5) how to exercise authority.

Which of these five are seen in the following examples. Place
the number(s) in the blank.
____ a. The Centurion in Luke 7:1-10.
____ b. Request for James and John in Matthew 20:20-28.
____ c. The disciples in Luke 8:22-25 when Jesus calms the sea.
____ d. Disciples in Luke 5:17-26 at the healing of the
         paralyzed man.
____ e. Miriam and Aaron in the incident involving jealousy
         over Moses' authority in Numbers 12:1-16.

2. Choose one of the examples of exercise 1. Explain it in terms
of the authority insights process item.

3. Give here an illustration from your own life of an authority
insights process item. Describe the incident and point out which
of the five areas of insights was in focus. Then explain exactly
the "authority insight" that was of profit to you.

ANSWERS----------
   1. __1,3__ a. The Centurion in Luke 7:1-10.
      __5__ b. Request for James and John in Matthew 20:20-28.
      __3__ c. The disciples in Luke 8:22-25 when Jesus calms
              the sea.
      __3,4__ d. Disciples in Luke 5:17-26 at the healing of the
              paralyzed man.
      __1,4__ e. Miriam and Aaron in the incident involving
              jealousy over Moses'authority in Numbers 12:1-16.
   2. e. In addition to the submission lesson, Miriam and Aaron
learned that God disciplines when authority is violated. This is
an incident of authority conflict in which Miriam and Aaron
wanted more authority and used self-efforts to get it. Note that
God defended Moses's authority, not Moses.
   3. Two are worth mentioning.(See also the feedback exercise
on the relationship insights process item.) The first concerned
submission to authority in regards to disciplinary actions. The
second concerned non-self-vindication of my spiritual authority.
That second lesson came through a literary process item in
conjunction with the relationship insights processing example I
mention in that section. I was reading Watchman Nee's biography
Against The Tide (Kinnear 1973) and along with it his book
Spiritual Authority. I learned that God is responsible to
vindicate (defend) a leader's spiritual authority. I saw that
principle repeated in Nee's life. I responded by accepting that
principle, not defending my own case, and waited for God's
vindication.

RELATIONSHIP INSIGHTS PROCESS ITEM   Symbol: P(RI)

introduction Influence depends on relationships with people.
              During growth ministry processing leaders will
              learn many lessons concerning influence and
              relationships with people. Many lessons will be
              the result of negative experiences. A developing
              leader will profit by lessons learned through both
              negative and positive experiences. The ability to
              establish relationships and see God use them to
              accomplish His purposes is an art and a skill.
              Leaders must learn the importance of relationships
              with others. The relationship insights process
              item focuses on expansion of this leadership
              capacity.

definition   The relationship insights process items refer to
              those instances in ministry in which a leader
              learns lessons via positive or negative experiences
              with regard to relating to other Christians or non-
              Christians in the light of ministry decisions or
              other influence means; such lessons are learned so
              as to significantly affect future leadership.

combination   The Centurion with Jesus. The Centurion recognized
relation-   spiritual authority and saw his relationship to
ship and   Jesus based on that insight. And he could act in
authority   faith based on his recognition.

Barnabas   1. Barnabas concerning Paul and his need to be
examples   related to the Jerusalem church (Acts 9).
              2. Barnabas with Paul concerning leadership
              transition (Acts 13).

Pauline   1. Paul and Barnabas and Antioch Church with
examples   Jerusalem Church. 2. Paul with Peter concerning
              the Galatian incident. 3. Paul with Barnabas
              concerning Mark. Both the immediate lessons seen
              in Acts 13 and the later lesson (Colossians 4:10).
              4. Paul with the Corinthians. I and II Corinthians
              are filled with relationship insights between Paul
              and the members of that church. Loyalty,
              obedience, spiritual warfare, and spiritual
              authority are key issues underlying the
              relationship insights.

via negative Often the relationship insight comes as a result of
experiences   authority clash, a submission lesson, or ministry
              crisis.

specific   The insight may be a specific one in regards to
or   relating to people in a given situation, or it may
general   be a more general one such as a principle for
insights   relating to people and structures so as to promote
              more efficient leadership.

FEEDBACK ON RELATIONSHIP INSIGHTS PROCESS ITEM

1. Consider the example of Barnabas with Paul concerning leadership transition. If you need refreshing read Acts 11:19-30; 13:1-12 and then contrast the leadership with that depicted from Acts 13:12 on through to the end of chapter 14.
    a. What was the relationship insight that Barnabas saw?

    b. How did this affect his future leadership?

2. What is the most important relationship insight you have learned to date in your leadership ministry?   How was it learned?

ANSWERS----------
    1. a. Barnabas had been in a mentoring relationship with Paul since Paul's first trip to Jerusalem as a Christian. He linked Paul into the Jerusalem church's leadership (Acts 9:27ff) and into the Antioch church (Acts 11:25,26). While ministering in Cyprus it became evident to Barnabas that Paul was at the point where he needed to be released in leadership. From Acts 13:13 and onward, with only three exceptions, the biblical record always refers to Paul and Barnabas. Prior to this Barnabas was always mentioned before Paul. It is clear that Paul was leading from then on. It takes real grace and maturity for a man such as Barnabas to not only allow such a leadership switch but actively work to make it a success. It is also clear that Mark could not handle the leadership switch. The relationship insight that Barnabas saw was that Paul needed to lead. He no longer needed a mentoring relationship, a subordinate relationship, nor even a co-equal relationship with Barnabas.
b. Barnabas submitted to that leadership with one exception (the Mark dispute).
    2. a. The most important relationship insight I have learned is that subordinates must be very careful in their correction of those in authority over them. One needs to be more than just right on issues in order for it to be appropriate to correct a person in leadership over them. Rightness or wrongness is not the whole show. One may be tactically correct but strategically wrong. Sometimes being right on certain issues is less important than maintaining a positive relationship.   b. I have learned this on three separate occasions with three different leaders. Each time I gained insights. This lesson was learned negatively, the hard way, in all three cases. But it has stayed with me. Two very important personal lessons resulted from the discipline connected with one of the incidents. One, I learned I was not very flexible and God began a continuing work of increasing my flexibility. Two, I learned to give up the right to be right.

COMMENTARY ON PEOPLE INSIGHTS CLUSTER

combination processing	**Relationship** and **authority insights** processing often occurs in combination with the **ministry conflict** process item. This means, when we as leaders are experiencing ministry conflict, we should carefully search the issues to see the lessons the Lord is trying to teach us on authority and relationships. These lessons are probably more important than the issues on which the ministry conflict rest. For lessons learned here can be useful throughout our leadership.
submission cluster	The **people insights cluster** is really a sub-cluster of a larger cluster of process items called the **submission cluster.** Ministry conflict, authority insights, relational insights, and **leadership backlash** all deal fundamentally with a root problem of submission.
further explanation spiritual authority and other power bases	I said previously that the ultimate goal of authority processing is to bring a leader into an understanding of and use of spiritual authority as the primary authority used in leadership influence. I said further that this is not to negate other kinds of authority as legitimate, but to put them in proper perspective. Spiritual authority dominates a servant leader's influence means. The Stewardship Model, the Harvest Model, and the Shepherd Model show us that leaders also have tasks to accomplish. The demands of task behaviors, which dominate primarily the Harvest Model and secondarily the Shepherd Model, require power bases sometimes involving coercive authority, induced authority, legitimate authority, competent authority, as well as spiritual authority. Because the maturity levels of followers vary, power bases other than spiritual authority are necessary to move them, for their own good, toward God's purposes. As followers mature, the spiritual authority power base will dominate as an influence means. The **people insights cluster** helps maintain a balance in this dynamic tension between authority bases. **Authority insights** processing will teach about the necessity of using authority to accomplish God's purposes and keep task behavior in focus. **Relationship insights** processing will continue to bring back the concepts of servant leadership by keeping concern for people in focus.

SUMMARY-SOME FINDINGS ON GROWTH MINISTRY PROCESSING--PART I

2 Major Ministry Problems

During the growth ministry processing two problems often crop up. These two problems are often seen as barriers or bridges to growth depending on how a leader responds to them. The two clusters of processing items have as major purposes the confrontation of these problems early on in a leader's life.

1. **THE PLATEAU BARRIER**
   Leaders have a tendency to arrest development once they have developed some skills and gained some ministry experience. They may be content to continue ministry as is without discerning their need to develop further.

2. **THE AUTHORITY PROBLEM.** Leaders in growth ministry processing must learn to submit to authority. Many leaders throughout their ministry have problems accepting authority over them and submitting to it. This is an on-going challenge and becomes much more subtle as a leader matures. Leaders who have trouble submitting to authority will usually have trouble exercising spiritual authority.

A further word needs to be said about the plateau problem. Plateauing is one of the major reasons leaders don't move on to more effective ministry in the latter period of growth ministry period.

Often as a result of experiencing personal development cluster processing, leaders tend to "get comfortable." They find they can do ministry, at least at some acceptable level of performance, and tend to accept this level. Once they take on this attitude, it is easy to plateau without even realizing it.

When a leader has potential for leadership that is not yet developed or used, God will eventually providentially challenge that leader to take steps to develop and use that capacity for God's purposes and glory. Often a leader is unaware of this capacity until God brings unusual guidance to bear through people or events to channel that leader toward development. The expansion processing of the next chapter will deal with the plateau barrier problem. At this point in the study you should be aware that personal development processing may well lead to this barrier in your life.

A further word on the authority problem. Remember, you reap what you sow. If you do not learn authority lessons early and rebel against authority, then your ministry will produce after its kind. You will have followers who rebel in the same way. Authority clashes will prevail throughout your ministry with followers and leaders. Heed this early processing well. Where mistakes have been made then bring closure now in terms of these lessons.

Major Lessons Focused on By These Two Clusters

Four of the major lessons of leadership are touched upon by the processing of the personal development and people insights clusters.

1. Learning **EFFECTIVE LEADERS, AT ALL LEVELS, MAINTAIN A**
   Posture **LEARNING POSTURE THROUGHOUT LIFE.**

The personal development cluster deals with learning posture in terms of cognitive and experiential learning. The people insights cluster deals with learning posture in terms of affective lessons as well as cognitive insights. These clusters reinforce the importance of leaders continually learning from the pressures of life.

2. Spiritual **EFFECTIVE LEADERS INCREASINGLY VALUE SPIRITUAL**
   Authority **AUTHORITY AS THEIR DOMINANT POWER BASE.**

The people insights cluster gives basic training needed concerning spiritual authority.

4. Ministry **EFFECTIVE LEADERS WHO ARE PRODUCTIVE OVER A**
   Philosophy **LIFETIME HAVE A DYNAMIC MINISTRY PHILOSOPHY WHICH EVOLVES CONTINUALLY FROM THE INTERPLAY OF THREE MAJOR FACTORS: BIBLICAL DYNAMICS, PERSONAL GIFTEDNESS, AND SITUATIONAL DYNAMICS.**

Many of the lessons learned in the authority insights and relational insights processing will become the bedrock of a ministry philosophy and will be heeded throughout life.

7. Pace **EFFECTIVE LEADERS ARE PACE SETTERS.**
   Setters

Both the personal development cluster and the people insights cluster show the importance of the leader experiencing personal lessons that can later be used with followers.

CHAPTER 6. GROWTH MINISTRY PROCESSING--PART II

Overview

Chapter 4 discussed foundational processing which led up to transition into full time Christian leadership. Chapter 5 picked up at that point and discussed early ministry processing and its effects on growth of the emerging leader. This chapter points out the many process items God uses to expand a leader. **Growth ministry** is the term used to embrace the concepts of these two chapters. Ministry indicates that the leader is indeed in full-time Christian work. Growth indicates that most of what is happening in processing is intended to shape the leader, not the followers. In fact, ministry is still rather provisional at this point. But it is ministry which forms the context in which that growth takes place. Expansion will move a leader from the provisional stage of growth ministry to the competent stage.

After some initial ministry and much personal growth in ministerial formation God begins to expand the emerging leader toward yet unrealized potential. Several clusters of process items thrust the leader toward expansion. These clusters include **ordinary expansion items, pressure expansion items, challenge items** (divine initiative items), and **spiritual insights items.** This chapter will describe how God uses the first two of these clusters to move a leader from provisional ministry to competent ministry.

Preview of All the Ministry Expansion Items

At least four clusters are used by God to expand a leader. Each cluster has its essential characteristics and development tasks. Table 6-1 gives a preview of this chapter by noting the essential elements of these clusters.

Each of the items of the clusters accomplishes specific development tasks in terms of immediate context in which the processing happens. Notice also that there is a cumulative effect of each cluster, taken as a whole, toward general development tasks. Table 6-1 identifies at least some of the prominent development tasks resulting from the clusters.

A general familiarization with this table will aid you as you read each individual process item defined in this chapter and the next.

Some preliminary definitions are necessary before the spiritual authority discovery process item can be given. These include **authority, spiritual authority,** and **power base** definitions as well as characteristics of spiritual authority.

TABLE 6-1
EXPANSION CLUSTERS

Cluster	Processing	Characteristic	Purposes
ordinary	Word, Literary, Mentor, Contextual, Paradigm Shift, Spiritual Authority Discovery, Ministry Structure Insights, Ministry Assignment.	Spurred on by the context of the routine; hence, may be overlooked in terms of strategic impact.	1. Strengthen learning posture. 2. Develop ministry philosophy. 3. Give routine guidance. 4. Affect competency step-by-step.
pressure	Ministry Conflict, Leadership Backlash, Crises.	Learning from negative experiences.	1. Soften leader's receptivity to lessons. 2. Strengthen learning posture. 3. Test spiritual authority. 4. Develop ministerial Formation.
challenge	Destiny Revelation, Faith Challenge, Prayer Challenge, Ministry Challenge, Influence Challenge.	Difficult to discern as from God at first; all imply risk and failure. Touch of divine-- life giving.	1. Inspire vision. 2. Develop strategic formation. 3. Strengthen destiny lesson. 4. Strengthen spiritual authority lesson. 5. Strengthen pace setting lesson. 6. Affect competency in quantum leaps.
spiritual insights	Spiritual Warfare, 4 Power Items	Sensed and felt rather than understood logically. Making the unseen as real as seen.	1. Develop spiritual authority. 2. Develop ministerial formation. 3. Expand power base. 4. Develop discernment.

ORDINARY EXPANSION CLUSTER

introduction   Much of the development of a leader takes place via
                   faithful response to the routine of ministry. It
                   is in the context of faithful response to on-going
                   ministry that God does the most, cumulatively, to
                   develop a leader.

description   The ordinary expansion cluster refers to the set of
                   eight process items which occur throughout growth
                   ministry processing in the context of on-going
                   daily life and which teach specific lessons for
                   the immediate but which also focus on development
                   tasks affecting learning posture, ministry
                   philosophy, routine guidance, and overall
                   competency--all of which deal with long term
                   development.

essential   Each item has tactical significance. That is, it
character-   applies to the immediate context of ministry and
istic   can be discerned in that manner. Hence, the long
                   term or strategic impact which is cumulative,
                   builds and is not easily sensed.

Venn Diagram   The set of items making up the cluster include:
                   **Word, Literary, Mentor, Contextual, Paradigm Shift,
                   Spiritual Authority Discovery, Ministry Structure
                   Insights, Ministry Assignment.** Some of these share
                   common issues. Some are unique.

ORDINARY EXPANSION CLUSTER

WORD PROCESS ITEM Symbol: P(WI)

introduction   An essential characteristic of leadership is the
ability to receive truth from God. It is critical
in building a spiritual authority power base for a
Godly leader. It is also an integral part of a
leader's methodology for getting on-going daily
guidance for the ministry. Leaders greatly used of
God have evidenced a love for truth. They study the
written word to feed their own souls as well as to
help those to whom they minister. They are quick
to discern God's truth in everyday life. They
learn to hear the voice of God through the ministry
of other people.   So then, one would expect God to
develop a leader in his/her ability to appreciate
truth, to cultivate habits of intake of truth, and
to obey truth. The process item used to describe
this development is called the word process item.

definition   A word process item is an instance in which a
leader receives a word from God which affects
significantly a leader's guidance, committal,
decision making, personal value system, spiritual
formation, spiritual authority, or ministry
philosophy.

example   Daniel unfolds his high point in God's use of the
word in his life in Daniel 9 (This occurs in a late
leadership development stage). This example is full
of lessons of how God processes a leader with the
word.

example   Phillip's ministry to the Ethiopian eunuch in Acts
8 illustrates a word processing item which forever
changed a life. It occurred early in the eunuch's
life-history.

timing   Word items will occur throughout a lifetime of
processing. Early on, they are more likely to be
checks as they test and build character. Later
word items will become habitual and sometimes
almost unnoticeable as the leader responds almost
automatically to God's direction in the word items.

uses   Word process items which occur in the foundational
phase are most likely going to be used to establish
values. Word process items in the transitional
phase mainly will be word checks to test and
form character. In the provisional growth ministry
sub-phase word items will be used to build
spiritual authority, for spiritual formation, to
reveal spiritual dynamics, as part of the normal
exercise of word gifts, to affect decision making
and ministry philosophy. Word items are used
throughout all phases for guidance.

FEEDBACK ON WORD PROCESS ITEM

1. See if you can identify a Word Process Item from your own
experience for each of the various aspects mentioned in the word
processing definition. Check any which apply to the items you
can remember:

___ a. significantly affected your guidance,
___ b. significantly affected your committal to the Lord,
___ c. significantly affected your perspective on leadership,
___ d. significantly affected your decision making,
___ e. significantly affected your personal value system,
___ f. significantly affected your spiritual formation,
___ g. significantly affected your spiritual authority,
___ h. significantly affected your ministry philosophy.
___ i. significantly affected you in a specific way--you name it:

2. For any one you checked above describe the incident, the
source of the item, the function affected, and the results.

3. Interview a Christian leader concerning the Word Process Item
in general. Seek to identify several illustrations which were
important in his/her leadership development. Identify categories
affected such as guidance, committal to leadership, decision
making, personal value system, spiritual formation, spiritual
authority, ministry philosophy, or any other--you name it. Note
one of these process items and describe the incident, the source
of the word process item, the function affected, and the results.

4. Repeat exercise 3 for a biblical example of a word item.

ANSWERS----------
    1. I have process items for all of these.
    2. The source was Psalm 1 particularly verses 1,2. I was
studying this Psalm in my quiet time (and memorizing it during
the week). Later at work I was advised that I ought to change my
field so as to better myself in my career. The advise given
seemed logical enough on the service. However, the one giving
the advice was a scoffer, one who had turned his back on God and
now made fun of those who were serious about Christianity. As I
was walking down the hall Psalm 1 verse 1 reverberated in my
mind. "Blessed is the man who walketh not in the counsel of the
ungodly." I knew God was speaking to me. I did not put in for
that career change. Had I done so I do not believe I would be
where I am today and doing what I am doing.
    3. I'll leave this one for group interaction.
    4. The prophets in general are filled with word process
items. One illustration, Jeremiah 32, is especially insightful.
Incident: In a time when it was clear that Judah would fall, God
spoke to Jeremiah and told him to buy some property. Under the
circumstances it seemed foolish to buy the field. This was
confirmed externally, by the double confirmation process item.
Source: conviction or inner voice. Function: personal guidance,
and a symbol of God's future activity (a faith challenge).
Result: Jeremiah obeyed. God used this later to encourage
Daniel.

LITERARY PROCESS ITEMS   Symbol: P(LI)

introduction	I first noted the concept of a literary process item while reading Jim Elliot's biography. He was significantly helped by reading biographies. Amy Carmichael, a missionary to India for 55 years, influenced him deeply. I began to read her works. Her biography revealed the same phenomenon. She quoted many who had helped her. I began to regularly look for this kind of "vicarious learning" in biographies. I soon saw how many great leaders were widely read and greatly helped by the experiences of others.
definition	The <u>literary</u> <u>process</u> <u>item</u> refers to the means whereby God is able to teach leaders lessons for their own lives through the writings of others.
example	Watchman Nee had a hunger both for reading the Bible and other literary sources. He was greatly influenced by the literary process item.
example	Peter Kuzmic is another high level leader who has an amazing appetite for reading and learning.
essence of the item	The thrust of the literary process item is not just an appetite to read. Rather, it is the ability to have God teach lessons through the reading which can be applied to life and ministry.
varied uses	The literary process item is suited to supplement almost any of the developmental tasks of any of the expansion clusters.
primary causal source-- biography	The wise leader who recognizes the importance of the literary process item will cultivate, as early as possible, reading skills which will allow rapid learning of lessons that God has for them which otherwise might take years through experiential processing. Biographies ought to be a regular part of one's literary diet as they are a rich source of lessons already learned and are able to be integrated into one's life--a natural application of the leadership mandate of Hebrews 13:7,8.
timing	This item can occur throughout the entire growth ministry processing. But it is rare for a younger emerging leader, who is concentrating so heavily on doing in the provisional sub-phase of growth ministry to do necessary reflecting on a biography milking it for life changing insights. And then, too, the younger emergent leader often does not have enough ministry experience to properly discern the leadership lessons being read. As experience builds, biographies will take on added importance.

FEEDBACK ON LITERARY PROCESS ITEMS

1. Suggest some names of Bible characters who most likely profited from the literary process item.

2. Name a significant book, tract, or other written material that God has used greatly in your own life. Describe how it was used?

3. If one wanted to profit from this **literary process item** in a more deliberate fashion what could be done? What would be some first steps to take to do so?

ANSWERS----------

1. Moses, David, Daniel, Jesus, Paul.
2. **The Green Letters** by Miles Standford. I learned the concept of time and processing in developing Christ-likeness.
3. a. Read many Christian biographies. b. Find out what books have changed the lives of others. c. Learn to read as part of your devotional life.

MENTORING PROCESS ITEM   Symbol: P(M)
MENTOR   synonym: sponsor

introduction   God has given some people the capacity and the
                heart to see leadership potential and to take
                private and personal action to help the potential
                leader develop. That action usually becomes a form
                of significant guidance for the potential leader.

definition   Mentoring refers to the process where a person with
                a serving, giving, encouraging attitude (the
                mentor) sees leadership potential in a still-to-be
                developed person (the protege) and is able to
                promote or otherwise significantly influence the
                protege along to the realization of potential.

definition   A mentoring process item refers to the process and
                results of a mentor helping a potential leader.

Bible   Barnabas mentored Saul. Barnabas also mentored John
example   Mark, a New Testament author.

historic   Margaret Barber mentored Watchman Nee. Imitation
example   modeling was a primary means of mentoring for her.

historic   Charles Trumbull mentored Robert C. McQuilkin, the
example   founder of Columbia Bible College.

present   John Stott has found ways to send several leaders
day   from Burma to Fuller for further formal training.
example   This undoubtedly has broadened them.

mentor   ● can readily see potential in a person,
charact-   ● can tolerate mistakes, brashness, abrasiveness,
istics   etc., in order to see potential develop,
                ● is often a very flexible person,
                ● is patient, recognizing that it takes time and
                  experience for a person to develop,
                ● has vision and ability to see down the road and
                  suggest next steps that a protege needs,
                ● usually has a gift-mix including one or more of
                  the encouragement spiritual gifts: mercy, giving,
                  exhortation, faith, word of wisdom.

ways   ● give encouraging and timely advice,
mentors   ● risk a reputation to back the protege,
help   ● bridge between proteges and needed resources,
proteges   ● model--using Goodwin's Expectation Principle,
                ● give tracts, letters, books or other literary
                  information which opens up perspectives,
                ● give financially, to further the protege,
                ● co-minister to increase the proteges confidence,
                  credibility, status, and prestige,
                ● have freedom to allow and even promote the
                  protege beyond the mentor's own leadership level

FEEDBACK EXERCISE ON MENTORING PROCESS ITEM

1. Barnabas was a mentor for Paul and John Mark. Of the ways mentioned that mentors function, which of these were used for Paul and which were used for John Mark? Mark those used with Paul with a P and those used with John Mark with a JM.

_____ a. giving timely <u>advice</u> which encourages the protege,
_____ b. <u>risking</u> his/her reputation in backing the protege,
_____ c. <u>bridging</u> between the protege and needed resources,
_____ d. <u>modeling</u> and using Goodwin's Expectation Principle[1],
_____ e. <u>giving</u> tracts, letters, books, or other literary
         information which opens perspectives for the protege,
_____ f. <u>giving</u> financially, sometimes sacrificially to further the
         protege's ministry,
_____ g. allowing for <u>co-ministry</u> which will increase the protege's
         credibility, status, and prestige,
_____ h. having <u>freedom</u> to allow and even promote the protege
         beyond the mentor's own level of leadership.

2. A mentor is a "linker." That is, a mentor can build bridges between people. From a study of the following passages, suggest what Barnabas was linking.
      a. Acts 9:27   b. Acts 11:25   c. Acts 11:30

3. Identify a "mentor" in your own experience. Describe how the mentor functioned.

ANSWERS----------
    1. For Paul, the ones I know for certain are:
b. (Acts 9:27ff), c. (Acts 9:27ff and 11:25), g. (Acts 11:26), and h. (Acts 13:13ff). I also think a., d, and f. occurred but do not have as much proof for these.   For John Mark, the ones I am more certain about are: b., c., and g. Ones which I think probably occurred for John Mark are: a., d., and f.   **2. a.** Barnabas linked Paul into the Christian power base.
        b. Barnabas linked Paul into a cross-cultural ministry which would be the springboard to other cross-cultural ministry work.
        c. Barnabas (noted for his giving heart) spurred on the church at Antioch to heed the prophet's words and give to the church at Jerusalem. This would further bridge the almost totally Gentile church at Antioch with the almost totally Jewish church at Jerusalem. This linking of churches at regional level is an apostolic function.
    3. Chuck Kraft was a mentor for me. He bridged me from my missionary post with Worldteam to my present position with the School of World Mission.
----
[1]Goodwin's Expectancy Principle (adapted) states that, "A POTENTIAL LEADER TENDS TO RISE TO THE LEVEL OF GENUINE EXPECTANCY OF A LEADER HE/SHE RESPECTS." (Goodwin 1981:41) I first saw this in Goodwin and named it after him for labelling purposes. I have since seen this same idea in several leadership research articles which pre-dated Goodwin's work so perhaps I shouldn't have really named it after him.

CONTEXTUAL PROCESS ITEMS   Symbol: P(CXT)

introduction   Contextual items, that is the large factors
                relating to district, regional, national, and
                international influences, providentially play an
                important part in any leader's development. By and
                large these are factors over which a leader has
                little or no control. Yet he/she can recognize
                them, see the hand of God in them, and pro-act
                concerning them rather than reacting to them so as
                to develop according to God's intent in them.

definition   Contextual items refer to those providential
                factors arising in local, regional, national, and
                international situations during a leader's life-
                history which affect spiritual, ministerial, and
                strategic formations, and frequently give God's
                strategic guidance for the leader.

kinds   cultural heritage, educational opportunities,
                political structures, geographical factors, war,
                famines, floods, other natural disasters,
                linguistic situation, economic situation, various
                kinds of movements (religious, political, economic)

example   World War II brought numerous pressures to bear on
                Watchman Nee who was in China at the time.
                Economic pressures and geographical shifts are two
                examples of contextual items which resulted from
                the consequences of the Japanese invasion in China.

example   The communist movement in China brought persecution
                upon Christian leaders. Nee intensified training
                because of the impending doom he saw coming. He
                chose to go to prison rather than flee the country.

example   Many service men who served in World War II saw the
                needs of people without the Gospel in other
                countries. After the war they came home and started
                mission societies. Winter describes this time in
                church history as the third burst of protestant
                mission orders. Hugh Davidson, an Australian, was
                one who was caught up in the above pattern. His
                time in Papua New Guinea during World War II was
                followed by pioneer mission work there.

example   Children in the United States who came to
                adolescent years in the wild decade of the 1960s
                grew up with tremendous cultural pressure to throw
                off authority and to live freely. This affected
                the inner-life growth phase of many and delayed for
                them the entry function into ministry.

example   See Naisbitt's (1982) 10 mega-trends which affect
                regional, national, and international scenes.

FEEDBACK ON CONTEXTUAL PROCESS ITEMS

1. Previously we defined in the foundational phase the process item called entry context. What is the difference between the entry context process item and this process item, contextual process items?

2. What have been the major contextual factors that have affected your life over the past 25 years? List them along a time-line. Time--->

|---|

Factor:

3. What is the most important recent contextual process item you have experienced. Analyze it for any indications from God for your development as a leader.

ANSWERS----------
    1.   These process items are essentially the same. The entry context process item is a special case of the contextual process item applied to the foundational phase and particularly the situation into which a leader is born.
    2.   I was born just after the depression years. My folks were greatly affected by those years so that my childhood was filled with values which came out of my parents experiences. times. Those values have stayed with me and affected my thinking even today. I grew up in a country that had free education through high school years. My folks who did not finish high school wanted me to go to college. I was the first person on either side of the family for as far back as I know who finished college. Another major contextual factor came out of the years of the sixties and seventies. Because of the social movements and failure of government leadership, I have been deeply impressed me with the need for integrity in leadership. This has influenced my thinking as I studied leadership and spiritual authority.
    3. The adult education movement has had a deep impact on today's generations of which I am a part. I am part of a School of World Mission which has arisen primarily to teach mid-career missionaries. This is part of the general trend toward adult education which has been building for 50 years in this country. Today people come from all over the world to continue their education. My present ministry could not have been possible 30 years ago.

PARADIGM SHIFT PROCESS ITEM   Symbol: P(PS)

introduction   Frequently a leader has moments in which God brings an insightful idea or model which radically changes how the leader perceives issues. This ideation frequently is prompted by a divine contact or a literary item.   Experiential awareness may precede cognitive awareness. After this processing the leader never again views some aspect of leadership as he or she did previous to the ideation change. Adult conversion is frequently a special case of this kind of processing. Second works of grace or empowerment in terms of giftedness may have this processing at its root and usually fit this category.

definition   A <u>paradigm</u> shift item refers to God's use of an incident or series of incidents to impress upon the leader a major new perspective for use in ministry.

example   A radical adult conversion (Gripentrog 1987 or Finzel 1987) frequently falls into this category.

example   Powerful sanctification experiences (Chan 1987) or radical power items dealing with healing or spiritual warfare (Gripentrog 1987, Carlson 1985) frequently require major ideation changes for those of western worldviews.

example   The introduction of various models in interrupted in-service training whether formal or non-formal (church growth paradigm, anthropological insights, a major definition such as the one given in this manual for leader with its influence focus) often is the trigger incident for a paradigm shift.

often combined   Paradigm shifts frequently occur in combination with other process items. For example, the conversion or leadership committal process items frequently correspond with a paradigm shift, particularly if occurring in adult years.

causal source   Divine contacts (ones who themselves have experienced some paradigm shift), literary items, destiny items, spiritual insights cluster of items and isolation are the process items most associated with paradigm shifts.

timing   Older leaders tend to experience fewer shifts than younger leaders.

properties   ● a "release effect" (as having been bound, and then freed),
● a joyous discovery mode pervades activity,
● enhanced learning posture.

FEEDBACK ON PARADIGM SHIFT PROCESS ITEM

1. What is the New Testament classical example of a paradigm shift? (See Acts 9, 22, 26)

2. What was the causal source processing in the above example?
___a. divine contact   ___b. literary item   ___c. destiny item
___d. spiritual insights cluster item, if this, then which one:
___e. isolation

3. Can you think of any Old Testament process incident which illustrates a paradigm shift?

4. What is the causal source of processing for the Old Testament incident you gave in exercise 3.
___a. divine contact   ___b. literary item   ___c. destiny item
___d. spiritual insights cluster item, if this, then which one:
___e. isolation

5. What paradigm shifts have you experienced personally or seen in some leader?

ANSWERS----------
    1. Paul's adult conversion experience.
    2. c. Destiny Item (also a leadership committal as seen in further explanatory remarks in Acts 22 and 26.
    3. Jacob's wrestling experience with the Angel of the Lord the night before he was to meet Esau. Notice the name change—Jacob became Israel. Sanford (1974) so judges this as a paradigm shift in psychological individuation for Jacob. He became a different person in his relationship with God thereafter.
    Joshua's experience with the Captain of the Lord's Army was a paradigm shift from which Joshua emerged as a confident, faith expectant leader, with an unusual leadership strategy for taking Jericho. Jericho needed to be a model victory that would demolish the confidence of the enemies in the land. The faith strategy for taking Jericho was unlike any normal strategy for taking a fortified city.
    Elisha's servant in II Kings 6:15-17 went through a paradigm shift in viewing the reality of the unseen world.
    4. The causal source for Jacob was a destiny item. The causal source for Joshua was a destiny revelation item. The causal processing for Elisha's servant was from one of the spiritual insights cluster--spiritual warfare.
    5. Disputed practices issues--teaching freed me to view people with different practices differently than before; the shift from naive realism to critical realism has opened for me the use of my natural analytical abilities to conceptualize models for viewing reality; Two of my colleagues have gone through fairly radical shifts with regards to power items (particularly gifted power).

AUTHORITY/ SPIRITUAL AUTHORITY / POWER BASE

introduction	Leaders have a right to influence. That right can come in various legitimate ways. One important way is through spiritual authority.
definition	Power base refers to the source of credibility, power differential, or resources which enables a leader (power holder) to have authority to exercise influence on followers (power subjects).
definition	Authority refers to the right to exercise leadership influence by a leader over followers with respect to some field of influence.
definition	Spiritual authority is that characteristic of a God-anointed leader developed upon an experiential power base which enables a leader to influence followers through persuasion, force of modeling and moral expertise toward God's purposes.
examples power forms	Power is manifested in power forms (instruments or influence means) which bring about compliance such as force, manipulation, authority, and persuasion. Authority is further sub-divided into coercive, induced, legitimate, competent, and personal. Spiritual authority is a combination of persuasion and legitimate, competent, and personal authority.
examples power bases	Power forms depend upon power bases. Bases come from power resources--those individual and collective assets such as organization, money, reputation, personal appeal, manipulative skills, interpersonal skills, kinds of knowledge, information, indwelling Holy Spirit, giftedness.
central authority concept	The central concept of authority is the right to exercise influence. That right is recognized both by leader and follower. It is based upon common assumptions about the "field of influence." For a spiritual leader the "field of influence" has to do with God's purposes and His directions for accomplishing specific aims that He reveals. Morality, corporate guidance, and clarification of truth, are three aspects within the "field of influence" which define the leader's range of use of spiritual authority.
spiritual authority power base	Spiritual authority comes from a life and a ministry which demonstrates the presence of God. Credibility is demonstrated in a life when a leader is what he/she teaches. Credibility comes from a ministry which manifests results which are from God. A leader with spiritual authority knows God and His ways and demonstrates this in life.

POWER FORMS synonym: influence means, power instruments

introduction   The following definitions are prerequisite for
                understanding spiritual authority processing.

definition   Power forms refer to four general terms of
                influence means: force, manipulation, authority,
                and persuasion.

definition   A force power form refers to the use of physical
                and psychic influence means to gain compliance.

definition   A manipulative power form refers to any influence
                means whereby a leader gains compliance of a
                follower where the follower does not have
                awareness of the leader's intents and therefore
                does not necessarily have freedom to exert moral
                responsibility in the situation.

definition   A persuasive power form refers to any influence
                means such as arguments, appeals or exhortations
                whereby the leader gains compliance of the follower
                yet protects the freedom of the follower to
                exercise moral responsibility.

definition   An authority power form refers to influence
                means such as: coercive authority, induced
                authority, legitimate authority, competent
                authority, personal authority and spiritual
                authority.

definition   Coercive authority is the form of power in which a
                a leader obtains compliance by using influence
                means such as threat of force or of punishment.

definition   Induced authority is the form of power in
                which a leader obtains compliance by using
                influence means of promise of reward or some gain
                for the follower.

definition   Legitimate authority is the form of power in which
                a leader obtains compliance by using influence
                pressure consonant with common expectations of the
                role or positions held by the follower and leader.

definition   Competent authority is the form of power in which a
                leader obtains or can expect (but not demand)
                compliance by virtue of acknowledged expertise in
                some field of endeavor. The authority is limited to
                that field of endeavor.

definition   Personal authority is the form of power in which a
                a leader obtains or expects compliance (but can not
                demand it) by virtue of the follower's recognition
                of the leader's personal characteristics.

6 CHARACTERISTICS AND LIMITS OF SPIRITUAL AUTHORITY

introduction   The following combine insights from Nee (n.d.)
Harris (1976) and De George (in Harris 1976).

1. Ultimate Source
Spiritual authority has its ultimate source in Christ.   It
is representative religious authority. It is His authority and
presence in us which legitimates our authority. Accountability to
this final authority is essential.

2. Power Base
Spiritual authority rests upon an experiential power base.
A leader's personal experiences with God and the accumulated
wisdom and development that comes through them lie at the heart
of the reason why followers allow influence in their lives.   It
is a resource which is at once on-going and yet related to the
past. Its genuineness as to the reality of experience with God is
confirmed in the believer by the presence and ministry of the
Holy Spirit who authenticates that experiential power base.

3. Power Forms
Spiritual authority influences by virtue of persuasion.
Word gifts are dominant in this persuasion. Influence is by
virtue of legitimate authority. Positional leadership (usually
Type C, D, and E) carries with it recognition of qualities of
leadership which are at least initially recognized by followers.
Such authority must be buttressed by other authority forms such
as competent authority, and personal authority.

4. Ultimate Good
The aim of influence using spiritual authority is the
ultimate good of the followers.   This follows the basic Pauline
leadership principle seen in II Corinthians 10:8.   Momentary
judgment of leadership acts and influence means depends on this
criterion.

5. Evaluation
Spiritual authority is best judged longitudinally over time
in terms of development of maturity in believers. Use of coercive
and manipulative forms of authority will usually reproduce like
elements in followers.   Spiritual authority will produce mature
followers who will make responsible moral choices because they
have learned to do so.

6. Non-Defensive
A leader using spiritual authority recognizes submission to
God who is the ultimate authority. Authority is representative.
God is therefore the responsible agent for defending spiritual
authority. A person moving in spiritual authority does not have
to insist on obedience. Obedience is the moral responsibility of
the follower. Disobedience, that is, rebellion to spiritual
authority, means that a follower is not subject to God Himself.
He/she will answer to God for that. The leader can rest upon
God's vindication if it is necessary.

FEEDBACK ON AUTHORITY/POWER DEFINITIONS

1. Consider again the definition of spiritual authority.

> Spiritual authority is that characteristic of a God-
> anointed leader developed upon an experiential power
> base which enables a leader to influence followers
> through persuasion, force of modeling and moral
> expertise toward God's purposes.

In your experience you most likely have observed leaders who in
your opinion have utilized spiritual authority. Note the name of
one such leader. What influence means stood out in this leader's
life (persuasion, force of modeling, moral expertise)?   Be
prepared to share incidents which illustrate the influence means.

name: Explanatory Comments:

2. For the leader noted in exercise 1 what aspects of his/her
experiential power base are you aware of?   Note any which you
feel underlie his/her spiritual authority.

3. For the leader noted in exercise 1 and 2 check below power
forms you have observed used by that leader to influence
followers.   Check any which apply.

____ a. force   ____ e. authority--legitimate
____ b. manipulation   ____ f. authority--personal.
____ c. authority--coercive   ____ g. persuasion.
____ d. authority--induced

4. Power forms depend upon power bases. Bases come from power
resources. What power resources have you observed in the leader
described above? Check any which fit and be prepared to explain.

____ a. organization   ____ g. special kinds of
____ b. money   knowledge
____ c. reputation   ____ h. information
____ d. personal appeal   ____ i. powerful presence of
____ e. manipulative skills   Holy Spirit
____ f. interpersonal   ____ j. giftedness
       skills

5. Suppose a leader was considering inviting you to be a part of
his/her ministry and asked you the following question.   What
clear evidence do you have that you have spiritual authority?
What would you say?

ANSWERS----------

I am not going to answer these due to the personal nature of
the answers but will give them in my classes when we do these
exercises.

SPIRITUAL AUTHORITY DISCOVERY PROCESS ITEM Symbol: P(SAD)

introduction   The realization of spiritual authority as a power
                 form (influence means) gradually increases over a
                 lifetime. The rate of realization rapidly
                 increases as one moves toward unique ministry.

definition   The spiritual authority discovery item refers to
                 any significant discovery--insight or experience--
                 which advances a leader along the spiritual
                 authority development pattern (especially in stages
                 6,7 and 8).

pattern   The following, M.7 Spiritual Authority Discovery
affected   Pattern, is covered also in chapter 11 where
                 patterns are discussed. The emphasis here is on
                 the stimuli which cause movement from stage to
                 stage. The emphasis in chapter 11 is on
                 evaluation of development of the leader. Read
                 the arrow as implying, usually leads to.

order   1) discovery of personal authority as a power form
property   ---> 2) discovery of other forms (force,
8 stages   manipulation, persuasion) ---> 3) discovery of
                 other authority forms (legitimate, competent) --->
                 4) discarding of force/manipulation as forms; use
                 of persuasion as complementary throughout following
                 stages ---> 5) effectiveness in use of legitimate
                 authority, competent authority, and personal
                 authority with some spiritual authority ---> 6)
                 lessening of legitimate authority, competent
                 authority becoming dominant ----> 7) combination of
                 competent authority, personal authority and
                 spiritual authority as equally dominant ---> 8)
                 spiritual authority dominant, personal authority,
                 competent authority, legitimate authority, and
                 persuasion used as complementary.

focus   to move a leader toward spiritual authority

timing   The leader moves through stages 1, 2, 3, and 4 in
                 the provisional sub-phase of Growth Ministry
                 processing while Stages 5, 6, and 7 usually occur in
                 the competent sub-phase. Stage 8 is reached in
                 Unique Ministry processing.

causal   The pressure cluster items serve as triggers in the
processing   the early stages. The challenge cluster items,
                 followed closely by the spiritual insights cluster,
                 triggers primarily in the latter stages. Some
                 ordinary cluster items stimulate discovery
                 throughout all phases.

philosophy   Spiritual authority is a major power base of
                 servant leadership.

FEEDBACK ON SPIRITUAL AUTHORITY DISCOVERY PROCESS ITEM

1. Check any of the stages for which you have process incidents
which reflect the processing that moved you to that stage or from
it. You may wish to read commentary page 203 which discusses
spiritual authority and some of the definitions of power forms
listed in these stages (page 193).   This exercise should probably be
revisited after you have worked through chapter 11 on patterns and
chapter 13 dealing with evaluation measures.

___(1) discovery of personal authority as a power form property
___(2) discovery of other forms (force, manipulation, persuasion)
___(3) discovery of other authority forms (legitimate, competent)
___(4) discarding of force/manipulation as forms; use of
       persuasion as complementary throughout following stages
___(5) effectiveness in use of legitimate authority, competent
       authority, and personal authority with some spiritual
       authority
___(6) lessening of legitimate authority, competent authority
       becoming dominant
___(7) combination of competent authority, personal authority
       and spiritual authority as equally dominant
___(8) spiritual authority dominant, personal authority,
       competent authority, legitimate authority, and persuasion
       used as complementary.

2. Discuss the most important discovery about spiritual authority
that you have learned to the present time. What processing was
instrumental in stimulating that discovery. With which stage is
it most closely related? Sometimes discoveries don't directly
relate to the power-mix (combination of the authority bases) that
the leader is actually using at the time of the discovery.

ANSWERS----------

   1. I am presently in stages 5 and 6.
   2. The most important lesson I have learned about spiritual
authority is that Spiritual authority comes from God. He will
vindicate spiritual authority. I previously shared that I had
learned that a leader does does not have to defend spiritual
authority. (See page 173)   A second is close. The 2nd most
important lesson I've learned is that if followers do not
recognize spiritual authority, I do not have to force them via
other means. Failure to recognize spiritual authority and act
accordingly is a follower problem not a leader problem. God will
judge them. I was in stage 4 when I learned the first lesson. I
was in stage 5 when I learned the second lesson.

MINISTRY STRUCTURE INSIGHTS PROCESS ITEM Symbol: P(MSI)

introduction   Successful leadership usually involves a philosophy
               of how the ministry is to be organized and vision
               for what it is to accomplish. The organization of
               ministry will involve structures through which it
               will be done. Knowledge about group dynamics,
               organizational dynamics, and administration of
               these various structures, contributes to a leader's
               ability to oversee a ministry. A leader will
               discover through actual experiences ministry
               insights about the nature of these structures,
               communication between them, the administration of
               them, and practical means of motivating people to
               join and participate in them. This item focuses on
               how the leader gets these God-given insights and on
               the expansion of leadership capacity which results.
               Structural insights may be culturally specific.

definition   The ministry structure insight process item refers
               to those discoveries about the various
               organizational units through which ministry is
               channelled and the effects of those discoveries on
               leadership capacity.

example   Pastor Yonggi Cho's use of cell groups.

example   My first discovery was that of the one-on-one
               discipleship structure advocated in Navigator
               ministries. I have been able to use that basic
               structure adapted to my gift-mix over the years.

example   My second discovery came when I saw God's hand in
               home Bible studies through Pastor L. Thompson's
               ministry. That structure provided the stimulus for
               evangelistic and maturity growth in that church.

example   Some various kinds of generic structures include:
               small groups, committees, personal networks,
               seminars, workshops, conferences, musical groups or
               teams, ministry teams, mentoring relationships,
               executive leadership groups, community homes, and
               many others. Each of these basic kinds of
               structures will take on various shapes in specific
               ministries. It is this discovery of a particular
               shape, and God's hand of blessing in it, that is at
               the heart of this process item.

example   A valuable insight for me was the basic cognitive
               discovery of the sodality (parachurch) structure as
               a valid redemptive structure. Insight to concepts
               underlying sodality structures has allowed me to
               apply the same concepts very broadly within
               modality structures (churchly structures) as well
               as in new sodality formations.

FEEDBACK ON MINISTRY STRUCTURE INSIGHTS PROCESS ITEM

1. Read again the four facets of the leader definition.
   A __leader__, is a person
   ___ (1) with God-given capacity AND
   ___ (2) with a God-given responsibility
   WHO IS INFLUENCING
   ___ (3) a specific group of God's people
   ___ (4) toward God's purposes for the group.

Remember, processing will affect one or more of these aspects of a leader. Which of these major concepts of the leader definition do you think are affected by by the **ministry structure insights** process item? Check any which you feel are affected and give a brief answer as to why you feel it is affected.

2. Illustrate the following.
   a. Give here an example from your own ministry processing in which God has allowed or forced you to see some **ministry structure** insight.

   b. How did this affect your ministry philosophy?

   c. What new skills did this entail or suggest for you if you were to apply the insight to your own ministry?

   d. What are the long term ongoing influences from this **ministry structure insight** process item? That is, does your present leadership still profit from that process item? If so, how. If not, why not?

ANSWERS----------

1. (1) with God-given capacity. The first one is probably most affected since ministry structure insights often force the learning of new skills and strategies. New skills and strategies directly affect influence capacity. However, each of them are usually also affected. New structures also help clarify accountability and responsibility for influence. They specify more clearly the groups that are to be influenced. They will also force thinking through the purposes of God for them.

2. a. My initial training in discipleship was along the lines of the Navigator one-on-one discipling. The stress on this insight is to recognize that there are some around you who are hungry for, need, and can use more training than is ordinarily provided. They must be given individual attention even though your main thrust of ministry is in some other direction. b. Since then, in every ministry I have been engaged I have always been on the lookout for individuals to whom I could devote special attention along discipling lines. c. I was forced to develop Bible studies, practical helps for prayer and devotional life, questionnaires and the like for discovering gifts, etc. d. Today that structural insight of constant individual relationships has been adapted to fit mentoring and imitation modelling training which I constantly use.

MINISTRY ASSIGNMENT PROCESS ITEM   Symbol: P(MASG)

introduction   A leader's ministry history is made up of various
               ministry assignments. These assignments involve
               doing ministry, with one person, a group, or groups
               for a period of time to accomplish specific
               ministry goals. During a given assignment the
               leader learns new skills, new ideas of what
               ministry is, and helps those being ministered to.
               Various process items will occur during these
               ministry assignments which will work toward all
               three formations. Post reflection on a ministry
               assignment can prove valuable toward solidifying
               progress in the three formative areas and seeing
               future guidance concerning new assignments.

definition   <u>Ministry</u> <u>assignment</u> describes a ministry experience
               which is more permanent than a ministry task yet
               has the same basic pattern of entry, ministry,
               closure, and transition out of the ministry
               situation and through which God gives new insights
               to the leader so as to expand influence capacity
               and responsibility toward future leadership.

example   A 2 year position as a Sunday School teacher

example   Temporary position of Field Director
               (administrative work) in a mission while the
               present administrator is on furlough.

example   A three year assignment as a mission short termer

example   Taking the position of youth pastor in a church
               following graduation from some formal training.

focus   Reflection on ministry assignments can reveal
               patterns that will be helpful for future selection
               of assignments. Early ministry challenges and
               assignments or new kinds of ministry challenges and
               assignments are particularly instructive.

timing   A **ministry assignment** is a cumulative process
               taking place over a relatively short period of time
               (1-5 years) in which numerous other process items
               combine to teach lessons throughout the assignment.

essence   The essence of the **ministry assignment** process item
               lies in the post reflective discovery of what the
               assignment taught by way of development of the
               leader in the three formative areas: spiritual,
               ministerial, and strategic formations. Discoveries
               may be general or quite specific.

causal   Usually prompted externally in terms of ministry
               challenges given by other leaders.

FEEDBACK ON MINISTRY ASSIGNMENT

1. Briefly describe your most recent ministry assignment. Were there new ministry skills that were needed for it? Did you acquire these? If so, how. If not, in retrospect what would you do to acquire those skills? (If needed skills were many and varied choose just one for this exercise.)

2. What was the causal sources of this assignment? That is, what prompted you to take it. Was it external or internal? Was there any special processing?

3. What were the special leadership development discoveries seen in your post reflection evaluation of this process item?

ANSWERS----------

　　1. I taught an adult singles class in my local church for four years. I have been out of that assignment a year now. My single adult class in my local church has forced me to add more training skills (particularly imitation modelling and informal apprenticeships) to deal with training of teachers for the class.
　　2. I had an external challenge from several members of the class. One in particular specifically prayed me into the role as my initial response was not to accept the assignment. The one praying for me used strong expectation motivation with me. I had some negative preparation in connection with a very recent ministry assignment which released me to consider this opportunity.
　　3. My major development was in the area of spiritual formation. God gave me new perspectives on who singles were and a new acceptance of them. I became less judgmental of singles in general and particularly regarding those who had come out of bad marriage situations. A more empathetic spirit toward singles has made me more empathetic in general.

COMMENTARY ON ORDINARY EXPANSION CLUSTER

faithfulness
in the
ordinary,
the key
to long-
term
development

It is the ordinary processing (that which comes through the context of daily life) that God uses, more than any other, over a lifetime to develop a leader. God seems to bring along people, give a word, link a leader to some needed information, bring a radical new perspective for viewing things, and a host of other daily incidentals which change a leader little by little. Looking at each change individually one might not perceive much, but standing back and looking at the whole one can sense that it is through this ordinary processing that God is forming leaders. Process items such as pressure items, challenge items, spiritual insights items, guidance items, and life maturing items are more likely high or low points that occur rather infrequently as compared to ordinary items. The **ordinary items** reinforce the M.1 Foundational Ministry Pattern which highlights the little–big faithfulness principle of Luke 16:10. It is this steadfastness that will insure development over the long haul.

word items,
P(WI)
correlated
to word
gifts

Word gifts are those gifts which are specifically used by God to reveal and clarify truth about God and His purposes and which will edify the believers and instill hope in them concerning God's present and future activity. Leaders are those who have word gifts. Word processing goes hand in hand with word gifts. Therefore, leaders can expect to have many, many word items throughout a lifetime. A major symptom of a plateaued leader is one to whom word items are infrequent. A symptom of plateauing is a lessening effect of word processing in a life.

further
explanation
word item,
P(WI)
Daniel

It is evident that Daniel had been studying Jeremiah chapters 27 and 29 and the contexts around them. The events of Daniel 9, the great prayer, and the prophetical revelation were a result of the word item which expanded Daniel's perspective and brought on Daniel's prayer. You can see Daniel praying phrases from Jeremiah, a needed ministry skill that younger leaders should emulate. This word processing resulted in a faith challenge which Daniel accepted. God answered above and beyond Daniel's expectations.

P(LI),
increases
development
pace

Numerous higher level leaders are noted for their aptitude for reading widely and for their capacity to learn for their own lives the lessons they see in the writings. The ability to do this often short circuits the years it would take to learn the same lessons by personal experience.

COMMENTARY ON ORDINARY EXPANSION CLUSTER continued

P(LI),
a quasi-
divine
contact

While the **divine contact** process item refers mainly to a person who influences, it is also true that written information can serve the divine contact function. Mentors who serve as divine contacts often send just the right "book" or "tract" or "brochure" or some other written information which serves the divine contact function and significantly contributes to the developing leader.

P(CXT),
correlative

Contextual factors are a very important category of process items which should be noted in order to set the stage for analysis and correlation of items. These larger factors always have an impact on personal development. It is the sensing of the hand of God in them that makes the contextual items important.

P(PS),
further
explanation

The shift from naive realism to critical realism, which occurs frequently to students at the School of World Mission, is a cumulative form of this item. Frequently the shift occurs gradually. Models are taught in most classes which portray portions of, but not the whole picture. Gradually the concepts of critical realism are imbibed. The diversity of views from many different cultures concerning various perceived realities seeks to affirm the critical realism epistemology. Some shifts occur instantaneously (as was with the Apostle Paul). Others are cumulative with a powerful trigger incident as can be the case of someone seeking a baptism or filling of the Spirit.

spiritual
authority
defined,
character-
ized

Spiritual authority is the right followers give leaders to exert influence upon them because of the perceived spirituality of the leader. Spiritual authority is based on an experiential power base. That is, a leader's power resources for spiritual authority are intimately tied to his/her experiences with God. Followers perceive spirituality in leaders in terms of character, demonstration of power, and perceived knowledge of God and His purposes. Processing experiences which build Godly character, show that God works powerfully through the leader, and give the leader understanding of God's ways and purposes for followers, all build up spiritual authority in the eyes of followers. In short, spiritual authority is that characteristic of a God-anointed leader developed upon an experiential power base which enables a leader to influence followers towards God's purposes, through persuasion, force of modelling, and moral expertise.

PRESSURE EXPANSION CLUSTER

introduction   Much of the development of a leader takes place via
                 the faithful response to the routine of ministry.
                 Routine can dull a person. God interrupts the
                 routine frequently with conflict which usually gets
                 the attention of the leader and forces the leader
                 to depend afresh upon God. Three items are listed
                 under this cluster.

description   The pressure expansion cluster refers to the set of
                 three process items, ministry conflict, leadership
                 backlash, and crises, which frequently occur in
                 the growth ministry period in order to keep a
                 leader depending on God and to expand that leader
                 in ministerial formation.

major   Pressure items:
purposes   1. soften a leader so that he/she is open to learn
                    lessons that would not be received otherwise.
                 2. strengthen the leader's learning posture--
                    especially flexibility to learn from the
                    negative.
                 3. test the spiritual authority of a leader. In
                    pressure processing leaders tend to revert to
                    manipulation and force to overcome the
                    opposition.
                 4. develop ministerial formation. Pressure
                    processing will point out influence skills which
                    are lacking as well as confirm others, which are
                    present.

Venn Diagram

PRESSURE EXPANSION CLUSTER

not   Several other items (e.g. conflict, life crises,
exclusive   etc.) do contain the essential characteristic of
                 this cluster--God ordained pressure. From time to
                 time they could fit with this cluster but they are
                 listed under other clusters because of their
                 primary processing foci.

MINISTRY CONFLICT PROCESS ITEM   Symbol: P(MCONF)

introduction   Conflict inevitably arises when people influence
                other people. Particularly this is true during the
                growth ministry period where many decisions are
                made by an immature emerging leader. The **conflict
                process item** is a general process item which
                describes any conflict that is used to process a
                leader in terms of spiritual or ministerial
                formation. The **ministry conflict process item** is
                the special process item which describes conflict
                which takes place in the growth ministry period and
                which has its primary focus on ministerial
                formation. Spiritual formation is also affected by
                such processing. Conflict is a mighty weapon in
                the hand of God and can be used to teach a leader
                lessons that could not be learned in any other way.

definition   The ministry conflict process item refers to those
                instances in a ministry situation, in which a
                leader learns lessons via the positive and negative
                aspects of conflict with regards to

                    1. the nature of conflict,
                    2. possible ways to resolve conflict,
                    3. possible ways to avoid conflict,
                    4. ways to creatively use conflict
                    5. perception of God's personal shaping through
                       the conflict.

example   The Apostles in Acts 6 faced conflict from within
                the church between the converts who were Greek-
                speaking and the converts who were Jewish-speaking.

example   Paul faced conflict from without in the Ephesian
                situation with the silversmith, Demetrius.

causal   The conflict may come from without, that is, those
source   who are not believers, or from within, those who
                are believers. Sometimes the conflict from within
                is the most difficult to face since a leader has
                higher expectations for believers.

focus   The ministry conflict process item, like the
primary   general conflict process item and the crises
inner   process items, generally tests maturity in the
character,   inner-life. Someone has said, "In a crisis we are
secondary   what we really are." Therefore, conflict
ministry   processing, in general, and ministry conflict
lessons   processing, in particular are important not so much
                for learning the lessons of solving ministry
                problems but for their value in revealing one's
                character. For what we are in the conflict is
                probably much more vital than what we do.

FEEDBACK ON MINISTRY CONFLICT PROCESS ITEM

1. The following exercises will ask you to analyze several ministry conflict process items from your own personal experience. Jot down the last 5 or 6 conflict process items that have happened in your experience. Start with your most recent and work back. Perhaps previously you saw them only as problematic situations and didn't realize that God was in them and working for his purposes of developing you. This feedback will perhaps help you reflect on this conflict with new perspectives.

When	Conflict Item	From Within	From Without
(1)			
(2)			
(3)			
(4)			
(5)			

2. Ministry history refers to the identification and cataloging of ministry tasks, ministry assignments, or other closure ministry experiences sequentially so that certain aspects of leadership development can be analyzed. Notice those words "other closure experiences." Ministry conflict processing is one kind of example of those "other closure experiences." It is important enough that it should be traced and analyzed in a leader's life. A study of ministry history with a focus on just conflict processing can reveal important patterns. Often it is the case in conflict processing that "closure" is weak. Analyze your list of conflict items in terms of "closure." Were they "successfully resolved," "left unresolved," "partially resolved," or just "left?" For each item give your intuitive analysis of closure by putting a short word or phrase to capture how you feel about closure for the item.

(1)   (2)   (3)   (4)   (5)

3. Read again the definition of the ministry conflict process item. Note the five areas suggested for reflection. Closure in conflict processing involves two major aspects:
> 1) closure with regard to the actual conflict
> 2) closure with regard to learning leadership lessons from that conflict.

It is this second aspect that affects long term leadership development. One of the most important lessons to be learned in early growth ministry processing is awareness that God uses conflict for his purposes both for your ministry and for your personal life. It is bad enough just to go through conflict. It is worse to go through conflict and not profit from it. Take one of the items listed for exercise 1 and analyze it for closure 2.

FEEDBACK ON MINISTRY CONFLICT PROCESS ITEM continued

a. List some positive or negative lessons learned:

b. What do you think was God's intent for leadership development for you in this conflict?

c. How do you think this processing will affect your future leadership?

ANSWERS----------

Because conflict is so personal and usually involves other persons I think it best if I don't put my ministry history in regard to five conflict items in print. However, I will share personally on this feedback when I use this manual for teaching. The important thing is that you regard conflict in terms of lessons for your leadership. And as you look at several taken together you may see some overall patterns that you did not previously see in the midst of an individual conflict item.

LEADERSHIP BACKLASH PROCESS ITEM Symbol: P(LB)

introduction   Sometimes a leader feels convinced about a course
of action. He/she then convinces followers of that
action, even demonstrating that the action is from
God. The group then takes the action and it brings
unforeseen ramifications along with accomplishment
of its major purposes. Because of the ramifications
the followers turn against the leader in a backlash
action. This particular form of conflict
processing can be difficult to take unless one
is forewarned about it and responds properly.

definition   The <u>leadership backlash process item</u> refers to the
reactions of followers, other leaders within a
group, and/or Christians outside the group, to a
course of action taken by a leader because of
various ramifications that arise due to the action
taken. The situation is used in the leader's life
to test perseverance, clarity of vision, and faith.

example   See Exodus 5:20ff where the people react to Moses'
leadership when persecution comes. The backlash
cycle can be seen readily in this example.

example   See also Exodus 16:2,3 where backlash continues.

comment   Usually the unforeseen ramifications involve
persecution or hard times of some kind. And though
followers may have agreed originally that the
course of action was proper they now blame the
leader for having taken it.

order   The full cycle of this item includes the following:
property   1. The leader gets a vision (direction) from God.
              2. The followers are convinced of the direction.
              3. The group moves in the direction suggested.
              4. Then comes persecution, hard times, or attacks
                 from Satan--spiritual warfare is common.
              5. There is backlash from the group.
              6. The leader is driven to God to reconfirm the
                 action and get God's affirmation in spite of
                 ramifications.
              7. God reveals himself further: who He is, what He
                 intends to do. He makes it clear that it is God
                 who is going to deliver.
              8. God vindicates Himself and the leader.

basic   Success brings problems as well as solutions to
lesson   problems. Awareness of this enables one to
persevere through these times of trials associated
with effective ministry.

FEEDBACK ON LEADERSHIP BACKLASH PROCESS ITEM

1. What purposes do you see in this process item?

    a. for the leader

    b. for the followers

    c. for God Himself

2. Could you suggest other biblical examples of this process item?

3. If you have experienced this (personally as a leader or have seen it in someone else's leadership) would you share that experience?

ANSWERS----------

    1. a. A leader can easily be taken up with a plan of action and needs to be reminded who is really ultimately responsible for its success. Complications in general are a means God uses to teach inner-life maturity. Leadership backlash in general is a form of integrity testing in which the leader's real heart motivation for the direction can be revealed.
    b. The people need to realize that spiritual authority involves loyalty to the leader who follows God's direction. Sometimes loyalty is not tested until difficult times.
    c. God can use difficult times to set the stage for deliverance which can only come from Himself. He then can deliver, receive glory, and lay foundations for future work.
    2. Though I do not know for certain, there could have been leadership backlash in John Mark's decision to leave Paul and Barnabas before the completion of the first missionary journey.
    3. I'll leave this one for group discussion.

CRISIS PROCESS ITEMS   Symbol: P(CR)

introduction   A crisis is a time of increased pressures due to
numerous situations such as: 1. threatening of
loss of life, property, or way of life, 2. conflict
of various kinds, 3. perceived situations requiring
urgent change, 4. inner turmoil in a life, 5.
sickness, 6. the need to see God's character
vindicated, 7. the need to have God's guidance or
special intervention, 8. persecution, or suffering.
The key to this process item is to see that these
human situations are often used by God to test and
teach a leader dependence on God. God will indeed
meet a leader in all of the major experiences of
life with a solution that is tailor made for the
leader. It is this ability to learn the lessons
concerning the sovereignty of God in crisis events
that make this process item important in regards to
leadership emergence. These crisis lessons will
prove extremely valuable in the effective ministry
of the unique ministry period.

definition   Crisis process items refer to those special intense
situations of pressure in human situations which
are used by God to test and teach dependence.

example   See Paul, II Corinthians 1:3,4 etc.

example   See Paul, II Timothy 3:10,11, for examples of
crises and how modelling can impact others.

example   See Jephthah, a crisis leader, in Judges 10, 11.
His crises processing included: crisis 1--family
conflict and ostracism, crisis 2--forced isolation,
crisis 3--survival as para-military band in foreign
country, crisis 4--ministry power, crisis 5--power
encounter, crisis 6--integrity check, crisis 7--
civil war.

result   Crises in the foundational phase can, as seen in
in   Jephthah, develop an inner character which is
Jephthah   strong and independent and can later be used for
forceful leadership situations.

two major   Crises can **drive one to God** or **drive one away.**
results   Crises early on tend to drive emerging leaders away
and perhaps out of the ministry (abbreviated entry
pattern). Crises in the latter growth ministry
period tend to drive a leader more deeply into the
heart of God. A willful intent to move deeper into
the heart of God in the early stages of a crisis
can carry one through it, with the end result of a
stronger leader with a deeper experience of God and
spiritual authority that accompanies it.

FEEDBACK ON CRISIS PROCESS ITEMS

1. Mr. Frank Sells, one of my Bible College teachers, used to say, "We are in a crisis what we really are!" And that seems often to be the focus of God's teaching in a crisis. How we react in the crisis is often more important than our solving the crisis. A major crisis that David faced was the revolt of Absalom (see II Samuel 15:13-17:22). David, in spite of his faults at this time of life, responded well. What was the major response of David in the crisis? (see Psalm 3 to pick up the inner-life response of David)

2. According to James 1:2-4 what is a major thing God wants to do in a leader through a crisis?

3. Paul suggests in II Corinthians 1:3,4 and II Timothy 3:10,11 how God uses crisis process items in a leader's life. What principles concerning crisis do you see in these passages?

4. When God wants to train someone how to handle crises or to prepare them for a major crisis of Christianity in a country what do you think will be the training methodology?

ANSWERS----------

1. In the Psalm we see that he: A. admitted his overwhelming situation (verse 1), B. related the physical situation to that of its spiritual roots (verse 2 God will not help him), C. claimed by faith God's protection and God's encouragement for his inner attitude (verse 3,4), D. acted on his faith and slept believing in God's protection (verses 5,6) E. Claimed God's intervention and asserted it by faith. In I Samuel we see he also took action by influencing the counsel that Absalom would receive. David was a man who had been trained in crises by on-the-job training.

2. Build endurance and persistence as qualities in the inner-life. We thus exhibit a maturity that others can follow in the many pressures of life.

3. In the II Corinthians 1:3,4 we see that we experience God's deliverance first hand. This allows us to minister to others with real spiritual authority because we minister out of experience. We also see in II Timothy 3:10,11 that our reactions in crises are models for others.

Summary of Expansion Processing--Ordinary and Pressure Clusters

This chapter has suggested that God challenges leaders, even those barely established in ministry, to grow. These challenges come first of all in the routine of ministry. A variety of means are used by God. In the daily preparation for ministry in the word the leader will be met sometimes unexpectedly by God so as to affect guidance, deeper committal, decision making, a personal value or information to meet some situation prompted in ministry (**WORD PROCESS ITEM**). An important book or other written material arrives with timely affect (**LITERARY PROCESS ITEM**). A leader further along in ministry takes a personal interest and gives some important advice (**MENTORING PROCESS ITEM**). Some major trend in society forces an openness with people previously non-receptive to the Gospel (**CONTEXTUAL PROCESS ITEM**). A peer shares a life changing idea (**PARADIGM SHIFT PROCESS ITEM**). A situation of ineffective leadership causes reflection which leads to a desire for spiritual authority (**SPIRITUAL AUTHORITY DISCOVERY PROCESS ITEM**). A key insight for starting a special group emerges (**MINISTRY STRUCTURE INSIGHT PROCESS ITEM**). A challenging temporary assignment sparks a new beginning in ministry (**MINISTRY ASSIGNMENT**).

The process items illustrated above occur in the daily working out of ministry. They are not necessarily sought for or planned on. But they happen. And God uses them to sovereignly expand a leader who is learning to hear and respond to God in these many ways that He is speaking.

But beyond the routine happenings in life there are those startling events or times when things don't go right. A decision is made to do something which upsets several church members who then raise a stink about it. Lines are drawn. Maybe the decision was unwise but it is difficult now to admit that. Some unhappy members leave the church. The young leader now has a reputation tarnished somewhat at least in the eyes of some (**MINISTRY CONFLICT PROCESS ITEM**). Perhaps a lawsuit threatens the very existence of the church. Or maybe funds have been mishandled so that at the least the integrity of the church and its leadership is called into question or at the most threatens to bankrupt the church (**CRISES PROCESS ITEM**). The young leader gets an unusual idea about ministry. He/she becomes convinced that God is in it. He/she uses his/her developing persuasive influence skills to convince followers to accept his radical ministry proposal. At first things go well. The young leader feels affirmed. Then a few things, not expected, force some of the followers to reconsider. They turn against the idea and eventually the young leader. The young leader even now questions whether the idea really came from God. In fact, his/her ability to hear God is being questioned (**LEADERSHIP BACKLASH PROCESS ITEM**). These startling often unexpected or unwanted times certainly break up the routine. More than that, they test leadership character and stretch a leader to grow.

These pressure times can intensify growth and speed up the

development of a leader if that leader is responding to them and knows how God uses them for development.

The effects of these two clusters can be missed due to their very obscurity. They are buried in the regularity of normal ministry activity. Sensitivity to God in this processing signals a growing leader.

Some Findings On Growth Ministry Processing--Part II

Some Problems

Four problems, that can impede a leaders development are addressed by the ordinary and pressure expansion clusters. Two were previously mentioned. Two are new.

1. **THE PLATEAU BARRIER**
   Leaders have a tendency to arrest development once they have developed some skills and gained some ministry experience. They may be content to continue ministry as is without discerning their need to develop further.

2. **THE AUTHORITY PROBLEM.** Leaders in growth ministry processing must learn to submit to authority. Many leaders throughout their ministry have problems seeing authority and submitting to it. This is an ongoing challenge and becomes much more subtle as a leader matures. Leaders who have trouble submitting to authority will usually have trouble exercising spiritual authority.

3. **THE MINISTRY CLOSURE PROBLEM**
   Leaders need to bring closure on ministry assignments. Many leaders leave one ministry assignment for another without bringing adequate closure to the previous ministry assignment. This is true of very small ministry assignments as well as larger long term ones. Closure will not always be satisfactory in terms of relationships and structures. But it definitely can be in terms of lessons learned so as to affect future ministry.

4. **THE MINISTRY PHILOSOPHY PROBLEM**
   Leaders frequently pursue ministry without a clear understanding of a ministry philosophy. That is, either they do not learn lessons in ministry processing or they fail to identify these lessons into a unified system that can undergird future ministry decision making.

The Plateau Barrier Problem

Leaders can become too comfortable. These two clusters have, as a by-product, a stimulus to overcome any arrested growth. The word, literary, mentor, and paradigm shift items of the ordinary cluster will stimulate growth. All of the pressure cluster items--ministry conflict, leadership backlash, and crises--challenge the status quo which becomes catalytic in terms of moving off a plateau.

The Authority Problem

Conflict almost always leads to questioning of authority. Leaders in conflict are forced to examine their own use or abuse of authority. Leadership backlash certainly focuses on a leader's authority. Ministry crises frequently have at the root a leadership authority problem. The pressure cluster will not resolve the authority problem but it will force it to be seen. Leaders can respond positively and learn lessons of authority in pressure processing or they can respond negatively and continue to the detriment of later ministry.

The Ministry Closure Problem

There is a tendency for all leaders to move on from situations to new ones without adequately learning all that could be learned from previous ministry. The ministry assignment process item has as its focus closure development. Leaders should move on from one ministry assignment wiser and better prepared as leaders for the next one.

The Ministry Philosophy Problem

The pressure cluster frequently stirs a leader to question what ministry is all about. Its processing can do much to cause a leader to reflect on ministry philosophy. While the ordinary cluster will bring a step-by-step accumulation of ministry philosophy lessons, it is the pressure cluster which will bring to bear the need for understanding this ministry philosophy.

Major Lessons Focused on By These Two Clusters

Five of the major lessons of leadership are touched upon by the processing of the ordinary and pressure expansion clusters.

1. Learning   **EFFECTIVE LEADERS, AT ALL LEVELS, MAINTAIN A**
   Posture   **LEARNING POSTURE THROUGHOUT LIFE.**

The word, literary, mentor, and paradigm shift process items all deal with learning posture. The pressure cluster items frequently open a leader up to learn because of the needs they bring.

2. Spiritual   **EFFECTIVE LEADERS INCREASINGLY VALUE SPIRITUAL**
   Authority   **AUTHORITY AS THEIR DOMINANT POWER BASE.**

Conflict and leadership backlash frequently teach about
ineffective use of power bases. Frequently they occur in
combination with the spiritual authority discovery process item.
Usually these combinations of processing items point out to a
leader lack of spiritual authority. They can motivate a leader
to desire spiritual authority as a power base.

3. Leadership   **EFFECTIVE LEADERS RECOGNIZE LEADERSHIP SELECTION**
   Emergence   **AND DEVELOPMENT AS A PRIORITY FUNCTION.**

Frequently, but not always, conflict happens because
potential leaders are not being developed and released and thus
they resort to confrontation to circumvent their frustrations.
Much ministry conflict comes due to a leader failing to recognize
a rising leader and freeing or releasing that leader. Continual
recognition, development, and release of rising leaders will do
much to avoid unnecessary conflict.

4. Ministry   **EFFECTIVE LEADERS WHO ARE PRODUCTIVE OVER A**
   Philosophy   **LIFETIME HAVE A DYNAMIC MINISTRY PHILOSOPHY WHICH**
                 EVOLVES CONTINUALLY FROM THE INTERPLAY OF THREE
                 MAJOR FACTORS: BIBLICAL DYNAMICS, PERSONAL
                 GIFTEDNESS, AND SITUATIONAL DYNAMICS.

Conflict and leadership backlash often leave a leader with
deep lessons that mold a leadership philosophy.

7. Pace   **EFFECTIVE LEADERS ARE PACE SETTERS.**
   Setters

Frequently a source of conflict arises when followers
perceive leaders are not willing or can not do what they are
demanding of followers.

Foundational Ministry Pattern

A major development pattern (discussed more fully in chapter
11) should be mentioned at this point in the explanation of
processing since it is tied so closely with ordinary expansion
cluster processing.

Jesus reveals an important principle in his application
remarks concerning the Unfaithful Steward Parable of Luke 16:1-
13. Verse 10 contains the principle.

Luke 16:10 LITTLE-BIG PRINCIPLE.

FAITHFULNESS IN A SMALL RESPONSIBILITY IS AN INDICATOR OF
FAITHFULNESS IN A LARGER RESPONSIBILITY.

This basic principle seems to be foundational to all of ministry processing. From observations of repeated application of this principle comes the foundational ministry pattern.

FOUNDATIONAL MINISTRY PATTERN

FAITHFULNESS IN MINISTRY TASKS AND MINISTRY ASSIGNMENTS, ALONG WITH POSITIVE RESPONSE TO THE TESTING ELEMENT OF MANY OF THE MINISTRY PROCESS ITEMS, LEADS TO EXPANDED MINISTRY AND RETESTING OF FAITHFULNESS AT THAT NEW MINISTRY LEVEL.

Of course the converse is also repeatedly seen. Unfaithfulness in small responsibilities is an indicator of unfaithfulness in larger responsibilities. The ordinary processing cluster has as its intent the stimulating of a leader along this pattern.

CHAPTER 7. GROWTH MINISTRY PROCESSING--PART III

Overview

Chapter 4 discussed foundational processing which led up to transition into full time Christian leadership. Chapter 5 picked up at that point and discussed early ministry processing and its effects on the growth of the emerging leader. Chapter 6 touched on the processes that God uses in the routine of ministry and the special pressures of ministry to expand a leader. This chapter points out the special discernment process items that God uses to expand a leader. Expansion will move a leader from the provisional stage of growth ministry to the competent stage.

Preview

Two clusters of process items make up the special discernment process items. The **challenge cluster** includes those process items that carry a special sense of the divine initiative: destiny revelation, faith challenge, prayer challenge, ministry challenge, influence challenge. Each of these require sensitivity on the part of the emerging leader to hear the voice of God. The **spiritual insights cluster** groups those process items which deal with special power issues and discernment of the spiritual realm. They include: spiritual warfare, power encounters, prayer power, gifted power, and networking power. Causal activity for the challenge cluster is the inward working of God. Causal activity for the spiritual insights cluster is mixed including spirit forces, divine initiative, and people.

The **challenge cluster** occurs throughout the whole time period of growth ministry. Destiny revelation can occur in early, middle, and latter parts of growth ministry. Usually destiny revelation will occur early in a general way and then will repeatedly occur each time clarifying and making more specific the destiny of the leader. The faith and prayer challenges can occur throughout. Frequently they will be in combination with other processes. The faith challenge may be part of the working out of destiny revelation processing. The prayer challenge may be in combination with pressure expansion cluster processing or any of the ordinary expansion cluster of items. Ministry challenge usually portends a new spurt of expansion. It can occur usually after an initial ministry assignment and from time to time in the middle and latter portion of the growth ministry period. Influence challenge usually occurs after a leader is operating more competently.

The **spiritual insights cluster** also occurs throughout the entire growth ministry period. Spiritual warfare and power encounters can occur throughout and can be in combination with the pressure cluster items. Some leaders coming out of dominant secular worldviews may require a paradigm shift in order to even sense these items. Prayer power, gifted power, and networking power all usually require some extended time in ministry and previous expansion before they are sensed.

Both clusters, challenge and spiritual insights, require expansion in **discernment**. Leaders who are very active, self-directed, and confident will tend to do things in their own strength. They will find it difficult to discern God in the challenge cluster. Frequently it takes some unusual experience, like failure or brokenness, or negative pressure cluster processing in order for a leader to begin to sense God in the challenge cluster. All of the challenge cluster items are fraught with risk. Timid leaders may require repeated remedial processing in order for the challenges to be accepted and expansion to occur. But in the challenges there is that touch of the divine that sparks new life and expands a leader and gives meaning to life and ministry. The challenge cluster inspires vision, develops strategic formation, and takes a leader further in the major leadership lessons of spiritual authority, pace setting, and sense of destiny. If growth via ordinary and pressure clusters can be called step-by-step growth, then growth via the challenge cluster is like quantum leaps or large steps. A leader advances rapidly in terms of competency via challenge processing.

Special discernment is needed in order to profit from the spiritual insights clusters. Leaders learn to sense and feel, more so than logically understand, the issues underlying the spiritual insights cluster. Logical understanding will come, but it is secondary. They learn to make the unseen as real as the seen. This cluster more than any other, except perhaps for one or two of the guidance items or life maturing items, develops depth in spiritual authority. A leader's power base expands significantly in this processing. Besides spiritual authority other development tasks of this processing include development of discernment and ministerial formation.

Preliminary definitions are needed to understand the influence challenge process item. These include **sphere of influence, three kinds of influence, influence-mix,** and the **influence continuum.**

CHALLENGE CLUSTER   synonym: Divine Initiative Cluster

introduction   God's intent is for each leader to develop to
                potential.   When Christ calls leaders to Christian
                ministry He intends to develop them to their full
                potential.   Each of us in leadership are
                responsible to continue developing in accordance
                with God's processing all our lives.   The challenge
                cluster describes processing which spurs leaders on
                to realize their potential.

description   The <u>challenge cluster</u> includes those major process
                items which stimulate a leader to take steps of
                risk and accomplish new things for God and result
                in expanded capacity to influence.

Venn Diagram
of Cluster

4 essential   All of the items are destiny items.   That is, they
charac-   are touched with the special presence of the Lord
teristics   so as to inspire a leader to build toward an
                ultimate contribution for the Lord.   All of the
                items are difficult to discern as from God, at
                first.   All imply risk and failure.   All require
                expansion in faith.

6 major   Challenge process items,
purposes
                1. inspire vision.   Influencing God's people
                   toward His purposes (the very core of
                   leadership) requires vision.
                2. develop a leader in strategic formation.
                   Clarification of ministry philosophy requires
                   destiny processing in general and specific
                   vision.
                3. give the leader a growing awareness of his/her
                   sense of destiny.
                4. give deeper experiences with God which are one
                   of the major credibility factors for spiritual
                   authority.
                5. require the leader to act before followers so as
                   to model the reality of the unseen living God.
                   This is at the heart of the major leadership
                   lesson on pace setting.
                6. result in major advances in the leader's
                   confidence and ability to influence and hence
                   significant advance in competence.

DESTINY REVELATION/CONFIRMATION PROCESS ITEM Symbol: P(DR)

introduction   The Destiny Pattern moves through three aspects.
One, God's preparatory work brings a growing
awareness of a sense of destiny. Two, the awareness
moves to conviction as God gives revelation and
confirmation of it. Three, there is movement in
accomplishment of that destiny which often
culminates in destiny fulfilled. Destiny
revelation/ confirmation describes the category of
process incidents or items which are operative in
aspect 2 of the destiny pattern, God's confirming
of a destiny. God begins to reveal more definitely
what it may be, or at least give hints that there
will be a destiny, and that the leader will be used
in a special way to accomplish special purposes for
God.

definition   The destiny revelation/confirmation process item
describes a grouping of incidents or process items
with an unusual sense of God's presence working in
them, and which are significant acts, people,
providential circumstances, or timing which confirm
a future destiny and perhaps begin to clarify its
nature.

examples   Bertelsen (1985) lists the following specific kinds
of destiny revelation process incidents or items:

- revelatory act
- revelatory
  dream/vision
- revelatory
  prophecy
- destiny insight
- word, obedience,
  integrity,
  faith checks
- divine affirmation

- all forms of sovereign,
  guidance: double,
  confirmation, divine,
  contacts, mentors
- spiritual authority
  affirmation,
- leadership backlash
- power items
- convergence

example   Moses' experience at the burning bush was a
revelatory act in which God attracted Moses'
attention and then revealed to him the next steps
in his destiny.

example   Joseph's dreams in Genesis 37 are examples of
revelatory dreams and revelatory prophecy.

example   The voice from heaven in John 12:27-29 illustrates
divine affirmation used as destiny confirmation.

example   Ananias' vision in Acts 9:10-16 is an example of
sovereign guidance given for Paul (double
confirmation) which was destiny revelation.

FEEDBACK ON DESTINY REVELATION/CONFIRMATION PROCESS ITEM

1. What destiny revelation incident or item occurs in Acts 16:6-10? Identify it; then tell its basic function in Paul's destiny pattern.

2. Can you think of incidents from the Bible which illustrate any other of the destiny revelation process items listed? (I realize that you are not yet familiar with some of the process items. But for the ones which are descriptive or self-evident, do this exercise.) Check any you can and give scripture references.

___ a. revelatory acts,
        dreams/vision, prophecy
___ b. word, obedience,
        integrity, faith checks
___ c. divine affirmation
___ d. spiritual authority
        affirmation

___ e. guidance items: sovereign
        guidance, double
        confirmation, divine
        contacts, affirmation
___ f. leadership backlash:
___ g. power items:
___ h. convergence:

3. Later we will come back to this exercise after more of these process items have been defined. But for now can you describe any incidents in your own life which you believe may have been destiny revelation/confirmation?

ANSWERS----------
1. Revelatory dream or vision. From Acts 9, 22, and 26 we know that Paul had a destiny to take the Gospel to Gentiles. Here God gives clear guidance as to the next segment of Gentiles to receive the Gospel. This was guidance as well as confirmation to Paul that he is doing the right thing and fulfilling another step in his destiny.
2. c. divine affirmation: the voice on the Mount of Transfiguration; Mark 9:7,8. g. power items: resurrection of Lazarus in John 11.
3. I have identified several. I'll relate one. In a boundary phase in which I needed specific guidance I set aside a day of prayer to get alone with the Lord and seek his specific guidance. I worshiped and prayed and reflected on my past ministry experiences and then asked the Lord to give me specific guidance as to what he wanted me to do. Within the next week I had three unsolicited requests concerning possible ministry situations for me. These along with two I knew about made up five choices. Now the three unsolicited requests in response to specific prayer gave tremendous divine affirmation of destiny. But the major destiny confirmation item that came was a destiny insight. My reflection on past ministry and how God had moved me in boundary times revealed a pattern. All major boundary decisions in the past had reflected an increase in sphere of influence potential. I then ordered the five opportunities in light of this destiny insight and made my decision which God later further confirmed.

FAITH CHALLENGE PROCESS ITEM   Symbol: P(FCHG)

introduction   Ministerial formation involves attitudes toward ministry as well as skills in doing ministry. Leaders are people with God-given vision. Response to that vision is manifest in terms of faith that accepts and sees that vision worked out. The faith challenge process item recognizes the essential importance of that function of leadership which inspires followers with hope of God's working. An attitude which is aware that God will challenge to steps of faith and which responds to such challenges is the goal of this process item.

definition   The faith challenge process item refers to those instances in ministry where a leader is challenged to take steps of faith in regards to ministry and sees God meet those steps of faith with divine affirmation and ministry achievement in such a way as to increase the leader's capacity to trust God in future ministry.

example Abraham   The classic Old Testament faith challenge process item concerns a series of encounters over more than 25 years with Abraham. See Genesis 12, 15, 17, 18, 22 and the New Testament commentary on it--Romans 4:20,21 and Hebrews 11:11-12, 17-19. The combination obedience check/ faith challenge in the Genesis 22 incident is particularly instructive.

example Moses   A subtle faith challenge often missed because of the prominent obedience/ sense of destiny experience occurs in Moses' call at the burning bush. Exodus 3:11,12 couch it. Moses wants some proof that what he is hearing is really of God and will happen. God tells him he will not know for certain until he comes back to this mountain having accomplished it. See Exodus 19 (especially verse 3) for the fulfillment of this faith challenge.

examples Joshua   Joshua 3:7,8: The crossing of Jordan.
Joshua 6:1-5: The fall of Jericho.

example Esther   Esther 4:12-14. Mordecai's challenge to Esther.

order property-- threefold pattern   The essence of a faith challenge involves three elements: 1) a revelation from God concerning some future intent, 2) a realization by the leader that God is challenging to act on the basis of this revelation, and 3) a resultant mind-set which makes leadership decisions based on this firm conviction. A faith challenge may come in one act or be given in a process over time in which the intent of God is slowly clarified and realized.

FEEDBACK ON FAITH CHALLENGE PROCESS ITEM

1. I didn't illustrate faith challenges from the New Testament. Suggest at least three giving the following information:

Who   How Challenge Came   Response--Leadership Decisions

a.

b.

c.

2. Aspect three of the faith pattern describes a positive response by the leader. The question must be asked, "What happens when a faith challenge is not sensed or refused?" What would you say in response to that question? Illustrate from Scriptures or your own life?

3. Give an illustration of a faith challenge from your own life.

When   How Given   Positive Response: Indications

ANSWERS----------
1. I'll leave these for you to do. But don't overlook Luke's opening chapters where some excellent faith challenges occur. You may wish to discuss your answers or get some answers from a knowledgeable friend.
2. As with testing items in general the negative or slow response can bring a repeated attempt at the challenge, instruction on the issue, discipline, or finally--a setting aside. Jonah is the classic Old Testament example. But the incident is a combined with such a strong obedience check that the faith challenge is often overshadowed. Zechariah in Luke 1 is an example of one who did not respond immediately and needed further proof. The angel gave him a disciplinary sign. See also the disciples in the storm, the disciples trying to heal a demon possessed boy after the Transfiguration, Martha at Lazarus' resurrection, Peter walking on the water, Rhoda and disciples at Peter's deliverance, two disciples on the road to Emmaus, Thomas after the resurrection.
3.

When	How Given	Positive Response
1967	inward conviction regarding support after committal to leave engineering job to go off to Bible School, followed by sign--telephone call from my brother-in-law Thad Hawkins with promise for support.	We resigned position, sold our house (at slight loss), went to Bible College and trusted God for financial support. And God met us faithfully over the three years we were there.

PRAYER CHALLENGE PROCESS ITEM   Symbol: P(PC)

introduction   At the heart of leadership is communication between
               God and the leader.   A leader's central thrust
               is to influence groups of people toward God's
               purpose for them.   Communication is involved.   In
               the busyness of doing ministry vital communication
               with God via prayer often is overshadowed.   God
               will from time to time bring a leader back to this
               foundational necessity of ministry.   This is one of
               the major "being" items that is constantly
               re-emphasized by God in this primarily "doing"
               phase. The prayer challenge may be stimulated by
               pressing personal needs or ministry needs but the
               essence of this processing item is more than the
               answer to those needs. It is the necessity and
               responsibility of prayer as a leadership habit
               which enhances communication with God and receipt
               of vision for ministry.

definition   Prayer challenge process items refer to those
               instances in ministry where God, in an unusual way
               impresses a leader with the essential spiritual
               dynamic lesson of ministry--a leader in ministry
               must pray for that ministry--and in which there is
               positive growth that will affect later ministry.

example   Samuel's last public leadership act. See I Samuel
               12, especially verse 23.

example   See also the illustration of Epaphras in Colossians
               4:12,13 in light of the Colossian problem.

example   The Psalms frequently portray David as seeing God's
               challenge to get apart and meet God.

example   Numerous historical giants in missionary history
               (Hudson Taylor, Jonathan Goforth) give repeated
               testimony to this item.

focus   An ultimate goal of this process item is not so
               much a burden (an early growth ministry conviction)
               but a release (a latter growth ministry conviction
               leading to unique ministry) to do so joyfully as a
               matter of life and ministry sustaining communion.

order   The essence of a prayer challenge involves several
property--   elements: 1) a growing sense of the need to meet
several   God in prayer usually prompted by pressure items or
aspects   an strong inward desire to get away from it all,
               2) trigger incidents which press toward this
               desire, 3) a desperate sense of need for God to
               work, 4) a meeting with God in prayer--usually in
               solitude but sometimes demonstrated in public
               5) God's answer or strong affirmation.

FEEDBACK ON PRAYER CHALLENGE PROCESS ITEM

1. Give a specific biblical illustration of a prayer challenge process item and analyze the cause and result of this prayer challenge in the life of the leader.

2. Read quickly through I Samuel 12. How did God vindicate Samuel's leadership? What was the people's response? What was Samuel's? What does verse 23 tell us about Samuel's long ministry?

3. Give a specific illustration in your own life of the prayer challenge process item. Be sure you explain the <u>unusual</u> <u>way</u> and <u>the</u> <u>positive</u> <u>growth</u> aspects of this definition.

ANSWERS----------
      1. A classical prayer challenge process item is seen in the Genesis 18 vignette in which Abraham pleads with God for Sodom. God uses two angelic visitors to reveal God's personal purposes for Sarah and Abraham concerning a child. Then immediately following that he informs Abraham (perhaps through the two angels, perhaps directly) of his intended judgment upon Sodom. Verses 23 through 33 show the result of the challenge. The vignette is especially instructive in terms of leadership. God reveals his purposes to a leader, challenges him to pray concerning that revelation and thus involves him in the outcome.
      2. God vindicated Samuel's leadership (which apparently had been rejected by the people in their demand for a centralized integrated leadership) by the power praying incident during the dry season in which a rain storm came in answer to specific prayer by Samuel. The people properly responded by recognizing Samuel's spiritual authority. They were in fear of God and repentant of their own previous actions. Samuel responded by encouraging them and warning them. In verse 23 there is a personal response. He, himself, though rejected as leader will continue his ministry of prayer for them. The phrase, ceasing to pray, indicates that throughout his ministry he had been one who prayed for these people.
      3. I'll forego this answer. Be prepared to share your answer with others.

MINISTRY CHALLENGE PROCESS ITEM Symbol: P(MCHG)

introduction Most initial ministry assignments come because some
one challenges us. A variety of ministry challenges
accepted will usually expand a leader greatly in
terms of giftedness discovery. The heart of the
ministry challenge process item is threefold: the
sensing of God's hand in the challenge, exercising
the faith to accept the challenge, and the joy in
discovering what it means to be a channel through
which God works.

definition Ministry challenge describes the means whereby a
leader or potential leader is prompted to accept a
new ministry assignment and sense the guidance of
God into service.

example Barnabas' recruitment of Paul to help at Antioch.

example Typical ministry challenges occurring in early
ministry processing in a local church include calls
for people to: teach sunday school classes, be a
committee member, help someone else do some service
ministry, lead a small group, do evangelistic
visitation, do organizational support work,
organize social functions for groups within the
church, or plan retreats.

example Typical ministry challenges in parachurch groups
might include: campus witnessing, discipling
others, leading Bible study groups, or various
types of youth work.

causal Sources for ministry challenge can be external or
source internal. External means some person other than
self. Internal means a self-recognized challenge
in terms of needs, situations, or other perception
of ministry opportunities.

entry Responses to challenges usually involve working in
patterns existing ministry structures or roles, or adapting
or changing those existing structures or roles, or
creating new ministry roles or structures within
existing ministries, or creating new ministry roles
and structures altogether. (See also M.8 MINISTRY
ENTRY PATTERNS in chapter 11.)

focus Frequently, ministry challenges are God's major
means of guidance and giftedness development.
Leaders tend to be content with operating
reasonably well in a known situation. The ministry
challenge serves to move one off a plateau.

SPHERE OF INFLUENCE

introduction   The phrase, "measure of faith," in Romans 12:3,6 implies a potential level of effective use of gifts varying according to God's unique gifting of individuals. Sphere of influence seeks to capture that notion. It applies the "measure of faith" from a leadership emergence standpoint. Leadership emergence is completed when a leader reaches that maximum level for which he/she is gifted and is continuously operating in convergence. The stewardship model also reinforces the Romans 12 concept. Those responsible for developing leaders should continuously seek to identify sphere of influence and make selection and training decisions which challenge trainees to reach their God-given ministry potential.

definition   <u>Sphere of influence</u> refers to the totality of people being influenced and for whom a leader will give an account to God.

3 kinds   The totality of people influenced subdivides into three domains called direct influence, indirect influence and organizational influence.

3 measures   Sphere of Influence can be measured in terms of
1. **extensiveness**--which refers to quantity;
2. **comprehensiveness**--which refers to the scope (breadth) of things being influenced
3. and **intensiveness**, the depth to which influence extends to each item within the comprehensive influence. Extensiveness is the easiest to measure and hence is most often used or implied when talking about a leader's sphere of influence.

importance   Sphere of influence focuses on two essential
two   concepts of the definition of a leader: capacity
reasons   and accountability. Leaders will answer to God for what they have done with the potential to influence that has been given them. They will also answer to God for those who have been influenced by them through their ministry. Sphere of Influence brings a more objective evaluation to accountability.

convergence   Convergence refers to a point in the unique ministry phase where there is very effective ministry and a proper fit between a leader's capacity and people being influenced.

caution   A leader should not consciously seek to expand his/her sphere of influence as if bigger were better. Rather, a leader responds to God's challenge to accept varying sphere of influences in order to find God's proper sphere of influence.

3 KINDS OF INFLUENCE

introduction   Sphere of influence requires leaders to be aware of
                followers being influenced. Three domains of
                influence are helpful in assessing this.

definition   Direct influence is that domain of sphere of
                influence which indicates a measure of people being
                influenced by a real presence of the leader,
                usually occurring in focused and structured
                situations where feedback between follower and
                leader is possible and necessary, and carries a
                high level of accountability for influence.

definition   Indirect influence is that domain of sphere of
                influence which indicates a measure of people being
                influenced by non-time-bound miscellaneous
                influences a leader exerts through others, through
                media, or through writing, and for which feedback
                between the leader and those being influenced is
                difficult, if not impossible, and where
                accountability is primarily for the content of the
                influential ideas.

definition   Organizational influence is that domain of sphere
                of influence which indicates a measure of people
                being influenced by a person in organizational
                leadership via indirect, direct and organizational
                power.

example   direct   indirect   organizational

                individuals   committee   supervisory group
                small groups   advisory board   program director
                local church   executive board   department head
                churches   writing   organizational head
                seminars   radio ministry   policy formulator
                conferences   networking   board member

3 measures   Measures of influence include extensive (quantity),
                comprehensive (scope, areas of influence), and
                intensive (depth of influence in a given area).

example   A type A or B leader in a western church might
                develop as follows: 1. direct influence with
                individuals 2. direct influence with small groups
                3. increase extensiveness of direct influence
                beyond just small groups 4. indirect influence
                through committees 5. increase of extensiveness of
                indirect via more committees or more important
                committees. Extensiveness in both direct or
                indirect may go all the way up to the entire local
                church. Organizational influence usually does not
                apply (except indirectly through committees) until
                the leader accepts a paid position in the church.

INFLUENCE-MIX

introduction   One characteristic potentially denoting development
                 is change in sphere of influence. This change can
                 be in degree (more), or kind (influence means).
                 Influence-mix is the term which evaluates the
                 different configuration of means of influence.

definition   Influence-mix is a term describing the combination
                 of influence elements--direct, indirect or
                 organizational--in terms of degree and kind at a
                 given point in time.

example   A. W. Tozer's change in influence-mix is given
                 below. The phases refer to a time-line which will
                 be explained later in chapters 9 and 10.

INFLUENCE-MIX

Phase	Title	Direct	Indirect	Organ.
I	Inner-discipline	none	none	none
II	On-The-Job Training/ New Beginnings			
	Sub-Phase A			
	Morgantown	small	none	none
	Sub-Phase B Toledo	larger	none	none
	Sub-Phase C			
	Indianapolis	larger	none	none
III	City Leadership/ Expanding National Influence			
	Sub-Phase A			
	Early City	larger	small	none
	Sub-Phase B			
	Middle City	largest	larger	small
	Sub-Phase C			
	National/City	same	largest	significant
IV	Wrap-Up/ Reflection	smaller	same	smaller

primarily   The degree above was limited to a general
extensive   description of extensive (numbers) and did not
                 include changes in comprehensive (scope) and
                 intensive (degree within scope factors). These
                 changed also but are difficult to show.

explanation   A. W. Tozer primarily worked through a local
                 church. His ministry focus was public communication
                 (teaching/ preaching). His organizational
                 influence was largely indirect and had two foci:
                 writing/editing for the major magazine of the
                 denomination and service on an executive committee.
                 His indirect influence was large in scope but
                 varied in intensiveness: He taught in nearby Bible
                 colleges and seminaries. He had a radio ministry
                 which became national. His writings of articles,
                 and eventually books,influenced very many.

THE INFLUENCE CONTINUUM

introduction   Just how accountable (Hebrews 13:17, etc.) is a leader for his/her influence? Kauffman (1986) suggested an influence continuum for noting the influence a person is exerting which includes the 4 responsibility influence criteria: 1) time of the influence, 2) presence or absence of the influencer, 3) feedback access of followers, and 4) accountability factors. At stake here is an understanding of what one will give account to God for in terms of influencing followers. According to Kauffman any influence a person has can be placed at some point on this continuum. He defines four points of reference along the continuum. Questions focusing on the 4 responsibility factors include:

1. Time factor: Is the time of influence immediate or delayed? focused or informal? structured or unstructured?

2. Presence factor: Is the influence face-to-face or indirect? personal/impersonal? no longer needed?

3. Feedback factor: Does the influence input allow or not allow feedback? or is feedback necessary?

4. Accountability factor: Is the accountability factor there/not there, for content and/or application?

Kauffman answers these questions for each major point on the continuum. Notice that Kauffman uses only direct and indirect influence. He considers that any organizational influence can be distilled to these two basal types.

	Highly	Mostly	Mostly	Highly
	|------------|	------------|	------------|	-------|
	Indirect	Indirect	Direct	Direct
Factor	Accountability generally increases ---------------->			
1. Time	very delayed	delayed, short, structured, focused	immediate or delayed, unstructured, focused	immediate, focused structured
2. Presence	internalized unknown	indirect, normally impersonal	personal but indirect	direct and personal
3. Feedback	unnecessary, internalized	not usually possible	necessary but only possible	possible; necessary
4. Account-ability	yes for immediate person	yes, for content	yes; content, application	yes; content, applicatior

FEEDBACK ON INFLUENCE DEFINITIONS

1. See if you are familiar with the various influence concepts by matching the influence term with a statement which relates to it. Place the letter of the influence term in the blank beside the statement describing, illustrating or defining it.

A. sphere of influence
B. direct influence
C. indirect influence
D. organizational influence
E. extensive

F. comprehensive
G. intensive
H. influence-mix
I. responsibility criteria

___ (1) that domain of the sphere of influence which indicates a measure of people being influenced by a person in organizational leadership via both indirect and direct influence means via organizational structures and personal relationships.

___ (2) that domain of the sphere of influence which indicates a measure of people being influenced by a real presence of the leader, in focused and structured situations where feedback between follower and leader is possible and necessary and for which there is high accountability.

___ (3) a term describing the combination of influence elements-- direct, indirect or organizational--in terms of degree and kind at a given point in a development phase.

___ (4) Pastor Paul preaches to 3200 people each Sunday morning.

___ (5) refers to the totality of people being influenced and for whom a leader will give an account to God.

___ (6) that domain of the sphere of influence which indicates a measure of people being influenced by non-time-bound miscellaneous influences a leader exerts through others, through media, through writing, etc. and for which feedback between the leader and by those being influenced is difficult if not impossible and where accountability is primarily for the content of the influencing ideas.

___ (7) Dr. Wagner teaches 400 students in classes each year; he reaches an additional 2 or 3 thousand through seminars and conferences; his 21 books sell in the thousands; he has occasional spots on TV, he is on advisory boards and executive boards of several important organizations, he writes regular articles for several magazines of wide circulation and other articles for other magazines. He is on several international committees which plan strategically to influence evangelism and church planting around the world.

___ (8) 1) time of the influence, 2) presence or absence of the influencer, 3) feedback access of followers, and 4) accountability factors.

___ (9) Jim Jones influence was such that he could demand followers to do almost anything.

___(10) Leaders of isolated communities (such as Amish, etc.) can influence schooling, recreation, family values, or vocational choices.

FEEDBACK ON INFLUENCE DEFINITIONS continued

2. Is there any biblical rationale underlying the general
influence concepts that have been introduced? Jot down any
biblical passages or contexts which bear on influence concepts.
What is the basic thrust of the biblical imperatives?

3. What is your present (or most recent) influence-mix? Indicate
at least the extensiveness of your influence-mix for the three
kinds of influence. Use terms that fit your situation and show
who and how you are influencing in these three domains.

    a. Direct--

    b. Indirect--

    c. Organizational--

4. Where would you place the following kinds activities on
Kauffman' Influence Continuum? A. intense mentoring B. small
group leader C. TV ministry D. writing of a book   E. a mentoree
in active ministry F. teacher G. radio ministry H. preaching
I. writing of an article. Place the letter on the continuum.

```
Highly Indirect  Mostly Indirect Mostly Direct    Highly Direct
|--------------|----------------|----------------|------------|
```

ANSWERS----------
     1.   <u>D</u> (1)   <u>B</u> (2)   <u>H</u> (3)   <u>B,E</u> (4)   <u>A</u> (5)
            <u>C</u> (6) <u>H,E</u> (7)   <u>I</u> (8)   <u>G</u> (9)   <u>F</u> (10)
     2.   The biblical passages dealing either directly or
indirectly with influence concepts include: Luke 10 Parable of
Pounds, Matthew 25 Parable of Talents, Romans 12:3-7
giftedness/capacity, Hebrews 13:17 pointing out accountability
for influence, Acts 20 farewell to Ephesian elders dealing with
accountability, I Peter 1:1-5 dealing with rewards for
leadership, the general judgment passages such as 2 Corinthians
5:10ff (and others). I am sure there are others. These come to
mind readily. The thrust of the biblical rationale behind
influence concepts is twofold: 1) simply that leaders will be
responsible for those they influence; 2) they will be
responsible for developing their potential and using it for God.
The actual influence definitions are not scripturally given and
only are used as helpful aids in understanding and evaluating
thrusts 1) and 2).
     3. I'll not put my own down as it might not be of general
help to readers. Be prepared to share your own analysis in a
group or with an interested person.
    4.

```
Highly Indirect  Mostly Indirect     Mostly Direct  Highly Direct
|---------------|-------------------|-------------|-----------|
E                 D       I           G C     H     F   B      A
```

INFLUENCE CHALLENGE PROCESS ITEM   Symbol: P(ICHG)

introduction   All leaders have capacity to influence. God seeks
                to develop that capacity over a lifetime. When a
                leader has potential for leadership that is not yet
                developed or used, God will eventually challenge,
                providentially, that leader to take steps to
                develop and use that capacity for God's purposes
                and glory. Sometimes a leader is unaware of this
                capacity. God's unusual guidance through people or
                events channels the leader to expand. Often the
                influence challenge process item comes in the form
                of a destiny process item.

definition   The influence challenge process item refers to
                those instances in which a leader is prompted by
                God to take steps to expand leadership capacity in
                terms of sphere of influence.

comment   The influence challenge comes in terms of an
                increase of ones present influence-mix in regards
                to extensiveness, intensiveness or scope. It can
                also come in terms of expanding the influence-mix
                to include new kinds of influence. Or some
                combination of these aspects.

example   The Acts 13:1-4 vignette was an influence challenge
                process item for both Barnabas and Saul. The
                influence-mix was expanded in terms of target
                groups (cross-cultural). The basic kind of
                influence remained direct.

example   The challenge to help encourage the Thessalonian
                church via an epistle was a move toward adding an
                indirect influence thrust to Paul's influence-mix.

example   The use of Titus, Timothy, Epaphroditus and others
                on various ministry tasks to various churches
                illustrate the concept of expansion of influence-
                mix along indirect thrusts.

discernment   It is likely that an influence-mix challenge can
                come, and not be perceived as such, and yet be
                acted upon by the leader in the normal course of
                things. However, awareness of the stretching
                process, and the meeting of God in it by faith, can
                be a significant ministerial formation growth item.

focus   The influence challenge process item is a major way
                that God challenges the Plateau Barrier problem.
                Leaders who have learned some basic skills and have
                had some ministry experience tend to want to rest
                on those abilities and that experience. God, in
                order to continue development, brings along the
                influence challenge process item.

FEEDBACK ON INFLUENCE CHALLENGE PROCESS ITEM

1. Looking back, perhaps you can now identify an influence-mix challenge process item. If so, explain how the challenge came about, the actual expansion in influence-mix, and the leadership development that resulted.

2. Examine again the influence-mix development of A.W. Tozer (see page 225). With nothing more to go on than the information displayed and your own experience of how things happen, can you suggest ways the influence-mix challenge process item may have occurred between any of the sub-phases. Try to guess how at least one influence-mix challenge may have come.

3. As you look to the future what needed influence-mix change do you see for yourself? What might be a way that God would challenge you toward moving into that new influence-mix?

ANSWERS----------
1. For me one influence-mix challenge came when I was designing and implementing a theological education by extension program at the Jamaica Bible College. I was forced to prepare programmed instruction texts (**Puzzles With a Purpose**, a book on the study of parables, came out of this processing). I did not recognize the value of this until much later. My teaching on parables no longer was bound by my presence. This self-study text could communicate the information as well as I could teach it personally. This was my first effort in indirect influence though I did not realize it at the time. I was just solving an everyday ministry problem. Later I was able to profit from the experience and extend it to other applications.
2. For each of the sub-phases in Phase II, I imagine the challenge came through a standard "call" from a pulpit committee. Each of the churches was a bit larger than the previous church. Tozer's pulpit ministry became better with each new church. In the change of influence-mix in Phase III, from the early city phase to the middle city phase, I imagine the challenge came through invitations to speak outside his own church and by requests to put in writing some of what he was teaching and preaching in the pulpit. His increased proficiency in his pulpit ministry probably stimulated some interested groups to finance a radio ministry.
3. For me I see two challenges in the future concerning influence-mix. One is a greater exposure of direct influence to many more people via an expanded seminar and workshop ministry in several countries. I see also a need for a greater indirect influence ministry through writing. The challenges have already come. I see God's challenge and hand in the pressures I am receiving from my peers concerning popular writing and from the promotion system which is forcing me to reflect theoretically and capture my ideas in texts that will influence many.

COMMENTARY ON CHALLENGE CLUSTER

clarifi-
cation on
destiny
incidents
or items

Bertelsen (1985) lists numerous process items or incidents, almost all of which are defined in this manual. The revelatory act, dream/vision, or prophecy are self-evident items especially in light of the previous examples given. One which will not be defined, and perhaps needs clarification, is the destiny insight process item. Destiny insight refers to a sudden clarification in understanding of some ministry focus. It is perceived as coming from God and carrying future implications. Spiritual authority affirmation can be a special case of ministry affirmation or a result of some of the power items. Convergence refers to a time of increased blessing of the Lord in ministry due to a number of factors coming together. (This is explained more fully in chapter 13.)

faith
challenge
not
exclusive

The faith challenge is not limited to leaders who possess the gift of faith. Faith is essential to leadership. Hebrews 11:6 makes this clear. "But without faith it is impossible to please God. He that cometh to God must believe that He is and that He is a rewarder of them that diligently seek Him." However, those with the gift of faith will see faith challenges becoming a habitual part of their ministry.

prayer
challenge
and
discipline
of
solitude

In the New Testament record we do not always see the means of the challenge that God uses but can assume it on the basis of need, for leaders to frequently get alone with God and pray for their ministries. Repeatedly, Christ was confronted with the prayer challenge regarding major decisions or crises in his ministry. His time away from crowds, alone with God, buttressed him and gave vision for future ministry.

prayer
challenge,
major
philosoph-
ical
principle

Samuel, in the closing days of his ministry is reminded of this vital issue and serves as the prototype for leaders. In a final public leadership act Samuel's spiritual authority is vindicated by God. Then comes the prayer challenge with its on-going lesson of responsibility to pray for one's ministry. See I Samuel 12, especially verse 23. A major principle drawn from this passage, and buttressed in the New Testament in many lives of leaders, is this:

**IF GOD CALLS YOU TO A MINISTRY THEN
HE CALLS YOU TO PRAY FOR THAT MINISTRY.**

COMMENTARY ON CHALLENGE CLUSTER continued

ministry
challenge,
explanation
causal
source

The majority of ministry challenges are those that
deal with needs in existing ministry structures.
Usually such challenges are externally given by
leaders perceiving the need. Sometimes they are
internally sensed and self-initiated. Less
frequently an emerging leader internally senses a
need and creates some new structure to meet it.
Self-initiated challenges, whether to meet a need
in an already existing structure or to create a
structure to meet that need, are the watermarks of
leadership. Leaders who are developing in
discernment increasingly manifest this trait. (See
also M.8 Ministry Entry Patterns in chapter 11.)

sphere of
influence,
explanation
Romans 12
metonymy

The phrase "measure of faith" is a figure of speech
called a metonymy ("Faith" stands for gift and
emphasizes the quality of exercising the gift;
"measure" would imply a degree of quantity.) Our
definition "sphere of influence" seeks to capture
this idea. That is, some people will influence
more people with the use of their gifts than will
others. Each is exhorted to make a correct
assessment of themselves, their gifts and
abilities, and to use them for God's glory and the
benefit of Christians. The Stewardship parables
also show differing levels of capacity and
resulting responsibility.

EXPANSION--SPIRITUAL INSIGHTS CLUSTER

introduction   Paul points out in several key places (especially
                 Ephesians 6:12) that the unseen world impacts the
                 seen. Leadership issues are more than what appears
                 on the surface. An expanding leader will be
                 processed in discernment in order to better assess
                 ordinary and superordinary causes. The spiritual
                 insights cluster does this processing.

description   The spiritual insights cluster is comprised of five
                 process items which have a cumulative effect of
                 teaching sensitivity to "behind the scenes
                 activity" of the spirit world on the physical world
                 and enable a leader to influence situations
                 involving these issues. The five process items
                 are: spiritual warfare, power encounter, prayer
                 power, gifted power, and networking power.

Venn Diagram   SPIRITUAL INSIGHTS CLUSTER
of Cluster

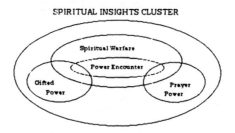

4 major   All of the items require discernment. This
purposes   discernment brings with it,

                 1. development of spiritual authority.
                    Demonstration of God's power is one of the
                    credibility power bases of spiritual authority.
                 2. develops ministerial formation, particularly
                    teaching the leader how to influence in
                    situations concerning the unseen world and its
                    effects.
                 3. expands the leader's power mix. It certainly
                    enlarges spiritual authority and most likely
                    expands competence authority and psychic force.
                 4. forwards the discernment development task that
                    is necessary for competent ministry.

different   Different kinds of discernment are developed.
kinds of   Spiritual warfare and power encounters teach
discernment   ability to discern root causes. Prayer power and
                 gifted power involve discernment of Spirit power in
                 the life of the believer. Networking power
                 requires discernment of God's sovereign activity in
                 human networks to accomplish His purposes.

SPIRITUAL WARFARE PROCESS ITEM Symbol: P(SW)

introduction   Spiritual warfare embraces a wide array of power
                incidents sometimes overlapping with power
                encounters, gifted power, and infrequently
                networking power. Spiritual warfare occurs
                throughout the entire growth ministry time period.
                However, maturity in discernment of spiritual
                warfare processing usually occurs later.
                Discernment is a leadership quality that God seeks
                to develop in a leader during the growth ministry
                phase. It is needed particularly with spiritual
                warfare.

definition   The spiritual warfare process item refers to those
                instances in ministry where the leader discerns
                that ministry conflict is primarily supernatural in
                its source and essence and resorts to various power
                items to solve the problem in such a way that
                leadership capacities, notably spiritual authority,
                is expanded.

example   John 8. Jesus in dialogue with "the Jews." (Note
                especially Jesus' accusations in verses 44ff.)

example   Daniel 10. The angel's explanation to Daniel about
                his delay in answered prayer shows the reality of
                the unseen spiritual warfare that is surrounding
                the physical scene.

example   Matthew 16:22,23. Jesus in admonishing Peter.

example   Acts 5. Peter confronting Ananias and Sapphira.

example   Acts 8. Peter in the incident with Simon.

example   Acts 13:6-12. Paul's confrontation with Elymas the
                magician.

example   Acts 16. Paul's confrontation with the slave girl
                who predicted future happenings via demonic
                knowledge.

causal   Spirit activity, good and evil, are involved in the
                spiritual warfare and power encounter process
                items. Holy Spirit activity is directly involved
                in gifted power and prayer power. Indirect
                sovereign activity of the Holy Spirit is involved
                in networking power.

patterns   The following patterns are affected by this
                cluster: M.7 Spiritual Authority pattern, M.6
                Giftedness Development, M.8 Ministry Entry
                (sometimes), UM.2 Upward Development, UM.1
                Reflective/ formative Evaluation (sometimes).

FEEDBACK ON SPIRITUAL WARFARE PROCESS ITEM

1. Choose 1 or 2 of the following. Glance at the scripture relating to them. Then answer these questions. What was discerned indicating that it was spiritual warfare? How was it discerned (if it is given or implied)? What was the result of the spiritual warfare process item--immediate? long-term?

a. John 8. Jesus in dialogue with "the Jews." Note especially Jesus' accusations in verses 44ff.
b. Daniel 10. The angel's explanation to Daniel about his delayed answer to prayer.
c. Matthew 16:22,23. Jesus in admonishing Peter.
d. Acts 5. Peter confronting Ananias and Sapphira
e. Acts 8. Peter in the incident with Simon.
f. Acts 13:6-12. Paul's confrontation with Elymas the magician.
g. Acts 16. Paul's confrontation with the slave girl who predicted future happenings via demonic knowledge.

2. According to Ephesians 6:10-20 what is the main sources of discovering spiritual warfare and means for overcoming it?

3. Give an example of a spiritual warfare process item in your own life with particular attention to the expansion of your leadership capacity via the whole process.

ANSWERS----------

1. c. Matthew 16:22,23. What was discerned? Jesus saw in a statement from Peter which could well have been a statement of genuine concern for Jesus' behalf the insertion of a Satanic thought--that of persuasion away from the cross and suffering entailed in it. How was it discerned? We do not know but something like word of knowledge in conjunction with discernings of spirits was obviously working. What was the result of the spiritual warfare immediately? Satan was rebuked; Peter corrected. The cross and suffering ahead plainly faced. Long term? Believers are cautioned that thoughts and spoken words may be influenced by spirit beings. Hence, we must be careful of our thoughts and words. And we must be attune to the Spirit's promptings as we hear others talk.

2. Paul is advocating the power of spirit-led praying both as a weapon in spiritual warfare and as a means for sensitizing ourselves to discerning spiritual warfare.

3. I'll leave confirmation for this one to discussion in a small group or with a friend.

POWER PROCESS ITEMS   Symbol: general meaning any one, P(PI)

introduction   At some time or other during growth ministry processing, usually toward the middle or latter part of the phase, a leader will question his/her own ministry concerning power. The power quest or search for power in one's ministry seems to be a frequent process item. Power lessons will be learned. Sometimes they will be in regards to gifted power, prayer (fasting) power, power in spiritual warfare, or power encounters to demonstrate and authenticate God's working in the ministry. Power process items, is sometimes used as a label to cover any of the individual power items or other incidents involving power which are not so easy to categorize.

definition   Power items refer to those demonstrations of God's intervention which convinces followers that God is indeed supporting the leader in the ministry for which the leader is responsible.

definition

symbol:
P(PE)

The power encounter process item represents a crisis ministry situation in which there is confrontation between people representing God and people representing other supernatural forces in which the power is the determining issue, God's credibility is at stake, and vindication is made by an unusual demonstration of God's power.

definition

symbol:
P(PP)

The prayer power process item involves the specific instance of the use of specific prayer to meet a situation in such a way that it is clear that God has answered the prayer and demonstrated the authenticity of the leader's spiritual authority.

definition

symbol:
P(GP)

The gifted power process item involves the specific instance of the use of a spiritual gift in which it is clear that the Holy Spirit is channeling power in terms of the use of the gift.

definition

symbol:
P(NP)

The networking power process item is the unusual use by God of mentors, divine contacts, or other related leaders, to channel power in order to open doors or accomplish influence goals for a leader so that the leader senses the importance of relationships with other leaders and knows the touch of God through networks of people.

O.T.
examples

Power encounter: Jephthah (Judges 11:14-28 pre-conditions, 11:32-33.); Samuel (I Samuel 7:10,11 Prayer power); Elijah on Mt. Carmel

POWER PROCESS ITEMS continued

example Pauline	Power encounter: See Acts 13:6-12 for Paul illustration
example	Prayer power: See I Samuel 12 for Samuel illustration. Samuel was a man of prayer. His prayer released power into his ministry. One of the finest examples of spiritual authority being backed by release of power is the answer to Samuel's prayer in I Sam 12:18.
example	Gifted power: See Acts 11:27,28; Agabus prophecy.
example	Gifted power: Acts 14:8-13; Paul heals cripple.
example	Networking Power: See Acts 9:25-27 Barnabas links Paul to Jewish Christianity.
causal	God's direct release of power may come through giftedness, a powerful prayer life, spiritual warfare, or power encounters. His indirect release of power often comes through networking.
distinction, gifted power	Giftedness when referring to power usually means the miraculous sign gifts. However, it can also mean the use of non-miraculous spiritual gifts with unusual power manifested.
order property, two power patterns	A leader's experience with each of the power items usually has with it a two-fold pattern. Power pattern 1 is the **temporary acquisition pattern.** Power pattern 2 is the **confident usage pattern.** The "temporary acquisition" pattern is as follows: 1) not aware of or at least have no need for 2) recognition of need for 3) situation forcing a seeking for 4) insightful moment when God meets the leader with the particular power item 5) return to normal status. The "confident usage pattern" is as follows: 1) constantly aware of need for power 2) insightful moment when God prompts for usage of power followed by 3) confident acceptance of power item by faith 4) God's channeling of the power for situation. Power items describe the "insightful moments" when God meets the leader with power to meet the situation's need. Usually the temporary acquisition pattern is repeated several times before a leader begins to move in power pattern 2. It is not clear how closely these power items are correlated to power gifts. Apparently some leaders not manifesting power gifts regularly move in terms of the power items as well as those who have power gifts which stimulate use of pattern 2.

FEEDBACK ON POWER PROCESS ITEMS

1. What major power lesson was learned in the power demonstration of Acts 5:1-13?

2. What category of power process item is represented in the Matthew 4:1-11?
___ a. gifted power   ___ b. prayer power
___ c. spiritual warfare   ___ d. power encounter

3. What category of power process item is represented in Mark 9:14-29?
___ a. gifted power   ___ b. prayer power
___ c. spiritual warfare   ___ d. power encounter

4. What function of power is described by Paul in I Corinthians 2:1-5?

5. Give an example of any one power item incident from your personal ministry or observation of another leader.

6. In what area(s) of ministry have you either already sought power from God? In what area(s) are you presently seeking God for power? What will you need to move further into competent ministry?
___ a. gifted power   ___ b. prayer power
___ c. spiritual warfare   ___ d. power encounter

ANSWERS----------

    1. The lesson concerned integrity in the inner life and the discipline of God where integrity is concerned. God's leaders must be able to discipline in power.
    2. c. spiritual warfare
    3. b. prayer power (see Mark 9:29) c. spiritual warfare
    4. Authentication of Paul's spiritual authority. Evidently the power was giftedness and validated Paul's message.
    5. Your choice
    6. I have sought a. gifted power (not miraculous giftedness, but power in the gift-mix I have. I have been seeing the power of God increasingly released through my gift-mix.) and b. prayer power (I am also exploring the combination of fasting and praying--I have identified 5 major kinds of fasts and have already experientially learned about one of them.)

COMMENTARY ON EXPANSION--SPIRITUAL INSIGHTS CLUSTER

spiritual
warfare
principle

PHYSICAL SITUATIONS MAY WELL BE CAUSED OR CONTROLLED OR INSTIGATED BY SPIRITUAL BEINGS. See Ephesians 6:10-20 especially verses 12. See also I John 4:1-3 where it is clear that the source of teaching may be spirit beings.

balance
principle,
spiritual
warfare

Two cautions must be heeded concerning this process item: 1) Don't underestimate the amount of spiritual warfare behind apparent physical situations. 2) Don't overestimate the amount of spiritual warfare behind every situation. Leaders can easily go to either extreme.

spiritual
warfare,
discernment
not ex-
clusive

This process item occurs with leaders regardless of whether or not they possess discernings of spirits as a spiritual gift. Those with that gift will see spiritual warfare process items becoming a normal part of their activity.

spiritual
insights
cluster,
awareness

Plotted on the process awareness continuum, prayer power and power encounters occur far to the left (high sovereign intervention); spiritual warfare and gifted power toward the left (sovereign intervention acknowledged); networking power is to the left of center (sovereign/providential mid-point).

classic
power
encounter,
6 stages

A power encounter refers to a special test in which God is on trial as to His reality or power. A classic power encounter has several elements as follows:

   1. A crisis between people representing God and others.
   2. There must be a recognition that the issue is one of power/confrontation in the supernatural realm.
   3. There must be public recognition of the pre-encounter terms (If...then...).
   4. There is an actual crisis/confrontation event (the more public usually the better will be the aftermath).
   5. There must be confirmation that God has done the delivering as the power encounter resolves.
   6. Celebration to bring closure and insure continuation of God's purposes in the power event is helpful.

prayer
power and
fasting

Mature leaders usually are people with an effective prayer life who can move people by moving God in prayer. Frequently, fasting is a means of release of power both via prayer and in and of itself.

SUMMARY ON SPIRITUAL INSIGHTS PROCESSING

This chapter has suggested that a competent leader is one who has developed discernment. **Discernment** will come from any given process item whenever a leader has a learning posture. But beyond normal development of discernment, God uses the spiritual insights cluster to stretch a leader's discernment.

The **SPIRITUAL WARFARE** and **POWER ENCOUNTER** process items teach a leader how to discern spiritual activity behind human actions and situations. The **GIFTED POWER** process item teaches a leader to confidently use power with elements of his/her giftedness set. Confident use depends upon an attitude that discerns God's working through giftedness. **PRAYER POWER** teaches a leader how to discern the divine initiative in prayer, how to sense God's timing in a situation, and how to release God's power into a given situation via intercession alone. **NETWORKING POWER** teaches a most subtle type of discernment. God providentially works though relationships with other people. Power can be released via linking a leader with resources, timely advice, opportune situations, and knowledge. People are often the bridge that God uses to take a leader to a new level of power.

The overall effect of the spiritual insights cluster is to produce a confident effective leader. The processing expands the leader's power base. He/she can use spiritual authority with a greater effect than ever before. Discernment brings with it power which is released into ministry.

Competent ministry will require power. A leader's experience with each of the power items usually follows two patterns.

Power pattern 1. Temporary Acquisition Pattern

The temporary acquisition pattern is as follows:

1. not aware of or at least have no need for special use of power,
2. recognition of need for,
3. situation forcing a seeking for,
4. insightful moment when God meets the leader with the particular power item,
5. return to normal status.

Power pattern 2. Confident Usage Pattern

The confident usage pattern is as follows:

1. constantly aware of need for power,
2. insightful moment when God prompts for usage of power followed by,
3. confident acceptance of power item by faith,
4. God's channeling of the power for situation.

SOME FINDINGS ON GROWTH MINISTRY PROCESSING--AS A WHOLE

A Discernment Problem

One significant discernment problem that can be a barrier to expansion involves the spiritual warfare process item. I call it the two-fold spiritual warfare problem. Much of the Christian life involves maintaining balance in two opposite tensions (kingdom now, kingdom then; position in Christ, practice in Christ; Christian freedom, Christian discipline; doing, being; sovereignty of God, human responsibility, etc.). One such dynamic tension is captured in this problem.

> **THE TWO-FOLD SPIRITUAL WARFARE PROBLEM**
> Leaders must learn discernment with regards to spiritual warfare. Two poles of divergent attitude/actions must be avoided. (1) The tendency to blame all conflict and problems on spiritual warfare; (2) The tendency to see nothing of spiritual warfare in the conflict and problems of ministry.

Major Lessons Focused On By These Two Clusters

Four of the major lessons of leadership are touched upon by the processing of the ordinary and pressure expansion clusters.

1. Learning   **EFFECTIVE LEADERS, AT ALL LEVELS, MAINTAIN A**
   Posture   **LEARNING POSTURE THROUGHOUT LIFE.**

Discernment is the climactic step of the learning process. A learning posture indicates a predisposition to want to learn. Discernment involves bringing closure to that learning bent and thus making it productive. Discernment is a major trait developed by the challenge and spiritual insights cluster.

2. Spiritual   **EFFECTIVE LEADERS INCREASINGLY VALUE SPIRITUAL**
   Authority   **AUTHORITY AS THEIR DOMINANT POWER BASE.**

Spiritual authority is essentially an experiential power base. That is, a leader's power resources for spiritual authority are intimately tied to his/her experiences with God. Three major credibility power bases underlying spiritual authority: 1. demonstration of power, 2. demonstration of character, 3. demonstration of knowledge of God and His ways. The challenge cluster focuses on developing aspect 3. The spiritual insights cluster focuses on developing aspect 1. These clusters will significantly expand a leader's spiritual authority.

4. Ministry   **EFFECTIVE LEADERS WHO ARE PRODUCTIVE OVER A**
   Philosophy   **LIFETIME HAVE A DYNAMIC MINISTRY PHILOSOPHY WHICH**
                EVOLVES CONTINUALLY FROM THE INTERPLAY OF THREE
                MAJOR FACTORS: BIBLICAL DYNAMICS, PERSONAL
                GIFTEDNESS, AND SITUATIONAL DYNAMICS.

5. Sense of   **EFFECTIVE LEADERS EVINCE A GROWING AWARENESS OF**
   Destiny   **THEIR SENSE OF DESTINY.**

     The challenge cluster deepens a leader's sense of destiny.
All of its items carry a touch of destiny. Some are more
immediate to a given situation. Some are long term. But all
move a leader forward in awareness of an ultimate contribution
for God.

Four Development Tasks

     At least two different approaches could be taken in
analyzing growth ministry. The first is to group process items
occurring throughout and identify what development tasks they
accomplish. That has been my approach. I have identified
**testing clusters, personal development clusters, people insight
clusters,** and four types of **expansion clusters: ordinary,
pressure, challenge** and **spiritual insights.** I have identified
the process items of each of these clusters and shown what each
process item does individually. And I have suggested a more
cumulative effect of the cluster taken as a whole.

     A second approach I could have taken involves analysis of
the entire growth ministry period for major development tasks
followed by identification of any individual process items which
add to development of the task. If I were to use this approach I
would identify **four cyclic tasks** which repeatedly occur throughout
growth ministry: the **entry task,** the **training task,** the
relational task, the **discernment task.**

     Analysis of the growth ministry period as a whole shows that
entry is the first task that must be accomplished. Once a leader
has entered ministry there follows training which enables some
stabilization in ministry. Then if the leader is to increase in
influence effectiveness he/she must learn the importance of
relationships with people. Finally, leaders mature in
discernment. Now these tasks overlap in time but do generally
follow the order I have suggested.

     But not only must God develop a leader in these basic areas
over the entire growth ministry period, He must also repeat this
cycle at a lesser level in each significant new ministry
assignment or challenge. The tree diagram which follows, Figure
7-1, groups process items in terms of their dominant focus in
regards to these four tasks.

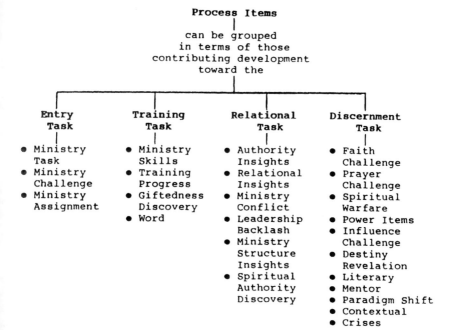

Process Items

can be grouped
in terms of those
contributing development
toward the

Entry Task	Training Task	Relational Task	Discernment Task
• Ministry Task	• Ministry Skills	• Authority Insights	• Faith Challenge
• Ministry Challenge	• Training Progress	• Relational Insights	• Prayer Challenge
• Ministry Assignment	• Giftedness Discovery	• Ministry Conflict	• Spiritual Warfare
	• Word	• Leadership Backlash	• Power Items
		• Ministry Structure Insights	• Influence Challenge
		• Spiritual Authority Discovery	• Destiny Revelation
			• Literary
			• Mentor
			• Paradigm Shift
			• Contextual
			• Crises

Transitioning From Growth Ministry

Some leaders do not ever progress beyond growth ministry processing. Three kinds of patterns explain this situation.

1) **The Abbreviated Entry (Drop Out) Pattern**
   People in this pattern do not negotiate the entry into ministry successfully and opt out of serving in leadership responsibilities. A large number of would be leaders fail last beyond one or two ministry assignments.

2) **Plateaued Leaders Pattern**
   This pattern refers to those who plateau at some level of ministry competency and show relatively little growth in ministerial or spiritual formation. They fail to respond well to the expansion clusters.

3) **Disciplined Leaders Pattern**
   This pattern describes those who are disciplined and thus constrained in ministry or set completely aside from it. Failure in character processing brings on this pattern.

Progress beyond growth ministry into unique ministry requires positive response to the expansion clusters, as well as the deep processing and guidance clusters to be discussed in the next chapter.

(This page deliberately left blank)

CHAPTER 8. PROCESSING TOWARD UNIQUE MINISTRY

Overview

Chapter 4 discussed foundational processing which leads up to transition into full time Christian leadership. Chapter 5 picked up at that point and discussed early ministry processing and its effects on the growth of an emerging leader. Chapter 6 touched on the processes that God uses in the routine of ministry and the special pressures of ministry which serve to expand a leader. Chapter 7 pointed out special discernment process items that God uses to expand a leader. Such processing often moves a leader from the provisional stage of growth ministry to the competent stage. These chapters taken together show how a leader progresses into full time Christian leadership and becomes a competent leader. This chapter first looks at processes that occur throughout the whole growth ministry period and provide guidance for that leader on his/her road to competency. Second, it points out processes that focus on maturity which eventually will transition the leader into a **unique ministry.**

Preview

Two clusters of process items are discussed: the **Guidance Cluster** and the **Maturity Cluster.**

Daily or routine guidance comes via normal guidance means along with many of the expansion process items. Unusual guidance, for exceptional situations, comes via the **guidance cluster.** It is this cluster that will mark milestones along the overall guidance path. This cluster will also give assurance that the leader is moving along God's destiny for him/her. Three sub-clusters representing various different functions in guidance make up the guidance cluster. The **Confirmation Sub-cluster** is God's surety guidance for critical junctures, usually occurring early in the growth ministry period. Such guidance may occur only a very few times in a leader's whole life. But when it does, it is at an important crossroad when a major choice must be made. The **Assurance Sub-Cluster** is God's approval of progress. It will occur many times in a leader's life and will give a sense of continuity and rejuvenation often when most needed or in preparation for a time of need to come. The **Negative Sub-cluster** will occur usually early or at junctures where change in ministry is needed. It uses negative experiences to teach dependence upon God in guidance.

Personal guidance processing in a leader's life paves the way for the leader to get corporate guidance for ministry. Vision from God is an essential ingredient for a leader. Learning to hear from God on personal decision making is a basic leadership skill which bridges a leader to exercise responsibility in getting vision for others.

The **maturity cluster** deepens a leaders walk with God. Two sub-clusters describe this time of processing. The **deep processing sub-cluster** describes three major kinds of chisels that chip away at a leader to shape him/her into a finished product. All of these teach dependence upon God. All are negative in terms of how the leader will experience them. Leaders would not normally choose these processes. But these are the deep processes ordained by God to form leadership character and bring about a paradigm shift.[1] Leaders must see that ultimately, effectiveness in leadership flows out of being. Character formation results highlight this deep processing.

A second sub-cluster of the **maturity cluster** deals with maturing in discernment. The leader who moves into unique ministry must not only have a character for it but also must operate effectively at the capacity for which he/she is gifted. The **convergence sub-cluster** gives insights to a leader that enable effective ministry. Questions such as: What role fits "who the leader is" in giftedness and being? What kind of influence should the leader have? Who should be influenced? are answered by the convergence sub-cluster.

Taken together, the guidance cluster and maturity cluster, accomplish two big goals. They prompt a leader toward fulfilling challenge 1 and toward experientially learning lesson five.

WHEN CHRIST CALLS LEADERS TO CHRISTIAN MINISTRY HE INTENDS TO DEVELOP THEM TO THEIR FULL POTENTIAL. EACH LEADER IS RESPONSIBLE TO CONTINUE DEVELOPING IN ACCORDANCE WITH GOD'S PROCESSING ALL HIS/HER LIFE.

EFFECTIVE LEADERS EVINCE A GROWING AWARENESS OF THEIR SENSE OF DESTINY.

These clusters test the reality of the living God in the leader's life.

Chapter 8 is the final chapter on the processing variable. For that reason I will include a final section which reviews the processing variable and adds some further information concerning other clusters and the nature of a process item.

----

[1]The transition from the growth ministry time period to the unique ministry time period requires a paradigm shift. During growth ministry, processing focuses on ministerial formation. Spiritual formation and strategic formation are important but secondary. The thrust of development is toward ministerial competency. "Doing" is in focus. As a leader becomes more competent in doing, the cumulative effect of processing, in general, on spiritual and strategic formation and the special effect of deep processing brings about a subtle shift in the basis of ministry. The leader moves from a "doing" base where success is uppermost to a "being" base where character and ultimate purpose are more important. That is, ministry flows out of being. Spiritual formation and strategic formation now become primary with ministerial formation secondary.

THE GUIDANCE CLUSTER

introduction   A leader is a person with God-given capacity and
God-given responsibility who is influencing a group
of followers towards God's purposes for the group.
The central element of this definition of a leader
is influencing toward God's purposes. Leaders must
know how to get corporate guidance for the groups
they are leading. How do they do that? The basic
guidance pattern is simple. A leader first learns
about personal guidance for his/her own life.
Having learned to discern God's direction for
his/her own life in numerous crucial decisions, the
leader can then shift to the leadership function of
determining guidance for the group that is being
led. I assume that much guidance will come through
one's on-going, obedient, daily walk with God. The
guidance process items given here are beyond these
routine aspects. They are unusual guidance means,
not the norm. The guidance cluster contains eight
process items which heighten a leader's discernment
for guidance.

description   The guidance cluster refers to the set of eight
process items which occur throughout growth
ministry processing and provide benchmarks by which
a leader is assured of God's continued guidance in
his/her development.

Venn Diagram

SOVEREIGN GUIDANCE

essential   All of these guidance items assume the intervention
character-   of the living unseen God in the lives of leaders at
istic   special points in their lives to provide external
                guidance for leadership.

major   1. Give certainty guidance on critical decisions.
purposes   2. Give assurance that the leader as a person is
                   pleasing God.
                3. Give assurance that the leader's ministry is
                   pleasing God.
                4. Give indications that a change in ministry
                   assignment is imminent.
                5. Give discernment lessons on the aspects of God's
                   will (what, how, when).

FOUR IMPORTANT GENERAL GUIDANCE FACTORS

introduction   The biblical thrust in guidance is moral guidance
and not decision-making guidance. The majority of
admonitions toward guidance reflect conduct for
living. A basic framework for viewing guidance is
given in the following diagram first introduced to
me by Frank Sells, one of my Bible college
instructors. A daily obedient walk with God will
allow for guidance to come via these four channels.
Those Seeking **GUIDANCE** must learn to discern God's
voice via these basic guidance channels.

GOD'S VOICE IN CIRCUMSTANCES	GOD'S VOICE IN THE HEART	GOD'S VOICE IN THE CHURCH
G O D ' S V O I C E IN T H E W O R D		

circumstances   Christians use the the phrases "open doors" and
"closed doors" to indicate that God sovereignly or
providentially controls circumstances to give
direction concerning guidance. Open doors mean:
special opportunities appear; something becomes
available at a timely moment; the way to do
something is clear and unhindered. Closed doors
mean: the opportunity to do something is not
available; something desired becomes unavailable;
the way to do something is blocked.

the heart   Christians use the phrase "God's voice in the
heart" to mean convictions or feelings or desires
assumed to be from God.

the Church   The Church, in this diagram, stands for counsel
from Christians as corporate groups to whom the
believer is responsible as well as individual
believers who can give wise counsel.

the Word   The Word is used here to mean both the written Word
and revelatory Word. Hearing God's voice in the
written Word means knowing and applying Bible truth
on a given guidance matter. This will include
guidance drawn from direct teaching on the matter,
principles derived from teaching and illustration,

FOUR IMPORTANT GENERAL GUIDANCE FACTORS   continued

and/or the sensing of God intending a specific
message to be personally applied upon reading a
passage concerning its relevance to a situation.
Revelatory Word means the direct intervention of
God to give a special word of application or
clarification on a situation. Such words may be
given directly to the believer (audible, sensed
inwardly, dreams, visions, angelic visitations, or
by impression) or may come via some of the
spontaneous word gifts such as word of knowledge,
word of wisdom, word of faith, or prophecy.

caution   God's voice in the written Word is foundational. A
word   revelatory Word should never contradict the written
                 Word. Revelatory word for major decisions should
                 be confirmed. Once confirmed, revelatory word and
                 written word are foundational and carry priority
                 over the superstructural factors.

caution   Circumstances can be engendered both by God and
circum-   Satan. Major decisions should never be made on
stances   circumstances alone. However, timely circumstances
                 do give a tremendous boost to confidence especially
                 when one is praying along the exact lines and the
                 circumstance happens.

caution   What God is saying to us inwardly must be tested.
the heart   The desires of the heart can not always be trusted.
                 What we think God is saying may be confused with
                 what we wish He would say. Inner convictions must
                 be honored unless they violate biblical
                 principles--that is a major biblical principle.

caution   While we want to take every advantage of what God
Church   has taught others, we must remember that we alone
                 will be responsible for our decisions. Where
                 counsel shows biblical principle, of course, we
                 need to take that in to account. And in general,
                 we will heed wise counsel. But others are not
                 responsible for understanding God's will for us.

basic   Normally major decisions should not have any
guideline   contradictions between guidance via the different
                 factors. On some decisions there may be silence
                 from some of the factors. But at least there
                 shouldn't be contradictions. If there are, wait
                 for clarification. In fact, a safe guideline is
                 this. **On major decisions the guidance via all the
                 factors should line up and confirm each other.**

normal/   Most guidance comes via this model. Leaders will,
unusual   however, need unusual direction via the Guidance
                 cluster.

GENERAL SOVEREIGN GUIDANCE PROCESS ITEM   symbol: P(SG)

introduction   Sometimes God gives guidance even more directly by divine revelation, or circumstantially blocking alternatives until the way to go is clear. We title this more direct intervention in the guidance process of a leader as sovereign guidance.

definition   Sovereign guidance is the general category of guidance which refers both to the superintending of God over a leader's guidance as well as the direct intervention of God into a leader's guidance choices through divine revelation or circumstantial arrangement of affairs and events so that it is unmistakably clear that God is directing.

example   In Genesis 12:1-3 we see divine revelation as God's direct intervention into the guidance process for Abraham.

example   In Genesis 24:12-67 (see especially verses 12-14) God providentially directs circumstances as Abraham's servant selects Rebecca.

example   Repeatedly in the life of Moses, God gave divine revelation to guide Moses as he led the people.

example   Guideon's fleece in Judges 6:36-40 is an example of divine guidance.

example   In Acts 8:26 Phillip received sovereign guidance concerning witnessing to the Ethiopian Eunuch.

example   In Acts 9 God's direct intervention channeled Paul into a life of ministry. His direct revelation to Paul to go unto the Gentiles became the touchstone for all that Paul did.

example   Acts 16:6-10 contains 3 different sovereign guidance instances.

inclusive   All the guidance items would fall under the category of sovereign guidance as special cases of it. When an item of guidance is significant to leadership development and does not fit one of the labels given in this chapter we use the generic designation--sovereign guidance. In attempting to identify guidance cluster process items use the specific items where they fit. If something does not essentially fit under one of the seven specific items (divine contact, double confirmation, divine affirmation, ministry affirmation, destiny fulfillment, negative preparation, flesh act) then use the general category sovereign guidance.

NEGATIVE PREPARATION PROCESS ITEM   symbol: P(NEG)

introduction Someone has said that while it may appear that the grass is always greener on the other side of the fence, in fact, it is really brown on both sides of the fence. A frequently seen process item, particularly in the boundary conditions between development phases, is the guidance process item called negative preparation. God often prepares someone to accept the next steps of guidance by first allowing them to go through negative experiences during their present development phase. The negative experiences make the "grass look greener" and often gives a high motivational incentive to move on and seek the next thing God has. Without the negative processing many would be satisfied to stay and not move on to develop, expand, or to sense God's next steps.

definition Negative preparation refers to the special processing which involves God's use of events, people, conflict, persecution, or experiences, all focusing on the negative, so as to free up a person from the situation in order to enter the next phase of development with a new abandonment and revitalized interest.

example The pre-Exodus persecution made the Israelites open to Moses leadership and promise of deliverance.

example See Exodus 13:17,18 for God's special use of this processing.

example Hannah's experience in I Samuel 1. Hannah was willing to give Samuel into the Lord's service, which was God's means of raising up a prophet/judge--transitional leadership into the kingdom phase of Israel.

example Robert C. McQuilkin's (founder of Columbia Bible College) transition from Development Phase II (Organizational Leadership Training) to Development Phase III (Implementing a Life Vision--Threefold Thrust) involved negative preparation.

uses 1. Signal a boundary phase.
2. Give release to move to a new development sub-phase or phase.
3. Point out limitations of influence-mix or role.
4. Point out areas of needed maturity.

timing Negative preparation occurs most frequently in early growth ministry and occasionally in latter growth ministry time period. As a leader matures in character and skills it is less frequent.

NEGATIVE PREPARATION PROCESS ITEM continued

kinds
1. Dissatisfaction with inner-life.
2. Dissatisfaction with present role.
3. Isolation--self-reflection.
4. Conflict with other Christian workers.
5. Problems in marriage relationships.
6. Problems with children.
7. Crisis in job or ministry.
8. Limiting possibilities thwarting sphere of influence development.
9. Limiting possibilities thwarting role.
10. Adverse living conditions in a given geographic area.
11. Sickness due to geographic conditions.

causal
1. Self-initiated (dissatisfaction).
2. Relational problems--people engendered (wife, husband, children, co-workers, nationals, followers, unbelievers).
3. Job related causes--long term development is limited.

discernment guideline
Negative preparation for guidance can easily be confused with negative processing to deepen character. James 1:2-4 shows that negative experiences often are used to mature character. A guideline for discernment: All negative processing is used to mature character; some is also used to give release for a new assignment. Do not move until character processing is appreciated and guidance is clearly confirmed. Or to give the guideline in another way: Don't just use negative processing as a scapegoat to move on to something else.

FEEDBACK ON NEGATIVE PREPARATION PROCESS ITEM

1. Which of the following represents a corporate application of the negative preparation process item?
    ___ a. Acts 10
    ___ b. Acts 8:1
    ___ c. John 1:48,49
    ___ d. none of the above

2. Which of the following is an example of negative preparation which resulted in guidance that significantly affected church history?
    ___ a. Acts 2:1-4
    ___ b. Acts 6:1-6
    ___ c. Acts 15:36-41
    ___ d. none of the above

3. Consider again the purposes behind use of process items.

    Processing is used by God to,
    ___ A. indicate leadership potential,
    ___ B. develop that potential,
    ___ C. confirm appointment to a role/ responsibility,
    ___ D. move the leader along to God's appointed ministry
         level for the realized potential.

Negative preparation process items would most likely be used in conjunction with which of the foci of this definition. Check any which apply.

4. Give a personal experience with a negative preparation process item used in your life for guidance. Indicate which components were in focus. Identify kind, use, and causal source.

ANSWERS----------
    1. b.
    2. c.
    3. All of them, though B and D will probably have the majority of negative preparation process items.
    4. My own conflict with a leader in my mission made me open to inner-life growth (B) and my need for a role (D) which would allow further development of my sphere of influence.

FLESH ACT PROCESS ITEM   symbol: P(FLESH)

introduction   Learning to discern the voice of God can be a
                difficult process when seeking His guidance during
                difficult situations. The flesh act process item
                teaches discernment via negative experience, a most
                valuable reflective process. Using hindsight can be
                a valuable process through which God teaches us to
                recognize His direction and guidance. The flesh
                act can be seen most clearly in cases where we
                presume guidance and move ahead of God. Another
                common instance of the flesh act process item is
                where we have a part of God's guidance but not the
                complete picture (like what we are to do but not
                when we do it or how we do it). We often try to
                help God work things out.

definition   A flesh act refers to those instances in a leader's
                life where guidance is presumed and decisions are
                made either hastily or without proper discernment
                of God's choice. Such decisions usually involve the
                working out of guidance by the leader using some
                human manipulation or other means and which brings
                ramifications which later negatively affect
                ministry and life.

example   See Genesis 16. Previously, God had promised Abram
                and Sarah that they would bear a son and be parents
                to a nation. For over twenty years this promise
                from God was not fulfilled. Sarah had a plan. Sarah
                had an Egyptian maid named Hagar. Sarah sent Hagar
                to Abraham that she might bear them a child. Hagar
                conceived and bore a son--Ishmael. This practice
                though culturally acceptable in that era was not
                God's plan. Later in his own way God did fulfill
                the promise. Negative ramifications from this
                flesh act are still with us today.

example   Joshua's treaty with the Gibeonites in Joshua 9.
                Notice in verse 14, that they did not consult the
                Lord about it.

guidelines   1. "What," "when," and "how" are all important
                   facets of guidance. Certainty on one or two
                   without the other(s) often leads to presumption
                   about the other(s) and to a flesh act.
                2. Presumptuous faith (assuming God will do
                   something that He has not communicated to a
                   leader) can lead to a flesh act.
                3. Taking action (in major decision times) without
                   consulting God often results in a flesh act.
                4. Failing to act according to sovereign guidance
                   which has been given and choosing an alternative
                   to what God has communicated is also classified
                   as a flesh act.

FEEDBACK ON FLESH ACT PROCESS ITEM

1. Examine the flesh act of Joshua 9. What guidance lessons do you think Joshua learned in retrospect?

2. Give here some other biblical example of a flesh act process item. Point out one or two lessons seen in it.

3. A synonym for a "flesh act" could be a "presumptuous faith act." What do you see connoted by that label that is not necessarily implied by "flesh act?"

4. Give here, if you can some flesh act process item that you have personally experienced or seen in the life of some leader. What have you learned from this item?

ANSWERS----------

1. One lesson: Everyday affairs are fraught with appearances which are not what they seem like. Two, When we are following hard after God on something He has clearly revealed for us to do we can expect detractions to occur. We can not presume to understand them but must analyze them in the light of the clear guidance we are following.
2. Hezekiah in Isaiah 39. He entertained the messengers from Babylon and showed him all his wealth and military equipment. Isaiah rebuked Hezekiah in verse 5-8 with a word from the Lord condemning this seemingly innocent action. Lesson one: Everyday affairs can lead to flesh acts if we are not alert and discerning in our actions. Lesson two: Pride (like wanting to show our accomplishments or boast of our possessions.) can lead to flesh acts.
3. It describes a condition where a leader presumes that he/she knows the "what" of the guidance but in fact is wrong.
4. I'll reserve this one for sharing with the class.

DIVINE CONTACT PROCESS ITEM symbol: P(DC)

introduction   At the "right moment" God brings across the path of developing leaders just what is needed such as a tract which challenges or explains some truth, a book which gives new perspectives, or a person who will be greatly used by God in that leader's life. All of these fall under the general category of Guidance Process Items. The divine contact process item refers to the unusual way that God brings people of significance across a leader's path at the right time.

definition   A <u>divine</u> contact is a **person** whom God brings in contact with leader at a crucial moment in a development phase in order to accomplish one or more of the following (or a related function):
1. to affirm leadership potential,
2. to encourage leadership potential,
3. to give guidance on a special issue,
4. to give insights which may give guidance indirectly (e.g. broadens the leader),
5. to challenge the leader God-ward (indirect guidance--a move toward leadership committal),
6. to open a door to a ministry opportunity,
7. other similar purpose which helps the emerging leader make guidance decisions.

example   Barnabas, Paul's divine contact (Acts 9:27, 11:25)

example   Peter was a divine contact for Cornelius (Acts 10)

example   Paul, divine contact for Timothy, Priscilla and Aquila, and a host of others.

timing   Divine contacts appear throughout all time periods but are especially prevalent early on in ministry or transition to ministry. Some divine contacts are interwoven into the lives of leaders and will reappear at needed times. Sometimes the relationship is mutual and each helps the other.

causal source   Leaders, because of their ability to influence, need to recognize that they often will be divine contacts for others they meet. They should be especially sensitive to the Holy Spirit's use of them as divine contacts and recognize this special way of influencing.

special divine contact, mentor   The mentor is a special kind of divine contact used to help encourage the developmental process of a leader or potential leader. Guidance may be given but the main focus is facilitating development and expanding the leader. Hence, it is categorized with the expansion process items.

FEEDBACK ON DIVINE CONTACT PROCESS ITEM

1. Look at Acts 18:24-28.

a. Identify its purpose (check the appropriate items).
____ (1) To affirm leadership potential.
____ (2) To encourage leadership potential.
____ (3) To give guidance on a special issue.
____ (4) To give insights which may give guidance indirectly (e.g. broadens the leader),
____ (5) To challenge the leader God-ward (indirect guidance--move toward leadership committal),
____ (6) To open a door to ministry opportunity.
____ (7) other similar purpose which helps the emerging leader make guidance decisions.

b. Describe the divine contact process item seen in Acts 18:24-28. Who was affected, and what was the result?

2. Identify a divine contact in your own experience. Describe the item and how God has used it in your leadership development.

ANSWERS----------
    1. a. (1), (2), and (3) guidance on doctrine.
        b. Priscilla and Aquila were divine contacts for Apollos. Apollos was a young leader with great potential. Priscilla and Aquila were Bible teachers who had enjoyed an informal apprenticeship under Paul. They were people who were ready to clarify Apollos' grasp of truth and help develop his "truth" base. Notice the "linking" provided for Apollos in verse 27.
    2. Harold Dollar, now a professor at the School of Missions of BIOLA, was a divine contact, for me in 1964. His timely arrival into my life was used by God to start me on the road to discipleship. Several times since then God has used one or the other of us to challenge, give guidance, counsel, or whatever, to the other. These repeated process items have significantly influenced each of our development phases.

DOUBLE CONFIRMATION PROCESS ITEM symbol: P(DBLC)

introduction	At crucial moments when major guidance decisions are to be made a leader often needs to know for certain that the decision is the will of God. One way God gives clear guidance in just such situations is via the double confirmation item.
definition	<u>Double confirmation</u> refers to the unusual guidance process item in which God makes clear His will by giving the guidance directly to a leader and then reinforcing it by some other person totally independent and unaware of the leader's guidance.
example Moses/ Aaron	Exodus 3 and 4 speak of God's dealing with Moses to get him to lead the Israelite people. Ex 4:27 is an example of the Aaron double confirmation in which God gives Aaron a word which will affirm what Moses has already heard.
example Saul/ Samuel	I Samuel 9 reveals how God worked in both Saul and Samuel to bring them together. God was having Samuel anoint a king. See especially verses 15-18.
example Paul/ Ananias	A most famous double confirmation is Paul's conversion. See Acts 9,22, and 26. Note how God worked through Paul and confirmed it independently through Ananias. See especially 9:10-18.
example Peter/ Cornelius	A significant example of double confirmation concerned God's revelation of Christianity for the Gentiles. See Acts 10:1-8 where God worked with Cornelius and then 10:9-18 where God works with Peter. The rest of the chapter gives the details for this famous double confirmation.
steps	The classic pattern for double confirmation 1. A crucial moment in the leader's ministry where direction needs a sure word from God, 2. God gives the direction to the leader sometimes directly, sometimes indirectly, 3. God then confirms this direction through someone else. The further outside the influence of the first person, the more spectacular is the double confirmation. 4. God then brings the two together in some unmistakable sovereign way.
uses	Double Confirmation has the following uses: 1. gives divine affirmation to some important decision. 2. will validate a leader's spiritual authority. 3. gives a renewed sense of destiny. 4. serves as a sign to outsiders as well as insiders.

FEEDBACK ON DOUBLE CONFIRMATION PROCESS ITEM

1. The double confirmation guidance process item follows a long standing biblical pattern. Can you give the general principle?

Hints: See I Timothy 5:19
            I John 4:1,2
            I Corinthians 14:13ff
            Genesis 37:5-9
            Daniel 2:5
            Genesis 41:17-32 see especially verse 32

2. Which spiritual gifts need to be sure and take into consideration the basic principle identified in question 1 which underlies the double confirmation process item?

3. Give from your own experience, if you can, a double confirmation guidance process item.

ANSWERS----------
   1. Confirming a significant truth amongst more than one source is a strong indicator of its credibility.
   2. Apostleship, words of knowledge, words of wisdom, discernings of spirits. tongues, and words of prophecy are all gifts which serve as sources through which truth comes. To be credible, there needs to be outside or multiple confirmation, particularly when the gift is revealing truth from God which will affect other's lives.
   3. I am always on the alert for various process items in people's lives. When doing a short leadership study on George Pitt, a New Zealand Baptist minister, I unearthed a double confirmation process item. In connection with two fasting periods of some length, George was led of God to experientially claim ground for God. He literally walked neighborhoods and prayed over ground, families, etc. The passage that God used to bring conviction was the Joshua 1 passage where God challenged Joshua, "Every place that the sole of your foot shall tread upon, that have I given you, as I said unto Moses." It was during this experiential learning of possession that George was attending a women's meeting with his wife in which husbands were invited. There was a speaker from the United States named Larry Allen. Toward the end of the meeting he began giving words of knowledge. He turned to George, pointed a finger at him and quoted Joshua 1:3 and said that God indeed wanted him to possess the land.

DIVINE AFFIRMATION PROCESS ITEM   symbol: P(DA)

introduction   Over a lifetime of ministry there will be times in which a leader will need reassurance from God. This involves a psychological need for acceptance as a person loved by God, as well as approval regarding ministry.

definition   Divine affirmation is a special kind of sense of destiny experience in which God gives approval to a leader so that the leader has a renewed sense of ultimate purpose and a refreshed desire to continue serving God.

example   At least three times in Jesus' ministry one can
Jesus   observe God's divine affirmation. See Matthew 3:17, 17:5, John 12:27,28.

example   From Genesis 12:1-3 onward for more than 25 years
Abraham   God repeatedly gave divine affirmation to Abraham a-periodically. See especially Genesis 15 where God renewed Abraham's purpose and also revealed great truth.

example   I Samuel 12:13-19 is a great passage illustrating
Samuel   divine affirmation of Samuel's ministry which is primarily external.

example   Acts 18:9,10 and 27:23-26 are divine affirmations
Paul   regarding Paul's ministry.

kinds   Divine affirmation can come through:
                1. an inner voice or other direct revelation,
                2. an angelic visitation,
                3. a vision,
                4. a miraculous sign,
                5. a prophetic word,
                6. a dream,
                7. a sense of God's blessing on a life as attested to by external testimony (see Joseph, Genesis 39:2,3 39:21-23).
                8. sovereign arrangement of circumstances,

uses   1. To renew a leader's desire to serve God,
                2. To give confirmation of acceptance, especially when there is a sense of rejection due to ministry or personal circumstances.
                3. To give external support for ministry purposes.
                4. To expand the spiritual authority power base.

timing   Can occur anytime throughout ministry.

causal   Dominantly perceived as directly from God. May come through people who perceive God's blessing on the leader's life.

FEEDBACK ON DIVINE AFFIRMATION PROCESS ITEM

1. Divine affirmation relates to several other process items.   To which of the other guidance process items is it most closely related.

___ a. DIVINE CONTACTS   ___ b. DOUBLE CONFIRMATION
___ c. NEGATIVE PREPARATION   ___ d. FLESH ACT

2. To which of the other guidance process items is it least closely related. Explain why you chose the one(s) you did.

___ a. DIVINE CONTACTS   ___ b. DOUBLE CONFIRMATION
___ c. NEGATIVE PREPARATION   ___ d. FLESH ACT

3. Analyze the following divine affirmations for focus. Put "I" if you feel the divine affirmation was internally focused or "E" if you feel the divine affirmation was externally focused. Describe the method by which the divine affirmation came, as well.

Example   Focus   Method

a. Matthew 3:17 (cf.
   John 1:32ff)

b. Matthew 17:5 (cf.
   II Peter 1:16-18)

c. Acts 18:9

d. Acts 27:23-26

e. I Samuel 12:13-19

f. Genesis 15

4. I have said that the divine affirmation process item is closely related to spiritual authority. Glance at the spiritual authority definition given below and explain why I said this.

> Spiritual authority is that characteristic of a God-anointed leader, developed upon an experiential power base, which enables a leader to influence followers through persuasion, force of modeling and moral expertise toward God's purposes.

5. Give an example of a process incident in which God gave you divine affirmation.

ANSWERS----------
See next page.

ANSWERS TO FEEDBACK ON DIVINE AFFIRMATION continued

1. __x__ a. DIVINE CONTACTS   __x__ b. DOUBLE CONFIRMATION
         (and its closely
         related counterpart,
         MENTORING)

    Affirmation is part of the methodology that a mentor uses
with a mentoree. Often the sovereign guidance item is an
affirmation of a direction. Divine contacts frequently are used
to give direction. Divine affirmation will also frequently come
via an internal focus and via an external focus which is in
actuality a double confirmation form of divine affirmation.

2. __x__ c. NEGATIVE PREPARATION   __x__ d. FLESH ACT

    Divine affirmation is almost always a positive experience.
While the end result of negative preparation is positive (great
release into the next steps for one's life), the experience itself
is usually negative. A flesh act would in no way have God's seal
of approval.

3.

Example	Focus	Method
a. Matthew 3:17 (cf. John 1:32ff)	I,E	visible sign, audible voice
b. Matthew 17:5 (cf. II Peter 1:16-18)	I,E	visible sign, audible voice natural phenomena
c. Acts 18:9	I	vision
d. Acts 27:23-26	I	angelic visitation
e. I Samuel 12:13-19	E	natural phenomena (rain storm)
f. Genesis 15	I	vision

4. Note the underlined words: Spiritual authority is that
characteristic of a God-anointed leader developed upon an
experiential power base which enables a leader to influence
followers through persuasion, force of modeling and moral
expertise toward God's purposes.
    At the very heart of spiritual authority is the sense of
closeness to God by the leader. Divine affirmation is one
manifestation of God-anointed. It is clear evidence of the touch
of God upon a life. The experiential power base refers to
experience with God. Divine affirmation is a special experience
with God. Divine affirmation gives the external backing to
spiritual authority; the testimony of the leader's life and
ministry gives internal evidence of spiritual authority.

5. Your choice. I'll share one or two of mine in class.

MINISTRY AFFIRMATION PROCESS ITEM   symbol: P(MAF)

introduction   During ministry processing many lessons are learned
via negative experience. These lessons are
valuable when seen in terms of an overview of a
lifetime of development. But in the midst of the
ministry processing that overall perspective is
often hard to see so that these negative lessons
can be discouraging. Leaders need to be encouraged
concerning proper leadership which is pleasing to
God. The ministry affirmation process item provides
that needed encouragement. It is a special form of
the more general divine affirmation process item.
It encourages a leader and gives a renewed sense of
ultimate purpose in leadership. It is God's "pat on
the back."

definition   The ministry affirmation process item is a special
kind of destiny experience in which God gives
approval to a leader in terms of some ministry
assignment in particular or some ministry
experience in general which results in a renewed
sense of purpose for the leader.

example   Acts 18:9-11. Paul in Corinth. Special vision given
to encourage ministry and show God's protection.

example   Paul and Barnabas. Their apostolic ministry
confirmed. See Galatians 2:1-10 especially verse 9.

example   Elijah. God meets Elijah in the midst of his
depression. See I Kings 19:1-18

example   Peter. Jesus' testing in John 21 is a significant
restorative ministry affirmation.

example   Jesus in the Lazarus resurrection incident. See
especially John 11:41-42.

example   Moses in the incident of rebellion with Korah,
Dathan and Abiram. See especially Numbers 16:27-
30. This is a complex process incident involving
authority, power, and affirmation process items.

kinds   Ministry affirmation means include: a vision, sign,
inner voice, inner conviction, successful ministry
incident, human expressions of appreciation, inner
satisfaction in reflection on some aspect of
ministry history, a word of knowledge or wisdom,
prophecy, promotion, or expansion of sphere of
influence.

focus   Primarily, ministry affirmation serves as
encouragement. Secondarily, it often serves as
confirmation of guidance.

FEEDBACK MINISTRY AFFIRMATION PROCESS ITEM

1. Examine at least two of the following examples for the "apparent need" prompting the ministry affirmation and the "means" through which ministry affirmation came. You will most likely need to read more of the context than I have given.

	Apparent Need	Means of Affirmation
a. Acts 18:9-11. Paul in Corinth.		
b. Galatians 2:1-1Ø. Paul and Barnabas.		
c. I Kings 19:1-18. Elijah.		
d. John 21. Peter.		
e. John 11:41-42 Jesus.		
f. Numbers 16:27-3Ø Moses		

2. Describe an important ministry affirmation process item you have personally experienced? Give the details.

When	Apparent Need	Means	Results

ANSWERS----------

1.

	Apparent Need	Means of Affirmation
b. Galatians 2:1-1Ø Paul, Barnabas	recognition of unique ministry	Human beings approve. Leaders in Jerusalem church, James, Peter, and John give approval to Barnabas and Paul's ministry
e. John 11:41-42 Jesus.	Proof of: in- timate communion with God; divine mission	A Miracle. Word of faith honored. Lazarus raised from dead.

2.

When	Need	Means	Results
Winter 1981	Guidance in a major boundary phase	day of prayer alone with God; 3 unsolicited ministry requests; via phone calls.	Not only did I receive guidance but I also knew that God was with me and wanted to use me. There was a great joy and a sense of anticipation.

DESTINY FULFILLMENT PROCESS ITEM   symbol: P(DF)

introduction   The Destiny Pattern contains three aspects. One,
                God's preparatory work brings a growing awareness
                of a sense of destiny. Two, the awareness moves to
                conviction as God gives revelation of it. Three,
                there is confirmation and movement toward an
                accomplishment of that destiny which often
                culminates in destiny fulfilled. Destiny
                fulfillment describes the category of process items
                which are operative in aspect 3 of the destiny
                pattern--the confirmation and growing sense of
                awareness of God's completion of a specific
                destiny.

definition   The destiny fulfillment process item describes a
                grouping of process items which are significant
                acts, people, providential circumstances, or
                timing which represent the completion of destiny
                processing that has gone on previously.

example   Joseph. See Genesis 30:22-24 for destiny
                preparation item. See Genesis 37:5-8, 9-11 for
                destiny revelation. See Genesis 42-47 for destiny
                fulfillment.

example   Paul. See Acts 9:15,16 for destiny revelation. See
                Acts 26:19 and all the Pauline epistles for various
                aspects of destiny fulfillment.

kinds   Bertelsen (1985) lists the following specific kinds
                of destiny fulfillment process items:

                1. promise realization.
                2. divine affirmation
                3. obedience process items
                4. word process items
                5. faith acts
                6. prophecy fulfillment.

use   Probably no greater satisfaction, from a ministry
                standpoint, can be derived than that of destiny
                fulfillment. To see destiny items occur over a
                lifetime (including preparation items and various
                revelation items) and then to see them come to
                fruition is to know that one's life counted for
                Christ. Destiny fulfillment is God's "well-done"
                while still here on earth. It is God's closure on
                a life that counted.

timing   Ultimate destiny fulfillment occurs late in life,
                usually in the unique ministry time period. Mini-
                fulfillments can occur any time in Growth or Unique
                Ministry (e.g. fulfillment of a prophecy,
                realization of a promise, etc.).

FEEDBACK ON DESTINY FULFILLMENT PROCESS ITEM

1. What words indicate a destiny fulfillment process item in John 19:29,30? Trace at least one destiny item from destiny preparation and destiny revelation which show progress leading to this destiny fulfillment item.

    a. words symbolic of destiny fulfillment:

    b. destiny preparation item:

    c. destiny revelation item:

2. Can you think of incidents from the Bible which illustrate any of the items suggested by Bertelsen as occurring in destiny fulfillment? Choose one, identify, and explain briefly the item.

    ___a. promise realization
    ___b. divine affirmation
    ___c. obedience process items
    ___d. word process items
    ___e. faith acts

3. Have you experienced incidents indicating destiny fulfillment? Describe.

ANSWERS----------

    1. a. It is finished. Jesus had accomplished what the Father had sent him to do. b. See Luke 1:32,33 and Luke 2:33-35. c. John 12:27-33
    2. e. faith acts. See Joseph. Genesis 50:25,26 along with Joshua 24:32
    3. Promise realization. In 1967 God affirmed a promise that someday I would be able to visit and preach in a chapel to be constructed at Christian Leader's Training College in Papua New Guinea. Students at Columbia Bible College were raising money to construct this chapel. My wife and I gave sacrificially to this project. In 1983 the promise was fulfilled. It was a moving moment for me which confirmed God's continued goodness in my life.

COMMENTARY ON GUIDANCE CLUSTER

balance   Guidance development is complicated and delicate. God must teach a leader to discern guidance, without thwarting the leader's personal initiative. While God is creating commitment to follow His guidance He must also teach the leader to sense individual responsibility for making decisions. This is not an overnight lesson. It takes place slowly, through many process items, over an extended period of time.

applying   Leaders who influence followers toward God's
Hebrews   purposes must be able to discern with certainty
13:7,8   God's purposes. The guidance cluster items described give some perspectives as to how leaders in the past have sensed God's hand in their lives.

P(SG)   Sovereign guidance, in all its facets, is extremely
and   important to the concept of spiritual authority.
spiritual   It is experiencing God in the crucial decisions of
authority   life. Normally a leader will not experience sovereign guidance on most of the leadership decisions of everyday life. But one who has spiritual authority can point to a track record of significant sovereign guidance both for personal life and for ministry. This is one of the elements which lends credence to spiritual authority.

P(FLESH)   Reflection on the flesh act process item is not an exercise in negative thinking. It is a process through which God can sharpen our discernment skills and strengthen our ability to recognize His voice. As we reflect on guidance instances, both our own and others, we are not looking to criticize the actions taken but to learn from them. We should look for lessons concerning how God communicates His guidance so that in the future we will be able to discern His guidance more clearly.

awareness   Sometimes divine contacts are unaware that God has
P(DC)   used them at a special time in some one's life. Often a "phrase" or a message given in ministry is a key at the right moment. Years later it may come to light how "at a given moment someone was specially used" by God in a divine contact function.

COMMENTARY ON GUIDANCE CLUSTER continued

P(DBLC) and certainty guidance	Some crucial decisions, issues, or junctures in life are so important that they warrant extra certainty in guidance. Such a case is Paul's conversion. See Acts 9, 22, and 26. Note how God worked through Paul and independently through Ananias. See especially 9:10-18. This conversion was so important to worldwide Christianity that there needed to be no question of or room for accusations of self-delusion. God gave certainty confirmation through someone who could only have known by God's revelation.
P(DBLC) application	As a leader, when you are confronted with a crucial decision, ask God to give double confirmation. This may in turn force a faith challenge upon you.
P(DBLC) variations	Gideon's famous fleece is an alternate kind of double confirmation. It points out the essence of the processing--getting certainty guidance so that God's guidance is absolutely clear. There will be other variations which do not follow the exact steps or format but provide the essential function.
P(DA) inclusive of P(MA)	Usually the affirmation is an inward thing which satisfies the leader alone that God is indeed with him/her and that the life-purpose of serving God is real and vital and worthwhile. However, sometimes the affirmation is external for others to know and see. The external divine affirmation usually is in connection with validation of spiritual authority.
P(DA) renewal, a commonly needed item	The routine of ministry needs to be a-periodically broken by the unusual. There is a genuine need to know that one's ministry is relevant and worthwhile and that one's life is indeed counting toward God's purposes. This reaffirmation is usually an inward need which will infuse new life to the leader. Occasionally, this affirmation is outward to confirm to followers that the leader does indeed have spiritual authority. The process item which describes this special approval from God is called divine affirmation. It is closely linked with spiritual authority.
P(MA) causal	Frequently, divine affirmation comes when a leader seeks God in isolation from present ministry. Deliberate times of fasting and days of prayer spent alone with God are the seedbed of ministry affirmation. The need for ministry affirmation is not a sign of weakness but a harbinger of renewal and refreshment that will motivate further service.

MATURITY CLUSTER Synonym: Deep Processing

introduction   Deep processing focuses a leader to evaluate life
                 and ministry for its deeper meaning. The maturity
                 cluster does this. Its two sub-clusters achieve
                 this reflective focus. The deep processing sub-
                 cluster utilizes isolation, conflict, and life
                 crises to force the leader to evaluate what life is
                 about and what ministry is accomplishing
                 ultimately. They are used to shape and to shift
                 his/her focus towards a whole lifetime of effort
                 and to what is of ultimate importance. Deep
                 processing focuses essentially on experiential
                 learning. Cognitive understanding is an important
                 secondary by-product. The convergence sub-cluster
                 focuses primarily on cognitive understanding of
                 what effective ministry could be.

description   The <u>maturity cluster</u> refers to a set of five
                 process items which magnify the importance of
                 "being" as the primary base for ministry. These
                 concentrate on teaching a leader about the
                 importance of character and personal essence as the
                 basis for what ministry is.

Venn Diagram   MATURITY CLUSTER

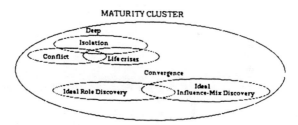

essential   All of these guidance items assume that God is
character-   concerned with shaping the leader toward effective
istic   ministry. Efficiency (doing things right) has been
                 a major goal of growth ministry processing in
                 general. Effectiveness (doing the right things,
                 and doing them for the right reasons and from the
                 right basis) characterizes these processes.

shared   Processing involving conflict and crises also
processes   occurs as part of ministerial formation processing.
                 When analyzed with the priority of ministerial
                 formation the focus is on what was being learned in
                 order to develop the person in ministerial
                 effectiveness. Here, the focus is on the leader
                 learning about himself/herself, and ultimate
                 accomplishment from a "being" base rather than a
                 "doing" base. Spiritual authority via exemplary
                 character is in focus.

ISOLATION PROCESS ITEM Symbol: P(I)

introduction   A recurring process item seen in leadership studies
                is the special kind of crisis item called
                isolation.   Several times in a leader's life time
                the leader may be set aside from his/her normal
                direct ministry involvement. Causes may include
                crises, disciplinary action, providential
                circumstances (such as war, oppressive government
                action, illness), or self choice. The thrust of the
                processing focuses on recognition that the
                isolation is God's work and that it is a call to a
                deeper relationship and experience of God.

definition   Isolation processing refers to the setting aside of
                a leader from normal ministry involvement in its
                natural context usually for an extended time in
                order to experience God in a new or deeper way.

why   Isolation process items are often greatly used by
important   God to teach important lessons that could not be
                learned in the pressures of normal ministry.

kinds   **type**   **lesson observed**

                sickness   ● dependence upon God
                               ● learning about supernatural healing
                               ● urgency to accomplish
                               ● deepening of inner-life, especially
                                 intercessory praying

                prison   ● dependence upon God
                               ● use of mental facilities, memory
                               ● submission to God's will
                               ● indirect influence through modeling
                                 and a widened intercessory life

                person-   ● submission to God
                ality   ● submission to spiritual authority
                conflicts   ● lesson of non-vindication of one's
                organi-   spiritual authority
                zational   ● value of other's perspectives
                discipline   ● dependence upon God

                self-   ● new perspective on ministry
                choice for   ● rekindling of sense of destiny
                renewal   ● power of prayer
                               ● inner convictions from Word
                               ● guidance

                self-   ● new perspective on ministry
                choice for   ● rekindling of sense of destiny
                education,   ● more open to new ideas and change
                training   ● dependency upon wider body of Christ
                               ● broadening through exposure to others

FEEDBACK EXERCISE ON ISOLATION PROCESS ITEM

1. Describe here any isolation process items you have personally experienced. Then describe what God was able to teach you in these process items. Do you think these lessons could have been readily learned in your normal ministry context?

2. If you are aware of any other types of isolation process items, list them here.

3. List here any Biblical illustrations of isolation process items that you can think of.

ANSWERS----------

1. In a leadership conflict in my own mission I was brought face to face with my own inflexibility. I was disciplined and set aside from the normal ministry I had been doing. For the first time I saw that I was inflexible. During the next year and a half I saw God work a marvelous change in my personality which included learning to bend and be flexible. I also learned some deep lessons on spiritual authority. The major one being--God vindicates spiritual authority. I don't have to do it.

2. Psychological isolation. In the midst of situations, though not physically isolated from some ministry, people can be isolated from the ministry they want to perform for a number of reasons.

3. John on Patmos. Paul in prison.

CONFLICT PROCESS ITEM   symbol: P(C)

introduction   The conflict process item is a general process item
                  which describes any conflict that is used to
                  process a leader in terms of any of the formations.
                  It is a preliminary form of a crisis process item.
                  Usually when it occurs in the growth ministry time
                  period we call it ministry conflict and give it a
                  special definition since lessons learned tend to
                  affect ministerial formation. But conflict occurs
                  in all phases and often is as much personal,
                  focusing on spiritual formation, as it does on
                  ministry formation. The thrust of the conflict
                  process item in the convergence sub-cluster is on
                  the lessons learned by the leader which primarily
                  affect spiritual or strategic formation.

definition   The conflict process item refers to those instances
                  in a leader's life-history in which God uses
                  conflict, whether personal or ministry related, to
                  develop the leader in dependence upon God, faith,
                  and inner-life.

example   Jeremiah is a book filled with conflict processing
                  including both ministry conflict and general
                  conflict items. The personal conflict items have
                  to do with Jeremiah's self-image and the
                  persecution he faced. The ministry conflict related
                  to various ministry tasks or assignments which he
                  received and the reaction to that ministry.

combination   Conflict process items usually will occur in
processing   combination with other items and will often be the
                  stimulus for learning the other item. Some
                  important combinations include conflict and,

                  ● destiny insights;   ● structure insights;
                  ● basic skills;   ● leadership backlash;
                  ● ministry challenge;   ● isolation;
                  ● faith challenge;   ● spiritual authority;
                  ● authority insights;   ● guidance items.

focus   Conflict processing accomplishes the normal
                  functions of ministry conflict and also focuses on

                  1) the leader's character as exposed by conflict,
                  2) God's intents on shaping character via the
                     conflict,
                  3) seeing conflict as the stimulus for other
                     processing.

purpose   The emphasis on the conflict item is not just the
                  insights learned about conflict but the intended
                  development orchestrated by God in those conflict
                  situations.

FEEDBACK ON CONFLICT PROCESS ITEM

1. The following exercises will ask you to analyze several conflict process items which may have occurred during foundational, transitional, or growth ministry processing. Jot down several conflict process items. Perhaps previously you saw them only as problematic and didn't realize that God was in them and working for his purposes of developing you. This feedback will perhaps help you reflect on this conflict with new perspectives. Describe lessons that you can now see (faith, dependence upon God, revelation of insights about self, etc.).

<u>When</u>   <u>conflict item</u>   <u>Lessons Seen in Reflecting Back</u>

(1)

(2)

(3)

2. Identify a given biblical illustration of conflict with its development intent. What lesson can you see in it for you?

3. Note again the comment concerning conflict often occurring in tandem with some other process item. Then check any combinations of conflict among following items which you yourself have personally experienced or have seen in a leader.
___ a. destiny insights   ___ f. structure insights
___ b. basic skills   ___ g. leadership backlash
___ c. ministry challenge   ___ h. isolation
___ d. faith challenge   ___ i. spiritual authority
___ e. authority insights   ___ j. guidance items

Choose one. Jot down the basics and be prepared to share.

ANSWERS----------
1. I'll reserve my answer to this question for my personal sharing in class.
2. David had conflict with Absalom which was primarily personal but escalated to ministry. Lesson for me: A leader too busy to take care of personal family problems will eventually reap ministry problems.
3. j. My own conflict with one of my former leaders was negative preparation for moving on into an expanded ministry. Without the conflict and a prophetical word I would not have accepted the ensuing influence challenge. I have seen illustrations of all, either in biblical characters, other leaders, or my own life.

LIFE-CRISIS PROCESS ITEM   symbol: P(LC)

introduction   Life-crisis is a special kind of general crisis
               process item. It contains the basic ideas of the
               crisis process item but its focus is on deepening
               spiritual authority. It may be used in conjunction
               with other process items to accomplish other things
               but it primarily draws a leader into a closer
               relationship with God.

definition   A life-crisis process item refers to a crisis
               situation characterized by intense pressure in
               human affairs in which the meaning and purpose of
               life are searched out with a result that the leader
               has experienced God in a new way as the source,
               sustainer, and focus of life.

example   II Corinthians 1:8-11 describes Paul's insights
Paul   resulting from several life-crises process items.

example   In II Corinthians 4:7-12 Paul shows that this
Paul   process item deepens one's understanding of God's
               power. A leader is only a channel for it.

example   Genesis 15 is the narrative disclosure of a life-
Abraham   crisis process item which shows how God reveals
               himself, uses the processing to expand the leader,
               and to give tremendous expectation toward God's
               future working. Abraham had just returned from a
               victory in battle. He had given his portion of the
               loot to Melchizedek. He was afraid of retaliation.
               In that moment of crisis God met him with a
               symbolic vision assuring protection, provision, and
               renewal of promise with further enlightenment of
               that destiny promise. Note the combination
               processing involving destiny revelation.

focus   Life and death situations certainly qualify for
               life-crisis processing. They cause reflection on
               the deeper meaning of life. The awareness of the
               temporary nature of life forces evaluation of life
               goals.   These in turn, drive one into deeper
               dependence upon God and the desire to do and be
               what God wants in whatever time is remaining. But
               life-crisis items are not limited to life and death
               situations. They can be any kind of crisis which
               causes reflection on ultimate purpose and a
               deepening of a relationship with God which sees
               that relationship as more important than any of
               life's attainments.

power   Life crisis processing points out the need for a
resource   deeper relationship with God. The experiencing of
               that relationship, itself, is a major power
               resource for spiritual authority.

FEEDBACK ON LIFE-CRISIS PROCESS ITEM

1. Examine the life-crisis process item given in Acts 27 for Paul. Identify the crisis. Point out how Paul met God. What was the end result of this processing?

2. Give here at least one biblical illustration of this process item other than those I have mentioned.

3. Describe a life-crisis process item you have personally experienced or have seen in the life of another. Be prepared to share this item and lessons seen in it with someone else.

ANSWERS----------
   1. Acts 27 describes the famous shipwreck incident which is part of Paul's journey to Rome. Paul had been caught up in an inexorable sovereign process of several years which had as its goal witness of the living God before rulers at Rome, the major capital of the world. It appears as if that process will end. But God intervenes with a word (verses 23, 24) of protection and renewal of that destiny promise. The result was a leader who was confident that God's purposes through him would be accomplished. This was a man whose many experiences such as this one gave him spiritual authority. He is the classic New Testament prototype of a leader with spiritual authority. It is just such processing which gave him power resources for spiritual authority.
   2. The Psalms are filled with numerous incidents in the life of David in which God met him in life-crisis processing and deepened the relationship between David and Himself. See especially the complimentary Psalms 3 and 4 and the end result of the deepened relationship.
   3. I will reserve this one for personal sharing. I have seen a number of these in my study of life-histories and reading of biographies.

IDEAL INFLUENCE-MIX

introduction   Significant change in sphere of influence signals a
                   change in a time period of development. This
                   change can be in degree (more), or kind (means of
                   influencing). Influence-mix is the term which
                   evaluates the different configurations of influence
                   means. Several patterns of influence-mix are
                   commonly observed. There is no fixed best
                   influence-mix. An influence-mix will change
                   depending on the time period and leadership
                   potential that has been developed to date. The
                   ideal influence-mix describes the "best" influence-
                   mix during the unique ministry time period when
                   convergence is being experienced.

definition   Influence-mix is a term describing the combination
                   of influence elements--direct, indirect and
                   organizational--in terms of degree and kind, at a
                   given point in a development time period.

definition   Ideal influence-mix refers to the influence-mix
                   combination which occurs when major and minor
                   convergence factors harmonize.

example   large organizational influence, direct influence
profile   (extensiveness small, intensiveness large,
                   comprehensiveness small), large indirect influence
                   (writings, boards).

example   large organizational influence, direct influence
profile   (extensiveness medium, intensiveness minor,
                   comprehensiveness small), large indirect influence
                   (writings, associations).

example   indirect organizational influence, regular direct
profile   influence (extensiveness medium, intensiveness
                   medium, comprehensiveness medium), a-periodic
                   direct influence (conference--large, seminars--many
                   and large), large indirect influence (writings--
                   books, magazines, crucial international committees)

logical   The idea of "measure of faith" (Romans 12:3-7)
extension   taken to its logical conclusion results in an ideal
Romans   influence-mix concept. This is a concept that is
12:3,6   tied directly to the stewardship model. The ideal
                   influence-mix is an idealized standard for
                   measuring one kind of development.

see also   CONVERGENCE FACTORS in chapter 11 give further
                   insight into ideal influence-mix.

IDEAL INFLUENCE-MIX DISCOVERY PROCESS ITEM symbol: P(IMD)

introduction   In the unique ministry time period, the leader
                knows and uses giftedness with a best influence-
                mix. The discovery of this ideal influence-mix is
                usually not instantaneous but grows over a period
                of time. As discoveries of effective influence
                means (kind) and opportunities for expansion of
                influence among specific follower groups (degree)
                arise role is usually modified to fit these new
                findings. Ideal influence-mix discovery is part of
                that process of role modification.

definition   The idea influence-mix discovery process item
                refers to any significant discovery or use of the
                combination of influence-mix which results from
                harmonizing of major and minor convergence factors.

example   The following is the ideal influence-mix of one
ideal in-   international leader in convergence:
fluence-mix
                indirect organizational influence, regular direct
                influence (extensiveness medium, intensiveness
                medium, comprehensiveness medium), a-periodic
                direct influence (conference--large, seminars--many
                and large), large indirect influence (writings--
                books, magazines, crucial international committees)

insights   Some of the key influence-mix discoveries which led
leading   to this ideal influence-mix include:
to
ideal   1. Key insight: Discovered writing ability. Now has
influence-   over 20 books in print (one of which has gone over
mix   100,000). Books now pave the way for conferences
                and awareness seminars.

                2. Key insight: Discovered lack of direct
                organizational management skills or aptitude
                (Negative preparation: headed two organizations and
                learned that was not the best use of his abilities).

                3. Key insight: Discovered that intensiveness and
                comprehensiveness should remain at low level. He
                does not apply truth well to individuals. His
                strength lies in ability to bring awareness and to
                motivate people to appreciate his ideas. He leaves
                application of them to others.

                4. Key insight: Discovered a marketing means for
                packaging his ideas in conferences and seminars. It
                allows for large a-periodic high extensiveness yet
                with low intensiveness and comprehensiveness.

                5. Key insight: Discovered how to modify role to
                facilitate a judicious use of scheduling.

FEEDBACK ON IDEAL INFLUENCE-MIX DISCOVERY PROCESS ITEM

1. Give any instances of your own discoveries toward your ideal influence-mix. What personal examples can you give from your own development up to this point concerning the ideal influence-mix discovery process item?

2. Examination of mini-convergence patterns leads to insights about ideal influence-mix. Examine the following list of mini-convergence factors. Check any which you have personally experienced. For at least one of those checked, discuss implications for influence-mix. What can you learn from that mini-convergence experience about your own personal influence-mix?
____a. giftedness matched with ministry task
____b. giftedness matched with role
____c. giftedness matched with influence-mix
____d. role matched with geographic location
____e. role matched with experience
____f. destiny matched with special opportunity
____g. destiny matched with experience
____h. destiny matched with geographic location
____i. other matched with other

3. What is the most important lesson you have learned to date about your influence-mix? Kind? Degree? Implications for role?

4. Contextual factors will affect ideal influence-mix. How do you think this happens?

ANSWERS----------
    1. a. In home Bible studies and in small group work in my early Navigator training, I learned that my direct influence had to have a strong intensive component. That is, application of what I teach had to be foremost. It is at least equally important with the content of what I teach. This pattern of the need for heavy intensiveness has pervaded all my ministry. b. Every major ministry I have had in my ministry history has involved an in-depth ministry to at least one person. Each of those persons in turn has impacted many others. I have learned therefore that majoring in-depth with at least one person from

FEEDBACK ON IDEAL INFLUENCE-MIX DISCOVERY PROCESS ITEM continued

time to time will bring large indirect influence. c. My
exposure to theological education by extension and self-study
materials (workbooks, programmed materials, and information
mapped materials) have shown me the efficient use of self-study
materials as a strong means of indirect influence. d. Recently I
have been serving on three boards and several important
committees. I have seen that I can have a powerful
organizational influence by exerting direct influence on leaders
in the organization. I have learned that my most powerful
organizational influence comes through intensive direct influence
on individual leaders. Positional influence is not necessary but
does enhance this intensive effort.

  2. b. Match between giftedness and role. Because of my
gift-mix (exhortation, teaching, and word of wisdom) I need a
role that allows for strong intensive direct influence and access
to leaders of organizations and churches (since my indirect
influence also requires in-depth intensiveness through few
individuals). My teaching role allows direct and highly
intensive contact with leaders, opening doors for counselling
concerning their personal and organizational leadership.

  c. Match between giftedness and influence-mix. I am more
comfortable, due to personality and giftedness, with smaller
groups (below 125). My direct influence group should usually be
this size or below.

  f. Match between destiny and special opportunity. Home Bible
study incident with a prophetic word (the destiny incident
described earlier) showed me that later I would need a doctorate.
Implication: My target group, that is, people I should be
influencing will be high level leaders for whom my doctorate will
be a door opener. When the opportunity to pursue a doctorate
came (through negative preparation processing) I responded to the
opportunity even though it would not normally have been my first
choice.

  f. Match between destiny (prophecy) and special opportunity,
as well as geographic locations. A divine affirmation prophecy
at Columbia Bible College in 1967 indicated that God would use me
around the world. Since then every major ministry guidance
decision has been made in light of that prophecy. This has
indicated to me that my influence-mix will require access to
people from around the world.

  3. Indirect influence via individuals upon whom I have had
intensive and comprehensive direct influence will be my most
important means of lasting and wide-spread influence. This has
meant that I deliberately seek formal and informal mentoring
relationships.

  4. In a country where there is social mobility, economic
mobility, and mobility in terms of ministry opportunities,
influence-mix can be a helpful concept. In countries where
social, economic, and ministry mobility is limited, leaders may
have little or no control over roles through which their
influence-mix will operate. Knowledge of influence-mix and ideal
roles will, at best, frustrate leaders in those kinds of
situations.

IDEAL ROLE DISCOVERY PROCESS ITEM   symbol: P(IRD)

introduction   Finding a role which enhances a gift-cluster
results in effective ministry. Leaders usually do
not find such a role. They create it from what they
have. There is the touch of the divine in pointing
out, enabling role modification, and releasing the
leader into that role. On the human side there is a
process of discovery. This process item relates to
that discovery process.

definition   The ideal role discovery process item refers to any
significant discovery or use of a role which
enhances a leader's giftedness and maximizes
influence-mix effectiveness.

example   The following describes an ideal influence-mix and
an ideal role of an international leader.

ideal
influence-
mix
profile   indirect organizational influence, regular direct
influence (extensiveness medium, intensiveness
medium, comprehensiveness medium), a-periodic
direct influence (conference--large, seminars--many
and large), large indirect influence (writings--
books, magazines, crucial international committees)

ideal role   The ideal role which matches this influence-mix is:
Tenured professor at a leading missiological school
with choice of courses, formats, scheduling of
same; freedom to travel in and around the
scheduling of courses; minimum organizational
entanglement in the school; committee work limited
to those committees through which his role can be
enhanced. Generous sabbatical policy which fits
well with his writing ability; freedom to be
involved or not in local church ministry. He
chooses to be involved and has strong prayer
support from this local church.

discovery,
over time,
step-by-
step   Discovery of this role (that is, modification of
it) has been gradual and in line with influence-mix
discovery. It has also been providential following
various guidance and destiny items and includes
unusual sensitivity to the minor convergence factor
of special opportunities. This leader has the
ability to see special opportunities and to take
advantage of them where others often do not see
such opportunities, nor do they have the drive to
follow-through on them if they do.

balance
pattern,
UM.4   This leader has an unusual sensitivity to the
balance pattern. He consistently selects
appropriate ministry opportunities that fit
giftedness. He refuses others. He stays within his
understanding of his appropriate influence-mix.

FEEDBACK ON IDEAL ROLE DISCOVERY PROCESS ITEM

1. Give any instances of your own discoveries toward your ideal role. What personal examples do you have so far of the ideal role discovery process item?

2. Analyzing giftedness and ideal influence-mix will prompt one towards ideal role discovery. Use your answers to previous questions involving gift-mix identification and ideal influence-mix to stimulate you to reflect on what kind of role would fit what you have discovered about them. Jot down any insights toward ideal role that you see from this analysis.

3. What is the most important lesson that you have learned to date about your ideal role? You might consider how various past roles have hindered or enhanced your ministry.

4. What is a major hindrance today to the concept of ideal role in churches and Christian organizations?

ANSWERS----------

1. Observation 1. Early giftedness drift showed me that eventually I would need a teaching role. Observation 2: Experience as the head of an institution showed me I was more effective not as the head but in some supportive role in which my ideas could be implemented from below. Observation 3: My personality is such that some people are drawn to me and deeply appreciate me. Others are turned off. I need a role in which people can be free to accept or reject my ministry. Observation 4: I need a role which will allow initial penetration of my ministry with freedom for in-depth follow-up later should a person accept my ministry. I have actual process items from my ministry history confirming these observations toward ideal role.

2. Gift-mix = exhortation, teaching, word of wisdom; Ideal influence-mix = regular direct ministry (fairly high intensiveness and comprehensiveness with extensiveness limited to 125 or under); a-periodic direct ministry (workshop, seminar, extensiveness of 50 and below with potential for follow-up); indirect influence (through heavy intensive direct influence of individuals, writing of self-study materials, writing of other materials); organizational influence (primarily indirect not positional via direct influence of key individuals, or design of key philosophical statements or training programs; board influence).

3. I must have freedom to ideate and try out ideas on people who can give helpful feedback. This means the role has to provide access to high level leaders.

4. Role expectations.

COMMENTARY ON MATURITY CLUSTER

ideal influence-mix, descriptive example, A. W. Tozer	A. W. Tozer in the latter portion of his third development time period, City Leadership, molded a pastoral role which stimulated the use of his word gifts (direct influence--public exhortation--size several hundred in extensiveness), while minimizing his personal relationships (freed from pastoral functions). His role allowed for use of word gifts in secondary direct influence through teaching experiences from time to time in Bible schools. His role also permitted a large indirect influence through a radio ministry (probably thousands). Indirect influence was facilitated also through writing (prophetic gift exercised) as editor of a denominational magazine and contributions to other periodicals. His books captured the highlights of his personal experience with God and provided further indirect influence in the thousands. His role also embraced organizational influence (local church in terms of leadership, but not administrative details; denominationally among executive leadership).
further explanation maturity cluster	Convergence is discussed in Chapters 10 in conjunction with the time variable. The unique ministry development phase describes the period in a leader's life when convergence happens. The unique ministry patterns, UM.1 Reflective/Formative Evaluation, UM.2 Upward Development, UM.3 Gift-cluster Ripening, UM.4 Balance, and UM.5 Convergence Guidance, all give further insights into maturity cluster processing.
data, P(IMD), P(IRD)	Data for the ideal influence-mix and ideal role discovery process items is not as plentiful as for other process items. Most research comes out of the study of historical biographies. Contemporary studies usually have not reached the latter growth ministry period or the unique ministry period and as a result not much information is included which gives insight concerning these items.

SUMMARY ON PROCESSING VARIABLE

The goal of Christian leadership development is the production of a leader who is mature in leadership character, leadership skills, leadership values and accomplishes the purposes of God. The **processing variable** is core to that development. Its two major elements the process incident and the process item, must be carefully distinguished.

Process incidents represent reality. They flow from real life **critical spiritual incidents.** Christian leaders recognize that certain events and happenings in their life are touched with the divine. They can sense that these incidents are critical to their leadership development though just how this is so is not always clear. Retrospective reflection especially when viewed over time usually identifies some of the ways an incident contributed toward leadership development.

Process items represent constructs which help describe and interpret the reality of process incidents so as to focus on leadership development issues. Researchers need to bear this in mind for they can not always easily identify process items from given process incidents. Several characteristics with explanatory observations detail this difference and give the essential nature of process items.

Characteristic 1. Non-Absolutes

Process items are not absolutes; they do not define reality. They describe it. Reality defines them. Constant comparison of data--new process incidents--may well clarify definitions and modify or add new properties.

Characteristic 2. Heuristic

Process items can be heuristic in nature. They often allow us to discover and see more in the reality than would be normally the case without these guiding perspectives. Though they don't define reality they allow us to see more of what is there by their suggestive descriptions.

Characteristic 3. Specificity

Process items vary in levels of specificity. Some are unique and apply to a well defined set of similar process incidents (e.g. integrity check). Others are more umbrella-like and embrace numerous kinds of process incident manifestations (e.g. spiritual authority discovery). Some are made up of a series of incidents in which a final incident triggers the processing--a cumulative process. Others occur in one incident-- a point process.

Characteristic 4. Overlap

Process incidents do not necessarily map one to one with

process items. That is, a given process incident may include
several process items going on concurrently.   Of these, one or
more may be in focus and may dominate. Several of the process
incidents used in the integrity check example have this overlap
property.[2] Or a given process item might be reflected over some
aspects of several process incidents.   Life incidents are usually
very complex and do not always neatly fit exact process item
categories.

Characteristic 5. Immediate Perception

Point process items (single striking incidents) are usually
perceived more easily and more rapidly and with greater self-
authentication than are cumulative process items (those extended
over time with several incidents contributing). The point action
(e.g. obedience check) items also tend toward the sovereign
intervention side of the process item awareness continuum.

Characteristic 6. Delayed Reflective Perception

Cumulative process items are usually perceived less easily
than point action items.   That is so because point process items
can usually be grasped as a whole (less incidents and time
involved).   Cumulative process items require reflection over a
period of time and require putting together separate incidents
for their processing effect. Usually trigger incidents will prod
retrospective reflection, and hence, identification of buildup
incidents involved in the total process.   These extended time
process items tend toward the providential intervention side of
the process awareness continuum.

Characteristic 7. Correlation To Expansion

The desired end result of analyzing a process incident is
not the exact identification of the process item but the
correlation of it to leadership development issues, the actual
leadership development functions being accomplished. Of course,
a researcher wants to be as accurate as possible in describing
the processing seen in process incidents.

---

[2]Several of the process incidents in Chapter 3 illustrate this.
The Student 4 example illustrated the mentoring process item,
the crisis process item, the conflict process item, hints of the
literary process item, as well as the integrity check which he
felt was in focus for him. The Student 6 example illustrated an
obedience check, word check, and perhaps a faith challenge, as
well as the integrity check. The Student 8 example illustrated
an obedience check as well as the integrity check.

Process Awareness Continuum

I have been using the Process Awareness Continuum to point out how leaders naturally, at first occurrence, perceive process items in terms of God's intervention. This continuum helps give further perspective on characteristics 5 and 6 above. The continuum suggests that awareness of processing varies with kinds of process items.

Christian leaders are generally much more aware of incidents which they attribute to sovereign intervention as being significant to their development than they do to incidents which are more providential (God's circumstantial arrangement of factors). The continuum simply recognizes that certain incidents toward the left are more easily attributable to God's intervention than those to the right. Recognition that incidents all along the continuum can indicate God's involvement is a step forward to further development. A heightened awareness of processing and various kinds of process items allows the leader to more effectively work with that processing towards its goal for his/her life. That is, knowledge of process items with their properties (kinds, uses, steps, etc.) allows the leader to shift those process items more to the left on the continuum in terms of sensing God in them. The numerous classes that have studied leadership emergence theory have confirmed this. This is one indication of the importance of this theory. Understanding of God's processes helps bring more effective processing toward leadership development issues.

General Nature of Properties of Process Items

Comparative analysis of similar incidents representing a given process item result in properties. Comparative analysis of all process items in terms of properties allows for generalizations to be given concerning properties of process items. Knowledge of properties of a given process item, when a leader is going through processing, amplifies the leader's sensitivity to God in it. These properties are especially helpful to a mature leader who is mentoring or counselling an emerging leader. Their potential predictive force carries power and use of them is a direct application of the leadership mandate of Hebrews 13:7,8.

Clusters

In explaining processing, I have found it helpful to group some process items into clusters. Clusters are usually sets of items which have strong common features which work towards certain development goals. Within clusters there can be sub-clusters, smaller groupings of items which contain similar development tasks.

Clusters other than the ones I have identified in this chapter have also been identified. Some of these clusters which might prove helpful to your analysis, include:

1. **CALLING CLUSTER**: ministry task/ministry challenge, ministry affirmation, destiny revelation.

2. **SUBMISSION CLUSTER**: ministry conflict, authority insights, relational insights, leadership backlash.

3. **POWER CLUSTER**: ministry skills, giftedness discovery, power items.

4. **ADMINISTRATIVE CLUSTER**: ministry skills, ministry relationship insights, ministry structure insights, faith challenges.

5. **WARFARE/VICTORY CLUSTER**: external conflict, spiritual warfare, power encounter, spiritual authority.

The **processing variable** is the **key variable** for leadership emergence theory. Its major concepts include critical incidents, process incidents, process items, properties of process items, the process awareness continuum, and clusters of items. I have described it in these several chapters with minimum reference to the other two variables, **time** and **response patterns**. The chapters which follow introduce the basic concepts of those two variables. Understanding of them will broaden one's understanding of processing.

CHAPTER 9. OVERVIEWING THE TIME VARIABLE

Integrative Overview

Leadership emergence Theory (LET) can be explained for the most part, in the life of a given leader by the use of three important variables: processing, time, and leader response. Chapters 3-8 explained the core variable of the theory, processing. Processing was seen to contribute to development of spiritual formation, ministerial formation, and strategic formation. This chapter shows how the time variable relates to the processing variable. It gives overall perspective for pinpointing processing in a leader's life. It sets the stage by giving a panorama of a lifetime so that response patterns which make up the response variable can be seen.

Preview

The **time variable** refers to that set of concepts which seek to describe a time orientation for the process variable. Development inherently carries within it the concept of change measured across time. All of the case studies involved in the research made attempts to recognize change in a leader's ministry and life by using some form of time measurement.

The dominant concept of the time variable is the **time-line**. It will be defined in terms of its major components: **development phases, subphases, boundary phases, development tasks,** and **boundary tasks**. The notion of **unique time-lines** and **generic time-lines** will be introduced. Several types of generic time lines will be given. Two of these, the **generalized time-line** and the **ministry time-line**, are particularly helpful for viewing the overall development of leaders. They will be explored more fully in the next chapter.

The time variable serves three very important roles in leadership emergence theory. **First,** it provides a backdrop for identifying when various processes are most likely to occur. This allows for scheduling and can prevent overscheduling or mis-scheduling (Whitehead and Whitehead 1982:35,36).[1]

----

[1]The Whiteheads use the word crisis similar to my notion of critical incident. They see a crisis in a developmental sense. It is a turning point or crucial period of increased vulnerability and heightened potential (1982:8). They analyze the structure of a developmental crisis as entry, duration, and resolution. Further, they hold that crises can be expected or unexpected. A basic premise which flows from this viewpoint is that a critical transition that occurs on schedule is most likely to be negotiated smoothly. From that notion a natural concept emerged, that of scheduling. Scheduling involves expectation of a given crisis. Crises can be scheduled, mis-scheduled, or overscheduled. These ideas suggest the predictive value of the processing variable in my own theory and

The **second** role is to provide a panorama of a lifetime which allows recognition of leader's response patterns in or across time periods. This second role will be recognized more fully when the response variable is explored in chapter 11. The **third** is to provide an integrating framework upon which to measure development. Time-lines provide an integrating framework for analysis of development. At any given point in a life, specific measures of development (such as sphere of influence, power-mix, and giftedness development) can be assessed. The natural time to do this is during a boundary or transition time between phases. Comparisons of measures done at various boundaries allows for recognition of development, seen as change in the various measures of development. Chapter 13, which discusses evaluation measures, will exploit this third role of the time variable.

Major Concepts of Time Variable

Comparative studies of numerous case studies with the time concept in mind led to several useful concepts:

1) notion of time-line,
2) unique time-line,
3) development phases,
4) sub-phases,
5) characteristics of development phases,
6) the development task,
7) boundaries,
8) characteristics of boundaries,
9) boundary tasks
10) generic time-lines,
11) compression-overlap,

This chapter will define the first nine of these concepts. The next chapter will give details of the remainder.

---

the importance of boundary processing. Being forewarned of certain kinds of processing that will occur during certain periods of time can enable a smoother transition and learning of lessons.

TIME-LINE

introduction   The integrating concept of a leadership emergence
               study is the time-line around which the
               study is oriented. Usually this time-line is given
               along a horizontal axis. The time-line is broken
               into increments referred to as development phases,
               identified with Roman numerals. Where possible
               these increments are dated or in some way marked in
               terms of time. These phases are usually labeled
               with descriptive phrases which point out the
               central thrust of the development that happened in
               the phase.

definition   The time-line is the linear display along a
               horizontal axis which is broken up into development
               phases.

Example 1. Time-line--Peter Kuzmic,
           Type D/E Contemporary Leader in Yugoslavia

I. SOVEREIGN	II. LEARNING	III. GOD'S	IV. ACCEPTING
FOUNDATIONS	BY DOING	PROVISION	AN
AS A PEASANT	WITH MINIMUM	OF TRAINING	EXPANDING
YOUNGSTER	RESOURCES	WITH GREAT	MINISTRY
		RESOURCES	

```
|----------------|----------------|----------------|------------|
1946             1961             1967             1972        1982
```

Example 2. Time-line--Watchman Nee,
           Type D Historical Leader in China

I. CHANGE	II. FOUNDATIONAL	III. DIRECT TO	IV. MATURITY
DYNAMICS	LESSONS	INDIRECT	YEARS
FOUNDATIONS		MINISTRY	

```
|-------------|-----------------|--------------|----------------|
1903          1921              1927           1941             1972
```

Example 3. Time-line--Dawson Trottman,
           Type D Historical Leader in United States

I. RESTLESS	II. DEVELOPING	III. BROADENING THE
FOUNDATIONS	THE MODEL	VISION: CUT-OFF

```
|-------------------//-----|----------//-------|----------|
1906                       1933              1948       1956
```

comment   A time-line can only be constructed after much
               study is done on the leader in order to identify
               the development phases.

UNIQUE TIME-LINE   synonym: often shortened to time-line

introduction   A given leadership emergence study on a leader will
produce a time-line that is unique to that leader.
There will be a foundation period in which God
works sovereignly. There will be a transition time
into full time Christian work. From there on, time
periods will vary with each leader. They will fit
God's development for that leader. Development
phases should be labeled to capture that
uniqueness.

definition   A unique time-line refers to a time-line describing
a given leader's lifetime which will have unique
development phases bearing labels expressing that
uniqueness.

Example 1. Peter Kuzmic, Type D/E Contemporary leader

I. SOVEREIGN FOUNDATIONS AS A PEASANT YOUNGSTER	II. LEARNING BY DOING; MINIMUM RESOURCES	III. GOD'S PROVISION; GREAT TRAINING RESOURCES	IV. ACCEPTING AN EXPANDING MINISTRY

```
|--------------|---------------|-----------------|-----------------|
1946          1961          1967             1972            1982
```

Example 2. Dawson Trottman, Type D Historical leader

I. RESTLESS FOUNDATIONS	II. DEVELOPING THE MODEL	III. BROADENING THE VISION: CUT-OFF

```
|-------------//----------|-----------//------|-----------------|
1906                    1933              1948            1956
```

Example 3. Apostle Peter, Type D/E Biblical Leader

I. RUGGED FISHERMAN FOUNDATIONS	II. RUGGED TRAINING FOR HEADING A MOVEMENT	III. OPENING DOORS FOR THE MOVEMENT	VI. AFTERGLOW REFLECTIONS ON THE MOVEMENT

```
|------------|-------------------|------------------|-------------|
```

Early life	A. Three calls	A. Jerusalem Jews	Writings
	B. Growing	B. Samaritans	
	C. Attachment	C. Gentiles	
	C. Brokenness	D. Antioch Gentiles	
		E. Jerusalem Council	

comment   On the first two examples, no sub-phases were
given. Notice that on the Apostle Peter time-line
the sub-phases were given and listed vertically.
Where there is room these would normally be given
sequentially in a horizontal manner so as to agree
with the actual time markers.

EXAMPLES OF CONTEMPORARY UNIQUE TIME-LINES

Example 1. Brian Newton, Unique Time-Line (Newton 1983:6)

```
I.              II.            III.           IV.         V.
PRE-            AWARENESS      SECULAR        FORMAL      MISSIONARY
CONVERSION      OF GOD         TRAINING/      TRAINING    EXPERIENCE
                               EXPERIENCE
|------------|------------|---------------|----------|-----------|
1944         1953         1959            1971       1974        1983
```

Example 2. Duane Wetherby, Unique Time-Line (Wetherby 1983:6)

```
I.  EARLY        II. PARA-CHURCH   III. CHURCH        IV. MISSION
    FORMATION        EXPERIENCE         EXPERIENCE        PREPARATION
|--------//-----|-----------------|----------------|-------------|
1952            1971              1979             1982          1983
```

Example 3. Nicholas Woodbury, Unique Time-Line (Woodbury 1984:6)

```
I. EARLY-LIFE            II. FORMAL        III. INITIAL    IV. OVERSEAS
   FORMATION                 TRAINING           MINISTRY        MINISTRY
|--------------------|-----------------|----------------|--//-----|
1939                 1957              1964             1969     1984
```

Example 4. Margaret Burt, Unique Time-Line (Burt 1989:1)

```
I. FOUNDATIONS     II. PASTORAL      III. TEACHING      IV. CROSS-
   LAID                MINISTRY           MINISTRY           CULTURAL
|------------------|-----------------|----------------|----------|
1939               1964              1970             1978       1989
```

Example 5. Greg Gripentrog, Unique Time-Line (Gripentrog 1987:2)

```
I. PRE-CONVERSION   II. PREPARATORY            III. INITIAL
   INFLUENCE            MINISTRY EXPERIENCE          VISION REALIZED
|-------------------|------------------------|-------------------|
1947                1965                     1977                1987
```

Example 6. Elizabeth Myers (Myers 1989:1)

```
I. FOUNDATIONS                 II. EARLY TRAINING        III. BACK TO
                                   AND EXPERIENCE             SCHOOL
|-----------------------------|-----------------------|----------|
1955                          1970                    1987       1989
```

FEEDBACK ON UNIQUE TIME-LINE

1. Compare the three time-lines given on page 294.

   a. What items are common to all three?

   b. Which time-line has less development phases?
   Can you suggest why?

2. Examine the contemporary unique time-lines on page 295.

   a. Which of these has the most phases?

   b. What is the shortest phase?

   c. What is the longest phase?

   d. What are the implications of a short or long development
   phase or sub-phase?

ANSWERS----------
   1. a. All have the word FOUNDATIONS as part of the
descriptive phrase for development phase I. But other than that
they are different. And that is the whole point of unique time-
lines. They should use phrases which uniquely fit the person
being studied.
   b. Dawson Trottman has less development phases. One reason
is suggested in the phrase "Cut-Off" in development phase III.
Trottman drowned in an accident trying to save someone.
   2. a. Example 1. Newton's time-line. Actually, the short
phase, IV, should probably be joined with II and III to make one
larger transitional phase into ministry.
   b. Example 1. Newton, Phase IV. 1971-1974, Example 2.
Wetherby, Phase III 1979-1982, Wetherby's last phase only shows
1 year but the phase had only begun. (The same is true for Myer's
last phase.) Again the short phases are more likely sub-phases
in a larger unit.
   c. Burt's foundational phase, 1939-1965. The longest non-
foundational phase is Myers II phase, 17 years.
   d. Normally a development phase will range anywhere from 7-
20 years on the average. If you have development phases of 2 or
3 years then they most likely should be treated as sub-phases of
a larger development phase. Look for a larger generic title that
will group the shorter phases (as sub-phases). Boundary
conditions can last from abrupt changes (occurring almost
instantaneously) to 2 years or more.

DEVELOPMENT PHASES
SUB-PHASES

introduction   A time-line representing the life-time of a leader
               can usually be broken down into units which are
               related to a significant segment of development.
               These significant portions of time are called
               development phases. Development phases are usually
               indicated by Roman numerals and a label describing
               the thrust of development going on in the leader
               during the phase. Further sub-divisions of
               development phases are called sub-phases, which are
               indicated by capital letters. Development phases
               and sub-phases have similar characteristics.

definition   A development phase is a marked off length on a
               time-line representing a significant portion of
               time in a leader's life history in which notable
               development takes place usually following a
               repetitive standard development pattern.

definition   A sub-phase is a marked off length on a time-line
               within a development phase which points out an
               intermediate time of development during the
               development phase.

Example 1. Development Phases and Sub-Phases for A. W. Tozer,

```
I. PRE-CONVERSION   II. ON THE JOB    III. CITY LEADERSHIP  IV. WRAPPING
   INNER-DISCIPLINE     TRAINING/          WITH INCREASING      IT UP
   FOUNDATIONS          EXPANDING          NATIONAL             REFLECTION
                        RURAL INFLUENCE    INFLUENCE            TIME
|------------------|--------------------|---------------------|------------
1897               1915                 1928                  1959        196:
<---A----><--B-->  <-A-><--B--><--C-->|  <--------A--------> |<----A---->
```

A. Rural   A. New Beginning   A. New Beginning   A. Convergenc
   Disciplines   Conversion,   City Work   Reflection
B. New Beginning   B. Negative Guidance   Prophetic Role,   Lasting
   City   C. New Beginnings   Indirect Influence Literary
                      Rural Pastorates   Gift-Mix Matures   Influence

Example 2. Development Phases and Sub-phases in the Life of Nee
           (Phase IV. is expanded below.)

```
I. SOVEREIGN    II. FOUNDATIONAL III. DIRECT TO       IV. MATURITY
   FOUNDATIONS      LESSONS          INDIRECT MINISTRY     YEARS
|--------------|------------------|--------------------|------//---|
1903           1921               1927                 1941     1972
```

```
IV.  MATURITY YEARS
|--------------|------------------|----------------------------------|
1941           1945               1952                              1972
A. Isolation   B. Urgency         C. Glory Years--Prison Isolation
   Years          Years
```

FEEDBACK ON DEVELOPMENT PHASES/SUB-PHASES

1. Examine the time-line given below for the Apostle Paul.

I. SOVEREIGN CROSS-CULTURAL FOUNDATIONS	II. INDIVID-UALISTIC TRAINING; MENTORED	III. TRANSITION LEADERSHIP; CROSS-CULTURAL MINISTRY	IV. DESTINY FULFILLED; FINISHING WELL

```
|---------------|---------------|-------------------|-----------|
2 B.C.?          37?            48?                 60?         69
                <-A--><--B-->   <-A-> <-B--> <--C--> <-A-> <--B-->
```

	A. Dynamic Reflection	A. Power Break Out Conflict; Change Dynamics	A. Isolation Rome/ Prayer, Dynamic Reflection
	B. Mentored By Barnabas	B. Conflict/ leadership development	B. Leadership Concerns
		C. Maturing Theologically	

a. How many development phases are given?

b. How many sub-phases are given?

c. What is the title of the last sub-phase listed?

2. Look again at the time-line for the Apostle Paul. Note that some of the labels for the development phases are a bit cumbersome? See if you can give a more concise label for development phases II and III?

a. your label for Phase II:

b. your label for Phase III:

ANSWERS----------

1. a. 4 b. 7 (Notice that the sub-phases are listed vertically. Where there is room they should be listed horizontally at the proper time indicated on the time-line.) c. Leadership Concerns
   2. Here are my attempts:
      a. Phase II: Early Ministry Efforts
      b. Phase III: The Leadership Vision Unfolds

3 CHARACTERISTICS OF DEVELOPMENT PHASES

introduction   A development phase represents a unit of time in a
                  person's life. It can be identified in one or more
                  of the following ways: 1. By observing the boundary
                  behavior similar to that of the standard
                  development pattern; 2. Noting major changes in
                  sphere of influence;   3. By noting the dominant
                  kind of process items happening.

definition   The standard development pattern involves a cycle
                  of transitional behavior, stabilizing behavior, and
                  boundary behavior.

definition   Sphere of influence refers to the totality of
                  people being influenced and for whom a leader will
                  give an account to God which includes those people
                  under direct personal influence (face-to-face
                  present ministry), those under indirect influence
                  (non-time-bound influence), and those under
                  organizational influence (influence flowing through
                  organizational structures.)

definition   Dominant process items refer to the kinds of
                  process items which are occurring which can be
                  correlated to early development phases, middle
                  development phases, and latter development phases.

standard   During the stable portion of a boundary phase a
development   person seeks to work out a lifestyle which agrees
3 stages   with the basic decisions made in the transition
                  period.   This continues until boundary behavior
                  forces reevaluation of those decisions and the
                  stabilizing lifestyle. The boundary behavior
                  usually leads back into transition behavior in
                  which decisions are made concerning the next stable
                  period to follow. The cycle repeats. Usually the
                  transition and boundary times taken together are
                  shorter than the stabilizing period sandwiched in
                  between them. See Boundary Processing.

sphere of   Sphere of influence usually differs both in degree
influence   and kind from one development phase to the next.
factors   Degree refers to the number of people being
                  influenced. Kind means the means of influence.
                  Influence-mix refers to the balance between direct,
                  indirect and organizational means of influence.

processing   Early development phases will have process items
and   which focus on basic lessons in spiritual
time   formation. Middle development phases will have
                  process items setting the direction for ministerial
                  formation. Latter development phases have process
                  items focusing on in-depth maturity in spiritual
                  formation and in ministerial formation.

CHARACTERISTIC 1--THE STANDARD DEVELOPMENT PATTERN

introduction   Below is given the time-line for A. W. Tozer (See
               also page 293), a type D, Christian and Missionary
               Alliance pastor. I will use this time-line to
               explain how characteristic 1 is seen. Phase II is
               expanded below.

```
I. PRE-CONVERSION    II. ON THE JOB      III. CITY LEADERSHIP  IV. WRAPPING
   INNER-DISCIPLINE      TRAINING/            WITH INCREASING      IT UP
   FOUNDATIONS           EXPANDING            NATIONAL             REFLECTION
                         RURAL INFLUENCE      INFLUENCE            TIME
|-------------------|--------------------|--------------------|-------------|
1897                1915                 1928                 1959        1963
<---A----><--B-->  <-A-><--B--><--C-->|  <--------A--------> |<----A---->
```

```
| II. ON-THE-JOB TRAINING: EXPANDING RURAL INFLUENCE                      |
|---------------|-------------|----------------------------------------|
|1915          1917          1919                                    1928|
A. New Birth    B. New          C. New Churches
                   Church          Morgantown  Toledo  Indianapolis
```

Explanation

     The phase as a whole demonstrates the standard boundary
pattern of transition, stabilization, and boundary turmoil. The
phase began with a major transition decision--conversion to
Christ. This decision led Tozer to join a church in which he
could work out his Christian commitment. This in turn led to a
deepening commitment and eventually ministry. Decisions to
minister led to rural churches, town church, and a large town
church. The final boundary condition involved Tozer's moving
from his town ministry to a city ministry. Each sub-phase also
demonstrates the same standard pattern. See table below.

Sub-phase	transition	stabilization	boundary
A. New Birth	conversion experience	joined Methodist church, began to grow as christian; spiritual formation	became too fundamental for Methodist church; evaluation led him to join another church
B. New Church	decision to join a church	began to grow not only in spiritual formation but ministerial formation; acquired ministry skills	growth in ministerial formation led to more ministry; finally led to pastoring a rural church
C. New Churches	needed bigger challenge	growth in minister-ial formation in each new church	called to new churches; this was repeated 3 times

CHARACTERISTIC 2--CHANGE IN SPHERE OF INFLUENCE

introduction A. W. Tozer's time-line for phase 2 and 3 will be
used to explain how characteristic 2, change in
sphere of influence, is important in identifying
different development phases. The influence-mix in
Phase II is limited to small direct face-to-face
influence. In Phase III it involves large direct
face-to-face influence, indirect influence, and
organizational influence.

Looking at Phase II and III in terms of Sphere of Influence

II. ON-THE-JOB-TRAINING	III. CITY LEADERSHIP; NATIONAL INFLUENCE
influence-mix--direct face-to-face: town church	influence-mix--direct face-to-face: city church; became large church
	indirect: teaching in Bible schools, radio ministry, writing books, articles, speaking in conferences,
	organizational: on major committee for denomination; networked with many important Christian leaders in other denominations, organizations, and other groups.

Explanation--Reflecting Sphere of Influence Change

Tozer's transition from Phase II, New Beginnings to Phase
III, City Leadership, Expanding National Influence, illustrates
variation in change of influence between different development
phases. In Phase II, Tozer's influence was only direct. It
concerned primarily face-to-face ministry to the same people. It
was relatively small numbers of people, being primarily a small
town local church. He moved in that phase from a new believer
influencing individuals to an ordained pastor. His pastorates
were all small churches: one was in Morgantown, West Virginia;
one in Toledo, Ohio; one in Indianapolis, Indiana. In Phase III,
his sphere of influence increased both in size and kind. Direct
ministry involved a large city church. But his influence also
changed beyond direct influence. In Chicago, probably the hub of
Christian activity in the United States during the period of his
ministry, he developed a large indirect sphere of influence
through radio, publishing articles, writing books, speaking in
conferences, and teaching in training institutions (e.g. Moody
Bible Institute, Wheaton College, and Fort Wayne Bible College).
In addition to word ministries, both direct and indirect, he
developed organizational influence in two ways. He was on a
major executive committee for his denomination which affected the
denomination throughout the United States. He also networked
with important leaders involved in many Christian organizations.
Of course the sphere of influence in Phase III did not develop
overnight. But it differed from Phase II even at the start.

CHARACTERISTIC 3--DOMINANT PROCESS ITEMS

introduction   A lesser characteristic for generally identifying differing development phases involves recognition of process items that dominate during the development phase. The diagram below lists those which correlate to these periods. Others not listed occur throughout.

Dominant Process Items

Early Phases	Middle Phases	Latter Phases
● destiny preparation	● ministry tasks	● life crisis
● entry context	● ministry challenge	● isolation
● family influence	● ministry skills	● spiritual authority
● basic skills	● ministry assignment	● ideal role discovery
● leadership committal	● training progress	● ideal influence-mix discovery
● word checks	● giftedness discovery	● destiny fulfillment
● obedience checks	● power items	
● integrity checks	● ministry structure insights	
	● leadership backlash	
	● influence challenge	
	● destiny revelation	
	● prayer challenge	
	● faith challenge	
	● spiritual warfare	
	● relationship insights	
	● authority insights	
	● ministry conflict	
	● ministry affirmation	

explanation   Early development phases will usually have process items which focus on basic lessons in spiritual formation (See Belesky 1987). Middle development phases will have process items setting the direction for ministerial formation (See Gripentrog 1987, Finzel 1987, and Waldner 1987 as typical examples). Latter development phases have process items focusing on in-depth maturity in spiritual formation and in strategic formation (see Clinton 1982d, study of Nee for a typical example).

relative   Of the three development phase characteristics,
importance   boundary analysis of the standard development phase pattern is most useful in specifying a development phase. Sphere of influence change is the next most useful. Dominant process items is weakest.

DEVELOPMENT TASK

introduction   Each development phase is characterized by general
                 and special accomplishments. These accomplishments
                 are called development tasks.

definition   A <u>development</u> <u>task</u> refers to the general and unique
                 goals of a development phase and to which
                 processing in the phase is directed.

example   A developmental task for the transitional period
                 into leadership involves God's working on inner
                 character formation including integrity, obedience,
                 and ability to hear and understand God.

example   A developmental task for the early growth ministry
                 time involves God's stimulation of the leader to
                 initially discover and develop giftedness via use.

general   Development phases have broad development tasks
development   which apply broadly to all leaders and specific
goals   unique goals applying to the individual leader.
                 Some general goals include the following.

<u>Phases</u>   <u>Developmental</u> <u>Tasks</u>

Early   1. Mold embryonic leadership personality.
                 2. Mold inner character.
                 3. Initiate discovery of leadership potential.

Middle   1. Facilitate development of leadership potential.
                 2. Develop ministry skills including initial
                    discovery and use of giftedness elements.
                 3. Develop ministry philosophy including an
                    experiential understanding of God's redemptive
                    structures and purposes.

Latter   1. Develop maturity both in spiritual formation
                    and in ministerial formation.
                 2. Develop spiritual authority as the foundational
                    power base.
                 3. Maximize leadership effectiveness toward
                    convergence.

primary   The standard developmental pattern involves
development   transition, stabilization, and turmoil (boundary)
task   behaviors. Described broadly, the primary task of
                 each stable period of a developmental phase is the
                 working out of a lifestyle which agrees with the
                 major decisions made during the previous transition
                 period. The working out of that task during the
                 "stable" period does not mean absence of stress
                 and problems and changes. But it does mean the
                 major direction has been set and will not change
                 until the next boundary period.

FEEDBACK ON DEVELOPMENT TASK

1. Examine the time-line given below for Dr. R. C. McQuilkin.

Time-Line for R. C. McQuilkin, Founder of Columbia Bible College

```
I. VICTORY            II. ORGANIZATIONAL  III. IMPLEMENTING LIFE-
   COMMITMENT             LEADERSHIP TRNG        VISION, THREE THRUSTS
|-------------------|--------------------|------------------------|
1886 1895  1898  1911       1917          1921                   1952
<-A-><--B-><--C-->  |  <--A-->  <---B---->|<----------A------------>
                                           <-------B------->
                                          <----------C------------>
```

A. Home   A. Organizational   A. Thrust 1. Bible College,
B. Church   Apprenticeship   Train Missionaries
   Training   B. Organizational   B. Thrust 2. Disseminate
C. Work/Informal   First Steps   Victorious Life Testimony,
   Training/   Ben Lippen, Conference
   Sodality   C. Thrust 3. Publish Victory
                                              Message

Even though you have not studied Dr. McQuilkin's life, from what
you know about the concept of a development task and from the
titles of the second development phase and its two sub-phases,
what would you say might have been a developmental task for Phase
II?

2. Refer to the time-line of A. W. Tozer on page 297. Suggest
one or two development tasks for phase II, On-the-Job Training:
Expanding Rural Influence.

3. Refer to the time-line of A. W. Tozer on page 297 (phases II
and III). Suggest one or two development tasks for phase III,
City Leadership; National Influence.

ANSWERS----------

     1. Develop facility with para-church organizations. It
appears to me that God was giving him training in Christian para-
church organizations which would later be used to build two major
Christian organizations in Phase III.
     2. Development tasks included: 1) learning basic public
communication skills before small groups, then larger ones. 2)
disciplines involving study of word and preparation of messages.
     3. Development tasks included: 1) preparation and giving of
Radio messages, 2) various literary skills--writing of articles,
editing articles, writing of books, 3) communication skills
before large audiences, and 4) networking skills.

BOUNDARY   synonym: boundary condition, boundary pattern

introduction   The standard developmental pattern includes
                 transition, stabilization, and boundary behaviors.
                 Boundary refers to the time period which ends the
                 stabilization period. You will remember that
                 stabilization refers to that time in which a leader
                 is outworking choices made during the transition
                 time. He/she does this until a boundary time--a
                 time of reflecting back on what has been done,
                 evaluation of the lifestyle of the stabilization
                 period, and searching for what God wants in the
                 immediate future. This searching usually leads to
                 alternative choices and another transition period
                 in which choices are made. Boundary length can be
                 abrupt or it can take place over a period of
                 several months or even a few years.

definition   Boundary is the label given to the time immediately
                 preceding the end of a sub-phase or phase which
                 usually is made up of an entry stage, transition
                 stage, and termination stage.

kinds of   Typically boundary times include boundary events
boundary   involving such things as **crises** (Palich 1987:42,
activity   birth of child with Down syndrome), **promotions**
                 (Gripentrog 1987:88, made regional director),
                 change to a new ministry (Finzel 1987:45 from
                 pastoral to Eastern European missionary), **change** of
                 organization (Wetherby 1983:6,26 Navigators to
                 secular and church involvement), **educational**
                 interlude which sets a new direction (Davis
                 1987:46, reflective study at School of World
                 Mission following relationship processing), an
                 isolation experience which brings on retrospective
                 evaluation (Clinton 1982d, Nee, sickness nearly
                 unto death), **a paradigm shift:** (Shelley 1985:10,22
                 change in views of leadership--influence, spiritual
                 authority, and gift-mix); **unusual religious**
                 experiences (Chan 1987:45, overwhelming by Holy
                 Spirit). **life-changing encounters with a person**
                 (Humble 1987:3,34; Sims 1987:71), a **divine guidance**
                 experience (Webb 1985:20, three housing miracles),
                 a geographic shift (Colquhoun 1987:41,42, move to
                 California). These events often contain one or more
                 process incidents which are significant in the
                 development of the leader.

common   Finzel's research (1988) on boundary processing
boundary   identified at least 10 process items associated
process   with boundary processing. These include: divine
items   contact, crisis/life crisis, ministry challenge,
                 faith challenge, conflict, leadership committal,
                 isolation, destiny revelation, negative
                 preparation, and training progress.

BOUNDARY TASK

introduction   Boundary tasks involve two general evaluation tasks
                 common to all leaders going through boundaries and
                 various specific tasks unique to the individual.

definition   Boundary tasks refers to the major developmental
                 tasks of a boundary condition which is to question
                 and reappraise the immediately preceding stable
                 period in terms of life and ministry with a view to
                 exploring various possibilities for change that God
                 intends and to move toward commitment to the
                 crucial choices that will form the basis for the
                 new stability period to follow.

3 kinds   Development task 1 involves retrospective
of tasks   reflection, analysis, and evaluation of development
                 in the previous development phase. Some sense of
                 closure is necessary in order to clearly evaluate
                 the future. Development task 2 involves
                 formulation and anticipation of future development
                 needed and guidance for next ministry. Development
                 task 3 involves decision making for the
                 individual's unique situation and could involve
                 several sub-tasks.

boundary   Finzel's Analytical Framework provides the backdrop
framework   for analysis of boundary tasks. It correlates
                 boundary processing with the standard development
                 pattern.

1. Development Pattern:

   STABILIZATION   **BOUNDARY BEHAVIOR**   **TRANSITION**

2. Boundary Stages

        ————————> entry ————> evaluation ————> termination
                  stage   stage   stage

3. Boundary Tasks

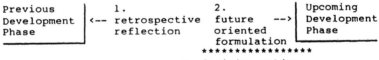

Previous	1.	2.	Upcoming
Development	<-- retrospective	future -->	Development
Phase	reflection	oriented	Phase
		formulation	

                         ****
                         3. decision making

   FINZEL'S ANALYTICAL FRAMEWORK FOR BOUNDARY ANALYSIS

EXAMPLE OF BOUNDARIES DISPLAYED

introduction   A. W. Tozer's time-line is used to indicate
                boundary times and show relative length. The major
                factors for each of the boundaries is briefly
                described.

symbol   A capital "B" enclosed in brackets, [B], is used to
                indicate a boundary for a development phase. A
                small "b" is similarly used to indicate a boundary
                for a sub-phase. If the boundary conditions lasts
                for a longer time, lines within the bracket
                indicate this, [-----B1-----].

example   From Tozer time-line

I. INNER-   II. ON-THE-JOB- III. CITY   IV. WRAP-UP;
   DISCIPLINE   TRAINING;   LEADERSHIP   REFLECTION
   FOUNDATIONS   NATIONAL
                                         INFLUENCE
|----------------|---------------|-------------------|-------------|
1897   1919   1928   1959   1963
                 [B1]   [-B2-]   [---B3-]

B1 = conversion experience, an abrupt boundary event which
     resulted in immediate transition choices

The major development task was to transition Tozer into full time
Christian leadership. Conversion brought a paradigm shift.
Activity in one church (more liberal in views than Tozer's
conservative views) led to his transferring membership to a
church more compatible. Activity in ministry eventually led to a
decision to be a rural pastor.

B2 = decision to accept call to Chicago ministry, a major change
     in ministry focus (large city church) and geographical shift
     from town to city.

The major development task was that of influence challenge
processing. Tozer had capacities beyond that of a town church.
God needed to move him into a geographic center where he could be
exposed nationally. The larger church provided a backdrop and
potential resources from which sphere of influence could be
expanded.

B3 = growing conviction to retire from the rigors of a large city
     pastorate to a ministry involving more contemplation, study
     and writing. The need for another building expansion was the
     termination event which hastened commitment to the crucial
     choice.

The major development task was via negative preparation. Tozer
needed to step down for the sake of the church's own need to
expand and for Tozer's own need to reflect and consolidate a
life-time of learning.

FEEDBACK ON BOUNDARY

1. Make sure you understand the concept of the boundary symbol.
Examine the time-line of Dawson Trottman given below. Remember
that in a boundary time the status quo is challenged, there is
reflecting back, evaluation of previous life and
ministry, and reflection forward including possible
alternative decisions.

example   From Trottman time-line

```
I. RESTLESS        II. DEVELOPING THE  III. BROADENING VISION;
   FOUNDATIONS         MODEL                CUT-OFF
|-----------------|--------------------|---------------|
1906              1933                 1948            1956
                  [---B1--]
```

Without knowing any of the details of this boundary other than
what can be observed from the time-line as a whole and the
boundary symbol itself, what could you say about the boundary and
boundary task?

2. Interview a leader whom you are certain has gone through some
boundary condition. Explain to the leader the general notion of
a boundary condition and then have that leader describe a major
boundary condition. As he/she describes the boundary condition
see if you can identify the length of the boundary time, the
entry, transition, and termination stages, the boundary task and
some of the reappraisal thinking and formulation of future
thinking that went on. In what way was there divine intervention
in the boundary pattern?

ANSWERS----------
    1. I happened to have studied this boundary condition in
detail and know that it was a major change in understanding of
ministry philosophy which shifted from evangelistic activity to
evangelism with in-depth discipleship (follow-up). This
transpired over a period of many months and included at least
three boundary process items worthy of note: a word process item,
a negative preparation guidance item, and a divine contact
guidance item. But even if I hadn't studied his life, just from
the time-line and symbol alone I could give some educated
guesses. I would suggest three things: (1) The boundary took a
long time, perhaps a year or two. (2) The boundary continued for
several months into the next development phase. Though there was
a definite shift toward the future it took time for it to
develop. (3) Probably since phase II speaks of a model being
developed the boundary task most likely involved the discovery of
that model.
    2. Your choice.

FEEDBACK ON ALL TIME-LINE CONCEPTS

1. Draw your own personal unique time-line and label the development phases and sub-phases.

2. Refer to your own time-line which you just constructed. Label a boundary on it. Then describe that boundary condition from your own life. See if you can indicate the entry stage, the transition stage, and the termination stage in the boundary processing. Indicate some of the retrospective reflection. Point out the future oriented formulation. What were some of the specific decisions that terminated the boundary? In retrospect what would you say was the major boundary task of that boundary condition?

3. Refer to your own time-line which you just constructed.

a. For your first development phase suggest briefly in what ways you see the following early developmental tasks indicated.

   (1) Indications of God's providential molding of embryonic leadership personality:

   (2) Indications of God's providential molding of inner character:

   (3) Indications of God's providential indications of leadership potential:

b. For your second development phase check any of the following general middle developmental tasks which you have seen God work on. Have a specific instance in mind and be prepared to share it with someone.

___(1) Facilitate development of leadership potential.
___(2) Develop ministry skills including initial discovery of giftedness
___(3) Provide opportunity for increasing use of gifts.
___(4) Develop ministry philosophy.

ANSWERS----------
      None given. These exercises should be shared with someone in order to bring closure to understanding of the concepts.

SUMMARY OF TIME-LINE CONCEPTS

The dominant concept of the time variable is the **time-line**.
All leaders can describe a time-line that is unique to them.
A **unique time-line** is broken up into division called **development
phases** which terminate with boundary events. Development phases
can themselves be subdivided into smaller units called **sub-phases**
which have boundary terminations.

Three characteristics help define development phases.   The
most important is the **standard development pattern**. Every
development phase involves three processes going on.   There is
stabilization behavior in which decisions from the previous
transition are being worked out.   Then there is boundary behavior
which signals the coming of a new development phase.   Finally
there is the transitional behavior that propels one into the new
development phase. Analysis of boundary processing is the most
helpful ide ntification aid for determining development phases.   A
second he¹pful characteristic involves recognition of **change of
sphere of influence**. Significant changes in sphere of influence
as to degree (more or less) and kind usually indicate a
distinction in development phases.   The changes may occur over a
period of time but it will be clear that at the end of that time
that sphere of influence is very different from what it was at
the beginning of that time.   A third characteristic less helpful
in identifying development phases recognizes that **dominant**
process items can usually be determined for different time
periods of development.   But process items are not always fixed
so closely to time. So this third characteristic, while serving
to confirm, is not as helpful in discovering development phases.

Development phases can be analyzed for overall development
accomplishments toward leadership. **Development tasks** describe
overall accomplishments in the leader's life.   These tasks are
described in terms of specific issues for development phases.
They also describe the general development of leadership
potential.   Boundaries can be analyzed for tasks also. Such tasks
are called **boundary** tasks.   Two general tasks are usually
accomplished.   One involves retrospective reflection concerning
the previous development phase.   The other looks forward to what
should happen next.   Decisions must be made concerning the upcoming development phase.   These decisions comprise the third
kind of boundary task.   They are specific to each individual
person.

After a time-line is constructed process incidents can be
identified all along it. The time-line can then be used as a
helpful tool for integrating evaluation measures.   The next
chapter discusses one of the first approaches which can be used
to evaluate.   That involves comparison of unique time-lines with
generic time-lines.   Generic time-lines are time-lines
synthesized from comparative studies of many unique time-lines.
Two such generic time-lines give a framework for the overall flow
of development and can be used as benchmarks to evaluate unique
time-lines.

CHAPTER 10. GENERIC TIME-LINES

Integrative Overview

Chapter 9 overviewed the concepts of the time variable. The essential concept was that of the time-line. The time-line forms the backdrop along which process items can be located and analyzed for development issues. Each leader has a unique time-line that describes his/her own life history in terms of development phases. Comparative study of many of these unique time-lines resulted in some general overall time-line patterns. These general overall patterns are called generic time-lines. They form the subject of this chapter.

Preview

Two major generic time-lines are introduced in this chapter. The more structured, the **generalized time-line**, is useful in describing leadership development primarily from a personal growth perspective. It is useful with lay leaders as well as full time Christian leaders. The **ministry time-line** views development of full time Christian workers. Neither time-line will precisely fit a given leader's unique time-line. But comparative study of a given leader's unique time-line with either of the generic time-line gives a sense of where a leader is in respect to other leaders. The lack of fit between a unique time-line and the generalized time-line is explained by **compression/overlap**. **Grouping** describes the effect of evaluating a unique time-line using the ministry time-line.

Each of the generic time-lines are explained in a running discussional format. Descriptive remarks are given concerning various development tasks along the way. Barriers to development and problems that leaders face in development are also mentioned in the running flow.

Several other generic time-lines are mentioned, in order to illustrate further the usefulness of this concept.

Generic Time-Lines Introduced

Integration efforts involving the time-variable led to comparative study of many unique time-lines which resulted in synthesis of patterns of time-lines. These are called generic time-lines and serve useful purposes for

1. integration,
2. analyzing various patterns,
3. stimulating one who is in the initial stage of formulating a unique time-line, and
4. for planning training designs.

In my research[1] I identified the following four generic
time-lines:

1. the Generalized Time-Line (a six stage personal
   growth time-line); for leaders types A-E, [1983]
2. the Ministry Time-Line (a three stage time-line with
   transitions focusing on full time-ministry
   development); primarily for leaders types C-E [1988].
3. a Korean pattern for type A, B, C Korean leaders
   (geographically located only in Korea) [1987].
4. a Singaporean pattern for type A, B Singaporean
   leaders (geographically located only in Singapore) [1987].

The first two, the Generalized Time-Line and the Ministry
Time-Line are the most useful when giving an overall explanation
of leadership development theory as they provide integrating
frameworks for discussing high level abstract concepts.

The Generalized Time-Line which focuses on personal
development (leadership character and leadership values) is
applicable to lay leaders (Type A and B leaders) as well as
middle and high level leaders (Types C, D, and E). It is
particularly useful in giving an overall preview for pre-service
leaders who are in the early stages of their leadership
emergence.

The Ministry Time-Line which focuses on development of the
leader particularly with reference to ministry effectiveness
(leadership skills and leadership values) contains great
explanatory power for full time mid-career Christian leaders
(Types C, D, and E). Since the ministry time-line is the most
applicable to mid-career full time leaders, it is used in
integrating the processing and response variables in this manual.

Generic time-lines 3 and 4 are most helpful for specific
studies dealing with early emergence patterns of lay leaders in
those specific cultures. They show that the foundational stage
differs in different cultures due to the societies' educational
patterns and family patterns.

----
[1]Dates in brackets indicate time when the concept emerged in the
research.

GENERALIZED TIME-LINE

introduction   Each individual leader's time-line is unique.
However, there are similarities in all leader's
time-lines. Comparative study has resulted in the
identification of common features. The generalized
time-line, given below is a synthesis of many
individual time-lines. While it rarely fits anyone
exactly, it does focus on the common development
issues of all leaders.

Generalized Time-Line

Phase I	Phase II	Phase III	Phase IV	Phase V	Phase VI
SOVEREIGN	INNER-	MINISTRY	LIFE	CONVERGENCE	AFTERGLOW
FOUNDATIONS	LIFE	MATURING	MATURING		
	GROWTH				

|-----------|--------|-----------|----------|------------|-------|

Table 10-1 Summary of Phases and Tasks

Phase	God's Developmental Tasks	Leader Response
Sovereign Founda- tions	• laying of foundations in the life including leadership potential	• respond positively • take advantage of these foundations
Inner- Life Growth	• identification of leadership potential • formation of basal leadership character through testing	• respond positively to testing • be prepared for expansion after test
Ministry Maturing	• initial identification: gifts and skills for ministry • release of leader to increasingly use and develop gifts and skills • teaching relationship lessons • unfolds ministry philosophy	• recognition of gifts and skills • take steps to use and develop gifts • learn & use lesson of submission and authority • catch the vision
Life Maturing	• deepened understanding of God • develop intimacy with God • focus on relationship with God as primary responsibility not success	• respond positively to deep processing • deepen communion • recognize ministry flows from being
Conver- gence	• guidance of leader into role and place of maximum contribution	• trust and rest and wait • make decisions toward convergence
After- glow	• bring glory to God for a life-time of leadership	• honor God's faithfulness

COMMENTARY ON THE GENERALIZED TIME-LINE

While it is true that each individual leader's time-line is
unique it is also true that there are similarities in all
leader's time-lines. Comparative study has resulted in the
identification of common features which relate to the personal
growth of a leader. The generalized time-line, given below in
Figure 10-1, is a synthesis of many individual unique time-lines.
While it rarely fits anyone exactly, it does focus on the common
development issues of all leaders. And it is the standard major
pattern, from a personal growth aspect, to which all unique time-
lines can be compared.

```
PHASE I       PHASE II    PHASE III    PHASE IV    PHASE V    PHASE VI
Sovereign     Inner-Life  Ministry     Life        Conver-    Afterglow
Foundations   Growth      Maturing     Maturing    gence
|-----------|----------|-----------|----------|---------|-------|
```

FIGURE 10-1
THE GENERALIZED TIME-LINE

Figure 10-1 depicts the Generalized Time-Line. Table 10-1
summarizes the Generalized Time-Line in terms of phases, general
development tasks, and suggested response from leaders to these
general development tasks. The following is a more detailed
discussion of the thrust of the development tasks listed in Table
10-1. It flows through each phase of the Generalized Time-Line.
Various process items are mentioned throughout each phase to show
how they fit in terms of a time perspective.

Phase I. Sovereign Foundations

In Phase I, **Sovereign Foundations,** God providentially works
through family, contextual background, and historical events
(including the timing of the birth of each leader) to establish
basic foundations in a leader's life. Sometimes it is difficult
for some leaders to believe that God was working through family
or environment, especially if these were not godly influences.
Personality characteristics and related experiences, whether good
or bad can be seen as used by God as well. Many times it is
later seen that personality traits correlate with the spiritual
gift-mix that God gives that person. The challenge of Phase I
through retrospective reflection is to identify the providence of
God. It is often difficult to see the importance of all these
items until later phases. Retrospective reflection will usually
allow an even deeper appreciation of His sovereignty.

The major developmental task of Phase I is the laying of
foundations in one's life. God sovereignly operates on this
developmental task. The potential leader has relatively little
control or determining influence over the majority of the
foundations which occur in this phase. The potential leader's
primary response to the major developmental task is to recognize
what has happened in the sovereign foundations phase and respond
positively in the present time, taking advantage, particularly in

guidance decisions, of the foundations God has laid.

Phase II. Inner-Life Growth

Following the foundation phase, a person who will emerge as a leader then goes through a time where the emphasis in his/her life is to know God in a more personal and real way. This phase is defined as Phase II, the **Inner-life Growth Phase**. The leader learns the importance of praying and hearing God. As he/she grows in discernment, understanding and obedience, such growth will be tested. Some of these early tests are crucial experiences that God will use to prepare the leader for the next steps in leadership.

Invariably, along with personal inner-life growth, the emerging leader gets involved in some kind of ministry. In the context of learning by doing, new inner-life lessons are seen and heeded. Even though the upcoming leader gets involved in ministry and does learn some ministry lessons, the dominant emphasis in this phase is inner-life growth.

The major developmental task in Phase II is the identification of leadership potential and the formation of character. God does this primarily through testing experiences. The potential leader's response to the major developmental task is to respond positively to these tests and to learn the fundamental lessons wrapped up in those foundational tests. The potential leader can expect God's expansions after testing and be prepared for tests involving larger responsibility.

Phase III. Ministry Maturing

In Phase III, Ministry Maturing, the emerging leader focuses on reaching out to others and helping them. The leader is beginning to experiment with his/her spiritual gifts though he/she may not even know what this doctrine is. Sometimes the budding leader will get non-formal training or even formal training in order to prepare for a more effective ministry. It is ministry which seems to be the focus of the rising leader at this stage.

Many of the ministry lessons will zero in on relationships with other people or on inadequacies in one's personal life. This will necessitate the continuation of inner-life growth testing as well. The testing items, dealing with inner-life growth, and the ministry items, dealing with important ministry lessons, dominate this stage of development.

The major developmental task of Phase III is twofold: one, the initial identification of gifts and skills and the increasing use of them in order to develop an increasingly effective ministry and two, the development of an experiential understanding of the body of Christ. This latter task will include many relationship lessons--some negative and some positive.

Reflective Comment on Phases I, II, and III

During Phases I, II, and III, God is primarily working in the leader and not **through** him or her. Though there may be much ministry activity and even fruitfulness, the major work is that which God is doing to and in the leader, not through him or her. Most often, emerging leaders don't recognize this. They are constantly evaluating productivity, activities, or fruitfulness. But God is quietly, often in unusual ways, trying to get the emerging leader to see that a **leader basically ministers out of what he/she is.** He is concerned with what the leader is in terms of being (character), more than doing (productivity).

Phase IV. Life Maturing

By Phase IV, **Life Maturing**, the leader has usually identified and is using his or her spiritual gifts in a ministry which is satisfying. The leader gains a sense of priorities through the lessons which are learned regarding how best to use giftedness. During this time the leader will focus on **what to do** and **what not to do** in ministry. This will result in a mature fruitfulness.

Such process items as isolation, crises, conflict, destiny experiences, and literary items take on a new meaning for the leader. The principle, that "ministry flows out of being" takes on new significance as the leader's character mellows and matures.

The major developmental task of Phase IV is the deepening of the leader's experiential understanding of God which in turn increases spiritual authority. The communion of the leader with God becomes foundational and more important than success in ministry. With this change the ministry itself takes on a deeper relevance and fruitfulness. The leader's response to this developmental task is to respond positively to the deep experiences which come in this phase and thus allow those items to deepen communion with God and become the base for lasting effective ministry.

Phase V. Convergence

In **Convergence**, Phase V, the leader is moved by God into a role which matches his or her giftedness set and experience so that ministry is maximized. Convergence roles not only free up a leader from doing ministry for which he or she is not gifted or suited, but also puts to use the best that the leader has to offer. Life maturing and ministry maturing peak together during this period.

Quite often though, many leaders do not actually experience convergence. There are various reasons for this. Sometimes they are hindered by their own lack of personal development. At other times, an organization may hinder a leader from realizing convergence by keeping him or her in a position that limits

potential. Some reasons are providential, and may be hard to
understand because we do not have the full picture. Convergence,
when realized, is maximized potential.

The major developmental task for Phase V, Convergence, is
the guidance of the leader into a role and place where maximum
ministry effectiveness can be reached for the leader. The
leader's response to the guidance efforts of God is to trust, to
rest, to watch, and to respond as God moves toward ministry which
takes advantage of the development which has gone on in the
preceding development phases. Convergence is not a goal,
something that one strives for, but rather a by-product,
something that manifests itself as a leader keeps on being
responsive to God.

Phase VI. Afterglow or Celebration

For a very few, there is **Afterglow** or **Celebration**. The fruit
of a lifetime of ministry and growth culminates in an era of
praise and indirect influence at very broad levels. The leader
at this stage of life has usually "retired" from formal ministry
positions and responsibility. But the leader in afterglow has
also built up a lifetime of contacts and will usually continue to
exert influence via these relationships. Others will seek them
out because of their consistent track record in knowing God and
seeing His work accomplished. Their storehouse of wisdom
gathered over a lifetime of leadership will continue to bless and
benefit many.

There is no recognizable developmental task in Phase VI,
Celebration, other than to allow a lifetime of ministry to
reflect the glory of God and to honor His faithfulness over a
lifetime of development.

THE MINISTRY TIME-LINE

introduction   Each individual leader's time-line is unique.
                However, there are similarities in all full time
                Christian leader's time-lines, especially when
                viewed from a ministry development perspective.
                Comparative study has resulted in the
                identification of common features. The ministry
                time-line, given below is a synthesis of many
                individual time-lines viewed from a ministry
                perspective. The ministry time-line assumes
                analysis of a full-time Christian worker while
                arbitrarily assigning the move into full time Christian
                work as the boundary between the foundational phase
                and the growth ministry phase.

Ministry Time-Line

Phase I	Phase II	Phase III
MINISTRY	GROWTH	UNIQUE
FOUNDATIONS	MINISTRY	MINISTRY

```
|-----------|---//-----|-------//--|---//-------|---------------|
A.           B.          A.          B.           A.        B.
Sovereign    Leadership  Provisional Competent    Role      Conver-
Leadership   Transition  Ministry    Ministry     Tran-     gence
Foundations                                       sition
```

                            [B1]   [-----B2-----]
                            full time   paradigm shift--"being"
                            ministry   as base of ministry;
                                              maturity in giftedness
                                              development, ministry
                                              philosophy, and discernment

distinctive   The time periods of the ministry do not
character-   necessarily coincide with boundary phases of a
istic   unique time-line. The provisional ministry sub-
                phase may last from 10-20 years and include 2 or
                more unique time-line phases.

Boundary B1   The move across the tactical barrier into a full
                time Christian worker position (type C leader)
                signals the shift from the MINISTRY FOUNDATION
                Phase to the GROWTH MINISTRY phase.

Boundary B2   Maturity in leadership character, leadership
                skills, and leadership values are expressed by
                operating out of a "being" base rather than a
                "doing/ success" base, development in giftedness,
                development in discernment, and a ministry
                philosophy in harmony with destiny processing.

MINISTRY TIME-LINE: PHASES AND IDENTIFYING FEATURES

Table 10-2 Phases and Identifying Features

Phase/Sub-Phase	Essential Characteristics	Patterns
I. **MINISTRY FOUNDATIONS**	God's early work of laying leadership foundations.	F.1, F.2, F.3, F.4, F.5
A. Sovereign Leadership	Same as SOVEREIGN FOUNDATIONS for generalized time-line.	
B. Leadership Transition	Some overlap with INNER-LIFE GROWTH Phase of generalized time-line; Focus here is on processing leading into ministry.	T.1, T.2, TR.1, TR.2, TR.3
II. **GROWTH MINISTRY**	Transition from a potential leader to a proficient leader.	
A. Provisional Ministry	1. Disappointment (role expectation and reality in dissonance). 2. Many leadership lessons learned via negative experience. 3. Trial and error approach to role and giftedness. 4. Large drop out. 5. Focus is on ministerial formation first and spiritual formation, second. Strategic formation is implicit and experiential. 6. Generally, inefficient ministry; inconsistent; some good, some bad.	M.1, M.2, M.3, M.4, M.5, M.6 M.7, M.8
B. Competent Ministry	1. Efficient ministry (doing things right). 2. Good basic knowledge of personal giftedness. 3. Experiential knowledge of mini-convergence; 4. Understanding of productive roles 5. Minister with confidence	M.6, M.7, M.8 UM.1, UM.2
III. **UNIQUE MINISTRY**	Effective ministry (doing the right things).	
A. Role Transition	1. Modification of role to enhance convergence.	UM.3, UM.4,
B. Convergence	1. Developed Ministry Philosophy. 2. Fulfilling of destiny.	UM.5

patterns	The patterns listed above are explained in detail in chapter 11. Table 10-2 should be used as a reference sheet when studying chapter 11.

EXAMPLE OF MINISTRY TIME-LINE RELATED TO UNIQUE TIME-LINES

introduction   The three examples which follow point out the
                distinction in time periods. The ministry time-
                line defines time periods in terms of measurement
                of leadership maturity. The unique time-lines uses
                "natural boundaries" to end development phases.

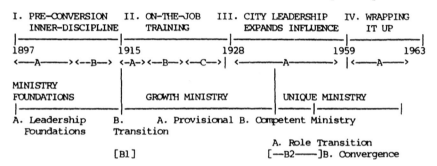

Figure 10-2. Tozer Time-Line Related To Ministry Time-Line


```
I.              II.           III.           IV.         V.
PRE-            AWARENESS     SECULAR        FORMAL      MISSIONARY
CONVERSION      OF GOD        TRAINING/      TRAINING    EXPERIENCE
                             EXPERIENCE
|-------------|-------------|---------------|----------|-----------|
1944        1953          1959            1971       1974        1983

                                                      GROWTH
MINISTRY FOUNDATIONS                                  MINISTRY
|----------------------------------------------|----------|-----------|
A. Sovereign Leadership Foundations           B. Tran-    A. Provisional
                                                 sition      Ministry
                                              [---B1----]
```

Figure 10-3. Newton Time-Line Related To Ministry Time-Line


```
I. EARLY-LIFE          II. FORMAL          III. INITIAL    IV. OVERSEAS
   FORMATION               TRAINING             MINISTRY        MINISTRY
|---------------------|------------------|----------------|--//-----|
1939              1957                1964             1969      1984
                                         GROWTH
| MINISTRY FOUNDATIONS                    MINISTRY
| ------------------------------------|-------------------|-----|
| A. Sovereign        B. Transition    |A. Provisional      B.
                      [----B1--------]                      Competent
```

Figure 10-4. Woodbury Time-Line Related To Ministry Time-Line

COMMENTARY ON THE MINISTRY TIME-LINE

The ministry time-line is a tool for viewing a leader's leadership development from a ministry perspective. It has three major phases: Phase I Ministry Foundations, Phase II Growth Ministry and Phase III Unique Ministry. The majority of leaders studied to date are in the growth ministry phase.

Ministry Foundations Phase

The **ministry foundations** phase corresponds roughly to two phases of the generalized time-line: the sovereign foundations phase plus the inner-life phase. Descriptive comments given explaining those two phases apply here also. This phase is viewed in two distinct sub-phases: sovereign leadership foundations and transition into full time leadership.

When using the ministry time-line particular emphasis is placed on analyzing processing from a ministry focus.

In addition to a special scrutiny of process items for ministry focus, the ministry time-line closely integrates response patterns into its analysis. These patterns especially concentrate on development from a ministry perspective. See also chapter 11 where these response patterns are defined in more detail. During the discussion which follows, enough of the pattern descriptions are given so that you can follow along with the flow of ministry development.

Sub Phase A, Leadership Foundations

Four foundational patterns describe the general backgrounds from which leaders emerge in the sovereign leadership foundations sub-phase: F.1 **Heritage**, F.2 **Radical**, F.3 **Accelerated**, F.4 **Delayed**. Each of the foundational patterns carries with it some inherent advantages and disadvantages. Each leader is unique and will reflect more or less, the advantages or disadvantages of each pattern.

The **heritage pattern** (F.1) is the **more common** pattern among Christian leaders. In the heritage pattern the leader comes from a Christian (or at least a nominal Christian) background. The leader is more or less processed into Christian values via the home and some church life.

Usually there is not a radical conversion experience (though there may be a growing awareness of God). Family life helps shape characteristics in the leader which will later be reflected in leadership. Normal schooling gives basic skills. Sports, clubs, or vocational experiences also teach competitiveness, perseverance, basic relational skills, organizational skills, entrepreneural skills or the like.

Toward the end of the teen years or during early collegiate years there is usually some sort of more radical commitment to

God (sometimes identified as conversion or as a surrender to do God's will) which frequently results in a desire to be a full time Christian worker. This can lead to on-the-job training or a choice for formal training.

The advantages of this pattern include those normally associated with heritage. There is the background of knowledge and values of Christianity which can be built upon. Frequently, there will be someone in the family line who has prayed for the new generation to become involved in God's work. Sometimes, there will be exemplary models of Christianity which will have influenced the person toward a sound implicit ministry philosophy. The person will have observed different gifts, natural abilities, and acquired skills in Christians so as to have an experiential foundation for giftedness development. Usually there will be support for the leader, though various family ambitions for the person may cancel this advantage. Usually few life style changes are needed as the leader moves into Christ an leadership since the basic Christian ethic is already intact.

Frequently this foundational pattern results in the person following training pattern one, TR.1, the transitional pre-service educational pattern.

The disadvantages are few. One of the most common is that familiarity with the things of Christianity may dull the spiritual realities of them. Enthusiastic committal to accomplishing God's work must be fostered by unusual experiences usually outside the routine of Christianity experienced while growing up. A second disadvantage may be that the routine of Christianity may not provide stimulus for on-the-job experience which can be vital to early identification of leadership potential. A third may be that ministry philosophy imbued via routine involvement in Christianity may be not challenging or apparently irrelevant in terms of reaching out to a lost world or cross-cultural involvement. Of the five typical cases, Waldner and Belesky and Baumgartner basically illustrate this pattern with some exceptions.

The radical committal pattern, F.2, refers to persons whose backgrounds are non-Christian or from very nominal Christian background. The person imbibes the values of the family, whether good or bad, as he or she grows up. Usually there is little or no knowledge of vital Christianity. Again normal schooling gives basic skills. Experience in sports, clubs, or part time jobs also teach competitiveness, perseverance, basic relational skills, organizational skills, entrepreneural skills, or the like. Usually the motivations built into the person are attainment of success or doing whatever gives enjoyment in life.

Then there comes an exposure to Christianity which involves a radical decision to follow Christ. Usually coincidental with this decision is a whole hearted committal to serve God. The experience can occur in high school, college, or during the

normal vocation. But it has decisive ramifications whenever it
occurs. All throughout life it will be looked back to as a major
marker event in life.

It usually results in very active on-the-job training which
involves giving of testimony about what has happened. Usually
the person is attracted to the means that brought about the
radical change whether it be a person or an organization. Early
on-the-job training usually follows that attraction. Ministry
philosophy flows from this exposure.

If the people are involved in the radical decision encourage
a learning-by-doing type of training, then the transitional
training pattern two (TR.2, the in-service pattern) is followed.
If they stress formal training then training pattern three (TR.3,
the modified in-service pattern) is often followed.

Advantages of this pattern involve a decisive leadership
committal process item which serves as foundational for all of
later leadership activity. Attitudes of committal involve
service to God right at the outset.

Another advantage involves early gift identification.
Frequently the radical experience will relate to giftedness or
acquisition of foundational skills which will be built upon. For
example, a conversion experience brought on by a gifted personal
evangelist may result in the new convert getting involved in
evangelism from the very first and eventually identifying and
using a spiritual gift of evangelism. If the radical conversion
came as a result of some small group experience where the Bible
was taught well, the emerging leader may well develop Bible study
and teaching skills and the gift of teaching or exhortation may
spring up.

Another advantage involves destiny processing, F.5. Because
of the radical nature of the committal frequently there is a
destiny preparation or revelation experience which will set the
tone for later development of focus in ministry philosophy.

A final advantage includes a fresh perspective on
Christianity. Since the person is usually unencumbered with a
Christian tradition frequently he or she is able to see new ideas
and create new kinds of structures and roles that would not be
thought of by a person of the heritage pattern.

Disadvantages include lack of Christian knowledge,
especially knowledge of the Bible. Frequently, there must be
radical lifestyle changes. Old habits are hard to break and may
result in early struggles regarding sanctification issues which
are taken for granted by heritage pattern persons. Early
leadership practices will follow the secular practices that have
been experienced whether good or bad. The emerging leader is
often unstable and vacillates between the old way of life and the
new.

The F.3 accelerated pattern and F.4 delayed pattern are response patterns observed about second generation (or more) leaders.

The F.3 **accelerated response pattern** describes the early rapid developmental pattern of generational Christian leaders. Such emerging leaders have a family heritage of Christian leadership and respond positively very early in life to ministry (often co-ministering with parents). It also describes some who do not come from a Christian heritage but are converted very early as in a child evangelism ministry or junior high or high school club and in which on-the-job training becomes an early experience which launches one into ministry with a running start.

The transitional testing patterns occur very early. Inner-life processing and ministry entry processing are compressed into the foundational phase so that the emerging leader is advanced even when beginning the ministry phase as compared to other emerging leaders moving along the generalized time-line. This rapid advancement means that by the time these accelerated leaders reach their thirties they are well into their ministry maturity phase. They have greatly accelerated ministry maturity development.

The in-service and modified in-service transitional training patterns usually correlate with the accelerated foundational pattern.

Advantages of this pattern include all the advantages of the heritage pattern. But beyond that there is a committal that has been tested by experience. Giftedness development occurs early. Ministry philosophy formulates early. The leader emerging from this pattern will move into unique ministry from five to ten years ahead of persons emerging via other patterns.

Disadvantages are few in this pattern. One disadvantage is a tendency towards over concern with activity, which may preclude mid-career formal training which could have a delayed negative impact concerning one's ability to move into convergence.

The **delayed** pattern, F.4, also describes the developmental pattern of generational Christian leaders. These emerging leaders have a family heritage of Christian leadership but initially rebelled very early in life to ministry but eventually have a deep leadership committal process item experience and enter the ministry phase later in life. This is often followed by rapid acceleration, though there has been a loss of time.

Numerous missionary kids and preacher kids have a tendency to rebel against the ministry because of perceived negative experiences during the foundational phase. Frequently the rebellion is turned around later (late twenties and early thirties) with a deep leadership committal experience. However, the period of time involved means that the ministry maturity phase of development starts late for them. But, due to early foundational background, movement in the phase is rapidly accelerated.

Advantages are few with one being that the person will usually have experienced some of the negative side of secular life. When recommittal comes they will experience a deliverance which allows them to identify with non-Christians in their needs and know the power of the Gospel. If they obtain formal training they usually learn more rapidly because of a learning posture created out of their life experiences. Many of the normal advantages of heritage belong to a person in this pattern but are not utilized until later.

Disadvantages often include overcoming of guilt attitudes (such as having wasted so much of life) and the lack of vital ministry experience. A further disadvantage usually involves having less options for formal training. The person is usually too old for Bible School and may not meet requirements for entrance into seminary.

Sub-Phase B, Transition into Leadership

Two classes of transitional patterns are helpful in analyzing how a leader moves into ministry. **Testing patterns,** deal with natural selection processes of a leader. **Training patterns** address steps an emerging leader will follow as part of entrance into ministry.

Two Testing Patterns

Early analysis of process items always involved identifying principles of truth. One principle that repeatedly occurred in comparative analysis was the Luke 16:10 Little-Big Principle (examples: Mann 1987:52; Shelley 1985:16; Wible 1982:33; Albrecht 1986:39; Loving 1987c:21,27; Claasen 1987:28,40; Petersen 1987:10). This important principle is given by Jesus in the application remarks following the Unfaithful Steward Parable of Luke 16:1-13. Verse 10 contains the principle.

Luke 16:10 LITTLE-BIG PRINCIPLE.
FAITHFULNESS IN A SMALL RESPONSIBILITY IS AN INDICATOR
OF FAITHFULNESS IN A LARGER RESPONSIBILITY.

Early comparative analysis of numerous examples of word checks, integrity checks, obedience checks, faith checks, and ministry tasks verified the essence of this little-big principle and identified two fundamental response patterns. Because of the testing nature of these patterns the four process items associated with them--the word, obedience and integrity checks and the ministry task--were labeled, the testing cluster. Two response patterns were derived based on the way in which God apparently used the testing cluster to test and expand potential leaders.

Each of the patterns involves three aspects: test, response, resultant action. The first, the failure pattern labeled negative testing/ remedial, T.1, involves test, negative response, and remedial action. The second, the success pattern labeled positive testing/ expansion, T.2, involves test, positive response, and expansion.

The first pattern, T.1, **negative testing/ remedial** pattern, describes God's use of integrity, obedience and word checks or ministry tasks to point out lack of character traits through a three step process which includes: 1) presentation of a test of character through a given incident in life experience, 2) a failure response in which the leader either does not perceive the incident as God's dealing and makes a poor choice, or a failure response in which the leader deliberately chooses to go against inner convictions or that which one knows pleases God's desires in the situation, 3) remedial action by God which tests again the leader on the same or similar issue, restricts the leader's development until the lesson is learned, or disciplines the leader. Supportive evidence of this pattern is given in Belesky (1987), Gripentrog (1987), Finzel (1987) and others.

The second pattern, T.2, **positive testing/ expansion** pattern, describes a three step process in which God's uses the testing cluster to form character in a leader: 1) presentation of a test of character through a given incident in life experience, 2) response of the leader first to recognize the incident as God's special dealing with him/her and then the positive response of taking action which honors inner convictions and God's desires in the situation, 3) expansion in which God blesses the positive response by confirming the inner conviction as an important leadership value and by increasing the leader's capacity to influence or situation of influence.

These patterns are important for leadership selection. They occur dominantly in the transition into leadership and early leadership time periods. In terms of the four foundational patterns the testing patterns occur normally after the heritage pattern person has made that second committal. They occur for the radical committal pattern person just after the radical committal. They occur for the accelerated pattern person co-terminus with early on-the-job training. They occur for the delayed pattern person early during the rebellion period which they usually fail, the negative testing/ remedial pattern, and again after the renewal committal.

Three Transitional Training Patterns

Foundational patterns usually correlate with a training pattern. The heritage pattern usually correlates with the **training pre-service** pattern, TR.1. This pattern involves moving straight into some formal training program with little or no ministry experience previous to the training.

Advantages of this pattern into ministry depend on the

quality of training received in the formal institution. That
training must provide an excellent experiential track since the
person entering this training pattern from the heritage pattern
will most likely not have much ministry experience nor knowledge
of giftedness. One major advantage seen repeatedly from this
pattern is the establishment of networks of relationships which
will be used by God in the future in terms of networking power.
Depending on the quality and relevance of the formal training, a
base may be laid for rapid and far reaching development during
the middle and latter ministry. Potential for developing along
strategic formation lines is laid with the broadened perspective
that comes with formal training. Progress in ministerial
formation includes word skills and communication skills and
perhaps training in small group dynamics--all of which contribute
to ministerial formation.

Disadvantages largely hinge around the quality of
instruction received in the formal institution. Spiritual
formation can be weakened through formal training and hence
shows up as a disadvantage in this training pattern. Where there
is a weak experiential track and the training tends to be
cognitive there is the danger of building an inoculation effect.
The sensed irrelevancy of such training can turn off these
emerging leaders toward further use of that material when it does
become needed.

The radical committal and accelerated patterns can correlate
with the **training in-service pattern**, TR.2. This pattern involves
a person moving gradually into leadership via lay involvement
with informal learning-as-you go training. When there is some
proficiency, and usually a sense of call, the leader launches
into full time ministry (without formal training).

Persons coming out of the radical conversion pattern are
most likely to transition into ministry via this training due to
their immediate involvement in ministry. An on-going active
ministry frequently keeps these persons engaged until they are
into their mid or late thirties. At that time they frequently
sense a need for some training but feel out of place in going to
institutions whose philosophy is basically pre-service. Hence,
they may not ever get formal training. This means they are
limited to in-formal and non-formal models. These may or may no
be adequate for advancement into effective latter ministry.

The advantages of this pattern include a match between informal or non-formal models and ministry needs. That is,
training that occurs is centered on real needs in ministry.
Spiritual formation usually develops rapidly at first but may
taper off due to lack of a solid theological base such as is
received in formal training. Ministerial formation occurs
rapidly but will usually be limited to the exposure of the
emerging leader to surrounding models.

Disadvantages hinge around latter ministry. Frequently
persons emerging from this pattern lack the base upon which to

mature in strategic formation. Many drop out of ministry due to various reasons (moral, financial, frustration, lack of training which would have enabled them to broaden their ministry, or inability to adapt beyond early ministry philosophy).

A few from the heritage pattern, radical committal pattern, and delayed pattern along with a larger number from the accelerated pattern follow the **modified in-service training** pattern, TR.3. This pattern stresses ministry experience and informal or non-formal training while learning ministry by doing until there is a transition into full time ministry. After some full time ministry experience there is a sensed need for full time training. This notion of interrupting ministry from time to time for bouts of special training continue throughout a lifetime.

Advantages in this transition training pattern involve selection of formal training which is apropos to the leader in terms of perceived relevancy. The leader selects the formal training in light of felt needs in the life based on ministry experience. The selection of training in mid-career also sets a pattern which will more likely be carried on in further repeated training. Another advantage of this training pattern involves the learning community. As contrasted with the pre-service pattern the learners in this formal training situation have learning agendas based on experience and resources to contribute to the learning process of the community.

Disadvantages are few other than disruption of family and often termination from a past ministry.

Growth Ministry Phase

The label for this phase is significant. The leader grows in ability to minister. Much of the emphasis during this long period of time is for the leader's growth, maybe more so than for the leader's accomplishments in ministry.

Two sub-phases comprise the **growth ministry** phase. The first, labeled **provisional ministry**, describes the potential conditional nature of ministry. The leader is ministering. But that ministry probably has more effect on the leader than on followers. Further, many leaders do not make it past this initial attempt into full time ministry. There is a rather large abbreviated entry, or drop out, in the first several years of full time ministry. The second, **competent ministry**, describes a leader who has made permanent entry and who develops through several ministry assignments so as to become proficient in ministering.

Provisional ministry

Both of the in-service transitional training patterns, TR.2 and TR.3, combine provisional ministry with transition into

full time ministry. After entrance into full time ministry the
provisional status continues but not as long as would be the case
for a pre-service transitional patter. The pre-service
transitional training pattern sees the leader move into
full time ministry out of a formal training program
with relatively little ministry experience.

For such leaders, provisional ministry is a shock. One, of
the earliest emotions to surface is disappointment. Full time
ministry does not seem to live up to its promise. This
disappointment occurs primarily for two reasons. One, there is
dissonance between the role expectations that the leader presumed
would be involved in ministry and the actual role. This
difference in role expectations is a continual thorn in the flesh
until the leader responds positively to the people insights
cluster of items and begins to understand at least implicitly
some implications of the servant leadership model. Two, the
leader usually quickly finds that formal training did not equip
for many functions that are required by the role.

During the provisional sub-phase, many lessons are learned
via negative experiences. Giftedness emerges out of attempts at
various kinds of ministry tasks and assignments. A trial and
error approach frequently describes how emerging leaders learn
lessons about giftedness. Emphasis during this sub-phase
primarily revolves around ministerial formation. The leader is
learning how to influence, how to use ministry skills, how to use
training skills, how to use giftedness, and how to perform as an
influencer. Much of the processing will focus on ministry
skills. Some processing usually overlapping with the ministerial
processing will deal with character.

For those who persevere during early provisional testing
there is growth in ministerial formation. A growing confidence
attaches itself to a leader who is progressing in giftedness
development, in use of power, and in discernment of appropriate
roles. Such a leader moves into the competence sub-phase of
growth ministry.

Patterns which are important during the provisional ministry
sub-phase include the M.1 Foundational Ministry pattern, the
various gift patterns (M.2, M.3, M.4, M.6). If the foundational
ministry pattern (learning of faithfulness) is not negotiated
successfully by an emerging leader, then there is little hope,
ever, of such a leader ever moving into unique ministry.

Competence Sub-phase

This sub-phase describes a leader who operates efficiently
in ministry. Such a leader has a good grasp of his/her
giftedness and has developed some competency with it. There is a
recognition of what kinds of roles will best enhance that
giftedness though choice of roles may not allow for those ideal
situations. There is a significant difference in discernment in
a leader in this sub-phase and the same leader in the early

provisional sub-phase.

Patterns important to this phase include M.8, Ministry
Entry, M.6 giftedness development (particularly movement
toward gift-mix and gift-cluster), and M.7 Spiritual authority
discovery. Movement into the latter stages of these patterns
signal maturity in ministerial formation. Toward the end of
competence two other patterns, UM.1 Reflective Evaluation and
UM.2 Upward Development, point out movement toward unique
ministry. These patterns deal with maturity in discernment.

Unique Ministry Phase

Few leaders actually reach unique ministry due to several
reasons: some leaders drop out of full time leadership early
during the provisional growth sub-phase; some leaders are
disciplined and set aside or limited due to the discipline; many
leader's plateau; many are in role situations which thwart
movement into unique ministry; some providential reasons
forego it. Two sub-phases describe movement in this
phase: role transition and convergence. These sub-phases
correspond roughly to the LIFE MATURING and CONVERGENCE
phases of the generalized time-line.

Role Transition

During this sub-phase the leader experiences clarification
of his/her gift cluster and appropriate roles for its use. A
mature discernment allows for selection of ministry which
balances giftedness, role, and appropriate influence-mix.

Processing associated with the UM.3, Gift-cluster Ripening,
UM.4 Balance, and UM.5 Convergence move the leader toward the
final sub-phase, convergence.

Convergence

This sub-phase corresponds to the CONVERGENCE and
CELEBRATION phases of the generalized time-line. Descriptions of
those phases are apropos here.

COMPRESSION-OVERLAP FOR GENERALIZED TIME-LINE

introduction   Generalized time-line phases are ordered in terms
                 of the natural sequencing of the appropriate
                 developmental tasks. These tasks usually are not
                 this clear cut in a unique time-line. Compression-
                 overlap describes how these tasks actually look
                 when fitted to a unique time-line.

definition   Compression-Overlap describes the expansion,
                 reduction, or overlap process which can be seen
                 when one traces the focus of each of the phases of
                 the generalized time-line on to a unique time-line.

Figure 10-4 Mapping of Generalized Time-Line on to Tozer Time-Line

Generalized Time-Line

```
I.            II.          III.        IV.       V.       VI.
Sovereign     Inner-Life   Ministry    Life      Conver-  Afterglow
Foundations   Growth       Maturing    Maturing  gence

|----------|-----------|----------|--------|-------|---------|
```

Tozer Time-Line

```
I. PRE-CONVERSION   II. ON-THE-JOB  III. CITY LEADERSHIP IV. CLOSURE
   DISCIPLINE           TRAINING         EXPANDS INFLUENCE
|----------------|----------------|-----------------|------------|
1897             1915             1928              1959        1963

  SF ------------> ILG ---------->- - - - - - - - -
                  MM------------------->- - - - -
                  LM------------------------------>- - -
                                       C------------->
                                          A--------->
```

Where abbreviations are: SF = Sovereign Foundations
                            ILG = Inner-Life Growth
                            MM = Ministry Maturing
                            LM = Life Maturing
                            C   = Convergence
                            A   = Afterglow

comment   The dash lines means there is some evidences of
                 these still seen but they are not major thrusts.

FEEDBACK ON COMPRESSION-OVERLAP

1. For the Apostle Peter's time-line given below. Do a comparison with the Generalized Phase functions and indicate with abbreviations, lines and arrows the Compression-Overlaps that you see just as I did with the Tozer time-line on page 331.

Time-line of Apostle Peter, Type D/E Leader

```
I.                II.               III.                  IV.
Rugged            Rugged Training   Opening Doors         Afterglow
Fisherman         For Heading A     For the               Reflections
Foundations       Movement          Movement              on the
                                                          Movement
|-----------|-----------------|---------------------|----------|
  Early life   A. Three calls   A. Jerusalem Jews     Writings
               B. Growing       B. Samaritans
                  Attachment    C. Gentiles
               C. Brokenness    D. Antioch Gentiles
                                E. Jerusalem Council
```

2. Do a Compression-Overlap plot for your own time-line which you constructed for exercise 1 on page 309. Follow the procedure indicated in the Tozer example.

ANSWERS----------

    1. Time-line of Apostle Peter, Type D/E Leader

```
I.                II.               III.                  IV.
Rugged            Rugged Training   Opening Doors         Afterglow
Fisherman         For Heading A     For the               Reflections
Foundations       Movement          Movement              on the
                                                          Movement
|-----------|-----------------|---------------------|----------|
  Early life   A. Three calls   A. Jerusalem Jews     Writings
               B. Growing       B. Samaritans
                  Attachment    C. Gentiles
               C. Brokenness    D. Antioch Gentiles
                                E. Jerusalem Council


SF----------> ILG ----------------------->- - -
                      MM --------------------->
                      LM -------------------->- - -
                                           C ? A------->
```

    2. Be prepared to share your analysis with someone.

GROUPING

introduction   The ministry time-line can be mapped onto a unique
                time-line. Usually when this happens several
                phases will be grouped under the various ministry
                time-line phases. Sometimes boundaries coincide.
                More often they do not. This is so since the
                criterion for ending the ministry time-line phases
                or sub-phases depends on evaluation of ministry
                efficiency or effectiveness and not the natural
                boundaries. Such a mapping gives helpful insights
                into the ministry development.

definition   Grouping refers to the effect of superintending the
                ministry time-line onto a unique time-line. Several
                unique time-line phases or sub-phases will be
                collected under each ministry time-line phases.

```
Ministry Foundation            Growth Ministry
     _____/\_____                 _____/_____
    /            \   /                               \
A.             B.    A. Provisional-------------| B. Competent---|

I. FOUNDATIONS    II. PASTORAL      III. TEACHING    IV. CROSS-
   LAID              MINISTRY            MINISTRY         CULTURAL
|-----------------|-----------------|-----------------|----------|
1939              1964              1970              1978      1989
```
Figure 10-5. Ministry Time-Line Mapped on Burt Time-Line

```
Ministry Foundation            Growth Ministry
     _____/\_____                 _____/_____
    /            \   /                              \
A.             B.    A. Provisional------------------|B. Competent

I. PRE-CONVERSION  II. PREPARATORY           III. INITIAL
   INFLUENCE           MINISTRY EXPERIENCE         VISION REALIZED
|-----------------|-------------------------|-------------------|
1947              1965                      1977               1987
```
Figure 10-6. Ministry Time-Line Mapped on Gripentrog Time-Line

```
         Ministry Foundation              Growth Ministry
     _____/_____            _____/_____
    /                      \          /                   \
A. Leadership Foundations   B. Transition  A. Provisional-------->

I. FOUNDATIONS                  II. EARLY TRAINING      III. BACK TO
                                    AND EXPERIENCE           SCHOOL
|-------------------------------|-------------------------|----------|
1955                            1970                      1987      1989
```
Figure 10-7. Ministry Time-Line Mapped on Myers Time-Line

FEEDBACK ON GROUPING

1. Map the ministry time-line onto the following unique time-line
as was done with the three examples of Figures 10-5, 10-6, 10-7.
Sketch in the ministry time-line phases above the time-line so as
to show the grouping effect.


```
I. EARLY-LIFE        II. FORMAL        III. INITIAL   IV. OVERSEAS
   FORMATION             TRAINING          MINISTRY       MINISTRY
|--------------------|-----------------|---------------|--//-----|
1939                 1957              1964            1969    1984
```

Woodbury, Unique Time-Line (Woodbury 1984:6)

2. 1. Map the ministry time-line onto your own time-line which
you constructed for exercise 1 on page 309.   Sketch in the
ministry time-line phases above your own time-line so as to show the
grouping effect.

ANSWERS----------
    1. Ministry time-line mapped onto Woodbury time-line.

```
          Ministry Foundation                Growth Ministry
                   _/\_                           _/\_
 /_____  _____\  /_____  _____\
/                                      \/                      \
A. Leadership Foundations  B. Transition  A. Provisional---->
                                                         B.
                                                         Competent

I. EARLY-LIFE        II. FORMAL        III. INITIAL   IV. OVERSEAS
   FORMATION             TRAINING          MINISTRY       MINISTRY
|--------------------|-----------------|---------------|--//-----|
1939                 1957              1964            1969    1984
```

Woodbury, Unique Time-Line (Woodbury 1984:6)

    2. Ministry time-line mapped onto your time-line.

Concluding Remarks on the Time Variable

Summary

The time variable refers to that set of concepts which seek to describe a time orientation for the process and response variables. The central concept of this variable is the **time-line**. Its components include **development phases** and **sub-phases**. Retrospective analysis of any given development phase for an individual's unique time-line results in identification of specific **development tasks** toward which the processing throughout the development phase was directed. Comparative analysis of many time-lines allowed the identification of general development tasks applying to all leaders.

Identification of development phases is usually done in three ways: 1) by recognizing the **boundary processing** of the standard development phase (transitional behavior, stabilizing behavior, and boundary behavior), 2) by noting significant **change in the sphere of influence**--that is, the influence-mix, either degree or kind or both, 3) by identifying the **unique processing** items which occur dominantly at different times.

Transitions from sub-phase to sub-phase or from phase to phase involve **boundary processing**. This is the most useful means of identifying development phases or sub-phases. Boundary processing follows a **threefold pattern** involving an **entry stage, a transition stage**, and a **termination stage**. Finzel identified a boundary cluster of ten process items which occur commonly during boundary processing. The occurrence of these process items forces the leader to do backward reflection of the passing development phase, to do forward formulation of the coming development, and to make decisions for moving into the coming development phase.

Characteristics of Time Variable

Any researcher doing analysis of time variable concepts should recognize the following four characteristics:

1. Time variable concepts are constructs for viewing reality. They are non-absolute in nature.
2. Time-line analysis varies depending on when the time-analysis is done.
3. Time variable concepts stimulate discovery of patterns.
4. Time-lines provide an integrating framework for analysis of development.

Time variable concepts are constructs. By this is meant that these definitions are simply perspectives through which time reality in a leader's life can be viewed. These constructs don't define the reality being observed; they simply describe it. Two equally proficient analysts doing separate studies of the same individual will usually not arrive at identical time-lines,

though there will most likely be quite a bit of agreement. In
either case each analysis will produce useful information
explaining the development of the individual.

     Time-line analysis varies depending on when the time-
analysis is done. For example, analysis done on a 35 year old
leader may identify three development phases, the foundational
phase and two shorter phases involving early ministry and a
change to a more expansive ministry. Analysis of that same
leader when he/she is 65 may integrate what were earlier
described as phases 2 and 3 into one more comprehensive phase
embracing them both as sub-phases. In general, the longer the
time span of an individual being analyzed, the more likely that
development phases will be longer and more integrative. In other
words, a full lifetime perspective tends to integrate smaller
time-spans into larger ones because larger boundaries can be seen
and more inclusive development tasks can be identified.[2]

Three Major Functions

     The time variable serves three very important roles in
leadership development theory. First, it provides a backdrop for
identifying when various processes are most likely to occur.
This allows for scheduling and can prevent overscheduling or
misscheduling (Whitehead and Whitehead 1982:35,36). The second
is to provide a panorama of a lifetime which allows recognition
of leader response patterns in or across time periods. The third
is to provide an integrating framework upon which to measure
development.

     Process items have been generally described in terms of when
they occur. Recognition that they do occur at certain times can
condition a leader to a proper response when they do occur. That
is the Whitehead's notion of scheduling.

     The Time variable stimulates discovery of patterns. A
pattern is an integrating term used to describe repetitive cycles
of happenings. When a person analyzes a given incident or series
of incidents when they are happening that person tends to
narrowly view the incident or incidents. But analysis of that
given incident or series of incidents in view of a time-line
stimulates the discovery of other similar incidents which have
previously happened.

     Comparisons of all of these incidents may well stimulate the
discovery of a pattern. Comparative studies of many time-lines
is useful to identify generic patterns. Knowledge of these
generic patterns can stimulate further discovery of similar or
contrastive patterns in a unique time-line.

---

[2]The Peter Kuzmic time-line, page 293, is a case in point.
Evaluation at age 50 or so might well conclude that Phases II
and III (note short time spans of each) really form a larger
Phase entitled Training--Informal and Formal with two subphases.

Time-lines provide an integrating framework for analysis of development. At any given point in a life specific measures of development such as sphere of influence, power-mix, and giftedness development can be assessed. The natural time to do this is at the boundaries of phases. Comparisons of measures done at various boundaries allows for recognition of development and change in the various measures of development.

The next chapter uses the ministry time-line as an integrating framework for viewing the important leader response patterns.

(This page deliberately left blank)

CHAPTER 11. THE RESPONSE VARIABLE

Integrative Overview

The development of a given leader can be explained for the most part by using the shorthand notation, $L = f(p,t,r)$. The processing variable, p, indicates that leadership for a given leader develops out of critical spiritual incidents which are used by God to process that leader and bring unique focus to that leader's life. The time variable, t, indicates that the processing can be identified and analyzed in terms of significant time periods in the leader's life. The response variable, r, indicates that patterns of response can be identified for a particular leader by analyzing the leader's overall response to processing in and across the various time periods. Indeed, patterns of response can be generalized from comparative study of many leader's responses which help any given leader to pinpoint development, recognize selection processes in emerging leaders (hence, speeding them up), and allow for more deliberate development in his or her own life.

This chapter will describe the generalized patterns that can be useful for early recognition of emergence of potential leaders, pinpointing one's own development, and suggesting what is needed for more deliberate approach to development. These patterns include the five foundational patterns and the five transitional patterns which are associated with the ministry foundations phase of the ministry time-line. Eight ministry patterns are associated with the growth ministry time period. Five unique ministry patterns signal the maturity processing that accompanies the unique ministry time period.

Preview--The Response Variable

Comparative study of many leadership emergence studies resulted in identification of extended repetition (or cycles) of items in leader's lives. These grouping of items sometimes followed steps or stages or some other time ordered feature. Having once identified these **patterns** it was found useful then to trace how other leaders exemplified them or failed to do so. In fact, a leader's response to various processing affects movement along a given identified pattern. The pinpointing of a given leader's development within a known pattern then became a form of comparative evaluation.

Table 11-1 lists the various response patterns that have been identified to this point in the research. It uses the ministry time-line as the basis for grouping the patterns. Each of these 23 patterns are then defined. Bibliographic references indicate one source where the pattern is noted. Others could have been given. Feedback maps are given after each grouping of patterns On these feedback maps you will be asked to identify where you are in terms of the patterns. This will form the backdrop for one of the evaluation measures given in chapter 13.

339

PATTERN

introduction   A comparative analysis of numerous leadership
                emergence studies results in common findings.
                Often these findings can be described in terms of a
                cycle of events, combination of sequential process
                items, repetitive stages making up a period of
                time or the like. These patterns, particularly
                when they are seen in numerous leader's lives in
                different cultures and situations are helpful not
                only for their evaluative insights but also for
                their predictive value.

definition   Pattern is the term used to describe a repetitive
                cycle of happenings seen from a comparative
                analysis of leadership emergence studies and may
                involve periods of time, combinations of process
                items, or combination of identifiable concepts.

example   The testing-expansion cycle. The developmental
                thrust in a leader's life during the transition
                into full time leadership often revolves around a
                testing-expansion cycle which develops character.
                God frequently uses five important process items
                (Word checks, obedience checks, integrity checks,
                faith checks, ministry tasks) to test an emerging
                leader's heart intent. Successful response on the
                part of the leader results in inner growth and
                expansion of ministry. The pattern usually has
                three parts: the challenge to consistency with
                inner convictions, the response to the challenge,
                and the results (either expansion or remedial
                processing).

example   Boundary Pattern. It involves three stages: an
                entry stage, a transition stage, and a termination
                stage. (See pages 305, 306.)

example   Both of the generic time-lines are examples of
                patterns.

example   Principles which operate at absolute levels of
                authority are specific illustrations of repetitive
                patterns.

major   Twenty three response patterns have been identified
patterns   and defined as part of the response variable.
                These include five foundational patterns (F.1-F.5),
                five transitional patterns (T.1, T.2, TR.1-TR. 3),
                eight ministry patterns (M.1-M.8), and 5 advanced
                patterns (UM.1-UM.5). These patterns help leaders
                schedule so as to maximize development through
                processing.

TABLE 11-1
RESPONSE PATTERNS ALONG THE MINISTRY TIME-LINE

I. MINISTRY FOUNDATIONS		II. GROWTH MINISTRY	III. UNIQUE MINISTRY

A. Leadership
   Foundations
	B. Transition	A. Provisional
		      B. Competent	

F.1 HERITAGE (Waldner 1987)	T.1 TESTING/ NEGATIVE-- REMEDIAL (Shelley 1985)	M.1 FOUNDATIONAL MINISTRY (Belesky 1987)	UM.1 REFLECTIVE/ FORMATIVE EVALUATION (Faber 1989)
F.2 RADICAL COMMITTAL (Dollar 1987)	T.2 TESTING/ POSITIVE-- EXPANSION (Clinton 1982a)	M.2 LIKE-ATTRACTS- LIKE GIFT (Finzel 1987)	UM.2 UPWARD DEVELOPMENT (Dollar 1987)
F.3 ACCELERATED (Hollis 1985)	TR.1 TRAINING PRE-SERVICE (Woodbury 1984)	M.3 GIFTEDNESS DRIFT (Finzel 1987)	UM.3 GIFT-CLUSTER RIPENING (Clinton 1989b)
F.4 DELAYED (Dutton 1986)	TR.2 TRAINING IN-SERVICE (Repko 1987)	M.4 ROLE/GIFT ENABLEMENT (Colquhoun 1987)	UM.4 BALANCE (Clinton 1989b)
F.5 DESTINY (Clinton 1985b)	TR.3 TRAINING MODIFIED IN-SERVICE (Smith 1983)	M.5 AUTHORITY INSIGHTS (Mueller 1987)	UM.5 CONVERGENCE GUIDANCE (Clinton 1989b)
		M.6 GIFTEDNESS DEVELOPMENT (Mueller 1987)	
		M.7 SPIRITUAL AUTHORITY DISCOVERY (Mann 1987)	

		M.8 MINISTRY
		      ENTRY --------------->
		      (many)	

critical   The **M.1 Foundational Ministry Pattern,** which
pattern   focuses on the leadership character trait of
             faithfulness, proves to be crucial to all continued
             development. Without this perspective, leaders
             will plateau and not reach advanced stages in many
             of the other patterns.

HERITAGE FOUNDATIONAL PATTERN   symbol: F.1

introduction   Leaders usually emerge out of one of four
foundational patterns or a modified version of
them. Each of the foundational patterns carries
with it some inherent advantages and disadvantages.
But each leader is unique and will reflect more or
less the advantages or disadvantages of the
pattern. accordingly. It is helpful to recognize
these patterns and implications of them in order to
make decisions for training or concerning
experiences which will build on the advantages and
minimize disadvantages. The heritage foundational
pattern is the most common pattern from which
Christian leaders emerge.

description   The heritage foundational pattern refers to the
F.1   early development of a leader in the foundational
development phase who comes from a Christian (or at
least nominal Christian) background in which the
leader is more or less processed into Christian
values via the home or some church life.

examples   Woodbury (1984), Dykstra (1983), Klebe (1982),
Wible (1984), Harris (1982b), Barnes (1987)

comment   Usually there is not a radical conversion
experience though there may be a growing awareness
of God.

comment   Family life helps shape characteristics in the
leader which are based at least in part on
Christian thinking.

comment   The educational pattern gives a prolonged time of
development before adult responsibilities must be
shouldered. This time of schooling allows for
development of basic skills, such as experience in
sports, clubs, or vocational efforts,
competitiveness, perseverance, basic relational
skills, organizational skills, entrepreneural
skills, or the like.

educational   Toward the end of the teen years or during early
collegiate years there is usually some sort of more
radical commitment to God than resulted from
previous conversion processing. Sometimes
identified as conversion, or as a surrender to do
God's will, this action frequently results in a
desire to be a full time Christian worker. This
can lead to learn-as-you-do-it training or an
opting for formal training.

HERITAGE FOUNDATIONAL PATTERN continued

Advantages of this pattern include those normally associated
                with heritage such as:

1. belief in God, knowledge of Him, and Christian values which
   can be built upon,
2. inheriting promises from faithful ancestors who have prayed
   and claimed God's working upon progeny (frequently destiny
   preparation processing is involved here),
3. having exemplary models of Christianity which will have
   influenced toward basic ministry philosophy concepts,
4. having an experiential foundation for understanding giftedness
   (having seen leaders with different natural abilities,
   acquired skills, and spiritual gifts),
5. usually having support for Christian leadership aspirations
   (though more nominal backgrounds may actually oppose because
   of secular career ambitions for the potential leader).
6. usually having fewer lifestyle changes as the person moves
   into Christian leadership since the basic Christian ethic is
   already intact.

Disadvantages are few and may include the following.

1. Familiarity with Christian things which may dull the spiritual
   realities of them.
2. Enthusiastic committal to the accomplishing of God's work must
   be fostered by unusual experiences usually outside the routine
   of Christianity experienced while growing up.
3. The routine Christian experience may not provide stimulus for
   on-the-job experience which can be vital to early
   identification of leadership potential.
4. Ministry philosophy imbued via routine involvement in
   Christianity may not have challenged or apparently was
   irrelevant in terms of reaching out to a lost world or cross-
   cultural involvement.

training   The heritage foundational pattern usually
                 correlates with the training pre-service pattern
                 and hence the advantages and disadvantages of that
                 training.

Use of   Those mentors or divine contacts who have influence
Goodwin's   in the lives of potential leaders emerging from
Expectation   this foundational heritage pattern and who are
Principle   sensitive to leadership emergence patterns do well
                 to influence these young potential leaders toward
                 apprenticeships or other significant ministry
                 experiences which may break the standard training
                 pre-service pattern.

RADICAL COMMITTAL FOUNDATIONAL PATTERN   symbol: F.2

introduction   Leaders usually emerge out of one of four
foundational patterns or a modified version of
them.   Each of the foundational patterns carries
with it some inherent advantages and disadvantages.
It is helpful to recognize these patterns and
implications of them. Future decision making should
build on the advantages and minimize disadvantages.
Christian leaders who emerged from a non-Christian
background fit this pattern. This pattern can offer
great advantages or disadvantages or combinations
of both upon which to emerge into leadership.

description   The radical committal pattern refers to the early
F.2   development of a leader in the foundational
development phase who comes from a non-Christian
background or at best a very nominal Christian
background in which the leader is more or less
processed into whatever values the environment
supports (usually those of the secular society of
the macro-context) and who makes a radical adult
decision for Christ which involves a significant
paradigm shift in terms of values and life-goals.

examples   Gripentrog (1987), Finzel (1987), Teng (1989a)

change of   Usually person's in this pattern were tracking
career   along some secular career path when the adult
conversion happened. The radical experience
frequently changes this direction.

values   The person imbibes the values of the family,
whether good or bad, as he or she grows up.
Usually there is little or no knowledge of vital
Christianity.

education   Educational patterns vary.   In the west the
educational pattern allows a prolonged time of
development before adult responsibilities must be
shouldered. This time of schooling allows for
development of basic skills, such as experience in
sports, clubs, vocational efforts, competitiveness,
perseverance, basic relational skills,
organizational skills, entrepreneural skills, or
the like. In non-western situations the educational
patterns vary and may or may not allow prolonged
time of development before adult responsibilities.
If not, the person usually learns via traditional
educational patterns the necessary basic and social
skills for the society.

comment   The turning point involves exposure to Christianity
which provokes a radical decision to follow Christ.
Usually coincidental with this decision is a whole

RADICAL COMMITTAL FOUNDATIONAL PATTERN continued

> hearted leadership committal to serve God. This
> radical experience can occur in high school,
> college, or during the normal vocation. But it is
> decisive whenever it occurs. Throughout life it
> will be looked back to as a major marker event.

comment
> On-the-job training, which often starts with sharing
> of testimony about what has happened, usually
> follows the radical decision. The person is
> attracted to the means that brought about the
> radical change whether it be a person or an
> organization. Early on-the-job training usually
> follows that attraction. Ministry philosophy flows
> from this exposure.

Advantages of this pattern involve:

1. a decisive leadership committal process item which serves as
   foundational for all of later leadership activity. Attitudes
   of committal involve service to God right at the outset.
2. early gift identification (frequently the like-attracts-like
   gift pattern is a common occurrence).
3. destiny processing. Because of the radical nature of the
   committal frequently there is a destiny preparation or
   revelation experience which will set the tone for later
   development of focus in ministry philosophy.
4. a fresh perspective on Christianity. Since the person is
   usually unencumbered with a Christian tradition frequently he
   or she is able to see new ideas and create new kinds of
   structures and roles that would not be thought of by a person
   of the heritage pattern.

Disadvantages include:

1. lack of Christian knowledge, especially about the Bible.
2. need for radical change of lifestyle. Frequently there must
   be extreme changes of lifestyle since the old is so
   incompatible with a Christian lifestyle. Old habits are hard
   to break and may result in early struggles regarding issues
   which are taken for granted by heritage pattern persons.
3. use of secular leadership patterns. Early leadership
   practices will follow the secular practices that have been
   experienced, whether good or bad.
4. instability. The emerging leader is often unstable and
   vacillates between the old way of life and the new.

training
> If the people who were involved in the radical
> decision put stress on on-the-job training then the
> transitional training pattern two, TR.2, the in-
> service pattern, is followed. If they stress
> formal training then training pattern three, TR.3,
> the modified in-service pattern, is often followed.

ACCELERATED FOUNDATIONAL PATTERN   symbol: F.3

introduction   Leaders usually emerge out of one of four
foundational patterns or a modified version of
them.   Each of the foundational patterns carries
with it some inherent advantages and disadvantages.
However, each leader is unique and will reflect
more or less of the advantages or disadvantages
accordingly. Recognition of a pattern helps in
future decision making.   One can choose training
and experience which will build on the advantages
and minimize disadvantages. The accelerated
foundational pattern is a special case of the
heritage pattern in which the heritage leads to
early ministry involvement and rapid early
development of ministry skills and basic character.

description   The accelerated foundational pattern describes the
F.3   early rapid developmental pattern of generational
Christian leaders, that is, emerging leaders who
have a family heritage of Christian leadership and
respond positively very early in life to doing
ministry (often co-ministering with parents).

examples   Hollis (1985), Metcalf (1987), I. Grant (1985)

comment   Hollis comes from a line of preachers. Expectancy
was high that he too would be in the ministry. He
began preaching and teaching at a very early age.
Grant was a missionary kid who went with his dad on
evangelistic treks and pastoral visits from the
time that he was a little lad. Metcalf was part of
a very active high school Christian movement in
which he learned evangelistic skills and early
organizational skills. His on-the-job training
continued right on through his secular college
experience.

comment   The pattern is often seen also in some who do not
come from a Christian heritage but are converted
very early as in a child Evangelism ministry,
junior high, or high school club and in which a
pseudo-parent (mentor) helps encourage on-the-job
training which launches one into ministry with a
running start.

comment   The transitional testing patterns occur very early.
Inner-life processing and ministry entry processing
are compressed into the foundational phase so that
the emerging leader is advanced even when beginning
the ministry phase as compared to other emerging
leaders moving along the generalized time-line.
This rapid advancement means that by the time these
accelerated leaders reach their thirties they are
well into their ministry maturity phase.

ACCELERATED FOUNDATIONAL PATTERN continued

Advantages   This pattern includes all the normal advantages of
the heritage pattern. But beyond that there is:

1. a committal that has been tested by experience,
2. giftedness development occurs early,
3. a basic ministry philosophy formulates early,
4. The leader emerging from this pattern will move
   into unique ministry from five to ten years
   ahead of persons emerging via other patterns.

Dis-   Disadvantages are few in this pattern with one
advantage   being the possibility that there may be an over
concern with ministry activity which may preclude
mid-career formal training. Such training gives
breadth and perspective that will later be needed
as the leader moves into convergence. Without this
perspective convergence may not be reached.

training   The in-service and modified in-service transitional
training patterns usually correlate with the
accelerated foundational pattern.

comment   Mentors should recognize the need for balance
between cognitive and experiential learning.
Over emphasis of ministry activity should be
countered by suggesting appropriate training which
will keep ministry momentum going yet balance it
with needed perspectives that will improve it.

DELAYED FOUNDATIONAL PATTERN   symbol: F.4

introduction   Leaders usually emerge out of one of four
                foundational patterns or a modified version of
                them. The delayed foundational pattern is a
                special case of the heritage pattern in which the
                heritage leads to an early rejection by the
                potential leader of that heritage later followed by
                a radical commitment (usually in late twenties) and
                then rapid development of ministry skills and basic
                character.

description   The delayed foundational pattern describes the
F.4   developmental pattern of generational Christian
                leaders (emerging leaders who have a family
                heritage of Christian leadership) who initially
                rebel against ministry very early in life but who
                eventually experience a deep leadership committal
                process item and enter the ministry phase late
                followed by rapid acceleration.

example   Dutton (1986)

comment   Numerous missionary kids and preachers have a
                tendency to rebel against the ministry because of
                perceived negative experiences during the
                foundational phase. This rebellion is turned
                around later (usually in the late twenties and
                early thirties) with a deep leadership committal
                experience. This late start, however, delays
                ministry entry. Rapid acceleration due to early
                foundational background often follows.

Advantages are few and include:

1. the person will usually have experienced some of the negative
   side of secular life. When recommittal comes they will
   experience a deliverance which allows them to identify with
   non-christians in their needs and know the power of God.
2. such a person who opts for formal training will usually
   learn more rapidly because of life experience upon which to
   relate input.
3. normal advantages of heritage belong to a person in this
   pattern but are not utilized until late.

Disadvantages often include

1. the overcoming of guilt attitudes for having wasted so much of
   life and for missing early vital ministry experience.
2. less options for formal training. The person is usually too
   old for Bible School and may not meet requirements for
   entrance into seminary.

training   Usually a modified in-service transitional
                educational pattern is followed.

DESTINY PATTERN   symbol: F.5

introduction   Destiny experiences refer to those experiences
                which lead a person to sense and believe that God
                has intervened in a personal and special way
                particularly in regards to encouraging the
                emergence of leadership toward some purpose of God
                during that leader's lifetime. A three stage
                pattern increasingly adds to a leader's sense of
                destiny over a lifetime. The pattern begins in the
                ministry foundation phase of the ministry time-
                line, increases in intensity during the growth
                ministry phase, and culminates either in the
                competent sub-phase or the unique ministry phase.

definition   Sense of destiny is an inner conviction arising
                from an experience or a series of experiences (in
                which there is a growing sense of awareness in
                retrospective analysis of those experiences) that
                God has His hand on a leader in a special way for
                special purposes.

description   The destiny pattern describes a spiritual leadership
F.5   pattern in which there is a growing awareness of a
                sense of destiny, progress seen in that destiny,
                and finally, culmination as the destiny is
                fulfilled. These three stages take place over all
                three phases of the ministry time-line.

                        The Ministry Time-Line

MINISTRY FOUNDATIONS   GROWTH MINISTRY   UNIQUE MINISTRY
|----------------------|----------------------|----------------|

                        The Destiny Continuum

Destiny To Be Fulfilled   Destiny Fulfilled
|
|--|
| |
time ------------->
emergence of leader unfolding -------------->

The Destiny Pattern

Stage 1   Stage 2   Stage 3

preparation   --->   destiny revelation   destiny realization--->
                        and confirmation --->

explanation   Stage 1, involves God's preparatory work bringing a
                growing awareness of a sense of destiny. In Stage
                2, the awareness moves to conviction as God gives
                revelation and confirmation of it. Stage 3, builds
                toward accomplishment of that destiny.

DESTINY PATTERN continued

Process items or incidents which correlate to the three stages
included the following.

The Ministry Time-Line

MINISTRY FOUNDATIONS   GROWTH MINISTRY   UNIQUE MINISTRY
|----------------------|----------------------|----------------|

The Destiny Continuum

Destiny To Be Fulfilled   Destiny Fulfilled

time -------------->
emergence of leader unfolding -------------->

Stage 1   Stage 2   Stage 3

preparation --->   destiny revelation   destiny realization--->
                         and confirmation --->

P(DP)   P(DR)   P(DF)

- prophecy   - revelatory act   - promise realization
- name   - revelatory dream   - divine affirmation
- prayer   - revelatory prophecy   - obedience checks
- contract (oath)   - destiny insight   - word checks
- faith act   - word, obedience,   - faith acts
- contextual   integrity and
  items   faith checks
- mentor   - divine affirmation,
- birth   - all forms of
  circumstances   sovereign guidance:
- preservation   double confirmation,
  of life   divine contacts,
- heritage   mentors
- parent's sense   - spiritual authority
  of destiny   affirmation
  for child   - leadership backlash
                         - power items
                         - convergence

FEEDBACK ON FOUNDATIONAL PATTERNS

1. Identify which one of the foundational patterns best describes
the background out of which you emerged.

___a. heritage foundational pattern
___b. radical committal foundational pattern
___c. accelerated foundational pattern
___d. delayed foundational pattern
___e. some combination--describe:
___f. other--altogether different, explain:

2. List the advantages of your pattern (you may wish to look back
to the advantages I listed for your pattern--feel free to add to
it).

3. List the disadvantages of your pattern.

4. Describe where you are in the destiny pattern by circling
any incidents or items you have experienced.

Stage 1	Stage 2	Stage 3
preparation --->	destiny revelation and confirmation --->	destiny realization--->
P(DP)	P(DR)	P(DF)
• prophecy • name • prayer • contract (oath) • faith act • contextual items • mentor • birth circumstances • preservation of life • heritage • parent's sense of destiny for child	• revelatory act • revelatory dream • revelatory prophecy • destiny insight • word, obedience, integrity and faith checks • divine affirmation, • all forms of sovereign guidance: double confirmation, divine contacts, mentors • spiritual authority affirmation • leadership backlash • power items • convergence	• promise realization • divine affirmation • obedience checks • word checks • faith acts

ANSWERS----------
All of these are your choices. Be prepared to share in class.

TESTING PATTERNS   T.1 Negative Testing, T.2 Positive Testing

introduction   An important transitional pattern features
               character testing. This pattern involves God's use
               of integrity, obedience, word and faith checks
               along with ministry tasks to test and expand
               potential leaders. The pattern involves three
               aspects: test, response, resultant action. Two
               sub-patterns occur. The success pattern involves
               test, positive response, and expansion. The
               failure pattern involves test, negative response,
               and remedial action.

definition   The negative testing/remedial pattern describes
T.1   God's use of the testing cluster of items to point
               out lack of character traits through a three step
               process which includes:

               1) presentation of a test of character through a
                  given incident in life experience,
               2) a failure response in which the leader either
                  does not perceive the incident as God's dealing
                  and makes a poor choice or a failure response in
                  which the leader deliberately chooses to go
                  against inner convictions or that which pleases
                  God's desires in the situation,
               3) remedial action by God which tests again the
                  leader on the same or similar issue, restricts
                  the leader's development until the lesson is
                  learned, or disciplines the leader.

definition   The positive testing/expansion pattern describes
T.2   God's use of the testing cluster of items to form
               character in a leader via a three step process:

               1) presentation of a test of character through a
                  given incident in life experience,
               2) response of the leader first to recognize the
                  incident as God's special dealing with him/her
                  and then the positive response of taking action
                  which honors inner convictions and God's desires
                  in the situation,
               3) expansion in which God blesses the positive
                  response by confirming the inner conviction as
                  an important leadership value and by increasing
                  the leader's capacity to influence or situation
                  of influence.

negative   King Saul's failure. See I Samuel 15. Disciplinary
example   action involved eventual removal from office.

positive   Daniel 1 (wine issue), Daniel 3 (idolatry issue),
examples   and Daniel 6 (worship issue) contain positive
               examples of the testing pattern.

FEEDBACK ON TESTING PATTERNS

1. Demonstrate that you understand the testing-expansion pattern
by analyzing it in conjunction with Daniel in chapter 1 of the
book of Daniel. Note the three stages (test, response,
expansion) of that pattern in your discussion.

2. Which testing patterns have you personally experienced?

___a. T.1 Negative Testing
        Circle the process items involved: integrity check
                                             obedience check
                                             word check
                                             faith check
                                             ministry task

___b. T.1 Positive Testing
        Circle the process items involved: integrity check
                                             obedience check
                                             word check
                                             faith check
                                             ministry task

ANSWERS----------

    1. All three elements of the integrity check are clearly
seen in the passage (Daniel 1:8-21). There is an inner
conviction, a religious conviction about certain foods, and there
is great pressure to violate this conviction. Daniel decided to
stick to his convictions. An amazing thing is that this is a
teen-ager away from home and parental influence who takes a stand
on religious convictions learned early in life. God gave
relationships that allowed him to work out a plan which did not
compromise his convictions. God honored that firmness of
character. Daniel and friends graduate with top honors. Notice
the expansion of ministry. Daniel is given a top job offer. And
God has strategically placed a leader who has character and will
testify upon God's behalf in increasingly tough situations.
    2. a. integrity check failed,   b. obedience and faith check
passed.

TRANSITIONAL TRAINING PRE-SERVICE PATTERN   symbol: TR.1

introduction   Foundational patterns usually correlate with
               training patterns. The heritage pattern often
               links to the training pre-service pattern. The
               emphasis on the pattern is training first and
               selection secondary. Selection of this pattern is
               usually via self-choice. Confirmation or rejection
               of this self-selection is determined after
               training. As a result there is usually a large
               drop out (abbreviated entry into ministry).

PRE-SERVICE EDUCATIONAL PATTERN (training first selection secondary)

```
I. FOUNDATIONAL          II. FIRST MINISTRY
|------------------|          (usually with established work)
                   |-------------------------------------->
               BOUNDARY PHASE
     |---------------| |-----------|
          EDUCATIONAL    RELATIVELY LARGE ABBREVIATED ENTRY
          TRANSITION     (drop-outs)
       (High School, college, seminary)
```

OVERALL PATTERN
```
|<----//------->||<-------------------------->||<------------------->
  PRE-MINISTRY    FORMAL MINISTRY TRAINING    FULL-TIME MINISTRY
```

examples   Woodbury (1984) followed this pattern into a
               successful missionary career and is now
               transitioning to training pattern 3. Others
               involved in this pattern (at least into the growth
               ministry phase) include: Dykstra (1983), Klebe
               (1982), Wible (1984), Harris (1982b), Barnes (1987).

Advantages include:

1. establishment of networks of relationships which will be used
   by God in the future in terms of networking power.
2. depending on the quality and relevance of the formal training,
   a base may be laid for rapid and far reaching development
   during the middle and latter ministry.
3. potential for developing along strategic formation lines is
   laid with a broadened perspective that comes with formal
   training.
4. Progress in ministerial formation includes word skills and
   communication skills as well as perhaps training in small
   group dynamics.

explanation   Advantages of this pattern into ministry depend on
               the quality of training received in the formal
               institution. That training must provide an
               excellent experiential track since the person
               entering this training pattern from the heritage
               pattern will most likely not have much ministry
               experience nor knowledge of giftedness.

TRANSITIONAL TRAINING PRE-SERVICE PATTERN   symbol: TR.1   continued

Disadvantages   depend upon the quality of instruction received in the formal institution and can include the following:

1. retrogression in spiritual formation,
2. the inoculation effect. Where there is a weak experiential track and the training tends to be cognitive there is the danger of building an inoculation effect. The sensed irrelevancy of such training can turn off these emerging leaders toward further use of the material (even though it may become needed later).

caution   Frequently, during college or seminary, persons coming out of the heritage pattern are tested concerning their faith. It is often the case that persons following this pattern come out of the formal training period with less devotion and fervor for Christ than they had going in. So that they actually retrogress in terms of spiritual formation and must go through a refurbishing time during the initial entry into full time ministry.

further   A helpful study concerning the drop-out pattern is **The Boundary--Meeting the First Years of Ministry** by Harbaugh, Behrens, Hudson and Oswald. Their initial findings indicate that intentional transitional programs during the start-up period help new clergy to make a more effective entry into ministry and make them less prone to terminate ministry prematurely. (1986:1). They discuss numerous models (several actually in practice and some ideal) which are very helpful in dealing with the early ministry entry pattern and hopefully preventing the drop-out pattern.

TRANSITIONAL TRAINING IN-SERVICE PATTERN   symbol: TR.2

introduction   The radical committal and accelerated patterns may
               correlate with this training in-service pattern.

IN-SERVICE PATTERN (selection dominates/ no formal training)

```
I. FOUNDATIONAL                  II. FIRST FULL-TIME MINISTRY
|-------------------|            |----------------------------->
```

may or may not include post-secondary
education; if so, it is incidental to ministry
```
        |-------------------------|
        MINISTRY TRANSITION
        BOUNDARY PHASE (on-the-job training)
```

OVERALL PATTERN
```
|<-------->||<--------------------->||<------------------->
PRE-MINISTRY  PART-TIME MINISTRY        FULL-TIME MINISTRY
              (ON-THE-JOB TRAINING)
```

examples   Atkinson (George 1982), Bresee (Tink 1982b), Taylor
            (Lee-Lim 1982), Studd (Morehead 1985), Trotman
            (Clinton 1984c), and Nee (Clinton 1982d) illustrate
            leaders who followed this training pattern.

comment   Persons coming out of the radical conversion
            pattern are most likely to transition into ministry
            via this training due to their immediate
            involvement in ministry. An on-going active
            ministry frequently keeps these persons engaged
            until into mid and late thirties. At that time
            they frequently feel need for some training but
            feel out of place in going to institutions whose
            philosophy is basically pre-service. Hence, they
            may not ever get any formal training. This means
            they are limited to in-formal and non-formal
            models. These may or may not be adequate for
            carrying the leader into effective latter ministry.

Advantages of this pattern include:

1. training centered on real needs in the ministry.
2. spiritual formation usually develops rapidly at first but may
   taper off due to lack of a solid theological base such as is
   received in formal training.
3. ministerial formation occurs rapidly but will usually be
   limited to surrounding models exposed to the emerging leader.

Disadvantages hinge around latter ministry.

1. lack of base upon which to mature in strategic formation.
2. drop out of ministry due to many reasons (moral, financial,
   frustration, lack of training which can broaden effectiveness,
   inability to adapt beyond early ministry philosophy).

TRANSITIONAL MODIFIED IN-SERVICE PATTERN   symbol: TR.3

introduction   A few from the heritage pattern, radical committal
               pattern, and delayed pattern, along with a larger
               number from the accelerated training pattern follow the
               modified in-service training pattern. Its
               emphasizes on-going training and retraining and
               their importance to continued development.

MODIFIED IN-SERVICE PATTERN (selection first/ then mid career forma
                    training later after solid entry)

I. FOUNDATIONAL   II. FIRST FULL   III. MID-CAREER
|-------------------| TIME MINISTRY   MINISTRY
      may or may not |-------------| |-----------|>
      include post-secondary
      education; if so, it is
      incidental to ministry
      |-------------------| |------| |------|
        MINISTRY TRANSITION   FORMAL   ONGOING
        BOUNDARY PHASE   MINISTRY   TRAINING
        on-the-job training   TRAINING

OVERALL PATTERN
|<----------->||<----------->||<----//--->||<----------->||<----->
PRE-MINISTRY   PART-TIME   FULL-TIME   INTERRUPTED   TOWARD
                MINISTRY   MINISTRY   IN-SERVICE   EFFECTIVE
                (on-the-job   TRAINING   LATTER
                training)   (formal)   MINISTRY

examples   Gripentrog (1987) illustrates this pattern ideally.
               Finzel (1987) and Metcalf (1987) are modified forms.

causation   Intense boundary processing often stimulates this
               pattern. Finzel (1987), radical committal pattern,
               illustrates that. Metcalf (1987), accelerated
               pattern, also demonstrates this pattern.

Advantages in this transition training pattern involve:

1. selection of formal training which is apropos to the leader in
   terms of perceived relevancy.
2. establishing a learning habit. Selection of training in
   mid-career sets a precedent which may later be repeated.
3. stimulation of an adult learning community. As contrasted
   with the pre-service pattern the learners in this formal
   training situation have learning resources based on experience
   to contribute to the learning process of the community.

Disadvantages

1. disruption of family and often termination from a past
   ministry and transition to a new one upon completion of the
   interrupted in-service training.

FEEDBACK ON TRANSITIONAL TRAINING PATTERNS

1. What transitional training pattern is illustrated by the following unique time-line? Check the correct answer.

```
I. EARLY-LIFE      II. FORMAL      III. INITIAL   IV. OVERSEAS
   FORMATION           TRAINING         MINISTRY       MINISTRY
|--------------------|----------------|---------------|--//-----|
1939                 1957             1964            1969    1984
```

Example 3. Nicholas Woodbury, Unique Time-Line (Woodbury 1984:6)

___ a. TR.1 Transitional Training Pre-service
___ b. TR.2 Transitional Training In-service
___ c. TR.3 Transitional Training Modified In-service

2. Identify your transitional training patterns.

___ a. TR.1 Transitional Training Pre-service
___ b. TR.2 Transitional Training In-service
___ c. TR.3 Transitional Training Modified In-service

ANSWERS----------

    1. a. From the time-line alone one would conclude "a." But actually Woodbury is now pursuing mid-career formal training so that "c" is absolutely correct.
    2. c. This is my pattern. Actually, my pattern is a modified TR.3.

THE FOUNDATIONAL MINISTRY PATTERN   symbol: M.1

introduction   Jesus reveals an important principle in his remarks
                following the Unfaithful Steward Parable of Luke
                16:1-13.

                Luke 16:10 The Little-Big Principle
                FAITHFULNESS IN A SMALL RESPONSIBILITY IS AN
                INDICATOR OF FAITHFULNESS IN A LARGER
                RESPONSIBILITY.

                This basic principle seems to be foundational to
                all of ministry processing. From observations of
                repeated application of this principle comes the
                foundational ministry pattern.

description   The <u>Foundational</u> <u>Ministry</u> pattern describes the
M.1   faithfulness expansion cycle that seemingly occurs
                throughout a life-time of ministry in which
                faithfulness in ministry tasks and ministry
                assignments along with positive response to the
                testing element of many of the ministry process
                items leads to expanded ministry and retesting of
                faithfulness at that new ministry level.

examples   Supportive evidence occurs in many case studies:
                See D. Belesky (1987), K. Waldner (1987), E.
                Baumgarnter (1987), G. Gripentrog (1987), H. Finzel
                (1987)

example   Lorne Sanny, Dawson Trotman's successor was cited
                by Trotman for this faithfulness quality. He
                became the architect for the second era of
                Navigator history.

Biblical   Paul's oft quoted leadership selection admonition
example   to Timothy points out this important quality. "And
II Timothy   the things that thou has heard of me among many
2:2   witnesses, the same commit thou to faithful men,
                who shall be able to teach others also."

comment   A logical extension of implications of the M.1,
                T.1, and T.2 patterns and the testing aspects of
                numerous process items is the response premise.

                RESPONSE PREMISE
                THE TIME OF DEVELOPMENT OF A LEADER DEPENDS UPON
                RESPONSE TO PROCESSING.   RAPID RECOGNITION AND
                POSITIVE RESPONSE TO GOD'S PROCESSING SPEEDS UP
                DEVELOPMENT.   SLOWER RECOGNITION OR NEGATIVE
                RESPONSE DELAYS DEVELOPMENT.

                This premise needs verification testing but
                indications to date suggest strong plausibility.

THE LIKE-ATTRACTS-LIKE GIFT INDICATOR PATTERNS   symbol: M.2

introduction   Effective leaders recognize that leadership
                selection and development is a priority function.
                They learn to recognize very early in the life of a
                potential leader symptoms and tendencies which
                indicate leadership. They then plan for training
                activities which will confirm, clarify or
                invalidate those early "selection guesses." An
                early ministry selection pattern is the like-
                attracts-like pattern. Potential leaders tend to
                be challenged by and attracted to experienced
                leaders who contain giftedness elements similar to
                their own embryonic giftedness.

description   The Like-Attracts-Like gift pattern describes an
M.2   early gift recognition pattern frequently seen in
                potential leaders in which those potential leaders
                are intuitively attracted to leaders who have like
                spiritual gifts.

examples   Supportive evidence for this pattern is seen in
                Baumgartner (1987), Gripentrog (1987), and Finzel
                (1987).

applies   This pattern is helpful for both mentors who tend
to   to attract proteges with like gifts and for
                emerging leaders as they seek to evaluate their own
                giftedness.

2 uses   A leader aware of the M.2 pattern can use it in at
                least two ways. One, the leader who knows well his
                or her own gifts can observe those people who are
                drawn to that leader's person and ministry and
                assume that there is the possibility of that person
                having one or more of those known gifts. The
                leader can then suggest ministry tasks which will
                aid development of those suspected gifts. The
                leader can also suggest disciplined self-study
                personal growth projects that personally helped
                his/her own development. Two, the leader can
                recognize that people drawn to another leader may
                well have one or more gifts of that leader. Again
                the same deliberate process of activities and
                growth projects can be suggested (except of course
                they should fit that other leader's gift
                development).

THE GIFTEDNESS DRIFT PATTERN   symbol: M.3

introduction   Effective leaders recognize that leadership
                selection and development is a priority function.
                They learn to recognize very early in the life of a
                potential leader symptoms and tendencies which
                indicate leadership. They then plan for training
                activities which will confirm, clarify or
                invalidate those early "selection guesses." The
                tendency for a potential leader, if given freedom
                or choice, to naturally drift toward ministry roles
                or functions which utilize that leader's embryonic
                gifts (even though these may not be explicitly
                known at the time) is helpful in early
                identification of giftedness.

description   The Giftedness Drift pattern describes the tendency
M.3   of a potential leader to most naturally respond
                to ministry challenges and assignments either that
                fit prior experience or perception of natural
                ability or intuitively, a spiritual gift.

examples   Waldner (1987), Gripentrog (1987), and Finzel
                (1987) indicate this pattern to be true of their
                development.

heuristic   This should encourage those who are emerging to
value   attempt ministry roles and activities toward which
                they feel drawn as they will most likely stimulate
                use of a latent gift or natural ability or point
                out the need to acquire a skill.

selection   This tendency should also point out to mid career
hint   leaders where and how to look for potential leaders.

central   This tendency is central to the notion of the
notion   giftedness development pattern which says that
                giftedness identification correlates strongly to
                ministry experience.

THE FORCED ROLE/GIFT ENABLEMENT PATTERN   symbol: M.4

introduction   Effective leaders focus on leadership
                selection and development. Tendencies and
                embryonic gifts are not the only thing a leader
                looks for in identifying gifts in a potential
                leader. Latent gifts emerge, or acquisition of new
                gifts sometimes happen, when God clearly leads a
                potential leader or developed leader into a role
                which requires gifts not seen in past ministry. If
                God clearly leads into a role then a leader can
                expect enablement for that role. The gifts may
                come to the leader (direct) or others associated
                with that leader (indirect).

description   The Forced Role/Gift Enablement pattern describes
M.4   the not so frequent M.4 pattern in which a person
                is placed in a role which requires some specific
                gift or gift-mix not previously known or
                demonstrated and in that role is met by the Holy
                Spirit so as to demonstrates one or more of those
                needed gifts while the role is active.

example   II Timothy 4:5. Paul's admonition to Timothy
                concerning evangelism, may illustrate this.

guidance   Normally guidance into a position or role is
implication   confirmed by some past experience. However, if God
                has, by other guidance, clearly led one to a role
                or function, notwithstanding former experience or
                demonstrated giftedness, then the leader can expect
                that giftedness will be given in the situation.

related to   The forced role/ gift enablement observation seems
tertiary   to correlate with the notion of tertiary spiritual
gifting   gifts. A gift is spoken of as vested if it appears
                repeatedly in a person's ministry and can be
                repeated at will by the person. A gift is spoken of
                as non-vested if it appears situationally and can
                not be repeated at will by the person. A gift is
                primary if it is a vested gift and currently being
                demonstrated as a significant part of the gift-mix
                or gift-cluster. A gift is secondary if at one
                time it was a vested gift but is now not
                demonstrated as part of the current gift-mix or
                gift-cluster. A gift is tertiary if it has been or
                is a non-vested gift or if it was manifested as
                necessitated by "role" responsibility in the past
                and is not now viewed as vested.

final   A gift experienced in a role situation may become
disposition   vested and used regularly on through life
                afterwards (hence be seen as a primary gift) or it
                may disappear after the time of the role finishes
                (a tertiary gift).

FEEDBACK ON BASIC GIFTEDNESS PATTERNS

1. Which of the following basic giftedness patterns have you experienced personally? Check any that you experienced.

___a. M.2 Like-Attracts-Like Gift Pattern
___b. M.3 Giftedness Drift Pattern
___c. M.4 Forced Role/ Gift Enablement Pattern

2. For any that you checked in exercise 1 list the gifts indicated or used in the pattern.

___a. M.2 Like-Attracts-Like Gift Pattern
      Gifts:

___b. M.3 Giftedness Drift Pattern
      Gifts:

___c. M.4 Forced Role/ Gift Enablement Pattern
      Gifts:

3. It was suggested that the M.1 Foundational Ministry Pattern was **the critical pattern**. Can you give any basis for that suggestion? In what way is it critical to the basic giftedness patterns?

ANSWERS----------
     1. a, b.
     2. a. teaching, exhortation b. teaching
     3. All of the gift patterns assume that discovery of a gift is for the purpose of ministry. That is, the stewardship model certainly applies to what ever gifts are discovered. Faithfulness in using what is discovered is the key to further development and new discoveries. In fact, faithfulness, the key element of the M.1 pattern is the core value of the stewardship model.

THE AUTHORITY INSIGHTS PATTERN   symbol: M.5

introduction   Leaders have a right to influence. That right can
                come in various legitimate ways. Authority refers
                to the right to exercise leadership influence by a
                leader over followers. Leaders learn about
                authority via numerous process items which relate
                to such issues as submission, interpersonal
                influence, interpersonal relationships, and
                organizational structures. Such process items as
                ministry structure insights, leadership backlash,
                relationships insights, authority insights, and
                ministry conflict are used by God to teach
                important lessons on how and how not to exercise
                authority as a Christian leader.

description   The Authority Insights pattern is a several stage
M.5   pattern describing an oft seen sequence of how a
                potential leader over a long period of time usually
                learns about the exercise of authority in ministry:
                1) negative lessons of authority lead to 2) a
                search for legitimate authority which leads to 3) a
                desire to model legitimate authority which gives 4)
                insights about spiritual authority which finalizes
                in 5) an increased use of spiritual authority as a
                foundational power base.

kinds of   As a leader moves along this pattern, processing
lessons   teaches either positive or negative lessons about:

                1) submission to authority,
                2) authority structures,
                3) authenticity of power bases underlying
                   authority,
                4) authority conflict or the like,
                5) how to exercise authority.

authority   Leaders in the Growth Ministry phase must learn how
problem   to submit to authority. This is a first step in
                learning how to use authority effectively. The
                "authority problem" refers to the repeated
                observation that many leaders throughout their
                ministry have problems in perceiving authority and
                submitting to it. This is an on-going challenge
                which becomes much more subtle as a leader matures.
                Leaders who have trouble submitting to authority
                will usually have trouble exercising spiritual
                authority.

followership   Authority is crucial to developing "followership."
                Improper use of authority will cause deterioration
                of "followership," eventually bringing about
                division, or will cower followers into submission,
                creating a false sense of "followership" which in
                effect hinders release of emerging leaders.

THE GIFTEDNESS DEVELOPMENT PATTERN   symbol M.6

introduction   A spiritual gift is a unique capacity for
                 channeling a Holy Spirit led ministry in and
                 through the life of a believer. Wagner (1979)
                 coined the term gift-mix to talk about multi-gifted
                 people. How a gift-mix is discovered and matures
                 as a gift cluster is the focus of this pattern.

description   The <u>Giftedness</u> <u>Development</u> pattern refers to the
M.6   process a leader goes through in moving from
                 initial discovery of a gift to convergence.

stages   The pattern includes: (read ---> as may lead to)
                 1. ministry experience -->
                 2. discovery of gift/natural abilities -->
                 3. increased use of that gift/abilities -->
                 4. effectiveness in using that gift/abilities -->
                 5. more ministry experience or new ministry roles
                 6. which stimulates further discovery of gifts to
                    meet the new situation -->
                 7. which over a period of time eventuates in
                    identification of gift-mix -->
                 8. development of gift-cluster -->
                 9. convergence.

explanation   **Gift-mix** is a phrase which is used to describe the
                 set of spiritual gifts a leader repeatedly uses in
                 ministry. **Gift-cluster** refers to a gift-mix which
                 has a dominant gift, supported harmoniously by other
                 gifts and abilities.   The **giftedness discovery**
                 process item describes any significant advance
                 along the giftedness discovery pattern and the
                 stimulus (trigger incident) that brought the
                 discovery. This might be an event, person or
                 reflection process. The repetition with increased
                 clarity of this giftedness discovery process item
                 is an important feature of the ministry phase.

giftedness   The **giftedness set** includes natural abilities,
set   acquired skills, and spiritual gifts. The pattern
                 above assumes that spiritual gifts are the focal
                 element (the central element of ministry focus).

inclusive   The pattern actually refers to all elements of the
pattern   giftedness set (natural abilities, acquired skills,
at lower   and spiritual gifts).   The latter stages refer only
levels   to spiritual gifts since most natural abilities and
                 acquired skills are discovered or obtained in the
                 foundational or transitional or provisional time
                 periods of the ministry time-line. As one matures
                 in giftedness the emphasis primarily involves
                 development of spiritual gifts or supplementary
                 skills related to them.

THE GIFTEDNESS DEVELOPMENT PATTERN   symbol M.6 continued

natural ability focal	If natural abilities are the focal element then steps 5, 6, and 7 most likely collapse into one step which seeks to subordinate acquired skills and spiritual gifts to symbiotically support it.
3 kinds of spiritual gift categories	Three kinds of gift categories which relate to corporate functions seen in various New Testament churches include: **word gifts, power gifts, love gifts.** Each of these clusters fulfill special functions essential to a church. The power gifts demonstrate the authenticity, credibility, power and reality of the unseen God. They stimulate faith in the unseen God. The love gifts manifest this God in practical ways that can be recognized by a world around us which needs love. The word gifts clarify the nature of this unseen God and His demands and purposes. They communicate about and for this God. They stimulate hope for the future. There is overlap in the clusters, that is, some gifts occur in more than one cluster.
power cluster	The power gift cluster includes: faith, word of knowledge, discerning of spirits, miracles, tongues, interpretation of tongues, healing, word of wisdom, prophecy.
word cluster	The word gift cluster includes: word of wisdom, prophecy, word of knowledge, faith, pastoring, evangelism, exhortation, teaching, apostleship, ruling.
love cluster	The love cluster includes: healing, word of wisdom, word of knowledge, governments, pastoring, giving, evangelism, mercy, helps, ruling.
two reasons for importance of clusters	These clusters are important for two reasons: 1. Leaders must constantly evaluate the corporate structures for balance and imbalance of giftedness. 2. In all cases studied, **Christian leaders always have at least one word gift in their gift-mix.**
leader types, stages	Type D and E leaders will reach stage 7, explicitly identifying at least a gift-mix. Often they will reach stage 8, the identification of a gift-cluster. If so, a leader will often make efforts to rearrange roles and priorities in terms of this gift-mix or gift-cluster (an important step towards convergence). Type C leaders reach stage 6, the level of discovery of other gifts. Type A and B leaders usually reach stage 4 with a few reaching stage 5. In either case, the gift may not be cognitively identified but usually intuitively identified in drift toward using it.

THE SPIRITUAL AUTHORITY DEVELOPMENT PATTERN   symbol: M.7

introduction   The Spiritual Authority Development Pattern
               involves the leader's experience with, use of, and
               understanding of power from the simplest forms
               involving personal power right on up to various
               combinations of power forms. The suggestive
               pattern, which is by no means normative involves
               8 stages.

description   The Spiritual Authority Development Pattern is an
M.7   8 stage pattern which reflects the changing power
               forms that a leader chooses to use ranging from
               one's initial use and discovery of power to a
               power-mix with spiritual authority as a dominant
               means.   The stages: 1) discovery of personal
               authority as a power form 2) discovery of other
               forms (force, manipulation, persuasion) 3)
               discovery of other authority forms (legitimate,
               competent) 4) discarding of force/manipulation as
               forms; use of persuasion as complementary
               throughout following stages 5) effectiveness in use
               of legitimate authority, competent authority, and
               personal authority with some spiritual authority 6)
               lessening of legitimate authority, competent
               authority becoming dominant 7) combination of
               competent authority, personal authority and
               spiritual authority as equally dominant 8)
               spiritual authority dominant, personal authority,
               competent authority, legitimate authority, and
               persuasion used as complementary.

goal   The ultimate goal of authority processing is to
               bring a leader into an understanding of and use of
               spiritual authority as the primary authority used
               in leadership influence. This is not to negate
               other kinds of authority as legitimate but to put
               them in proper perspective. Transition from the
               Growth Ministry phase to Unique Ministry phase of
               the Ministry Time-Line features significant
               progress toward this ultimate goal. This pattern
               describes movement toward dominant use of spiritual
               authority by a leader.

disclaimer   This is a tentative working description. Leaders
               may obviate this pattern due to early experience
               under other leaders who model some of the advanced
               power forms. The crucial portion of the pattern is
               the switch from competent or legitimate or personal
               authority as dominant to spiritual authority as
               dominant.

progression   The realization of spiritual authority as a power
               form (influence means) gradually increases during
               Growth Ministry. It begins in the provisional sub-

THE SPIRITUAL AUTHORITY DEVELOPMENT PATTERN symbol: M.7 continued

phase of the Growth Ministry Phase, continues in the competent sub-phase of the Growth Ministry Phases and deepens in the boundary processing leading to the Unique Ministry Phase. It peaks in the latter part of the Unique Ministry Phase. It is during the boundary leading into the Unique Ministry Phase that significant insights concerning spiritual authority are grasped and applied to situations. The deepening of the experiential power base (one's personal experience and knowledge of God) is gained through the maturity cluster of process items.

processing   The spiritual authority discovery item refers to
P(SAD)   the process by which gains are made towards
                 spiritual authority. The authority development
                 pattern helps measure stages in those gains. In the
                 provisional sub-phase of the Growth Ministry Phase,
                 competent authority, and legitimate authority, and
                 persuasion reign as dominant power forms. Spiritual
                 authority is a lesser power form. The conclusion
                 of the competent sub-phase of the Growth Ministry
                 Phase signals the insertion of spiritual authority
                 as a major power form.

explanation   The spiritual authority discovery item refers to
P(SAD)   any significant advance along the spiritual
                 authority development pattern (especially in stages
                 6,7 and 8) and any event, person, reflection
                 process or tandem process item that was
                 instrumental in bringing about the discovery.

experiential   Usually the discovery of insights is experiential
learning,   first, with cognitive understanding following much
primary   later. That is, leaders usually experience the use
                 of some power form in relation to leaders they are
                 under, or their own use of some power form, without
                 necessarily understanding it conceptually. Later
                 reflective thinking usually leads to understanding.

order   On a linear time-line the above stages most likely
                 corresponds to Phases as follows:

Boundary Into Growth Ministry	Provisional Growth Ministry	Competent Growth Ministry	Role Transition Unique Ministry	Convergence Unique Ministry
Stage 1	Stage 2 Stage 3	Stage 4 Stage 5 Stage 6	Stage 7	Stage 8

MINISTRY ENTRY PATTERNS   symbol: M.8

introduction   Ministry entry can refer to the initial ministry an
                 emerging leader takes part in or it can refer to
                 any new ministry task, assignment, or challenge
                 that a growing leader assumes. Most initial
                 ministry entry activities come while the emerging
                 leader is a lay person and is usually the result of
                 some sort of challenge. The challenge may come
                 from within (self-initiated by the emerging
                 leader). The resulting ministry may be something
                 entirely new created to meet the challenge. This
                 is relatively rare among early emerging leaders.
                 The challenge may be internally generated in
                 response to a need in an organization. This is less
                 rare than self-initiated ministry. The majority of
                 ministry challenges come from without (leaders
                 challenging potential leaders to fill needs within
                 existing ministry structures). A variety of
                 ministry challenges accepted will usually lead to
                 initial discovery of giftedness. Five process items
                 are closely related to the various ministry entry
                 patterns: **ministry challenge, ministry assignment,
                 ministry skills, training progress, giftedness
                 discovery.**

description   The ministry entry patterns describe the ways
M.8   challenges come to leaders and potential
                 leaders as they accept various ministry tasks and
                 assignments during early, middle and latter
                 ministry. They are a series of patterns relating
                 three factors: 1. how the challenge comes--
                 motivated externally or internally, 2. the
                 structures or roles that relate to the challenge--
                 existing structures/roles, modification of
                 structures or role, or creation of new structures
                 or roles, 3. the frequency of occurrence.

success   Successful initial ministry entry for full time
entry   Christian workers depends upon several factors:
criteria   previous experience as Type A and Type B leaders,
                 type of transitional training pattern, degree of
                 balanced learning in the training, time/ ministry
                 context perspectives.

caution   Leaders who by-passed Type A and Type B experience
by-passing   will find initial ministry entry more difficult and
Type A, B   stand a high probability of experiencing the
                 abbreviated entry pattern (drop out). This is
                 especially true if the transitional training
                 pattern is unbalanced toward the cognitive side
                 rather than experiential side. Harbaugh et al,
                 describe orientation training which attempts to
                 offset the large dropout.

MINISTRY ENTRY PATTERNS   symbol: M.8   continued

introduction   Tables 1,2, and 3 below show typical ministry
                challenges for the growth ministry phase. Tables 1
                and 2 apply more to the provisional sub-phase.
                Table 3 applies to the competent sub-phase.

Pattern   Challenge/Response   Frequency

                    Table 1. Early Processing

1   external work in existing
                       ministry structures/roles   most common
2   internal work in existing
                       ministry structures/roles   next most common
3   external create new ministry
                       roles or structures   rarer
4   internal create new ministry
                       roles or structures   rarest

                    Table 2. Middle Processing

1   external work in existing
                       ministry structures/roles   most common
2   internal work in existing
                       ministry structures/roles   very common
3   internal change existing ministry
                       structures/roles   very common
4   external change existing ministry
                       structures/roles   not so common
5   external create new ministry
                       roles or structures   occasional
6   internal create new ministry
                       roles or structures   rare

                    Table 3. Latter Processing

1   internal work in existing
                       ministry structures/roles   very common
2   internal change existing ministry
                       structures/roles   very common
3   external change existing ministry
                       structures/roles   not so common
4   internal create new ministry
                       roles or structures   rare

summary   Ministry challenge describes the means whereby a
                leader or potential leader is prompted to accept a
                new ministry assignment and sense the guidance of
                God into service. The most common pattern of entry
                into a ministry assignment is an external challenge
                to work in some existing role in a ministry
                situation. The rarest entry patterns involve self-
                initiated challenges to create new ministry roles
                and structures. An important entry pattern in all

MINISTRY ENTRY PATTERNS   symbol: M.8   continued

three stages involves usually internal (self-initiated) challenges to adapt present roles or ministry structures. This signals potential for high level leadership.

implications   Three implications come to mind. The first two are leadership selection insights and are for leaders selecting other leaders. The third is for any leader to consider for self-evaluation.

1. The majority of leaders will follow common entry patterns.
2. It is the self-initiation instinct of the internal entry patterns which indicates strong potential for upper level leadership.
3. Plateauing is indicated by a lessening frequency of interest in ministry challenges and ministry assignments.

application   Application of implication 1 is straightforward. A major function of all leadership is the selection and development of potential leaders. Thus, present leaders should openly and deliberately challenge potential leaders in terms of specific roles and the needs of existing ministries. Over the years the enthusiasm of ministry often wanes as leaders move toward latter ministry processing. As a result there is a corresponding lack of challenging and recruiting. This insight should help people in ministry, whether in early, middle or latter processing to see the value of continuing to enthusiastically challenge others for ministry.

indicator   Self-initiated ministry tasks or assignments carry with them the seeds of higher level leadership. Leaders should recognize that this quality is important and be on the alert for those who are constantly doing this kind of thing. One problem does exist. Often those who self-initiate ministry tasks and assignments are challenging the status quo and threatening leaders over them. Often when defensiveness arises in the midst of threatening situations, the sparkling quality of self-initiative is quickly by-passed and set aside for re-enforcing the status quo. Thus, implication 2 is very important. Later, in guidance processing, the mentor process item will be stressed. Mentors tend to be alert to this predictive quality and can patiently work to see it developed.

FEEDBACK ON MINISTRY PATTERNS--M.5, M.6, M.7, M.8

1. Examine the M.5 pattern in terms of your own personal
experience. Indicate any of the stages for which you have
experienced processing. Then check any of the kinds of
lessons you have experienced.
a. ___(1). negative lessons of authority
   ___(2) search for legitimate authority
   ___(3) desire to model legitimate authority
   ___(4) insights about spiritual authority
   ___(5) an increased use of spiritual authority so as to
           establish it as a foundational power base.
b. Lessons learned from either negative or positive experiences
about:
   ___(1) submission to authority,
   ___(2) authority structures,
   ___(3) authenticity of power bases underlying authority,
   ___(4) authority conflict or the like,
   ___(5) how to exercise authority.

c. For any one of the categories you checked relate an incident
and identification of processing that you see in it.

2. Examine the M.6 pattern in terms of your own personal
experience. Indicate any of the stages for which you have
experienced processing. Then indicate what element was
focal in your most recent ministry. Finally, indicate
your gift-mix and dominant gift. Be prepared to point out
processing which has influenced your movement along the
pattern.
a. ___(1) ministry experience
   ___(2) discovery of gift/natural abilities
   ___(3) increased use of that gift/abilities
   ___(4) effectiveness in using that gift/abilities
   ___(5) more ministry experience or new ministry roles
   ___(6) stimulated toward further discovery of gifts to meet
          a new situation,
   ___(7) identification of gift-mix over a period of time,
   ___(8) development of gift-cluster,
   ___(9) convergence.

b. Circle focal element which dominated most recent ministry
assignments: natural abilities, acquired skills, spiritual gifts.

c. Indicate your gift-mix by circling the spiritual gifts
identified as part of your gift-mix. Underline your dominant
gift.

apostleship	interpretation of tongues	miracles	giving
prophecy	kinds of healings	exhortation	tongues
pastoral	discernings of spirits	ruling	helps
teaching	word of knowledge	governments	faith
evangelism	word of wisdom	mercy	

FEEDBACK ON MINISTRY PATTERNS--M.5, M.6, M.7, M.8 continued

d. Identify any processing affecting this pattern.

3. Examine the M.7 pattern in terms of your own personal
experience. Indicate any of the stages for which you have
experienced processing. Then describe any authority insights,
spiritual authority discovery, relational, or power processing
that you have experienced in conjunction with this pattern.
a. Stages you have experienced:
___(1) discover personal authority as a power form
___(2) discover other forms (force, manipulation, persuasion)
___(3) discover other authority forms (legitimate, competent)
___(4) discard force/manipulation as forms; use of persuasion
        as complementary throughout following stages
___(5) effective in use of legitimate authority, competent
        authority, and personal authority with some spiritual
        authority
___(6) lessening of legitimate authority, competent authority
        becoming dominant
___(7) combining of competent authority, personal authority
        and spiritual authority as equally dominant
___(8) spiritual authority dominant, personal authority,
        competent authority, legitimate authority, and
        persuasion used as complementary.

b. Indicate here at least one process item from any authority
processing you have experienced in conjunction with this pattern.

4. Review again the M.8 Ministry Entry Patterns then underline
any you have experienced. Circle any of the entry patterns that
you have experienced either with ministry tasks, ministry
assignments, or other miscellaneous kinds of ministry
experiences. Be prepared to share the details of the causal
source (external or internal), roles, and structures involved.

a. Circle any ministry entry patterns you have experienced.

Causal Source	Dominant Response to Role or Structures
1 external	work in existing ministry structures/roles
2 external	change existing ministry structures/roles
3 external	create new ministry roles or structures
4 internal	work in existing ministry structures/roles
5 internal	change existing ministry structures/roles
6 internal	create new ministry roles or structures

b. What is your dominant causal source? Any observations
concerning it? What is your dominant response? Any special
processing?

ANSWERS----------
Your choices on all of these. Be prepared to share in class or
with a discerning friend.

THE REFLECTIVE/ FORMATIVE EVALUATION PATTERN   symbol UM.1

introduction   God uses a cluster of process items, the maturity
                cluster, comprised of destiny revelation, word
                items, literary items, contextual items, guidance
                items, life crisis, isolation, and spiritual
                authority discovery, to work on the major
                development task of the boundary phase overlapping
                into the Unique Ministry Phase. Such processing
                moves a leader to develop spiritual authority as
                the major power base of a leader. Spiritual
                authority is based on an experiential power base.
                That is, a leader's power resources for spiritual
                authority primarily depend on his/her experiential
                knowledge of God.   Three sub-tasks involve a
                deepened understanding of God, a deepened communion
                and intimacy with God, and a reversing of
                priorities from ministry success to relationship
                with God. The reflective/ formative evaluation
                patterns suggests some stages that occur throughout
                the processing involved with the maturity cluster.

descriptive   The Reflective/ Formative Evaluation pattern
UM.1   describes a 5 step leader response pattern to deep
                processing such as is experienced via the maturity
                cluster of process items and which has as its
                purpose the deepening of the leader's relationship
                with God and the ultimate shift of power base to
                spiritual authority. The five steps include:

                1. God initiates intense processing to gain the
                   attention of the leader.
                2. The leader is forced to do serious reflective
                   thinking about ministry, life, and ultimate
                   reality.
                3. The leader does evaluation of ministry and life
                   which results in formative thinking and
                   committal to growth measures learned in the
                   processing.
                4. The leader experiences a renewed determination
                   to know God more deeply.
                5. God blesses the committal and renewed
                   determination by deepening the relationship
                   between Himself and the leader. The whole
                   experience increases the spiritual authority of
                   the leader.

development   Throughout this pattern God seeks to develop
task of   spiritual authority as the major power base.
UM.1   a. A leader must know more about God.
                b. A leader must experience a deepened communion
                   and intimacy with God.
                c. A leader must focus on relationship with God as
                   one's primary responsibility rather than success
                   (the competent sub-phase's major motivation).

THE REFLECTIVE/ FORMATIVE EVALUATION PATTERN   symbol UM.1   continued

comment   The pattern above focuses on two important facets:

                    1) reflection as to the meaning of ministry and the
                       basis of God's involvement in it and
                    2) evaluation leading to a major philosophical
                       shift in basis for ministry from "competency in
                       doing" to "effectiveness flowing from being."

comment   One of the things that stimulates the philosophical
                    shift is processing which involves a leader in an
                    increasingly more intimate relationship with God.

processing   Process items which support this function include:
                    destiny revelation, word items, literary items,
                    contextual items, and guidance items. Significant
                    process items which directly affect this life-
                    maturity processing include: life crisis,
                    isolation, and spiritual authority discovery.

psychological   The boundary between the competent ministry sub-
paradigm   phase and the Unique Ministry Phase is a subtle
shift   one. It is primarily a psychological one and thus
                    may take place without change of ministry
                    assignment, location, role, or any other of the
                    most common things associated with a major boundary
                    change. It takes place in an increasing way as the
                    development task is progressively accomplished
                    though there may be a decisive moment in
                    conjunction with one of the 3 special life-maturity
                    process items which triggers the psychological
                    shift.

Biblical   A major book in the Bible which sheds much light on
example   spiritual authority and its relationship with life-
                    maturity process items is II Corinthians. This
                    book should be studied in depth utilizing
                    leadership perspectives seen in this manual.

example   See especially II Corinthians 1:3-11 which
                    describes some of Paul's processing which forced
                    the reflective/ evaluation pattern.

THE UPWARD DEVELOPMENT PATTERN   symbol: UM.2

introduction   The Upward Development pattern points out interplay
between spiritual and ministerial formation.
During certain times processing focuses on
leadership character ("beingness"). At other times
processing emphasizes leadership skills
("doingness"). A qualitative leap forward in
beingness usually leads to a more effective
ministry (doingness) which in turn forces need for
an ever deepening relationship with God.

description   The Upward Development pattern is a repeated
UM.2   spiraling of growth in beingness and doingness
extended over several phases. In each being cycle
an increased depth of experiencing God leads to
more effective ministry service ("doing"). The
more effective service ("doing") in turn points to
need for a deeper relationship with God (increased
need for "beingness"). Ultimately the final stage
fuses being and doing--union life.

focus   Ultimately, ministry flows out of beingness. Luke
10:17-20 prioritizes relationship with God over
success or power in ministry. The essence of this
pattern involves the deepening of vertical
spirituality (one's relationship with God) which
results in horizontal spirituality (one's
relationship with people).

duration   This pattern, time wise, includes all phases. The
and   foundational phase focuses on doing. A conversion
flow   experience for the F.2 Radical Committal Pattern or
a second committal experience (Lordship or
leadership committal) for the F.1 Heritage
Foundational Pattern signals an intense momentary
focus on beingness. A radical new relationship is
established with God. This results in reactions by
the developing leader to shift from the receiving
to giving mode--"In light of all He has done for me
I must do something for Him." The testing patterns
quickly return the emphasis to character. The
transitional training patterns shift back to doing
and ministry success. Early ministry failures
involving relationships point out character needs
though the emphasis during the provisional growth
sub-phase is on doingness. The competency sub-
phase along with deep processing experienced with
the maturity cluster leads to the deeper need for
beingness. During the Unique Ministry Phase the
psychological shift to ministering out of beingness
coincides with the deepened union experience. The
Unique Ministry Phase fuses being and doing as it
focuses on convergence.

THE GIFT-CLUSTER RIPENING PATTERN   symbol: UM.3

introduction   A leader moving toward convergence in the latter
               part of the competent ministry sub-phase or early
               portion of the Unique Ministry Phase frequently
               operates with a mature gift-cluster. Gifted power
               is habitual. The supportive gifts of the cluster
               synergistically support the dominant gift to
               produce the cluster effect. The cooperative
               interaction between the gifts of the gift-mix is
               such that the total effect is greater than the sum
               of the effects of each gift taken independently.

description   The Gift-cluster Ripening pattern expands in detail
UM.3   the advanced stages (7,8) in the giftedness
               development pattern and includes the following: 7a
               Selection of ministry based on dominant gift --->
               7b. experiencing supportive gifts in concert with
               dominant gift ---> 7c. gaining of insights into how
               supportive gifts relate to dominant gift ---> 8a.
               selection of ministry opportunities based on total
               gift-cluster ---> 8b. modifying of role to allow
               supportive gifts to operate in concert with
               dominant gift.

explanation   **Gift-cluster** denotes a dominant gift supported
               by other gifts so as to harmonize the gift-mix and
               to maximize effectiveness.

5 examples   *exhortation (dominant), teaching, word of wisdom
               *apostleship (dominant), word of knowledge, teaching
               *governments (dominant), exhortation, mercy
               *giving (dominant), governments, teaching
               *discerning of spirits (dominant), miracles, mercy

shift to   A major shift occurs in terms of gifted power at
power   the culmination of this stage of giftedness
pattern 2   development. The leader shifts from Power Pattern
               1, The Temporary Acquisition Pattern, to Power
               Pattern 2, Confident Usage Pattern.

explanation   The **temporary acquisition pattern** is as follows;
Power   1) not aware of or have no need for a special use
Pattern 1 of power, 2) recognition of need for, 3) situation
               forcing a necessity to obtain, 4) insightful moment
               when God meets the leader with the particular power
               item, 5) return to normal status.

explanation   The **confident usage pattern** is as follows: 1)
Power   constantly aware of the need for power,
Pattern 2 2) insightful moment when God prompts for usage of
               power followed by, 3) confident acceptance of power
               item by faith, 4) God's channeling of the power for
               situation.

THE CONVERGENCE BALANCE PATTERN   symbol: UM.4

introduction The definition of a leader as a person with God-
              given capacity and God-given responsibility who is
              influencing a group of God's people towards God's
              purposes for them, requires a strong view of
              leadership. If follows that God has in mind the
              development of that leader toward realized
              potential. Three convergence factors which
              manifest realized potential include gift-cluster,
              ideal influence-mix, and power-mix. The balance
              pattern recognizes the need to keep within the
              limits of capacity with regard to these three
              convergence factors when selecting ministry roles.

description   The Balance pattern describes a leader's processing
UM.4   toward convergence which seeks to assess capacity
              and fit between three major convergence factors: 1.
              ministry role which fits gift-cluster, 2. ministry
              role which allows ideal influence-mix (appropriate
              degree and kind), 3. ministry role which utilizes
              appropriate power-mix consonant with the leader's
              influence-mix and gift-cluster.

explanation   **Gift-cluster** denotes a dominant gift supported
              by other gifts so as to harmonize the gift-mix and
              to maximize effectiveness.

example   exhortation (dominant), teaching, word of wisdom

explanation   **Influence-mix** denotes the combination of influence
              elements--direct, indirect or organizational--in
              terms of degree and kind at a given point in a
              development phase. **Ideal influence-mix** refers to
              the influence-mix combination which occurs when
              major and minor convergence factors harmonize.

example   large organizational influence, direct influence
influence-   (small extensiveness, large intensiveness, small
mix   comprehensiveness), large indirect influence
              (writings, boards). See page 415 for explanation.

explanation   **Power-mix** denotes the combination of power forms--
              force, manipulation, authority (and its sub-forms),
              and persuasion--which are dominant in a leader's
              influence in leadership acts during a time period.

examples   *spiritual authority, competence authority,
                  persuasion power
              *manipulative power, coercive authority,
                  induced authority
              *legitimate authority, manipulation power,
                  persuasion power
              *spiritual authority, personal authority,
                  persuasion power

THE CONVERGENCE BALANCE PATTERN   symbol: UM.4 continued

explanation   A leader in convergence is aware (implicitly or
                    explicitly) of the need for maintaining balance
                    between ideal influence-mix, power-mix, and gift-
                    cluster. This means that ministry opportunities or
                    roles should allow the maximum possible combination
                    between these three convergence factors. The term,
                    fit, refers to this state.

related   The thrust of balance or remaining within
to   leadership capacity, influence-mix limits and
destiny   appropriate power forms for stated limits, relates
                    closely to divine guidance, and calling and destiny
                    experiences. Paul describes his own recognition of
                    balance limits in a context of exercising
                    authority.

Pauline   "As for us, however, our boasting will not go beyond
comment   certain limits; it will stay within the limits of
                    the work which God has set for us and this includes
                    our work among you." (II Corinthians 10:13)

convergence   A. W. Tozer, in the latter portion of his third
balance   phase, City Leadership, molded a pastoral role
example   which stimulated the use of his word gifts (direct
                    influence--public exhortation--size several hundred
                    in extensiveness), while minimizing his personality
                    shaping (freed from pastoral functions). His role
                    allowed for use of word gifts in secondary direct
                    influence like teaching from time to time in Bible
                    schools. His role also permitted a large indirect
                    influence through a radio ministry (probably
                    thousands) and an indirect influence through
                    writing (prophetic gift exercised) as editor of a
                    denominational magazine and contributor to other
                    periodicals. His books captured the highlights of
                    his personal experience with God and provided
                    further indirect influence in the thousands. His
                    role also called for organizational influence
                    (local church, in terms of leadership but not
                    administrative details, and denominationally among
                    executive leadership).

THE CONVERGENCE GUIDANCE PATTERN   symbol: UM.5

introduction   Convergence represents a period of time in which
                several development patterns peak. These include:
                giftedness development, upward development, and
                convergence guidance. Leadership potential has been
                developed and an "ideal role" emerges which allows
                that potential to be used at capacity in terms of
                "ideal influence-mix" and "power-mix."

description   The <u>Convergence</u> <u>Guidance</u> describes the tracing of
UM.5   God's guidance over a life-time toward convergence
                and includes such occurrences as: 1. experience of
                various mini-convergence patterns, 2. recognition
                of ideal influence-mix and ideal role, 3. guidance
                processing leading to ideal role or allowing
                modification of role toward ideal role, 4. merging
                of several mini-convergences, 5. synergistic
                combination of major and minor convergence factors.

explanation   **Convergence** refers to a period of effectiveness in
                a leader's life characterized by simultaneously
                reaching mature stages in several development
                patterns and seeing various convergence factors
                harmoniously supporting each other to bring about
                that effectiveness. (See also **Table of Convergence
                Factors** which follows.)

major and   For descriptive purposes convergence factors are
minor   classified as major (giftedness, role, influence-
factors   mix, upward dependence and ministry philosophy) and
                minor (experience, personality shaping, geography,
                special opportunity, prophecy, destiny).

mini-   Mini-Convergence is the term indicating that two or
convergence   more convergence factors (whether major, minor or
                some combination) are seen as supporting each
                other, increasing a leader's effectiveness and
                capacity to influence at a given point in time.
                Nine of the more common patterns of mini-
                convergence were suggested:
                1. giftedness matched with ministry task.
                2. giftedness matched with role.
                3. giftedness matched with influence-mix.
                4. giftedness matched with power-mix.
                5. role matched with geographic location.
                6. role matched with experience.
                7. role matched with personality.
                8. destiny matched with special opportunity.
                9. destiny matched with experience.
                10. destiny matched with geographical location.

guidance   An insightful leader notes carefully any mini-
                convergence patterns. Reflection yields important
                guidance indicators for future ministry.

TABLE OF CONVERGENCE FACTORS

MAJOR FACTORS	DESCRIPTION
1. Giftedness	Giftedness including natural abilities, acquired skills, and spiritual gifts has matured so that the leader operates with gift-cluster or focal element enhanced.
2. Role	The role of the leader has been adapted to maximize giftedness and fit influence-mix and power-mix.
3. Influence-Mix	The leader has reached appropriate capacity for influencing followers. Influence-mix has right combination and depth (i.e. appropriate extensiveness, intensiveness, and comprehensiveness).
4. Upward Dependence	The leader has a deep relationship with God and can confidently trust God for life, ministry, and chanelling of God's power in giftedness. Union life is the norm.
5. Ministry Philosophy	The leader has clear focus in what to accomplish and how to do so. Articulated values undergird ministry.

MINOR FACTORS	DESCRIPTION
1. Experience	Past experience which may not have made sense now fits together to provide new insights in convergent ministry.
2. Personality	Role and influence-means match the unique personality shaping of the leader. That is, they will take advantage of positive personality traits and minimize negative personality traits.
3. Geography	The leader is located in a place, and with a ministry structure, which allows for influence-mix and capacity to be realized.
4. Special Opportunity	God will open doors of special opportunity. His timing will be evident frequently.
5. Prophecy	Any past processing involving a prophecy will be realized in convergence.
6. Destiny	Previous destiny experiences will come to fulfillment in convergence.

FEEDBACK ON UNIQUE MINISTRY PATTERNS: UM.1-UM.5

1. For the UM.1 Reflective/ Formative Evaluation Pattern indicate by checking any stage in which you have seen processing; indicate one or more process items with date. [example: P(LC), 1982; P(I), 1985;] Be prepared to share details of the processing.

Stage   Processing

___(1) God initiates intense processing
        to gain attention of leader.

___(2) The leader is forced to do serious
        reflective thinking about ministry
        and life and ultimate reality.

___(3) The leader's evaluation of life
        and ministry results in formative
        thinking and committal to growth
        measures.

___(4) The leader experiences a renewed
        desire to know God more deeply.

___(5) God blesses the committal and the
        renewed determination by deepening
        the relationship between Himself
        and the leader. The whole
        experience increases the spiritual
        authority of the leader.

2. Which of the development tasks usually associated with the UM.1 pattern have you experienced either in part or whole? Throughout this pattern God seeks to develop spiritual authority as the major power base.

___a. Sub-task 1. a leader must gain knowledge about God.
___b. Sub-task 2. a leader must experience a deepened communion
        and intimacy with God.
___c. Sub-task 3. A leader must focus on relationship with God as
        primary responsibility rather than success (a competent
        sub-phase motivating factor) or other motivational factors.

3. The UM.1 pattern focuses on two important facets. Indicate by checking if any processing has prompted toward these facets. Be prepared to share processing and end results in terms of these facets.

___a. reflection as to the meaning of ministry and the basis of
        God's involvement in it and
___b. evaluation leading to a major philosophical shift in basis
        for ministry from "competency in doing" to "effectiveness
        flowing from being."

FEEDBACK ON UNIQUE MINISTRY PATTERNS: UM.1-UM.5 continued

4. The UM.2 Upward Development pattern is a repeated spiraling of
growth in beingness and doingness extended over several phases.
In each being cycle an increased depth of experiencing God leads
to more effective ministry service ("doing"). The more effective
service ("doing") in turn points to the need for a deeper
rel_   hip with God (increased need for "beingness").
Ultimately the final stage fuses being and doing--union life.
Describe in what way you have seen this pattern in your own life
or some modified form of it.

5. Check any stages of the UM.3 pattern which you have reached.
The Gift-cluster Ripening pattern expands in detail the advanced
stages (7,8) in the giftedness development pattern and includes
the following:
___(7a) selection of ministry based on dominant gift
___(7b) experience supportive gifts in concert with dominant gift
___(7c) gaining of insights into how supportive gifts relate to
        dominant gift
___(8a) selection of ministry opportunities based on total gift-
        cluster
___(8b) modifying of role to allow supportive gifts to operate in
        concert with dominant gift.

6. Usually movement toward and in the UM.3 gift-cluster ripening
pattern involves experiences with two power patterns. Indicate
if you have experienced processing dealing with either of these
patterns. Be prepared to explain.

a. Power Pattern 1. The temporary acquisition pattern:
___(1) not aware of, have no need for, special use of
       power,
___(2) recognition of need for
___(3) situation forcing a necessity to obtain,
___(4) insightful moment when God meets the leader with the
       particular power item
___(5) return to normal status.

b. Power Pattern 2. The confident usage pattern:
___(1) constantly aware of need for power
___(2) insightful moment when God prompts for usage of power
___(3) confident acceptance of power item by faith
___(4) God's channeling of the power for situation.

7. The UM.4 Balance pattern describes a leader's processing
toward convergence which seek to assess capacity and fit between
three major convergence factors: 1. ministry role which fits
gift-cluster, 2. ministry role which allows ideal influence-mix
(appropriate degree and kind), 3. ministry role which utilizes
appropriate power-mix consonant with the leader's influence-mix
and gift-cluster. Describe your present understanding of
capacity as to gift-cluster, influence-mix, and power-mix and an
ideal role which fits with them.

FEEDBACK ON UNIQUE MINISTRY PATTERNS: UM.1-UM.5

8. The UM.5 Convergence Guidance describes the tracing of God's guidance over a life-time toward convergence and includes such occurrences as: (1) experience of various mini-convergence patterns, (2) recognition of ideal influence-mix and ideal role, (3) guidance processing leading to ideal role or allowing modification of role toward ideal role, (4) merging of several mini-convergences, (5) synergistic combination of major and minor convergence factors.

a. Check any mini-convergence factors you have experienced, indicate the phase or sub-phase in your time-line when it occurred.

Mini-Convergence Experienced   Phase(s)

___(1) giftedness matched with ministry task.
___(2) giftedness matched with role.
___(3) giftedness matched with influence-mix.
___(4) giftedness matched with power-mix.
___(5) role matched with geographic location.
___(6) role matched with experience.
___(7) role matched with personality.
___(8) destiny matched with special opportunity.
___(9) destiny matched with experience.
___(10) destiny matched with geographical location.

b. Indicate any of the major convergent factors for which you have seen processing. Indicate (with process item symbols) the processing that has given you insights about the factor.

Factor   Processing

___(1) Giftedness
     Giftedness, including natural
abilities, acquired skills, and
spiritual gifts, has matured so that the
leader operates with gift-cluster or
focal element enhanced.

___(2) Role
     The role of the leader has been
adapted to maximize giftedness and fit
influence-mix and power-mix.

___(3) Influence-Mix
     The leader has reached appropriate
capacity for influencing followers.
Influence-mix has right combination and
depth (i.e. appropriate extensiveness,
intensiveness, and comprehensiveness).

FEEDBACK ON UNIQUE MINISTRY PATTERNS: UM.1-UM.5 continued

Factor   Processing

___(4) **Upward Dependence**
     The leader has a deep relationship
with God and can confidently trust God
for life, ministry, and chanelling
of God's power in giftedness.

___(5) **Ministry Philosophy**
     The leader has a clear focus as to
what to accomplish and how to do so.
Articulated values undergird ministry.

b. Indicate any of the minor convergent factors for which you
have seen processing. Indicate (with process item symbols) the
processing that has given you insights about the factor.

Factor   Processing

___(1) **Experience**
     Past experience, which may not have
made sense, now fits together to provide
new insights in convergent ministry.

___(2) **Personality Shaping**
     Role and influence-means match the
unique personality shaping of the
leader. Positive personality traits
are taken advantage of and negative
personality traits are minimized.

___(3) **Geography**
     The leader is located in a place,
and with a ministry structure, which
allows for influence-mix and capacity
to be realized.

___(4) **Special Opportunity**
     God will open doors of special
opportunity His timing will be evident
frequently.

___(5) **Prophecy**
     Any past processing involving a
prophecy will be realized.

___(6) **Destiny**
     Previous destiny experiences will
come to fulfillment in convergence.

ANSWERS----------
     Your choice. Be prepared to share your answers.

CONCLUDING COMMENTARY ON RESPONSE VARIABLE

General

Processing occurs throughout a leader's lifetime. Time-lines allow for integration of this overall processing. This integration includes identification of patterns. Comparative analysis of a leader's life with known patterns can provide further understanding concerning present happenings in a life as well as insights into scheduling for future aspects due to the predictive nature of these patterns.

The unique ministry patterns, UM.1-UM.5, are more difficult patterns to understand. These require a maturity in discernment. Maturity in discernment usually occurs late in life and is usually gained through much experience with and sensitive responses to God's processing.

The UM.2 Upward Development Pattern which sees cycling back and forth between processing that develops spiritual formation (being) and processing that develops ministerial formation (doing), has an added complication. That complication has to do with theological influence on one's understanding of spirituality, a concept dominantly involving being. Various theological positions on sanctification influence how a leader sees the being side of the upward development pattern. Even within such theological divergence there is a common pragmatic viewpoint. Almost all theological patterns whether catholic or protestant climax in various forms of union with God.

Summary of Major Response Variable Functions

The response variable basically serves four functions.

1. It **explains** where a leader is in terms of a number of factors which cross time-periods.

2. It **predicts** possible happenings useful for decision making with emerging leaders and developing leaders. These patterns can be especially helpful in leadership selection. By knowing past leader's experiences with various steps and stages, a leader can use the predictability inherent in the patterns to improve decision making.

3. The response variable also can help a leader **speed up development** by pointing out where scheduling can be helpful. If the leader is aware of where he or she is on various patterns and what kind of processing is most likely to happen the negotiation of that processing is enhanced.

4. Finally, the response variable **points** out the various kinds of **process items** associated with various patterns of development which relate to scheduling.

CHAPTER 12. THE GOALS OF PROCESSING

Integrative Overview

The development of a leader can be explained by the tracing of three variables over a lifetime: processing, time, response. The strategic effect of processing leads to three goals: formation of the leader in terms of **leadership character**, **leadership skills**, and **leadership values**. The formation of leadership character is referred to as **spiritual formation**. The shaping of leadership skills is called **ministerial formation**. The instilling of leadership values into a coherent ministry philosophy is labelled **strategic formation**. This chapter describes these three formations and indicates the overall expectations for them along the ministry time-line phases. These three strategic goals of processing provide the backdrop for chapter 13 which provides measures to evaluate a leader's development.

Preview--The Three Formations

Comparison of many cases over entire lifetimes has resulted in identification of three primary leadership development thrusts of processing: spiritual formation, ministerial formation and strategic formation.

Spiritual formation relates primarily to Christian character development. It refers to the development of the inner-life of a person so that the person experiences more of Christ as the source of life, reflects more Christ-like characteristics in personality and in everyday relationships and increasingly knows the power and presence of Christ in ministry.

Ministerial formation refers to development of ministry skills and knowledge. As a leader develops he/she grows in understanding of leadership skills and knowledge. There is a growing sensitivity to lessons taught by God in terms of the dynamics of leadership--leader, follower and situation. Further, this formation involves development of gifts and skills and their use with increasing effectiveness with followers. It describes the ability to motivate followers toward beneficial changes which will harmonize with God's purposes.

Strategic formation refers to an overall ministry perspective--a ministry philosophy. This ministry philosophy develops over a lifetime of processing and incorporates lessons and values learned from spiritual formation, ministerial formation, and destiny processing. It uniquely weaves together Biblical values of leadership, the challenges of the times, and the unique giftedness of the leader. It gives focus and direction to a leader's lifetime of ministry so that the leader senses his or her ministry as moving toward God's purposes.

Process items, viewed **individually** can be seen to contribute to selection purposes:
1. indicate leadership capacity (such as inner integrity, influence potential),
2. expand potential,
3. confirm appointment to roles or responsibilities using that leadership capacity, and
4. direct that leader along to God's appointed ministry level for realized potential.

When viewed **corporately** over a lifetime, process items can be seen to contribute to the broader goals of spiritual formation, ministerial formation and strategic formation.

Processing and Spiritual Formation

While it is partially true that any process incident affects character it is also true that some more than others focus on character shaping. Several clusters especially work on particular aspects of spiritual formation. These include the **foundational testing cluster**, the **ordinary cluster**, the **pressure cluster**, and the **maturity cluster**.

The **foundational testing cluster**, comprised of **integrity, word**, and **obedience checks** as well as ministry tasks and faith checks, centers on elementary character traits necessary to leadership. These include such things as basic morality, honesty, truthfulness, submission, perseverance, and responsibility. They teach the emerging leader basic lessons concerning flexibility of the will. Willingness to be used by God in ministry, to trust a truth God has shown, to forgive, to confess, or to right a wrong, are all common issues dealt with by the foundational testing cluster. The issue of basic holiness in one's relationship to God is a critical element of foundational testing. Allegiance, accountability, and sensitivity to God are all common aims of this basic testing. These lessons of foundational testing usually occur prior to or in the early stages of ministry. The essential trait developed by the cluster is integrity. The **critical process item** is the **integrity check**. Without integrity there is no credibility with followers, a necessary prerequisite to influencing them. The **critical patterns** are the **testing patterns**. This cluster dominates the transition sub-phase and the early provisional sub-phase.

The **ordinary cluster** works on disciplining the leader. Perseverance is its goal. Some of its process items are more focused on spiritual formation issues than others. The **word, literary, mentor, paradigm shift**, and **spiritual authority discovery** while accomplishing ministerial development also often build leadership character. The major thrust of this cluster in regards to spiritual formation is to discipline a leader's character so as to instill faithfulness. A leader can be counted on to attempt to carry out vision, to complete tasks, and to work diligently at assignments. Intent will be transmitted into action. Action will achieve vision unless obstacles are

insurmountable. No single process item dominates. The
cumulative effect of positive response to the many ordinary
cluster items builds perseverance, the discipline side of
faithfulness. The **critical pattern** is the **M.1 Foundational
Ministry pattern**. This cluster works throughout the entire
growth ministry phase.

The **pressure cluster** exposes character weaknesses of the
leader both to the leader and to followers. Its intent is to
create needs that will allow the leader to be receptive to
processing for character improvement. Poor leader response to
character pruning in the provisional sub-phase will limit a
leader's effectiveness in the competent sub-phase and may prevent
altogether entrance into the unique ministry phase. The **conflict
process item is the critical process item** for exposing character
weaknesses and firming or confirming of character strengths. The
M.5 Authority Insights and **M.7 Spiritual Authority Discovery**
patterns are **critical patterns** during this processing. Paul and
James state the goal of pressure cluster processing in two
scriptures which bring out genuineness and balance of character.

> The ultimate aim of the Christian ministry, after all,
> is to produce the love which springs from a pure
> heart, a good conscience and a genuine faith. I
> Timothy 1:5 (Phillips Version)

> When all kinds of trials and temptations crowd into
> your lives, my brothers, don't resent them as
> intruders, but welcome them as friends! Realize that
> they come to test your faith and to produce in you the
> quality of endurance. But let the process go on until
> that endurance is fully developed, and you will find
> you have become men of mature character with the right
> sort of independence. James 1:2-4 (Phillips Version)

This cluster works throughout the entire growth ministry phase.

Later on, after a period of ministry and more experience in
life in general God begins to again work on character. Whereas
the major thrust of early character testing was preparation for
ministry the latter character testing has as its function the
deepening of the leader's relationship with God. The **maturity
cluster** made of process items such as **crisis, life crisis,
conflict, ministry conflict, leadership backlash,** and **isolation**
all work to give a leader an experiential relationship with God
which overflows into ministry. This deepening of character
results in spiritual authority and puts a leader's ministry on a
higher plane. He or she learns to minister out of being. What
he or she is becomes more important than "successful doing."

While these kinds of process items can occur throughout all
of life they have a more powerful leadership developmental effect
during the middle and latter portion of the growth ministry
phase. The thrust of this processing is a deepened relationship
with God. Sometimes its effect can not take place until the

leader has been broken. A leader has to come to the end of his/her personal resources before this deepened level of trust can be appropriated. Strong leaders will operate out of ego strength until they encounter processing which leads to brokenness before God. The results of such brokenness is usually a paradigm shift of viewing success in ministry in terms of one's relationship with God, rather than in one's accomplishments for God. The **critical process items** for the maturity cluster are **isolation, crisis,** or **life crisis.** The **critical patterns** are the **UM.1. Reflective/ Formative Evaluation** and the **UM.2 Upward Development** patterns.

In summary, one views the **maturity cluster** as forcing a leader into a deeper relationship to God. From this deepened relationship with God arises a greater degree of spiritual authority. With heightened awareness of spiritual authority comes a paradigm shift which sees the leader ministering out of "beingness" rather than "doingness" as the primary criterion for successful ministry.

Summary of Spiritual Formation

The definition of a Christian leader assumed in this study is a person with God-given capacity and God-given responsibility who is influencing a specific group of God's people toward God's purposes. The processing described in this section has focused on character and spiritual formation which are intimately connected to the first two elements of that definition.

Christians in general are pre-disposed by theological notions of sanctification to recognize that God uses "all things" to form the character of Christ in them. Passages such as Romans 6-8 and Galatians 4:29 tend to reinforce this sensitivity. Leaders, even more so, are conscious of this God-given priority. They know through passages like Hebrews 13:7-8, Acts 20:17-38, Philippians 4:9 and I Peter 5:1-4 that leaders must model exemplary character. The process items described in this chapter simply attempt to categorize and describe the major ways that Christian leader's perceive God's accomplishment of character formation. Such identification and description not only provides explanation for leaders but also heightens their sensitivity to the purposes of development underlying the processes.

Ministerial Formation

Ministerial formation is defined as that development of a leader which relates to effective leadership--the capacity to influence followers and to minister to them. It refers to development of ministry skills and knowledge. Knowledge about leadership in general, about ministry in particular, and skills to use that knowledge are the essentials of this processing. There is a growing sensitivity to lessons taught by God in terms of the dynamics of leadership--leader, follower and situation.

For a Christian leader this formation specifically involves identification, recognition and development of spiritual gifts. It also involves development and use of other aspects of giftedness--natural abilities as well as acquired skills. The leader learns to rely on giftedness with increasing effectiveness in ministering to followers and motivating them toward beneficial changes which will harmonize with God's purposes as understood by the leader.

The ministerial formation process begins with the leader's entrance into ministry usually signaled by a **leadership committal**. It then follows a repetitive cycle of **entry** into roles, **training** for those roles, **relational learning** in those roles, and **discernment** of the leadership processes involved in those roles.

The decision for a potential leader to enter ministry is usually a crucial one. The process item which describes this important decision is called the **leadership committal process item**. The leadership committal process item is a destiny process item, either an event or process which culminates in an acknowledgment from a potential leader to God of willingness to be used in ministry in whatever way God shows. This item is the **critical item** in the whole process of ministerial formation.

Gripentrog describes his leadership committal incident pointing out the destiny sensed in that moment.

> Age 22
> Following my conversion I began to become quite active in the ministry of Campus Crusade for Christ on my college campus. Every week I was involved in personal evangelism, follow-up and various Bible studies. I became convinced that Christ was the answer to the basic problems of individuals and that therefore I wanted to commit my life to helping people come to know Him rather than pursuing my original goal of seeking a career in the field of social work. I made formal application to join the staff of Crusade but as the time of my college graduation and new staff training drew near I had not received any reply from Crusade. At this point I had a tremendous sense that serving Christ was all that I wanted to do with my life and therefore one evening I prayed, committing my life to Him and telling Him that I would do whatever He wanted me to as long as I could serve Him. Within a few days I received notice from Crusade telling me that I had been accepted on staff and inviting me to new staff training.
> Surrender to do the will of God is a vital qualification for a spiritual leader. God will work to bring a person to this point of surrender.
> In the years following this experience I have

often looked back at this experience as the moment
when I clearly felt that the Lord was calling me
into His service and as the time when I
surrendered myself to Him without reservation for
whatever purposes He had for my life and ministry.
The remembrance of this experience was a source of
strength during difficult times in ministry in the
years following (Gripentrog 1987:34,35).

The heart of the leadership committal process item is an
inward private agreement (though there may be some public
stimulus to this) between the potential leader and God. The
agreement pledges willingness by the potential leader to be used
by God in service for him as the major priority of life. In
essence, it is a Lordship decision with regard to service for
Christ. This does not necessarily mean a full-time Christian
vocation though that is often the case. But it does mean that
all vocational efforts will be subservient to whatever service
roles God gives.

For some who experience radical conversions like the Apostle
Paul, the leadership committal may be coincidental with
conversion. For others who were born into a Christian heritage
the agreement may not be related to the salvation experience but
to some other kind of Lordship challenge. The committal may be
in response to a perceived call from God to the mission field,
pastorate, or Christian organization. It may not be a specific
call but a willingness to be used with a gradual clarification
over time as to how. The committal may come after some ministry
has been experienced. And suddenly there is an inner
satisfaction and an inner knowledge that you want to be and will
be used by God in ministry. The desire to be deeply used is a
first step toward leadership emergence.

Paul's crisis experience (Erwteman 1983) in conversion
particularly emphasizes the destiny aspect of this process item.
His leadership committal process item was linked to a sense of
destiny call which forever changed his life work. The radical
nature of his conversion experience led him to have confidence in
the Gospel and its power to save. He believed it would work for
all kinds of people (see his descriptions in I Corinthians 6:9).
And he lived that conviction.

Kuzmic's conversion (Clinton 1982b) as an early teen-ager
from scientific-atheism through a miraculous power experience was
coincidental with committal to ministry and can be correlated to
his evangelistic ministry and his training ministry.

The committal process item can occur coincidental with
conversion or as a second committal after conversion. The
committal act may occur long before the actual leadership
potential emerges or it may initiate the process immediately.
Baumgartner's committal was coincidental with conversion and
immediately set the direction of his life--toward pastoral
ministry.

Age 17
        During a week of re-consecration I was deeply
moved by Christ's love and my own faithlessness.
I experienced conversion and a new sense of inner
peace. At the end of the week Pastor Krumpschmid
called on those willing to serve Christ wherever
he would lead them. That for me meant a call to
the ministry to which I now could respond without
reservation. Instead of becoming a medical
doctor, a biology teacher or a chemical
researcher, I became a pastor.
        The public response ended a longer process of
search for the direction of my life. Since the
committal happened in the immediate context of my
conversion it has provided a strong sense that God
called me specifically into His service.
        The committal became the foundation for my
life calling. Although I sometimes doubted that I
was fulfilling my destiny in the way God had
intended it, I never doubted this call which so
dramatically altered all the plans I had for my
life (Baumgartner 1987:26).

The committal may occur as result of a special challenge or
as a result of a special revelatory act or in terms of a growing
awareness which culminates in decisions reflecting steps toward
leadership. Palich's committal was a combination of challenge
and a growing awareness toward a specific kind of ministry--
cross-cultural.

Age 20
        I had never been challenged to missions,
outside of my contact with a missionary friend,
Ona Liles. My impression was that all mission
work was rural and boring (after seeing missionary
slides and hearing their presentations). While at
Manhattan Christian College, I heard Richard Hicks
speak in chapel. He was the first missionary I
had met that was working in an urban setting
(Campinas, Brazil), and he was interesting to
listen to. I was interested in discipleship in
the youth ministry--he was discipling in Brazil.
He challenged me to think seriously about mission
service in an urban setting.
        Shortly after that, our college choir sang at
our brotherhood's National Missionary Convention.
Most of the students returned to school the next
day, but I stayed for the convention. I was
challenged by the speakers, and on the closing
night, I went forward, committing myself to
mission service and evangelism. I'm not one to
make rash or emotional decisions and this one was
not. It was one that grew, as God worked on and
in my life.

Commitment is often a growing expression.
God works on and in a person's mind, changing his
view of reality, until He can redirect the willing
person, through active commitment, into the roles
He has in mind.
I knew that my life would be involved in
evangelism at this point, but I didn't know how.
I had followed the Lord's leading, stepped out in
faith to be used by Him; but it was unsettling to
not know where He would want me. But I knew the
role I would play, in general terms (Palich
1987:29,30).

In ministerial formation, the leadership committal process
item or its functional equivalent[1] are foundational to a
continued long term development that will last a lifetime. It
couples with the M.1 Foundational Ministry pattern to ensure
perseverance over a lifetime of ministry.

The major clusters which concentrate on ministerial
formation include the **ordinary cluster**, the **challenge cluster**,
the **personal development cluster**, the **people insights cluster**,
and **spiritual insights cluster**. These were all treated in depth
in chapters 5-8.

Comparative studies of descriptions of the ministry portions
of leader's lives have identified four kinds of functions which
cycle through most of ministry development:

1. entry,
2. training,
3. relational,
4. discernment.

These cyclic functions can be used to organize the presentation
of processing which affects ministerial formation. I chose in
chapters 5-8 to use an approach which identified clusters and
their specific leadership development tasks. But explanation of
the cycle gives added information important to understanding
ministerial formation.

---

[1]Percentage wise, 70% of the cases studied indicated a leadership
committal item as being significant in the emergence process of
their leadership. Either a leader has such an experience or its
functional equivalence (a growing sense of assurance that full
time ministry is right for a career). Such a growing assurance
can come through process items such as ministry affirmation or
destiny revelation.

   This cycle can be seen throughout a long period of ministry
if the ministry is analyzed as a whole. It can also be seen when
examining a given ministry task or assignment. In general, when
viewing a long period of ministry there is a change in emphasis
in the four cycles with progress moving from entry and training
in the earlier part of the ministry to relational and discernment
functions in the latter part. Figure 12-1 points out these
functions and the most important process items generally relating
to them.

   As a leader moves through several development phases he or
she can expect many of the indicated process items of Figure 12-1
to occur. The further along in ministry one is the more they
will cover incidents reflecting more of these process items. For
example, for five typical cases that were compared Belesky, the
youngest in ministry experience had 7 of the 17 described;
Baumgartner listed 8 of the 17 listed; Waldner has 11 of the 17;
Finzel had 13 of the 17; Gripentrog had 16 of the 17. As more
ministry is experienced the process items in the relational and
discernment functions begin to fill in.

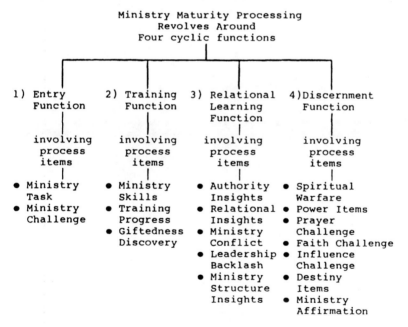

Ministry Maturity Processing
Revolves Around
Four cyclic functions

1) Entry   2) Training   3) Relational   4)Discernment
   Function   Function   Learning   Function
                                  Function

   involving   involving   involving   involving
   process   process   process   process
   items   items   items   items

● Ministry   ● Ministry   ● Authority   ● Spiritual
  Task   Skills   Insights   Warfare
● Ministry   ● Training   ● Relational   ● Power Items
  Challenge   Progress   Insights   ● Prayer
                ● Giftedness   ● Ministry   Challenge
                  Discovery   Conflict   ● Faith Challenge
                               ● Leadership   ● Influence
                                 Backlash   Challenge
                               ● Ministry   ● Destiny
                                 Structure   Items
                                 Insights   ● Ministry
                                                 Affirmation

FIGURE 12-1
CYCLICAL FUNCTIONS AND PROCESSING IN MINISTRY

The processing associated with these functions contain lessons which increase the leader's ability to perceive new ministry, adapt to needed training for it, increasingly relate to people more wisely in terms of that new ministry, and to increasingly evaluate ministry in terms of the seen and unseen realities of spiritual ministry. The entry and training function process items focus primarily on development of ministerial formation. The relational function process items focus equally on ministerial and strategic formation. The discernment function process items focus primarily on strategic formation though they are crucial to ministerial formation.

The major problem in ministerial formation is plateauing. A grasp of the learning posture lesson is a healthy antidote to plateauing.

EFFECTIVE LEADERS MAINTAIN A LEARNING POSTURE THROUGHOUT THEIR LIFETIMES.

The complexity of ministry demands a leader who is continuing to learn.

Summary of Ministerial Formation

A leader learns to minister effectively over a lifetime. This learning has a solid foundation in the critical process item, **leadership committal**. Faithfulness, as evidenced in the **M.1 Ministry Foundational Pattern**, is a key ministerial formation trait. Numerous clusters such as the **ordinary cluster**, the **challenge cluster**, the **personal development cluster**, the **people insights cluster**, and **spiritual insights cluster** provide the details of the learning. Four major patterns repeat themselves with each new major ministry assignment: entry, training, relational learning, and discernment. Some leaders plateau. They do not maintain a learning posture.

Strategic Formation

Strategic formation is the most complex of the three notions of strategic goals of processing. Strategic formation refers to an overall ministry perspective--a **ministry philosophy**. This ministry philosophy develops over a lifetime of processing and incorporates lessons and values learned from spiritual formation, ministerial formation, and destiny processing.

Strategic formation is unique for an individual for it uniquely weaves together the individual's perceived Biblical values of leadership, the challenges of the times that face the individual, and the unique giftedness of the individual. It gives focus and direction to a leader's lifetime of ministry so that the leader senses his or her ministry as moving toward God's purposes.

Strategic formation is the incarnation of a ministry

philosophy which uniquely fits the development of a given leader.
All process items contribute to lessons which impact the leader.
They contribute, at least implicitly if not explicitly to that
leader's ministry philosophy.

A number of developmental factors contribute to strategic
formation. The set of strategic formation factors include:
lessons learned generally from all process items--but especially
the **discernment function process items**, the **guidance process
items**, and **destiny process items**.

This section will discuss the set of factors that contribute
to strategic formation. It does so by first generally describing
ministry philosophy. It goes on to explain the discernment
function processes introduced in the previous section. Finally,
it will point out the place of guidance processing and destiny
processing toward giving focus to the leader's strategic
formation.

Ministry Philosophy

A well articulated lived-out ministry philosophy is the
final idealized goal of strategic formation. It is the core of
strategic formation. Ministry philosophy will be based on values
learned in processing which integrates spiritual formation,
ministerial formation, and destiny processing and which uniquely
weaves together Biblical values of leadership, the challenges of
the times, and the unique giftedness of the leader.

Ministry philosophy[2] refers to ideas, values and principles
whether implicit or explicit which a leader uses as guidelines
for decision making, for exercising influence, or for evaluating
his/her ministry.

An emerging leader usually operates on an unwritten
philosophy of ministry which was imbibed in earlier phases.
Somewhere in the ministry phase God will cause this former

---

[2]My thinking in part is based on D. Allen's special research
project on ministry philosophy which was an in-depth case study
of Charles Simeon. From it, and from comparisons with other
historical case studies, I have tentatively identified the
following theoretical relation. Ministry philosophy is a
function of three major variables: **blend** (an integration of past
and present leadership values), **focus** (destiny convergence,
giftedness), and **articulation** (the explicit or implicit
organization of leadership values into a strategy for ministry
which has the focus variable as its driving force). I devote an
entire chapter in my book, **The Making of a Christian Leader,** Nav
Press, to the topic of ministry philosophy. In it, I talk about
guidelines for developing a ministry philosophy, identifying and
grouping of principles, generic leadership functions, specific
and generic approaches to ministry philosophy.

philosophy to be questioned and evaluated, with the result that
it will be accepted or modified or discarded for a new one in
order for God to accomplish His purposes.

    In terms of an underlying ministry philosophy, most ministry
just happens as an emerging leader is taken step by step from a
place of no responsibility to one in which there is personal
responsibility. As the emerging leader begins to accept
responsibility and recognizes that there is an ultimate
accountability to God for ministry the need for a ministry
philosophy arises. It is then that process items which are
directed toward formation of ministry philosophy will be
recognized and responded to. Three major stages describe the
overall ministry philosophy pattern. These three can be broken
down further into 10 steps (which sometimes overlap).
Figure 12-2 depicts the three stages and 10 steps.

Stage	General Description	Some Functions
1. Osmosis	Leader learns implicit philosophy experientially.	1. Operate with implicit philosophy of sponsoring group.
2. Baby Steps	Leader discovers explicit philosophy through experience and philosophy.	2. Personal lessons in ministry. 3. Questioning/ evaluation of implicit philosophy of ministry. 4. Evolving of a modified philosophy; some implicit some explicit
3. Maturity	Leader formulates, uses and articulates his/her ministry philosophy. He/she passes on to others the key ideas and retrospective reflection of what ministry is about.	5. Develops a growing sense of uniqueness and ultimate accountability. 6. Sees need for evaluation of ministry. 7. Recognition of need for focus and unique ministry. 8. Formulation of focused ministry philosophy. 9. Internalization of the philosophy. 10. Articulation of the ministry philosophy which has been worked out in practice.
comment	The set of factors contributing to strategic formation includes lessons learned from all process incidents but especially those from the discernment process items, guidance process items and destiny process items.	

FIGURE 12-2
DEVELOPMENT OF MINISTRY PHILOSOPHY

Any process item, if it is sensed as a special intervention from God, causes serious reflection. Usually lessons are learned from this. The accumulation of these lessons over a lifetime build up the ministry philosophy. Note the following comments taken from process incidents described in case studies. These point out how processing lessons affect ministry philosophy. "Through these conflicts, God helped me clarify my own leadership philosophy as never before" (Student 9 1987:54). "I knew that my life would be involved in evangelism at this point, but I didn't know how. I had followed the Lord's leading, stepped out in faith to be used by Him; but it was unsettling to not know where He would want me. But I knew the role I would play, in general terms" (Palich 1987:29,30). "God will put us in situations which will help to develop our spiritual gifts and which will prepare us for future ministry" (Waldner 1987:35). "I learned a valuable lesson from this experience and from this point I began to use a different pattern in interacting with and seeking to influence Indonesian leaders in a group context" (Gripentrog 1987:66). "This authority insight is very critical in the development of my leadership philosophy. In whatever ministry I work in the future, I want to see a board at the top where the buck stops" (Student 16 1987:54). "Seeing the value of discipleship has caused me to develop my personal ministry philosophy around this concept" (Waldner 1987:39).

The lessons can deal with relationship with God, character and personal ethics, practical ministry guidelines, ministry ethics, guidance, destiny and other factors suited uniquely to the individual. The net effect of the accumulation of these lessons is a framework that guides the leader in actions, planning, and decision making.

Of the three major variables of ministry philosophy it is blend (an integration of past and present leadership values taught through processing) which is stressed when process items are analyzed for lessons. Blend is usually the first of the ministry philosophy variables sensed by a leader.

Discernment Function Processes

While all process items teach lessons that build toward strategic formation some especially force reflection on ministry philosophy in general and on focus and meaning of ministry in particular. The discernment function processes do just that. Like the ministry task they have a dual function. They give insights and help for present ministry while causing reflection and formulation of lessons for future ministry. They do contribute toward ministerial formation and thus were included in the four cyclic functions (entry, training, relational, and discernment) introduced in the last section. But they also contribute toward the focus element of ministry philosophy.

To develop a leader in discernment God enlarges the leader's perspectives concerning the spiritual dynamics of ministry. The leader must learn discernment in two major areas: 1. sensing spiritual reality (including discerning genuine from fake) and 2. recognizing need for personal expansion. The leader must learn to sense the spiritual reality (spiritual warfare process item) behind physical reality as well as to depend upon God's power (power items: gifted power, prayer power, power encounter, and networking power) in ministry. And the leader must learn to hear God's voice in the challenge process items (faith, prayer, influence) and the destiny items (destiny preparation, destiny revelation, destiny fulfillment and ministry affirmation process items) The leader will need this discernment ability throughout a lifetime.

The heart of the discernment function is the enlargement of the leader's perspectives. God develops discernment throughout the whole of a leader's ministry but it peaks toward the latter portion of ministry. Inner lessons from all of processing, but notably the special effects of discernment processing, give the micro adjustments to focus. They change the day-to-day attitudes and perspectives of ministry. It is through discernment that a leader learns to articulate a ministry philosophy.

Guidance and Destiny Processing

Guidance processing, giftedness development, and destiny processing all help a leader to sense the divine intent in ministry philosophy focus. Destiny processing gives a special sense of the divine touch that inspires a leader toward some ultimate purpose in life. At the core of motivation for Christian leadership is the sense that God is directing the leader to accomplish His purposes. Any one of the guidance process items can be **critical items** or a turning point in regards to development of ministry philosophy. The **F.5 Destiny Pattern** and the **M.6 Giftedness Development Pattern** are key patterns.

Guidance is one of the crucial elements of leadership. The need for guidance occurs throughout a leader's lifetime; so process items referring to guidance do not restrict themselves to just one portion of a leader's life. A second reason for its being crucial is that it deals with the fundamental notion of a leader. A leader is a person with God-given capacity and God-given responsibility who is influencing a group of followers towards God's purposes for the group. The central ethic of this definition of a leader is influencing toward God's purposes. This means leaders must know how to get corporate guidance for the groups they are leading.

Destiny processing and guidance give the macro corrections to one's focus. They are concerned with the major decisions of ministry. A major change of role, location, special ministry thrust, or major decision are issues dealt within guidance processing. In looking back over a lifetime it is the major guidance processes that a leader will point to as marker events in a life. These give the sense of God's having directed the leader toward God's purpose.

Summary of Strategic Formation

Christian leaders are those who are influencing people of God toward God's purposes for them. They must be people who can sense external direction for their leadership through basic processes used by God. The thrust of strategic formation is the direction of a leader into a continued ministry which utilizes that leader's uniqueness to accomplish God's purposes. The lessons learned in the normal process items partially give focus to an emerging ministry philosophy. But it is especially the discernment function processes with their focus on the ultimate reality underlying ministry and the challenges to expand a leader's ministry which give a leader perspective to realize a unique focus. And it is the guidance processes which will mark the major changes of a leader in terms of decision making, change in role, location, or thrust of ministry. The articulation aspect of ministry philosophy grows with discernment and as a leader experiences focus in ministry philosophy. It is the last of the ministry philosophy elements to develop.

Final Remarks On the Three Major Goals

All three formations develop concurrently. All process items help develop character, reflect lessons on doing ministry more effectively, and instill values that will affect later ministry. Even though all processing is complex and develops all formational aspects at all times, certain emphases can be discerned. Recognition of these emphases at different times helps a leader schedule more effective development. Figure 12-3 indicates relative ranking of emphases as plotted along the ministry time-line.

Ministry Time-Line

Phase I MINISTRY FOUNDATIONS		Phase II GROWTH MINISTRY		Phase III UNIQUE MINISTRY	
`|-----------|---//-----|-------//--|---//-------|---------------|`					
A. Sovereign Leadership Foundations	B. Leadership Transition	A. Provisional Ministry	B. Competent Ministry	A. Role Tran- sition	B. Conver- gence
Primary	SPIRITUAL	MINISTERIAL	SPIRITUAL	STRATEGIC	
Secondary	MINISTERIAL	SPIRITUAL	STRATEGIC	SPIRITUAL	
Tertiary	STRATEGIC	STRATEGIC	MINISTERIAL	MINISTERIAL	

FIGURE 12-3
FORMATIONS AND THE MINISTRY TIME-LINE

Over a lifetime spiritual formation develops leadership character. Ministerial formation develops leadership skills. Strategic formation develops leadership values which increasingly become a ministry philosophy. Development in any one or two of these formations can be arrested while there is limited progress in the other(s). The most common of these aberrant patterns is when development in leadership skills outstrips development in leadership character and leadership values. A gifted leader can still have an effective ministry even with character defects or unbalanced leadership values, at least for a limited time. However, such unbalance will eventually catch up with a leader. The ideal development should be:

1. formation of basic leadership character in the transitional sub-phase, notably an integrity base,
2. formation of leadership skills in the provisional sub-phase, while adding to the character base perseverance, faithfulness, and relational values; early leadership values begin to form,
3. formation of leadership character, notably a deepened dependence upon God, and perseverance in deep processing during the competence sub-phase; continued accumulation of leadership values,
4. formation of leadership values into a strategic ministry philosophy during the latter part of the competence sub-phase, and early part of the unique ministry phase.

Of these formational results leadership character is most foundational. Arrested development in it can be most disastrous in regards to ultimate accomplishment for God.

CHAPTER 13. TOWARD MEASURING LEADERSHIP DEVELOPMENT

Integrative Overview

The development of a leader can be explained by the tracing of three variables over a lifetime: processing, time, response. The strategic effect of processing leads to three goals: formation of the leader in terms of **leadership character, leadership skills,** and **leadership values.** Chapter 12 detailed the strategic effect of processing leading to those three goals. How does one measure progress toward these strategic goals? That is a major concern of this chapter. Evaluation is not entirely objective. Interpretation is always involved. However, seven measures are suggested which are helpful in determining progress.

Preview--Toward Measuring Leadership Development

This chapter suggests that seven categories of measurement are useful in evaluating measurement at any point along the ministry time-line. These categories include:

1. **major lessons,**
2. **development tasks,**
3. **giftedness,**
4. **sphere of influence,**
5. **influence means,**
6. **assessment along patterns**
7. **convergence.**

At any point in a leader's life, these seven factors can be interpreted by the leader or someone cognizant of the life history of the leader. Comparison of these interpretations at the given point of time with results from some previous point in time yields indications of progress. Admittedly assessment of the factors always involves interpretation.

Two other measures include subjective assessment of the overall contributions of a leader and ultimate contributions of a leader. Contemporary case studies always produce a synthesized evaluation of contributions of a given leader. This summary statement usually lists between four and nine accomplishments of the leader. Comparative studies of evaluative case descriptions of accomplishments of some 42 missiological giants resulted in a typology for assessing ultimate contribution of a lifetime. Recognition of these categories can suggest areas of "focus" for ministry philosophy. A leader can deliberately move toward ultimate accomplishments as he/she moves from the competence sub-phase to the unique ministry phase.

Leadership Measures

Several times I have referred to the shorthand notation, $L = f(P, T, R)$, meaning that the development of a leader to a large degree can be determined by evaluating the three major variables processing, time, and response. Chapters 3-10 discussed the right hand side of the equation. Chapter 11 broke ground toward the left side of the equation. It indicated three strategic goals that development should move toward: maturity in leadership character, skills, and values.

This chapter also focuses on the left hand side of the equation. In essence it is dealing with these questions: What does it mean for a leader to be developed? How can you assess it? Or in other words, what are the indications or manifestations of accomplishment of the strategic goals involving spiritual formation, ministerial formation, or strategic formation? What standards are there for assessing what is happening as a leader responds to processing over time?

This chapter suggests that goals are rather open ended and are a function of the leader and God's processing toward the focus element of ministry philosophy for that leader. Giftedness and destiny help determine the goals of development for a given leader. These goals toward which God is processing are explained at least in part by seven major development measures:

1. major lessons,
2. development tasks,
3. giftedness,
4. sphere of influence,
5. influence means,
6. assessment along patterns
7. convergence.

The conceptual framework for almost all of these has been laid previously in the chapters on the processing, time, and response variables. This chapter will explain how they help provide measures for evaluating development.

Development assumes change over time. Any or all of these measures of evaluation can be applied synchronically in time to a given leader's life history. These same measures can be applied synchronically at a later point in time. Comparison of the two different sets of measures will indicate development, lack of development, or even retrogression.

Development Measure 1--Immediate Lessons

Leaders learn lessons through processing. Sometimes these lessons are very explicit and can be articulated. At other times the lessons are more implicit and, even though they can not be articulated at the time, they affect the discernment of the leader in future leadership situations. Each lesson learned

through a process incident is an immediate measure of development
for that leader. It will have affected some value dealing with
character, skill, or ministry philosophy. This measure,
indication of learning God's lessons in process incidents, is
probably the most important of all the types of measures. A
leader who is constantly discerning God's lessons in life is a
developing leader. Other things being equal, that kind of leader
will develop in all the categories.

It remains then to know as much as possible about how
leaders learn to identify lessons in process incidents. There
are limitations in assessing immediate lessons. In Biblical or
historical case studies possible principles or lessons seen in
processing can be suggested, but not always confirmed, unless
there are statements in the description of the incidents which
interpret the lessons learned. In contemporary studies
researchers can confirm for themselves the actual lessons they
learned.

Development measures for indicator 1, immediate lessons, are
listed in Table 13-1 **Sub-indicators** point out categories of
development measure. **Manifesters** indicate the kind of fillers
for the given sub-indicator slot. The example column will give a
specific entry, such as would occur in a case study.

TABLE 13-1
DEVELOPMENT MEASURES FOR IMMEDIATE LESSONS

Sub-indicators	Manifesters	Example
1. **specific lessons**	statements of learning in specific application terms	Nee's leadership character was strengthened as he passed the early integrity test on cheating in class.
2. **generalized principles**	statements of learning using general language for transference	EXPECT AND USE TESTING ITEMS TO DEVELOP LEADERS.

Examples of indicator 1, specific lessons and generalized
lessons, from four different recent cases are given in Table
13-2. These principles refer to generalized statements of truth
which are observations drawn from specific instances of
processing. Principles can be asserted as absolutes, guidelines
or suggestions depending on the researchers understanding of
their validity according to several criteria[1] which have

---

[1]For Biblical sources of truth I specify eight questions dealing
with textual and then five factors based on genre of literature
and finally five suggestions for deriving the statement of the

developed in my study of derivations of principles. Principles
thus derived are usually written specifically in terms of the
context and process item involved (small letter). It is then
generalized for wider possible application (capital letter).

TABLE 13-2
EXAMPLES OF DEVELOPMENT INDICATOR 1

Name	event	principle(s)
Mueller (1987:40)		
1. Preparation for Destiny	car accident	a. God used a specific event to give me an awareness of the fact He had a special purpose for me. A. GOD WILL USE SPECIFIC EVENTS TO ALLUDE TO THE POTENTIAL LEADER OF THE SIGNIFICANT POTENTIAL OF OF HIS/HER LIFE. (guideline)
Nelson (1987:43)		
2. Faith Check	severe illness kept me away from our work for three months.	a. I reaffirmed my belief that God was in control of my ministry and received new insights during the isolation. A. PREPARE DEVELOPING LEADERS FOR TIMES OF ISOLATION BY STRESSING FAITH IN GOD'S CONTROL OF EVERY SITUATION.
Menees (1987:52)		
3. Alone in Jungle	two years of isolation in the rain forest of Bukavu	a. Turning to God in disciplined prayer helped overcome stress and conflict. A. A DISCIPLINED PRAYER LIFE IS FOUNDATIONAL TO COUNTERACTING CULTURE SHOCK AND STRESS. (guideline)
Collingridge (1987:49)		
4. Destiny Revelation; Divine affirmation	God used a dream that occurred much earlier in my life to affirm that what we were and what we were doing was in His purpose.	a. A clarification in purpose was uplifting during moments of discouragement. A. A LEADER CAN EXPECT GOD TO AFFIRM MINISTRY AT VARIOUS TIMES. (guideline) B. AWARENESS OF GOD'S HAND ON A LEADER'S MINISTRY BRINGS A RENEWED SENSE OF AUTHORITY. (guideline)

----

principle. For non-Biblical sources of principles I suggest five
screening questions as guidelines. See Clinton 1987b:94-106.

One of my early assumptions in my research of life history cases was that one could study leadership by studying leaders. It is this immediate development indicator--truth being learned in processing--which confirms that assumption. One of the most useful results of leadership emergence studies has been these observations of truth that can be applied to other leadership situations. They carry great explanatory force (a cognitive focus) and great transformational power (affective and conative focus) with researchers who have a perspective of God working sovereignly in leader's lives.

These truths help us understand other leadership situations and help us predict what ought to be in leadership situations. They also help us in the selection and training of leaders since they give guidelines that have successfully been applied in past leadership situations. These truths are usually seen first as specific statements concerning one leader in his/her situation. They are then generalized to cover other leaders and like situations. The question of how generally they can be applied to others is a genuine one. The certainty continuum and screening questions help caution one seeking to derive principles (Clinton 1987b).

Leaders develop experientially by learning lessons from process incidents. This is the most immediate development indicator. As leaders mature they develop a learning posture which makes them sensitive to learning lessons from life incidents.

Development Measure 2--Development Tasks

Once a time-line has been established for a leader each development phase can be analyzed for overall accomplishment of leadership development. This involves synthesizing development tasks that were accomplished by God. A **development task** refers to the general and unique goals of a development phase and to which overall processing in the phase is directed. Comparative studies show that there are general development tasks common to all leaders being developed. Several were suggested in Chapters 9 and 10. In the foundational phase some general tasks include: 1. mold embryonic leadership personality, 2. mold inner character, and 3. initiate discovery of leadership.

In the transition sub-phase two general tasks include: 1. working on inner character formation, and 2. developing ability to sense God's communication--especially to hear and understand God.

In the provisional sub-phase some general development tasks include: 1. facilitate development of leadership potential, 2. develop ministry skills including initial discovery and use of giftedness elements, and 3. develop initial ministry philosophy values including an experiential understanding of God's redemptive structures and purposes.

In the competent sub-phase, several development tasks provide initiative toward movement into the unique ministry phase. These include:

1. develop a deepened understanding about God,
2. develop intimacy with God, and
3. bring focus on relationship with God as primary responsibility of leader.

In the role transition sub-phase of the unique ministry phase the major task is guidance of the leader into a role and place of maximum contribution.

In addition to these very general development tasks unique tasks fitting the time periods of the leader can be derived. Unique development tasks emerge when the analyst examines a specific time period and asks, what was God doing over this time period to specifically free up a leader for advancement in general or in any of the four basic goals that processing attempts to accomplish. Process incidents are used by God to develop a person by shaping leadership character, skills, and values so as to:

1) indicate leadership capacity (such as inner integrity, influence potential),
2) expand potential,
3) confirm appointment to roles or responsibilities using that leadership capacity, and
4) direct that leader along to God's appointed ministry level for realized potential.

Table 13-3 illustrates unique tasks from a recent case study.

TABLE 13-3
UNIQUE DEVELOPMENT TASKS

Person	Phase or Sub-Phase	Unique Development Tasks
Strong (1989)	I. DIVINE DISCLOSURE	+to assure me of God's reality +to give me cross-cultural training +to show the vanity of a life without Christ +to provide a life partner
	II. GRACE ABOUNDING	+to correct lack of faith +to gain total allegiance +to teach that God provides all things
	III. DEEPENING LOVE	+to teach ministry is in being, not tasks +to give me empathy for the helpless +to instill spiritual realities

Analysis of development tasks requires a certain intuitive insight. This is a subjective measurement, yet a helpful one, in that it brings a post-reflective sense of closure to development phases and sub-phases previously completed. Seeing what God has accomplished also builds a sense of anticipation toward the present and future development phase.

Development Measure 3--Giftedness Indicator

The giftedness set includes three elements: natural abilities, acquired skills and spiritual gifts. Development of giftedness, then, means a recognition and use of these capacities in an increasingly effective way. Measurements of these usually involve a simple phase by phase listing of items which symptomatically indicate these three elements. Table 13-4 lists important categories for measuring development of giftedness, with a particular emphasis on spiritual gifts--an important facet of development in a Christian leader.

TABLE 13-4
DEVELOPMENT MEASURES FOR GIFTEDNESS

Sub-indicators	Manifesters	Example
1. natural abilities	specific descriptions	physically well coordinated, good in athletics
2. acquired skills	specific descriptions	basic entrepreneural skills; risk taking in small business ventures
3. spiritual gifts	listing of Biblical names	exhortation, word of wisdom
4. roles	specific description	coordinator of small seminars
5. gift-mix	list of primary vested gifts	apostleship, teaching
6. gift-cluster	list of primary vested gifts, dominant gift indicated	exhortation (dominant), teaching, word of wisdom
7. giftedness cluster	analysis of three elements taken together: natural, acquired, spiriutal	natural musical abilities dominant; many musical skills acquired; exhortation gift
8. focal element	identification of dominant giftedness element; explanation	natural abilities (descriptive analysis showing fit between elements)

Some explanation and several definitions related to the
ideas in Table 13-4 will be helpful in approaching assessment of
giftedness in a leader.

Giftedness Set

The giftedness set is composed of three elements, all of
which are important to the development of capacity of a leader.
Preliminary indications suggest that in a given life one or more
of the elements--natural abilities, spiritual gifts, or acquired
skills--will usually dominate the giftedness set. That dominant
element is called the focal element. The other elements will
usually operate symbiotically to enhance that element.
Preliminary indications from case studies and general
observations indicate that a leader's focal element could be any
one of the three. For Phillip Bliss, natural abilities were
focal (Clinton 1987d). D. H. Whittle, exhibited spiritual gifts
as focal (1987d). General observations from Henry Venn and Rufus
Anderson's lives indicate that acquired skills (organizational/
administrative abilities) dominated.

The giftedness set is complex. There may well be overlap
between the elements. Natural abilities may be reflected in
spiritual gifts. That is, a spiritual gift may relate to or be
based on some previously recognized natural ability which seems
to be closely related to it in function. Natural abilities may
not relate closely to a spiritual gift but may be a channel
through which it expresses itself. In other words, an apparently
unrelated natural ability may be the means for an unrelated
spiritual gift to operate. Example: People with natural
abilities along musical lines frequently have an exhortation
gift. Music is the channel through which that gift is exercised.
Natural abilities may involve mental abilities, social skills,
physical dexterity, or the like. Acquired skills may involve
mental skills, social skills, or physical skills.

Giftedness Awareness Continuum

It is helpful to use the sovereignty/ providential continuum
to help clarify the giftedness set. Figure 13-1 depicts this
continuum.

```
SPIRITUAL      NATURAL       EXPANDED NATURAL      ACQUIRED
 GIFTS         ABILITIES     ABILITIES             SKILLS
|-----------------------------------------------------------|
            LEVEL OF AWARENESS OF DIVINE INVOLVEMENT
  <------ INCREASES                   DECREASES------>
SOVEREIGN INTERVENTION           PROVIDENTIAL INTERVENTION
```

FIGURE 13-1
GIFTEDNESS AWARENESS CONTINUUM

Spiritual Gifts

The following information has emerged both from thorough

studies of the five Biblical passages on spiritual gifts, other passages in scripture illustrating use of spiritual gifts, and from the empirical study of many leaders via case studies. The descriptions and definitions are a necessary prerequisite to understanding assessment of the development of a leader in terms of the spiritual gifts portion of the giftedness set.

A **spiritual gift** is a God-given unique capacity, to each believer, for purpose of channeling a Holy Spirit empowered ministry through that believer for a momentary situation or repeatedly over time. Different analysts define different numbers of spiritual gifts. I identify 19 spiritual gifts[2] (arrived at from study of the five basic passages, and modified by my empirical studies of spiritual gifts in leaders). In my materials on spiritual gifts I list a central thrust, the essence of the definition, as well as a more technical definition for each of the spiritual gifts.

Gift-Mix and Gift-Cluster--Vested and Non-Vested Gifts

Studies of leaders have indicated that leaders at any given time in a development phase usually demonstrate more that one spiritual gift. **Gift-mix** is the label that refers to the set of spiritual gifts being used by a leader at any given time in his/her ministry. In time a gift-mix develops into a **gift-cluster**. Gift-cluster refers to a gift-mix which matures. It is a term used in explaining an advanced stage in the giftedness development pattern in which there is a dominant gift supported by other gifts and used so that the supportive gifts harmonize with the dominant gift to maximize effectiveness.

A gift is spoken of as **non-vested** if it appears situationally and can not be repeated at will by the person. Such a gift does not carry with it responsibility for development nor accountability for using over time.

A gift is spoken of as **vested** if it appears repeatedly in a person's ministry and can be repeated at will by the person. Such a use of a gift carries with it responsibility for development and accountability for using over time.

Observations of numerous leaders with large gift-mixes (Albrecht 1986, Collingridge 1987, Mueller 1987 et al) in terms of gifts exercised at any one given development phase leads to the following perspectives for viewing vested gifts over a

---

[2]Gifts that I have identified include: apostleship, prophecy, evangelism, pastoral, teaching, exhortation, word of wisdom, word of knowledge, faith, miracles, kinds of healings, discernings of spirits, tongues, interpretation of tongues, helps, governments, mercy, giving, and ruling. See Clinton 1985a, 1989a for further treatment of spiritual gifts and their development.

lifetime. Gifts can be thought of as primary, secondary, or tertiary in terms of the criteria of vested or non-vested and in terms of present demonstration.

Primary, Secondary and Tertiary Gifts

A gift is **primary** if it is a vested gift and currently being demonstrated as a significant part of the gift-mix or gift-cluster. A gift is **secondary** if at one time it was a vested gift but is now not demonstrated as part of the current gift-mix or gift-cluster. A gift is **tertiary** if it has been or is a non-vested gift or if it was manifested as necessitated by "role" responsibility in the past and is not now viewed as vested.

In my own teaching on spiritual gifts I have found it helpful to recognize three generic functions and group the gifts according to these generic functions: **power gifts, love gifts, and word gifts.** These three categories recognize crucial functions that must occur in corporate situations. These three categories are closely related to, but not identical with, the frequently repeated Pauline formula describing corporate traits of churches: faith, love, and hope. The power gifts demonstrate the authenticity, credibility, power and reality of the unseen God. They stimulate faith in the unseen God. The love gifts are manifestations attributed to God through practical ways that can be recognized by a world around us which needs love. The word gifts clarify the nature of this unseen God and His demands and purposes. They communicate about and for God. They stimulate hope for the future. Some gifts occur in more than one cluster and thus are said to be overlapping.

The power gift cluster includes the following gifts: faith, word of knowledge, discerning of spirits, miracles, tongues, interpretation of tongues, healing, word of wisdom, and prophecy. The word gift cluster includes the following gifts: word of wisdom, prophecy, word of knowledge, faith, pastoring, evangelism, exhortation, teaching, apostleship, and ruling. The love cluster includes the following gifts: healing, word of wisdom, word of knowledge, governments, pastoring, giving, evangelism, mercy, helps, and ruling. These clusters are important in terms of leadership for two reasons. Leaders must constantly evaluate the corporate structures for balance and imbalance of giftedness.

The second reason concerns an important empirical observation (for leadership selection) that resulted from a comparison of spiritual gifts in all the cases. **Christian leaders always have at least one word gift in their gift-mix.**

Examples From Researchers

Examples of giftedness from some of the later case studies are listed here. Bryant (1987:2) identifies teaching, exhortation, pastoring as primary spiritual gifts; mercy and evangelism as secondary; and ruling as tertiary. He identifies

major natural abilities as writing and public relations and major
acquired skills as oral communication. Hewko (1987:2) identifies
evangelism, exhortation, and administration as primary; helps as
secondary; and word of knowledge and healing as tertiary. He
describes his natural abilities as very personable with people,
and innovative. He describes acquired skills as: carpentry,
organizational ability, administrator capabilities. Mitchell
(1987:2) identifies her primary gifts as exhortation, teaching
and discernment. She does not identify any secondary gifts but
lists wisdom, prophecy, and pastoring as tertiary. Her natural
abilities include bent toward teaching, seeing the "big picture,"
deep care for oppressed people, seeing people as important, and
being extrovertish. She assessed major acquired skills as
writing, teaching, counseling, talking in front of groups, and
administration. Martinez (1987:1) lists teaching, apostleship
and prophecy as primary; discernment as secondary; and pastoral
as tertiary spiritual gifts. He describes his natural abilities
as creativity and analytical/ focused thinking. Acquired skills
include administrative, networking, organizational ability.

Comparison of giftedness indications at the beginning and
end of a development phase will be a strong measure of
development.

Development Measure 4--Sphere of Influence

Sphere of influence is the single most important indicator
of development of capacity. Table 13-5 lists typical categories.

TABLE 13-5
DEVELOPMENT MEASURES FOR SPHERE OF INFLUENCE

Sub-indicators	Manifesters	Example
1. direct influence	descriptive listing of people, groups influenced face to face; indication of size and degree	small group at university, young people at church
2. indirect influence	descriptive listing of people, groups influenced by non-time-bound miscellaneous influences; through others, media, writing, etc.	Junior High Department classes via preparation of S.S. materials
3. organizational influence	listing of structures and groups within organization	nominating committee; advisor to youth pastor
4. influence-mix	assessment of balance of influence means	small direct; small indirect; small organizational; direct is high intensive

Explanation of Rationale

Expansion in a leader's capacity to influence is usually reflected in three ways: 1. change in numbers of people being influenced, 2. change in ways of influencing, 3. change in intensity of influence. The easiest of these to identify is change in numbers. Change in means can be identified fairly easily. It is more difficult to identify change in intensity of influence. Identification of expansion by looking at numbers being influenced, variety of ways influence is exerted, or depth to which followers are affected, does not necessarily imply that the changes are good or bad.[3] Retrogression is likely to be reflected in a lessening of numbers of people being influenced and the use of influence means or intensity of influence. In either case, expansion or retrogression, assessment of people being influenced is an indicator of development (positively or negatively). **Sphere of influence** refers to the totality of people being influenced and for whom a leader will give an account to God which includes those people under direct personal influence (face-to-face present ministry), those under indirect influence (non time bound influence), and those under organizational influence (influence flowing through organizational structures.) The totality of people influenced can thus be described in three domains called direct influence, indirect influence and organizational influence.

Three Kinds of Influence

Direct influence is that domain of the sphere of influence which indicates a measure of people being influenced by a real presence of the leader, in focused and structured situations where feedback between follower and leader is possible and necessary, and for which there is high accountability.

Indirect influence is that domain of the sphere of influence which indicates a measure of people being influenced by non-time-bound miscellaneous influences a leader exerts through others, through media, through writing, or other means and for which feedback between the leader and by those being influenced is

---

[3]The first step in evaluating sphere of influence is the identification of who is being influenced, how and to what degree. That is as far as the theory has progressed to date. Value judgments as to good or bad of these measures awaits future research. The fact that a leader has an increase in numbers of followers does not mean that the leadership is necessarily good, nor does a decrease in numbers mean that leadership is bad. The fact that a leader has powerful intensity over followers is not necessarily good or bad (e.g. Jim Jones). Evaluation of the sphere of influence measure is at this point descriptive and not evaluative (at least not deliberately so). Most development theories first move through a descriptive phase before forming normative theory.

difficult if not impossible to occur, and where accountability is primarily for the content of the influential ideas.

Organizational influence is that domain of the sphere of influence which indicates a measure of people being influenced by a person in organizational leadership via both indirect and direct influence means via organizational structures and personal relationships. Table 13-6 gives typical examples of the three kinds of influence.

TABLE 13-6
KINDS: DIRECT, INDIRECT, AND ORGANIZATIONAL INFLUENCE

direct	indirect	organizational
individuals	committee	supervisory group
small groups	advisory boards	program director
local church	executive boards	department head
local churches	writing	head of organization
seminars	radio ministry	policy formulator
conferences	networking	member of board

Three Measures of Degree of Influence

Wrong (1979) points out that sphere of Influence can be measured in terms of **extensiveness** which refers to quantity, **comprehensiveness** which refers to the scope (breadth, areas of influence) of things being influenced and **intensiveness,** the depth to which influence extends to each item within the comprehensive influence. Extensiveness is the easiest to measure and hence is most often used or implied when talking about a leader's sphere of influence.

Looking At The Balance of Influence--Influence-Mix

One of the major characteristics denoting a development phase is change in sphere of influence. Measurement of that change is an assessment of development. This change can be in degree (more), or kind (means of influencing). **Influence-mix** is a term describing the combination of influence elements--direct, indirect or organizational--in terms of degree and kind at a given point in a development phase. Several patterns of influence-mix are commonly observed. An example of influence-mix as a development indicator is shown below in Table 13-7.

The degree measurement in Table 13-7 is limited to a general description of extensive (numbers) and did not include changes in comprehensive (scope) and intensive (degree within scope factors). These measures changed also within each of the kinds of influence.

TABLE 13-7
A. W. TOZER EXAMPLE OF EXTENSIVE INFLUENCE-MIX

		INFLUENCE-MIX		
Phase	Title	Direct	Indirect	Organiz.
I	Inner-discipline	none	none	none
II	On-The-Job Training/ New Beginnings			
	Sub-Phase A			
	Morgantown	small	none	none
	Sub-Phase B	larger	none	none
	Toledo			
	Sub-Phase C			
	Indianapolis	larger	none	none
III	City Leadership/ Expanding National Influence			
	Sub-Phase A			
	Early City	larger	small	none
	Sub-Phase B			
	Middle City	largest	larger	small
	Sub-Phase C			
	National/City	same	largest	major
IV	Wrap-Up/ Reflection	smaller	same	smaller

Since A. W. Tozer primarily worked through a local church and his ministry focus was public communication (teaching/ preaching) one would not expect a large organizational influence. His organizational influence was largely indirect and had two foci: writing/editing for the major magazine of the denomination and a prominent member of an executive committee. His indirect influence was large in scope but varied in intensiveness: He taught in nearby Bible colleges and seminaries. He had a radio ministry which became national. His writings, articles and books influenced very many.

Closing Comments on Sphere of Influence

Sphere of influence is important for two reasons drawn from essential concepts of the definition of a leader: capacity, accountability. Christian leaders perceive that they will answer to God for what they have done with the potential to influence that has been given to them. They will also answer to God for those who have been influenced in their ministry. Sphere of Influence more objectively focuses evaluation of capacity and accountability. It also points out the necessity of a leader's awareness of the followers being influenced both for purposes of accountability and for evaluation of leadership development.

An understanding of the general concept of sphere of influence will enable a leader to understand God's processing toward convergence especially in terms of influence-mix. However, one caution should be observed. A leader should not consciously seek to expand his/her sphere of influence as if bigger were better. Rather, a leader responds to God's challenge to accept

varying sphere of influences in order to find God's proper sphere
of influence for him/her.

Development Measure 5--Influence Means

A leader influences by using power to accomplish ends.
Power is manifested in power forms including force, manipulation,
authority, and persuasion. Authority can further be sub-divided
into five authority forms. The influence indicator attempts to
assess development as to what power forms or authority forms a
leader uses. Table 13-8 gives the major sub-indicator which is
power-mix. Substantial background concerning influence, power,
and authority concepts are necessary in order to understand the
use of the power-mix sub-indicator. The thrust of development
concerning influence means sees progress in movement toward
spiritual authority as a primary component of the power-mix.
Later in the convergence indicator I will return toward the
concept of development of power-mix toward a dominant element of
spiritual authority.

TABLE 13-8
DEVELOPMENT MEASURE FOR INFLUENCE MEANS

Indicator	Manifester	Example(s)
power-mix	combinations of power/ authority forms	1. spiritual authority, competent authority, persuasion power
		2. manipulative power, coercive authority, induced authority
		3. legitimate authority, manipulation power, persuasion power
		4. spiritual authority, personal authority, persuasion power

Various power and authority definitions are necessary in
order to understand assessment of influence means. See pages
192-194 where the terms used to describe power-mix are defined.

Power-Mix

The definition of leader as a person with God-given capacity
and God-given responsibility to influence a group of God's people
towards God's purposes for them requires a strong view of
leadership. This means that spiritual authority, the major power
form during convergence, will be supplemented by other power
forms if that influence is to be effective. The term describing
the combination of power and authority forms that make up a
leader's influence means is power-mix.

Power-mix is a term describing the combination of power forms--force, manipulation, authority (and its sub-forms: coercive authority, induced authority, legitimate authority, competent authority, personal authority), persuasion--which dominate a leader's influence in leadership acts during a given point of time in a development phase.

While it is difficult to give value to various specific power-mixes, in general two factors must be kept in mind. The leader must get the job done. His/her job is to influence followers toward God's purposes. A power-mix which will do this must be used. Yet it must be in accord with ethical guidelines which are part of the leadership values of the leader. Where possible it must respect followers and contribute towards their development. (Spiritual authority certainly does this.) Development is thus an assessment of a leader's ability to use the proper power-mix and maintain this balance.

Development Measure 6--Assessment Along Patterns

From the provisional sub-phase onward, certain patterns provide a degree of measure. Evaluation as to stages, steps, or definite increments of movement in the following patterns are indicators of progress:

1. M.5 Authority Insights,
2. M.6 Giftedness Development,
3. M.7 Spiritual Authority Discovery,
4. UM.1 Reflective/ Formative Evaluation,
5. UM.2 Upward Development,
6. UM.3 Gift-cluster Ripening,
7. UM.4 Balance,
8. UM.5 Convergence Guidance.

Development is indicated by a simple statement assessing the location in the pattern.

Development Measure 7--Convergence

An idealized development goal (that of a leader who has matured in leadership character, leadership skills, and leadership values, and is operating in convergence) flows from an extension of the logical implications of the definition of leader. A leader is a person with God-given capacity, and God-given responsibility, who is influencing a specific group of God's people toward God's purposes. It follows that if God is indeed in the process of developing that leader and the leader responds ideally to that processing, then the leader will mature in character, skills, and values and will accomplish effectively God's purposes. Convergence then describes the condition of ministry for an idealized development.

Major and Minor Convergence Factors

Convergence refers to a period of effectiveness in a

leader's life characterized by simultaneously reaching mature stages in several development patterns and seeing various leadership factors harmoniously supporting each other to bring about that effectiveness. I will discuss the factors first and then come back to the development patterns which suggest standards for evaluating convergence.

A number of factors contribute to this time of convergence. For descriptive purposes these factors are classified as major and minor convergence factors.

Major factors include: giftedness, role-match, influence-mix, upward dependence, and ministry philosophy. In convergence the leader is enjoying effective ministry because a number of these major factors are fitting together to enhance each other. **Giftedness**, including natural abilities, acquired skills and spiritual gifts, fits together with role and influence-mix. **Role- match** means that the role (or functional responsibility) of the leader enhances use of giftedness. **Influence-Mix** means that the leader is influencing followers who should be influenced with the right combination of influence-mix to the depth of influence feasible (i.e. appropriate extensiveness, intensiveness, and comprehensiveness). **Upward Dependence** is a measure of spirituality. It means that the leader is at height of maturity in experiencing the reality of God, trusting God for life and ministry, and channeling of God's power in giftedness. Union life is the norm for convergence. The **ministry philosophy** major factor means that the leader has experienced values concerning what ministry is about and how it should be done. These lessons from life involve the leader's own uniqueness and potential accomplishments. Stage 3, steps 8, 9, 10 (see page 398) describe the ministry philosophy in convergence.

Minor factors include: experience, personality, geography, special opportunity, prophecy, and destiny. The **experience** minor factor means that in convergence, past experience gives insights and wisdom for present ministry. Various ministry and life experiences in the past now take on new meaning and give a vital experience base from which to operate in convergence. People have unique personalities. They reflect Christ likeness through these unique personalities. The **personality** minor factor recognizes that uniqueness in personhood. In convergence the role and influence-means will match the particular **personality shaping** that has gone on. The role and/or functional responsibility will take advantage of positive personality traits and minimize negative personality traits. The **geography** points out the fact that location has much to do with widespread influence. The leader is located in a place, and with a ministry structure which allows for influence-mix and capacity to be realized to the appropriate capacity. Because a leader has an effective ministry in convergence God will frequently open up many doors of **special opportunity**--more than, would be the case of a leader operating in the competence sub-phase. Leaders in convergence are able to take advantage of these special opportunities. As God opens doors of special opportunity, His timing will be evident frequently. Some leaders, not all, have destiny processing which included a **prophecy** concerning ultimate usefulness. The fulfillment of that prophecy frequently coincides with convergence. Previous **destiny experiences** (in addition to prophecy) will point to convergence. Destiny fulfillment processing will be occurring in convergence.

In addition to the meshing of major and minor factors, convergence is also accompanied by advanced stages in several important advanced patterns. Table 13-9 lists these advance patterns and indicates stages usually accompanying convergence.

TABLE 13-9
CONVERGENCE AND ADVANCED PATTERNS

Pattern	Stage or Step in Convergence
M.7 Spiritual Authority Development	6,7,8 (see page 367)
UM.3 Gift-Cluster Ripening Pattern	8a,8b (see page 377)
UM.4 Balance	conditions 1,2 exist (see page 378)
UM.5 Convergence Guidance	conditions 3,4,5 exist (see page 380)

Evaluation of convergence has less meaning for a leader in provisional ministry. Such a leader will not have experienced many of the factors of convergence. At such a stage one can simply assess mini-convergence in terms of pairs of factors such as was described on page 380. Recognition of these factors will enhance perceiving convergence guidance later when it is needed. Leaders in the competent sub-phase should be aware of convergence as a measure of development and use it to both assess present leadership and formulate future decisions for ministry.

Measures of Development as Unique

Each Christian leader differs from every other Christian leader in terms of God-given capacity, God-given responsibility, influence capacity, groups to lead, and purposes to accomplish for God. It follows then that there is no absolute standard development to which all leaders must aspire. Development is open ended--the final development goal is a function of the individual. However, comparative study of many unique time-lines using the ministry time-line indicates an open ended ideal goal, that of a mature leader operating in convergence. Maturity is evaluated in terms of various development indicators just discussed.

Development is complex due to the uniqueness of each Christian leader, the time of assessment, and the complexity of subjective/ objective perspectives used in evaluation. Timing can be synchronic, diachronic, or at the end of a lifetime.

Immediate--Synchronic, is Limited

Evaluation at a given moment of time is limited. It can be done for the seven major development indicators. However, development can only be properly assessed by comparing synchronic analysis done at different times. Immediate lessons can always be assessed synchronically by simply evaluating lessons being learned in current processing. Their accumulation into a cohesive ministry philosophy can, again, only be assessed over a long period of time.

Longitudinal--Diachronic

It is the comparative evaluation of various synchronic evaluations of development that allow assessment of development (expansion or retrogression). In its essence, development can only be evaluated longitudinally. Comparisons of the various development indicators over time give an indication of development. Usually assessment of the seven indicators (as many as can be done) should be done on a sub-phase basis. Assessment at the end of development phases are helpful in pinpointing unique development tasks for a given leader.

Ultimate Assessment

Development can only be ultimately assessed after a life-time is over. And then evaluation is limited to what was actually done, not what could have been done. There is no way to assess capacity which was not developed that could have been. Development in the ultimate sense is indicated not only by final measures of development (analysis of the seven major indicators and changes in them over one's lifetime) but also by that which was actually accomplished for Christianity. Unfortunately, evaluation of accomplishments is difficult to do.

Complex--Approximate At Best

Evaluation of development, while aided by objective definitions as guiding perspectives, is still difficult at best. This is so for several reasons. One, evaluation is almost primarily subjective. Two, some of the measures (e.g. extensive influence, and comprehensive influence) at this point in the research, do not have practical means for applying. Sub-indicators of these concepts need to be developed. Three, the notion of arrested development (i.e. plateauing[4]) and reaching

---

[4]Leaders who fail to progress as they should are said to have hit the plateau barrier. Symptoms of the plateau barrier include: 1) no enthusiasm for leadership selection. (A major function of leadership which is the continual recognition of emerging leaders and facilitation of them in the early entry and training

maximum capacity may appear to overlap. Four, retrogression is
not always a negative indicator. Bigger and better is not a
criterion for development. Development up to capacity is a
measure which is not based on whether capacity is large or small.
Retrogression may be a normal means of finding one's capacity
level. Aspects of retrogression can usually be expected along
with aspects of expansion in some phases (e.g. a leader moving
into afterglow). Five, some of the higher level indicators (power
and authority; development patterns) are still being researched
and theories concerning them are presently in flux. Again, these
high level abstractions like power-mix and authority bases need
practical questionnaires and practical symptomatic statements
describing them so that use by practitioners can be facilitated.
At this stage of research of leadership emergence theory,
evaluation of development (except for sphere of influence and
giftedness evaluation) is one of the more tentative portions of
the theory and needs further research.

Case Study--Overall Assessment

    Each case study of a contemporary life history concludes
with a summary sheet which gives an overall view of the
development of a leader. That summary sheet includes sources of
the data, a time-line, an indication of giftedness development,
sphere of influence, and contributions to the Christian movement.
The section on contributions to the Christian movement is an
important **subjective evaluation** of the leader's development up to
that point in his/her history. Typical evaluation statements of
accomplishments are given in Table 13-10. One must bear in mind
that these statements represent only partially what will be
accomplished in a life since they are done on contemporary
leaders who are mid career. Assessment of the same leader at the
end of a career might conclude very different results.

    Usually a given case will have between four and seven
contribution statements. Both male and female students are
illustrated in the table.

----

functions), 2) no personal growth projects (the ministry skills
item and training progress item are relatively infrequent if at
all), 3) a lack of interest in basal formation aspects--
interaction with word, prayer, special personal communion times
alone with God, 4) a tendency to take the "easiest way" in
conflict situations 5) the fourth aspect of a leader,
influencing God's people toward God's purposes, is not being
reflected in the leader. A major symptom is a noticeable lack
of God's processing for development's sake and an increased
processing for discipline or for limiting the leader's
influence. This means that those aspects of processing which
transition the leader into the unique ministry phase are
conspicuously absent or not being perceived by the leader.

TABLE 13-10
CONTEMPORARY CONTRIBUTIONS

Source	Sample Contribution Statements

Source   Sample Contribution Statements

Student 9   +model the adventure of growing obedience
                      +Church planting: direct involvement in the
                       establishment of 5 churches and the
                       rehabilitation of one other--3 in Canada, 2
                       overseas.
                      +Church planting: indirect involvement in the
                       planting of 12 churches, 4 in Canada, 8
                       overseas.

Student 10   +revitalized and led St. Helen's Christian Union
                      +major musical contribution to life and ministry
                       of Lee Abbey community
                      +musical and creative administrative contribution
                       to St. Aldate's Oxford
                      +first woman clergy at St. Peter's Halliwell;
                       major contributions in music administration and
                       mission interest
                      +opening up potential new field (France) for CMJ;
                       also major musical contribution to Jews for
                       Jesus (USA); also first woman clergy at St.
                       Michael's Paris
                      +first administrator and editor for LCJE (linking
                       individuals and agencies involved in Jewish
                       evangelism worldwide with each other)

Student 11   +encouraging many individuals, youth and adults,
                       to a deeper experience and understanding of
                       God, commitment/ surrender to Jesus Christ and
                       to continued growth in Him. This is a
                       lifestyle commitment which has been augmented
                       and facilitated by various roles, jobs and
                       opportunities experienced from 1974-1989.
                       Mentoring a few individuals in-depth has led to
                       their involvement in ministry.
                      +vision for world mission has been shared and
                       strategies constructed for church/
                       ecclesiastical organizations in North Carolina
                       (Reynolds Presbyterian Church, Moravian
                       Provincial Mission Committee, Moravian Board of
                       World Mission (1980-1989)
                      +vicarious influence upon Chinese students,
                       administration, and ESL teachers by being key
                       person in the selection process of over 130 ESL
                       instructors. (1987-1989)

TABLE 13-10
CONTEMPORARY CONTRIBUTIONS

Source	Sample Contribution Statements
Student 12	+founded and developed one of the fastest (perhaps the fastest) indigenous church movements in Malaysia +founded Bible school +production of several magazines and publications
Student 13	+developed and expanded extension training ministries in Belgium for lay leaders +wrote program text entitled Communique La Foi (How to Communicate the Faith) for the training of Belgians in evangelism + developed missionary candidate training program of Grace Community Church. Missionaries are worldwide
Student 14	+established One-Way Agape, a ministry on the University of Alberta that is still in existence and has spawned a similar ministry on the University of Calgary campus +established Youth With a Mission Alberta +established Missionfest Conference in Calgary, now an annual event

Ultimate Contribution

The notion of development in leadership emergence theory connotes the idea of movement toward or progress toward some end. I have described generally an idealized goal--a leader mature in character, skills, and values who is operating in convergence. This end was derived as a logical extension of the definition of leader. Apart from that ideal generalized notion of a goal, development of a leader can also be asserted with a focus on the **final concept** in the leader definition. A leader is a person with 1) God-given capacity, and 2) God-given responsibility who is influencing 3) a specific group of God's people 4) **toward God's purposes for the group.** Accomplishment in terms of God's purposes for the group will differ and will be unique for each leader. Guidance processing, destiny processing, and strategic formation for a given individual leader will contribute toward the leader's understanding of God's purposes for the group.

Development then is not only toward general maturity but also toward **unique accomplishments for God.** Development measures in maturity will always be incomplete since potential capacity can never be assessed absolutely nor can the degree to which it was reached. Accomplishments can be evaluated more readily and development in terms of them can be ascertained to a degree.

Whitworth (1989b), in a special research project, did a comparative study of forty two legacy articles which were written essentially to show just that, unique accomplishments. The persons studied included an impressive array of missionary types: Roman Catholics, protestants, men, women, westerners and non-westerners, scholars, social workers, church planters, evangelists, founders of institutions and movements. [5]

The legacy articles were done by historians, missiologists, fellow missionaries, professors, other academic people, mission administrators, and other full time christian workers. No criteria were given these writers. They assessed the person they wrote on in terms of that person's unique contributions. Many of the writers were "experts" on the person for whom they wrote the legacy article. Because of the wide perspectives used to evaluate and lack of a fixed criteria for identifying achievement, one could assume that a comparative analysis would most likely result in identification of generic levels and would establish some general guidelines for approaching evaluation of the "ultimate contribution" of a leader, the final development measure. And that was the case.

Whitworth's analysis yielded some general categories of accomplishment--final means for evaluating development. I simplified her research findings as follows. Legacies, something precious left behind by these leaders for future leaders, included five broad categories: Character, Ministry, Catalytic, Organizational, Ideation. Some of these were broken down into further sub-categories. For each of these major categories one could further analyze the ultimate contribution as contemporary, that is, time-bound, applying more to the times of the leader while he/she lived or classic, that is, a contribution not time-bound, one that would have future ramifications beyond the life of the leader.

Table 13-11 displays the ultimate contribution categories and sub-categories.

----

[5]These included Florence Allshorn, Rufus Anderson, C.F. Andrews, V.S. Azariah, J.H. Bavinck, H.R. Boer, A.J. Brown, T.C. Chao, Pierre Charles, P.D. Devanandan, A. Duff, J.N. Farquhar, W. Freytag, A.J. Gordon, Bruno Gutmann, W.W. Harris, Barbara Hendricks, A.G. Hogg, E. Stanley Jones, J. Herbert Kane, H. Kraemer, K.S. Latourette, F.C. Laubach, D. Livingstone, D.B. Macdonald, John R. Mott, Stephen Neill, D.T. Niles, W. Paton, Joseph Schmidlin, Wilhelm Schmidt, Ida S. Scudder, Robert E. Speer, R. Kenneth Strachan, R. Streit, Johannes Dindinger, Johannes Rommerskirchen, J. Hudson Taylor, Henry Venn, Warneck Gustav, Max Warren and Samuel M. Zwemer. Certainly these were people who "learned how to number their days so as to apply themselves diligently with wisdom." (Psalm 90:12) Such is the intended impact of the ultimate contribution typology--help people to deliberately move toward lives that ultimately count.

TABLE 13-11
CATEGORIES OF ULTIMATE CONTRIBUTION

Category	Sub-category	Example	Explanation
A. Character	none	Samuel Brengle Jim Elliot	Person lived an exemplary life. Thought of as a saint or a model for others to emulate. The person usually is thought of as having a very intimate relationship with God. Frequently mystical experiences occur. He or she demonstrates the fruit of the spirit. The thrust of this accomplishment is vertical, upward, toward God.
B. Ministry	1. Personal	Robert McQuilkin Bob Munger	This is a person who has impact on individuals. He or she relates ministry down to a personal level. They are thought of as mentors, disciplers, and people who have a network of close followers. They will spend time developing people. There is heavy intensive and comprehensive sphere of influences.
	2. Public	D. L. Moody C.H. Spurgeon	This is a person who has public exposure and whose ministry is thought of as to the masses or large groups of people. They are usually mass communicators. They shine before large groups. They will motivate a large following. There is broad extensive sphere of influence though comprehensive and intensive influence may be nil.
C. Catalytic	1. Pioneer	J. O. Fraser Robert Jaffray	This is a person who creates something like a new religious structure, new religious institution, new church or denomination or organization, or works in a place where no one has gone or sees a special need and finds a way to meet it or breaks new ground by showing some new way to do something. The thing created or done is left behind as the legacy.
	2. Change	Mother Theresa Theresa of Avila John Woolman	This is a person whose desire is to correct things. They see problems in society or the church or a Christian organization and set about to bring change.

TABLE 13-11 continued
CATEGORIES OF ULTIMATE CONTRIBUTION

Category	Sub-category	Example	Explanation
D. Organization	none	Samuel Mills Hudson Taylor	This is a person who builds an organization and brings stability to it so that it will survive and will be effective.
E. Ideation	1. Researcher	Donald McGavran William Carey Roland Allen	This is a person who sees a situation and seeks to understand it and comes up with a framework for understanding it. This framework is usually considered a breakthrough which aids the Christian church as a whole. The research can focus on a contemporary issue and applies uniquely only to that time or it can deal with fundamental dynamics which are more timeless in their application. The basic thrust of the contribution is conceptualization.
	2. Writer	K. S. Latourette John Bunyan E. Stanley Jones	This is a person who produces a body of literature that affects a significant portion of Christianity either in a time bound way or in a timeless way—it is continually read by later generations. Sometimes one single work—a book, a tract, a sermon, an article—is significant enough that it lives on as an ultimate contribution. The basic thrust of the contribution is the written product.
	3. Promoter	John Mott Rufus Anderson Robert Speer F. C. Laubach	This is a person who may or may not have originated some conceptualization but who is adept at marketing it across the Christian market. The contribution then is the widespread acceptance and use of the ideation by Christians.

Factors Describing Ultimate Contributions

Ultimate contributions can be contemporary or classic. **Contemporary** simply means its major contribution was to the people and the time in which the leader lived. **Classic** means that the contribution was not time bound and lived on beyond the individual. Both contemporary and classic are important. The **nature** of the contribution can be a **tangible product** such as a book, or a theory, or an organization, or a changed institution or it may be an **intangible product** such as a model life or unknown numbers of people that came to know God. Ultimate contributions may also be judged in terms of **sphere of influence factors** direct, indirect, or organizational and levels within those factors of extensive, intensive or comprehensive

The value of categories of ultimate contribution lies in the suggestive power to bring focus to a life that is already contributing. Such futuristic thinking can help a leader to mold an ideal role and to focus more deliberately on that which God wants to accomplish through the leader.

Continued study of historical leaders for ultimate contribution is needed. There are some other ultimate contributions that do not fit easily into these major categories. This suggests that the typology needs refinement. Subcategories also need refinement. The ministry subcategories of private and public, while good, are not adequate to describe all kinds of ministry ultimate contributions. Such study will provide results to help judge overall development of leaders, give a broader framework for assessing sense of destiny fulfillment, and challenge leaders to assess response patterns in terms of their movement toward ultimate contribution.

Summary

Seven development measures were discussed in this chapter: 1. **major lessons**, 2. **development tasks**, 3. **giftedness**, 4. **sphere of influence**, 5. **influence means**, 6. **assessment along patterns**, and 7. **convergence.** It was suggested that evaluation of a leader for these categories be done at boundary times. Comparative analysis of successive boundaries or beginning and final boundaries gives an indication of development that has taken place in a leader's life. All of these measures occur throughout most of the cases.

It should be noted that these measures do not assess the leadership of the leader. They do not indicate, either, whether the development in learning of lessons, or the gain or loss in sphere of influence, development along a certain gift-mix is good or bad. These measures simply point out if these things are occurring. Future research, particularly Biblically based research, needs to be done in terms of values which can serve as standards for assessment of these measures. This research was empirically based and simply describes the measures that were observed.

Contemporary leaders have begun to make self-assessment of their accomplishments. These accomplishments seem, at least in embryonic form, to fit the general categories of Whitworth's ultimate contribution typology.

Absolute assessment awaits the judgment seat and a divine perspective which can see the whole and the parts and provide an unbiased analysis with eternal perspective.

CLOSURE

The Leadership Mandate and the Leadership Gap

When I began my own pilgrimage into the study of leader's lives I was personally challenged by the leadership mandate. Read it again.

Remember your former leaders, who spoke God's message to you. Think back on how they lived and died, and imitate their faith. Jesus Christ is the same yesterday, today, and forever. Hebrews 13:7,8

When I read those verses, two questions came to mind. The first question is how do I "think back on how they lived and died?" The second is how do I "imitate their faith?"

This manual emerged as I sought to answer these questions in detail. I believe the issues discussed in it are vital to the leadership gap.

Pressing Leadership Needs—The Leadership Gap

Leadership is a very relevant subject. I travel widely. I consult with mission organizations and national church leaders. I teach leadership subjects both in the United States and abroad. In all of these situations I see pressing leadership needs. If there is one need that it is echoed over and over it is this. "We need **more** and **better** leaders." Or otherwise stated, "we don't have trained leadership. Our church is growing so fast that we do not have enough trained leadership." Ministries, both at home and abroad, are reflecting what Jesus saw when he exhorted his followers,

As he saw the crowds, his heart was filled with pity for them, because they were worried and helpless, like sheep without a shepherd. So he said to his disciples, "The harvest is large, but there are few workers to gather it in. Pray to the owner of the harvest that he will send out workers to gather in his harvest." (Good News Bible: Matthew 9:37-38).

There was a leadership gap in Jesus' time. There is one today. The gap involves quantity and quality. Some churches are expanding so rapidly in these days that they are outstripping the "trained" leaders available. And studies show that growing churches will need many more leaders than can be produced by formal training institutes. What a pleasant problem!

But more than numbers are involved. We need quality leaders. While it is true that some leaders fail in leadership due to lack of ministry skills or ministry philosophy, it is not lack of ministry skills or ministry philosophy which is the major cause of failure. It is failure in leadership character. A number of recent nationally publicized Christian leadership scandals (and

many more not known or publicized) indicate that quality leaders
are needed. Leaders with God-shaped character and convictions
are needed to model for Christians and for the secular world what
leadership is. What can we do about the leadership gap?

Three Things To Do To Meet these Pressing Needs

I believe the answer lies first of all in an obedient
response to the leadership mandate. We need to know what good
leadership really is. The mandate emphasizes that fact. But it
does more. It points out that we can expect Jesus, the living
source of leadership, to instill in us those same leadership
qualities and to accomplish through us similar achievements
toward His purposes. Does the mandate work?

Many of us who are Christian leaders know full well how our
lives have been significantly impacted by stirring examples of
past missionaries or pastors or other Christian leaders.
Early in my own development I was deeply challenged by
reading about Hudson Taylor--particularly his many faith-
challenging exploits. I learned that I could trust God in my
ministry to supply funds and to open doors. I learned that
I needed to listen to what God wanted to do through me and
then to trust Him to do it. It is true! Jesus is the same.
He is the source of leadership. What He did for past leaders
He can do for today's leaders--and tomorrow's.

I like to interpret the command in this leadership mandate
this way. "Think back on how they have lived and died and
learn vicariously for your own lives."

This manual will help you obey the leadership mandate. By
applying its concepts you will learn how to assess good
leadership and to see how it emerges. You will learn how God
intervenes in a leader's life to shape that leader. You can
readily apply these concepts to your own life.

So **step one** in resolving the leadership gap is to obey the
leadership mandate and begin to understand what good leadership
is by studying how God develops it.

Ministry ultimately flows out of being. Once we begin to
see what good leadership is and how God develops it we must
become good leaders ourselves--working with God in His
development processes to shape us. Our alert, sensitive, rapid
response to God's processes will increase the rate of our
leadership development. We must **become** good models. The on-
going force of the leadership mandate applies here. We help
solve the leadership gap in a significant way when we model good
leadership. Good leadership attracts good emergent leadership.
So **step two** is to become the leaders we need to be in order that
God may utilize the power of the leadership mandate through us to
emerging leaders. If we "are ourselves becoming the leaders God

intends" then we can claim the promise of the leadership mandate
for others arising in our ministries.

Like-attracts-like. Once we are **becoming models worthy of
being emulated** we can expect God to bring around us emerging
leaders who long for what we have and are. We must then know how
to mentor them. In order to mentor we must be and we must have
eyes to recognize emerging leaders, and we must know how to
mentor. **Step three** involves mentoring emerging leaders.
Leadership today is more complex than ever. I am convinced that
young emerging leaders need spiritually mature mentors if they
are to make it in today's complex leadership situation.

The Right Kind of Mentors

If we are to be good mentors we will need to remember and
respond to the challenges I introduced in the preface. I repeat
them here for emphasis. A mentor is one who is growing toward
maturity in leadership character, skills, and values. Not a
finished product but one moving in the right direction. The four
challenges, if responded to, help insure that you are moving in
the right direction. Read them again and ask God to give you a
heart to respond to them.

CHALLENGE 1. **WHEN CHRIST CALLS LEADERS TO CHRISTIAN MINISTRY HE
INTENDS TO DEVELOP THEM TO THEIR FULL POTENTIAL.
EACH OF US IN LEADERSHIP IS RESPONSIBLE TO CONTINUE
DEVELOPING IN ACCORDANCE WITH GOD'S PROCESSING ALL
OF OUR LIVES.**

CHALLENGE 2. **A MAJOR FUNCTION OF ALL LEADERSHIP IS THAT OF
SELECTION OF RISING LEADERSHIP. LEADERS MUST
CONTINUALLY BE AWARE OF GOD'S PROCESSING OF YOUNGER
LEADERS AND WORK WITH THAT PROCESSING.**

CHALLENGE 3. **LEADERS MUST DEVELOP A MINISTRY PHILOSOPHY WHICH
SIMULTANEOUSLY HONORS BIBLICAL LEADERSHIP VALUES,
EMBRACES THE CHALLENGES OF THE TIMES IN WHICH THEY
LIVE, AND FITS THEIR UNIQUE GIFTEDNESS AND PERSONAL
DEVELOPMENT IF THEY EXPECT TO BE PRODUCTIVE OVER A
WHOLE LIFETIME.**

CHALLENGE 4. **MINISTRY ESSENTIALLY FLOWS OUT OF BEINGNESS. YOU
MUST CONTINUALLY ASSESS YOUR SPIRITUALITY AND
MAINTAIN IT IF YOU ARE TO GIVE SPIRITUAL LEADERSHIP
IN THE KINGDOM.**

By all means do not forget challenge 4. Maintain your
spirituality. Most leadership failures stem from failure to
guard one's spirituality.

Good mentors, who know the leadership mandate and believe
it, do well to carefully consider the seven major lessons I have
been emphasizing throughout the manual. They are synthesized
from numerous past leaders who have had worthy ultimate

contributions. Remember the lessons are only symptoms. Simply
attempting to apply the lesson may not work. Let me illustrate.
Someone in the 1960s noted that successful business leaders had
extensive vocabularies. Immediately their was a rash of books to
hit the market on how to improve one's vocabulary. The idea
behind it was that if you improved your vocabulary you would
become a more successful person in business. Building a
vocabulary does not insure a better leader. But it is
symptomatic of a good leader. It is the dynamics behind the
major lessons that are important. Ask God to make you to be the
kind of person who will demonstrate these lessons in your own
life. Again, I will repeat them to refresh your memory.

1. **EFFECTIVE LEADERS MAINTAIN A LEARNING POSTURE
   THROUGHOUT LIFE.**

2. **EFFECTIVE LEADERS VALUE SPIRITUAL AUTHORITY AS A
   PRIMARY POWER BASE.**

3. **EFFECTIVE LEADERS RECOGNIZE LEADERSHIP SELECTION
   AND DEVELOPMENT AS A PRIORITY FUNCTION.**

4. **EFFECTIVE LEADERS WHO ARE PRODUCTIVE OVER A
   LIFETIME HAVE A DYNAMIC MINISTRY PHILOSOPHY.**

5. **EFFECTIVE LEADERS EVINCE A GROWING AWARENESS OF
   THEIR SENSE OF DESTINY.**

6. **EFFECTIVE LEADERS INCREASINGLY PERCEIVE THEIR
   MINISTRY IN TERMS OF A LIFETIME PERSPECTIVE.**

7. **EFFECTIVE LEADERS ARE PACE SETTERS.**

Expanding the Twofold Purpose of the Manual

In the preface I stated a twofold purpose for producing this
manual. My treatment of Leadership Emergence Theory is purely
applicational in nature. I want mid-career leaders, both men and
women, to understand what God has done in shaping them in the
past and to confidently expect God to continue that shaping in
the future. I want them to believe that God will make them
quality leaders whom He will use to accomplish His purposes. I
further want these quality leaders to use leadership emergence
theory concepts to help select and develop the future leaders who
are emerging all around us. If we, first of all **become** the
leaders God wants us to be, and then secondly reach out to **mentor**
the more effective development of younger leaders, we will
decrease the leadership gap and do our part in hastening the
coming of the Kingdom.

Let me give five uses for leadership emergence
theory which expands these two major purposes. Kurt Lewin said

it long ago. "Nothing is as practical as a good theory." And conversely, nothing is as impractical as a poor theory (or worse, no theory). I believe leadership emergence theory is a good theory. It has biblical roots in the leadership mandate. Let me suggest the following practical ways it can be used:

1. **Self-analysis**
   First of all, the theory can be studied by leaders to apply its findings to their own lives. It will help them understand where they are in their own present development. Mid-career leaders need this sort of reflection. The manual can be studied in formal courses, in workshops, in small groups, with another concerned leader, or alone. Its concepts may give mid-course corrections that will make a leader's remaining leadership extremely effective.

2. **Explanation**
   Definitions, concepts, and descriptions of processes from the theory can be applied at a given moment in time to explain what is happening to leaders in given situations. People do not have to know the entire theory to profit from concepts. Knowing what is happening in a given situation can be as simple as explaining a kind of process that God uses to shape a leader or showing a series of stages that leaders go through in a given kind of learning situation. You can use concepts from this theory with others even if they do not know the theory. In fact, you should if you want to apply the leadership mandate more broadly and take advantage of its built in power.

3. **Scheduling**
   The Whiteheads did us a good favor when they conceptualized the notion of "scheduling." They assert that people can "negotiate" (handle much better with profit) a crisis in their lives if they know what is happening or about to happen. It is the old idea of "forewarned is forearmed." Or to say it in a biblical context, it is applying Proverbs 22:3 very broadly. "A prudent man foreseeth the evil, and hideth himself; but the simple pass on, and are punished." It pays to schedule. You can use ideas from leadership emergence theory expecting it to have predictive punch. You can't assert its ideas as absolutes but as important guidelines on how God has worked in the past. It can help leaders negotiate difficult processing they are facing so as to see God's lessons in it.

4. **Career Counselling**
   Organizations ought to be cognizant of the life histories
   of their people. Decisions should be made not only in
   the light of of organizational needs but in terms of a
   developmental appraisal of individual leaders. Career
   files should have life history information based on many
   of the concepts of leadership emergence theory.
   Top level personnel decision making should be
   made with an awareness of a lifetime
   perspective on people involved.

5. **Mentoring**
   You can use leadership emergence theory to help you
   mentor emerging leaders. Knowing the processes whereby
   leaders develop will greatly aid you in wisely mentoring
   emerging leaders.

I hope you will use leadership emergence theory. I believe that
we can significantly narrow the leadership gap if we do.

REFERENCES CITED

Allen, Daniel
  1988   Ministry Philosophy in the Life of Charles Simeon. Oral
          Report with research notes. Unpublished research
          project. Pasadena: School of World Mission of Fuller
          Theological Seminary.

Albrecht, Wallace
  1986   "A Study in Divine Initiatives--Wallace Albrecht: A
          Leadership Selection Process Self-study." Pasadena:
          Unpublished paper in the School of World Mission of
          Fuller Theological Seminary.

Barnes, John
  1987   "The First Thirty-Nine Years." Pasadena: Unpublished
          paper in the School of World Mission of Fuller
          Theological Seminary.

Baumgartner, Erich Walter
  1987   "Erich Walter Baumgartner Called For a Mission in
          Europe." Pasadena: Unpublished paper in the School of
          World Mission of Fuller Theological Seminary.

Belesky, David
  1987   "A Leadership Development Study on David Belesky."
          Pasadena: Unpublished paper in the School of World
          Mission of Fuller Theological Seminary.

Bennett, David William
  1988   "Review of the Literature." Pasadena: Unpublished
          paper in the School of World Missions of Fuller
          Theological Seminary.

Bertelsen, Walt
  1985   When God Gives A Sense of Destiny--A Biblical Study on
          Motivating Leaders. Pasadena: Unpublished Research
          Project in the School of World Mission of Fuller
          Theological Seminary.

Booth, Carlton
  1984   **On the Mountain Top.** Wheaton, IL: Tyndale House.

Bryant, Rees
  1987   "The Emergence of a Reluctant Leader." Pasadena:
          Unpublished paper in the School of World Mission of
          Fuller Theological Seminary.

Buchan, Jeff
  1987   Jeff Buchan: A Leadership Selection Process Study.
          Pasadena: Unpublished Data Notes in the School of
          World Mission of Fuller Theological Seminary.

Burt, Margaret
    1989   "LEP SKETCH." Pasadena: Unpublished Data Notes in the
            School of World Mission of Fuller Theological Seminary.

Butt, Howard
    1973   **The Velvet Covered Brick: Christian Leadership in An
            Age of Rebellion.** New York: Harper and Row.

Callender, R. Bruce
    1983   "Francis Asbury: Advocate Supreme." Pasadena:
            Unpublished paper in the School of World Mission of
            Fuller Theological Seminary.

Carlson, Dean W.
    1985   "J. O. Fraser--A Leadership Selection Process Study."
            Pasadena: Unpublished paper in the School of World
            Mission^] of Fuller Theological Seminary.

Chan, Geok Oon
    1987   "A Leadership Emergence Patterns Study of Geok Oon
            Chan." Pasadena: Unpublished paper in the School of
            World MIssion of Fuller Theological Seminary.

Chao, Peter
    1982   "Personal Leadership Selection Paper" Pasadena:
            Unpublished paper in the School of World Mission of
            Fuller Theological Seminary.

Chuang, James
    1982   "A.B. Simpson: A Dynamic Initiator of a New Movement."
            Pasadena: Unpublished paper in the School of World
            Mission of Fuller Theological Seminary.

Classen, Gordon
    1987   "Leadership Development Study on Gordon Classen."
            Pasadena: Unpublished Data Notes in the School of World
            Mission of Fuller Theological Seminary.

Clinton, J. Robert
    1975   **Puzzles with a Purpose.** Coral Gables, FL: Learning
            Resource   Center.

    1981   **Figures and Idioms.** Altadena: Barnabas Resources.

    1982a   "Daniel--A Model of Transitional Leadership"
            Unpublished notes. Pasadena: School of World Mission
            of Fuller Theological Seminary.

    1982b   "Leadership Selection Processes in the Life of Peter"
            Unpublished notes. Pasadena: School of World Mission
            of Fuller Theological Seminary.

    1982c   "Leadership Selection Processes in the Life of Peter
            Kuzmic." Unpublished notes. Pasadena: School of World
            Mission of Fuller Theological Seminary.

1982d   "Watchman Nee: A Model of Indigenous Leadership"
        Unpublished notes. Pasadena: School of World Mission
        of Fuller Theological Seminary.

1983a   **Leadership Emergence Patterns.** Altadena: Barnabas
        Resources.

1983b   **Leadership Training Models.** Altadena: Barnabas
        Resources.

1984a   Unpublished research notes on A. W. Tozer. Pasadena:
        School of World Mission of Fuller Theological Seminary.

1984b   Unpublished research notes on Robert C. McQuilkin.
        Pasadena: School of World Mission of Fuller Theological
        Seminary.

1984c   Unpublished research notes on Dawson Trottman.
        Pasadena: School of World Mission of Fuller Theological
        Seminary.

1985a   **Spiritual Gifts.** Alberta: Horizon House.

1985b   **Joseph--Destined To Rule, A Study in Integrity and
        Divine Affirmation.** Altadena: Barnabas Resources.

1986a   "Reflections on a Leadership Bibliographic Search"
        Unpublished Doctoral Tutorial. Pasadena: School of
        World Mission of Fuller Theological Seminary.

1986b   **Leadership Styles.** Altadena: Barnabas Resources.

1986c   **A Short History of Leadership Theory--A Paradigmatic
        Overview of Leadership Theory from 1841-1986.**
        Altadena: Barnabas Resources.

1987a   **Leadership Emergence Patterns.** 2nd ed. Altadena:
        Barnabas Resources.

1987b   **How to Do a Leadership Development Study.** Altadena:
        Barnabas Resources.

1987c   "Leadership Development Theory--Influence
        Perspectives." Unpublished Doctoral Tutorial. Pasadena:
        School of World Mission of Fuller Theological Seminary.

1987d   Phillip Bliss, Eliza Hewitt, and D. H. Whittle.
        Unpublished research notes on three 19th century hymn
        writers. Pasadena: School of World Mission of Fuller
        Theological Seminary.

1988a   "Leadership Development Theory: Comparative Studies
        Among High Level Christian Leaders." Doctoral Thesis.
        Pasadena: School of World Mission of Fuller Theological
        Seminary.

1988b   **The Making of A Leader.** Colorado Springs: Nav Press.

1989a   Developing Leadership Gifts. Pasadena: Unpublished
         Syllabus Notes for ML521, School of World Mission of
         Fuller Theological Seminary.

1989b   Unpublished Observation Notes on an International
         Leader. Pasadena: School of World Mission of Fuller
         Theological Seminary.

Clinton, J. Robert and Raab, Laura
    1985   **Barnabas--Encouraging Exhorter, A Study In Mentoring.**
            Altadena: Barnabas Resources.

Colquhoun, Rick
    1987   "Rick Colquhoun's Personal Pilgrimage: A Leadership
            Development Study." Pasadena: Unpublished Data Notes
            in the School of World Mission of Fuller Theological
            Seminary.

Collinridge, Richard
    1987   "Leadership Development Study on Richard Collingridge.
            Pasadena: Unpublished Data Notes in the School of World
            Mission of Fuller Theological Seminary.

Cook, Jennifer
    1987   "Charles Simeon A Study in Leadership. Pasadena:
            Unpublished paper in the School of World Mission of
            Fuller Theological Seminary.

Davis, Ray
    1987   "Leadership Emergence Patterns A Self-Study by Ray
            Davis." Pasadena: Unpublished Data Notes in the
            School of World Mission of Fuller Theological
            Seminary.

De George, Richard T.
    1976   "The Nature and Functions of Epistemic Authority." in
            Authority: A Philosophical analysis. Harris (ed).
            Tuscaloosa, Alabama: University of Alabama Press.

Dutton, Peter
    1986   "Personal Leadership Selection Process Paper."
            Pasadena: Unpublished paper in the School of World
            Mission of Fuller Theological Seminary.

Dykstra, Joan L.
    1983   "Personal Leadership Selection Study--Joan Dykstra."
            Pasadena: Unpublished paper in the School of World
            Mission of Fuller Theological Seminary.

Edwards, Robert Earl
    1986   "Leadership Development Process." Pasadena: Unpublished
            paper in the School of World Mission of Fuller
            Theological Seminary.

Elliston, Edgar J. (ed.)
  1989   **Christian Relief and Development Developing Workers
          for Effective Ministry.** Dallas, TX: Word Publishing,
          Incorporated.

Faber, Linda
  1989   "LEP SKETCH." Pasadena" Unpublished Data Notes in the
          School of World Mission of Fuller Theological Seminary.

Fiedler, Fred
  1967   **A Theory of Leadership Effectiveness.** New York: McGraw
          Hill.

Finzel, Hans
  1987   "A Leadership Development Study of Hans Finzel."
          Pasadena: Unpublished Data Notes in the School of
          World Mission of Fuller Theological Seminary.

  1988   "Developing An Awareness of Boundary Processing."
          Pasadena: Unpublished Research Paper in the School of
          World Mission of Fuller Theological Seminary.

George, William
  1982   "Leadership Selection Processes in the Life of Maria W.
          Atkinson founder of the Church of God in Mexico."
          Pasadena: Unpublished paper in the School of World
          Mission of Fuller Theological Seminary.

Goodwin, Bennie E.
  1981   **The Effective Leader--A Basic Guide to Christian
          Leadership.** Downer's Grove, IL: InterVarsity Press.

Grant, Ian L.
  1985   "The First Thirty-Four Years: Ian Grant--A Leadership
          Selection Process." Pasadena: Unpublished paper in
          the School of World Mission of Fuller Theological
          Seminary.

Gripentrog, Greg
  1987   "Greg Gripentrog A Leadership Development Study."
          Pasadena: Unpublished Data Notes in the School of
          World Mission of Fuller Theological Seminary.

Harbaugh, Gary L., et. al.
  1986   **Beyond the Boundary--Meeting the Challenge of the First
          Years of Ministry.** New York: Alban Institute.

Harris, Mike
  1982a   "Joseph--A Leadership Selection Paper." Pasadena:
          Unpublished paper in the School of World Mission of
          Fuller Theological Seminary.

  1982b   "Personal Leadership Selection Paper." Pasadena:
          Unpublished paper in the School of World Mission of
          Fuller Theological Seminary.

Harris, R. Baine (ed.)
   1976   **Authority: A Philosophical Analysis.** Tuscaloosa:
           University of Alabama Press.

Hersey, P. and Blanchard, K.H.
   1982   **Management of Organizational Behavior.**   7th Edition.
           Englewood Cliffs, N.J. Prentice Hall.

Hewko, Murray
   1987   "Leadership Emergence Patterns." Pasadena:
           Unpublished Data Notes in the School of World Mission
           of Fuller Theological Seminary.

Hiebert, Edmond
   1954   **An Introduction to the Pauline Epistles.**   Chicago, IL:
           Moody Press.

Hinton, Keith
   1982   Personal Leadership Selection Process Study. Pasadena:
           Unpublished Data Notes in the School of World Mission
           of Fuller Theological Seminary.

Holland,   Fredric L.
   1978   "Theological Education in Content and Change: The
           Influence of Leadership Training and Anthropology on
           Ministry For Church Growth." Pasadena: D. Miss.
           Dissertation in School of World Mission of Fuller
           Theological Seminary.

Hollis, Douglas
   1985   "Douglas Hollis--A Leadership Selection Process."
           Pasadena: Unpublished paper in the School of World
           Mission of Fuller Theological Seminary.

Humble, Arny
   1987   "An Autobiographical Leadership Development Study."
           Pasadena: Unpublished Data Notes in the School of
           World Mission of Fuller Theological Seminary.

Kauffman, Tim
   1987   "Influence Continuum." Pasadena: Unpublished research
           report. Pasadena: School of World Mission, Fuller
           Theological Seminary.

Kietzman, Robin
   1983   Life Study: Robin Kietzman. Pasadena: Unpublished Data
           Notes in the School of World Mission of Fuller
           Theological Seminary.

King, Roberta
   1982   "Charles Wesley--A Model of Background Leadership."
           Pasadena: Unpublished paper in the School of World
           Mission of Fuller Theological Seminary.

Kinnear, Angus I.
   1973   **Against the Tide The Story of Watchman Nee.** Ft.
           Washington, Pennsylvania: Christian Literature Crusade.

Kirkpatrick, John
   1988   **The Theology of Servant Leadership.** D. Miss Thesis.
           Pasadena: School of World Mission of Fuller Theological
           Seminary.

Klebe, Karen
   1982   "Karen Klebe--A Study of Leadership Selection and
           Development." Pasadena: Unpublished paper in the
           School of World Mission of Fuller Theological Seminary.

Knowles, Malcolm
   1980   **The Modern Practice of Adult Education.** Chicago:
           Follett Publishing Company.

Le Peau, Andrew T.
   1983   **Paths of Leadership.** Downers Grove, IL: InterVarsity
           Press.

Lee-Lim, Guek Eng
   1982   "James Hudson Taylor." Pasadena: Unpublished paper in
           the School of World Mission of Fuller Theological
           Seminary.

Loving, Richard
   1986   "Richard Loving--A Leadership Selection Process."
           Pasadena: Unpublished paper in the School of World
           Mission of Fuller Theological Seminary.

   1987   "Observations on Studies of Two PNG Leaders."
           Pasadena: Unpublished paper in the School of World
           Mission of Fuller Theological Seminary.

Low, Dexter
   1989   "LEP SKETCH." Pasadena: Unpublished Data Notes in the
           School of World Mission of Fuller Theological Seminary.

MacDonald, Gordon
   1985   "Lectures on the Life of Charles Simeon." Pasadena:
           Unpublished paper in the School of World Mission of
           Fuller Theological Seminary.

Mann, David P.
   1987   "Leadership Development Study: David P. Mann."
           Pasadena: Unpublished Data Notes in the School of
           World Mission of Fuller Theological Seminary.

Maranville, Randall R.
   1982   "Samuel J. Mills Jr." Pasadena: Unpublished paper in
           the School of World Mission of Fuller Theological
           Seminary.

Martinez, Juan
    1987   "A Loner Who Found A Friend." Pasadena: Unpublished
            Data Notes in the School of World Mission of Fuller
            Theological Seminary.

McGavran, Donald
    1981   Unpublished class notes from Advanced Church Growth
            Class. Pasadena: School of World Mission.

McConnell, Doug
    1985   "Doug McConnell--A Leadership Selection Process."
            Pasadena: Unpublished paper in the School of World
            Mission of Fuller Theological Seminary.

Menees, Richard
    1987   "Maverick for Mission A Leadership Development Study on
            the Life of Richard A. Menees." Pasadena: Unpublished
            Data Notes in the School of World Mission of Fuller
            Theological Seminary.

Metcalf, Sam
    1987   "Overview Draft of Own Emergence Patterns." Pasadena:
            Unpublished Notes in the School of World Mission of
            Fuller Theological Seminary.

Morehead, Peter
    1985   "C.T. Studd" Pasadena: Unpublished paper in the
            School of World Mission of Fuller Theological Seminary.

Mitchell, Linda
    1987   "A Leadership Development Study on the Life of Linda
            Mitchell." Pasadena: Unpublished paper in the School
            of World Mission of Fuller Theological Seminary.

Mueller, Karl
    1987   "A Leadership Development Self-Study." Pasadena:
            Unpublished Date Notes in the School of World Mission
            of Fuller Theological Seminary.

Myers, Elisabeth
    1989   "LEP SKETCH." Pasadena: Unpublished Data Notes in the
            School of World Mission of Fuller Theological Seminary.

Naisbitt, John
    1982   **Megatrends.** New York: Warner Books.

Nee, Watchman
    n.d.   **Spiritual Authority.** Fort Washington: Christian
            Literature Crusade.

Nelson, Randall
    1987   "A Leadership Development Study--Randall D. Nelson."
            Pasadena: Unpublished Data Notes in the School of World
            Mission of Fuller Theological Seminary.

Newton, Brian
1983   "Personal   Leadership   Selection   Process   Paper."
         Pasadena: Unpublished paper in the School of World
         Mission of Fuller Theological Seminary.

Newton, Robert D.
1983   "Personal Leadership Selection Paper." Pasadena:
         Unpublished paper in the School of World Mission of
         Fuller Theological Seminary.

Palich, Steven A.
1987   "Toward a Clearer Reflection." Pasadena: Unpublished
         Data Notes in the School of World Mission of Fuller
         Theological Seminary.

Pease, Richard B.
1983   "A. B. Simpson." Pasadena: Unpublished paper in the
         School of World Mission of Fuller Theological Seminary.

Petersen, Mitchell
1987   "Leadership Selection Processes." Pasadena:
         Unpublished paper in the School of World Mission of
         Fuller Theological Seminary.

Pierce, George Preble
1986   A Leadership Selection Process Study. Pasadena:
         Unpublished Data Notes in the School of World Mission
         of Fuller Theological Seminary.

Reid, Patricia and Van Dalen, Norma
1985   "Leadership Development in the Life of Amy Beatrice
         Carmichael." Pasadena: Unpublished paper in the
         School of World Mission of Fuller Theological
         Seminary.

Repko, Denny
1987   "LEP OVERVIEW and Back-up Notes." Pasadena:
         Unpublished notes in the School of World Mission of
         Fuller Theological Seminary.

Sanford, Agnes
1983   **The Healing Gifts of the Spirit.** Old Tappan, NJ:
         Fleming H. Revell Company.

Sanford,   John C.
1974   **The Man Who Wrestled With God--Light from the Old
         Testament on the Psychology of Individuation.** New
         York: Paulist Press.

Schambach, Sonna
1989   "LEP SKETCH." Pasadena: Unpublished Data Notes in the
         School of World Mission of Fuller Theological Seminary.

Senyimba, Michael
    1986   "A Leadership Selection Process for Michael N.
             Senyimba." Pasadena: Unpublished paper in the School
             of World Mission of Fuller Theological Seminary.

Shelley, Mark
    1985   "Leadership Selection Process Study of Myself: A
             Study in Conflict and Spiritual Authority." Pasadena:
             Unpublished paper in the School of World Mission of
             Fuller Theological Seminary.

Sims, Ronald John
    1987   "A Study of My Personal Leadership Development."
             Pasadena: Unpublished Data Notes in the School of
             World Mission of Fuller Theological Seminary.

Smith, Marvin
    1983   "Leadership Selection Paper for Marvin Smith."
             Pasadena: Unpublished paper in the School of World
             Mission of Fuller Theological Seminary.

Stalnaker, Cecil
    1989   "LEP SKETCH." Pasadena: Unpublished Data Notes in the
             School of World Mission of Fuller Theological
             Seminary.

Stanford, Miles
    1975   **The Green Letters.** Colorado Springs: published
             privately.

Strong, Cynthia
    1989   "LEP SKETCH." Pasadena: Unpublished Data Notes in the
             School of World Mission of Fuller Theological Seminary.

Takatori, Hironari and Kropp, Dick
    1983   "A. B. Simpson--Leadership Selection Process."
             (By Hironari Takatori and Dick Kropp.) Pasadena:
             Unpublished paper in the School of World Mission
             of Fuller Theological Seminary.

Teng, Kwang
    1989a   "LEP SKETCH" Pasadena: Unpublished Data Notes in the
             School of World Mission of Fuller Theological Seminary.

    1989b   "Personal Giftedness Analysis." Pasadena: Unpublished
             paper in the School of World Mission of Fuller
             Theological Seminary.

Tink, Fletcher
    1982a   "Personal Leadership Selection Paper." Pasadena:
             Unpublished paper in the School of World Mission of
             Fuller Theological Seminary.

1982b   "Phineas   F.   Bresee--Creator   of   Sodalities."
          (By Fletcher L. Tink.) Pasadena: Unpublished paper
          in the School of World Mission of Fuller
          Theological Seminary.

Tippett, A. R.
1969   **Verdict Theology in Missionary Thought.** Lincoln, IL:
          Lincoln   College Press.

Turkot, Jeff
1987   "A Leadership Analysis of the Lord's Donkey--David du
          Plessis." Pasadena: Unpublished paper in the School
          of World Mission of Fuller Theological Seminary.

Wagner, C. Peter
1984   **Leading Your Church To Growth.** Ventura, CA: Regal
          Books.

1981   **Church Growth and the Whole Gospel.** San Francisco,
          CA: Harper & Row Publishers.

Waldner, Kathy
1987   "Leadership Development Study of Kathy Waldner."
          Pasadena: Unpublished paper in the School of World
          Mission of Fuller Theological Seminary.

Warkentin, Marjorie
1982   **Ordination--A Biblical Historical View.** Grand Rapids:
          Eerdmans.

Webb, Joe E.
1985   "Leadership Emergence Patterns: Joe Webb." Pasadena:
          Unpublished paper in the School of World Mission of
          Fuller Theological Seminary.

Wetherby, Duane
1983   "A Personal Leadership Selection Paper." Pasadena:
          Unpublished paper in the School of World Mission of
          Fuller Theological Seminary.

Whitehead, Evelyn Eaton and James D. Whitehead
1982   **Christian Life Patterns.** Garden City, N.Y.: Doubleday.

Whitworth, Julia M.
1989a   "Summaries of 40 Christian Leaders From Legacy Articles
          Concerning Ultimate Contributions." Pasadena:
          Unpublished research notes in the School of World
          Mission of Fuller Theological Seminary.

1989b   "Giftedness Analysis and Development Strategy."
          Pasadena: Unpublished paper in the School of World
          Mission of Fuller Theological Seminary.

Wible, Steven M.
    1984   "Personal Leadership Selection Paper." Pasadena:
            Unpublished paper in the School of World Mission of
            Fuller Theological Seminary.

Willard, Dallas
    1988   **The Spirit of the Disciplines.** San Francisco, CA:
            Harper & Row.

Woodbury, Nicholas
    1984   "Personal Leadership Selection Paper." Pasadena:
            Unpublished paper in the School of World Mission of
            Fuller Theological Seminary.

Wrong, Dennis H.
    1979   **Power Its Forms, Bases and Uses.** San Francisco, CA:
            Harper & Row.

Zabriskie, Tyler
    1986   "Tyler Zabriskie--A Leadership Selection Process."
            Pasadena: Unpublished paper in the School of World
            Mission of Fuller Theological Seminary.